SUITABLY MODERN

Early morning view of the Kathmandu skyline, with monsoon clouds and snow-covered high Himalayas in the distance.

SUITABLY MODERN

Making Middle-Class Culture in a New Consumer Society

MARK LIECHTY

PRINCETON UNIVERSITY PRESS
PRINCETON AND OXFORD

COPYRIGHT © 2003 BY PRINCETON UNIVERSITY PRESS

Published by
Princeton University Press
41 William Street
Princeton, New Jersey 08540

In the United Kingdom
Princeton University Press
3 Market Place
Woodstock Oxfordshire OX20 1SY

Library of Congress Cataloging-in-Publication Data

Liechty, Mark, 1960–
Suitably modern : making middle-class culture in a new
consumer society / Mark Liechty.
p. cm.
Includes bibliographical references and index.
ISBN 0-691-09592-2 (alk. paper)
ISBN 0-691-09593-0 (pbk. : alk.paper)
1. Kathmandu (Nepal)—Social conditions. 2. Middle class—
Nepal—Kathmandu. 3. Consumption (Economics)—Nepal.
I. Title
HN670.9.K37 L543 2003
305.5′5′095496—dc21   2002029337

This book has been composed in Sabon

Printed on acid-free paper. ∞

www.pupress.princeton.edu

Printed in the United States of America

10 9 8 7 6 5 4 3 2 1

FOR JOHN S. OYER (1925–1998)
AND ATLEE BEECHY (1914–2000)

CONTENTS

ILLUSTRATIONS

FIGURES

MAPS

PREFACE

Nepalis experience modernity through a development ideology that
insists that they are *not* modern, indeed that they have a very long way
to go to get there.

—STACY PIGG, *The Credible and the Credulous*

This ethnography of middle-class life in Kathmandu illustrates one of the
paradoxes of global modernity at the turn of the millennium, a paradox
whereby a "Western" model or image of modernity is simultaneously the
object of intense local desire and always out of reach, seemingly by definition an unachievable condition for those in the "non-West." Transnational currents of modernity have daily consequences for the lives of people in Kathmandu, with satellite television, unemployed youth, beauty
pageants, mass tourism, and countless other examples linking the city to
worldwide trends. At the same time an ideologically weighted global politics of "development" and "progress" places Nepal and its capital in the
structural position of modernity's opposite. Nepalis are frequently reminded that among the world's "least developed countries" (LDCs),
Nepal ranks near the bottom. Yet hundreds of thousands of people in
Kathmandu lead lives riddled with both the problems and pleasures of
modernity.

This study offers insights into the experience of modernity on the
"Third World" periphery, an experience that is at once fully integrated
into the unprecedented movements of goods, ideas, people, and power
that characterize global modernity and conceptually excluded from that
modernity by a dominant political and cultural economy that continues to
require a "traditional" other against which to imagine itself as "modern."
Whether for orientalist scholars or anthropologists, development experts
or romantic tourists, Nepal has long been a favored site for Western projects of imagining "tradition." In almost all of these imaginings, "Nepal"
and "modern" end up on opposite ends of the conceptual spectrum. This
contradiction presents Nepalis with a challenge—at once emotional, intellectual, and material—to *produce themselves* as members of, and inhabitants in, a world that is both modern *and* Nepali. Paying particular attention to consumer practices and the role of commercial mediation, this
book examines the project of cultural production through which Kathmandu's middle class works to carve out a new sociocultural domain, and
fashion its own modernity.

Background and Methods

My interest in Nepal dates from 1969 when, during a year spent attending an international school in northern India, I traveled with my family from Patna (capital of the Indian province of Bihar) by horse cart, ferry, and bus north over the Himalayan foothills to Kathmandu. My fourth-grader's recollections include the stunning crystal clarity of the dark blue midwinter Kathmandu sky, and how the bright sun seemed to cast razor-sharp shadows separating the glowing brick and tile buildings from the dark, cool streets of the old city. I also reveled in the buff-burger (as opposed to beef!) and pie shops that characterized this nascent stage of Kathmandu's tourist industry.[1] In the late 1970s I returned to India for my senior year of high school and also spent several months in various parts of Nepal, including Kathmandu. In 1986, returning with my wife from a year in China, I again traveled overland to Kathmandu, but this time south from Lhasa, across the Tibetan plateau and high Himalayas into the green valleys of Nepal.

Although these early voyages to Kathmandu helped me gain an appreciation for the city's place in the cultural and geographic landscape of the subcontinent and spawned a lasting interest in the region, this book is based on sixteen months of field research conducted between 1988 and 1991, plus follow-up visits in 1996 and 2001. During the summers of 1988 and 1989 I lived in Kathmandu, studying language and working through ideas for research.[2] While living in several middle-class Nepali homes and "hanging out" at a center for youth with substance abuse problems, I became more and more intrigued with the relationships between mass media, consumer desire, and (at least for the young men at the center) the almost overwhelming challenges of being young and middle-class in Kathmandu. Typically from families broken by the stresses of the expanding local cash/consumer economy, these young men often turned to commercial media for visions of a modern future, and to hard drugs to help deaden the fear of being excluded from that seemingly impossible future. With these images and experiences in mind, I returned to Kathmandu in 1991[3] to explore how media, consumerism, and middle-class practice converge. This mutually constitutive intersection forms the nexus around which this book is organized.

---

[1] For more on early tourism in Kathmandu, see Liechty 1996a, Tomory 1996.

[2] These trips were made possible by a Foreign Language and Area Studies (FLAS) summer language study grant and a grant from the Department of Anthropology of the University of Pennsylvania.

[3] This year of research was funded by a Fulbright-Hays Dissertation Research Grant.

In addition to the "participant observation" of living in Kathmandu, the research base for this study consists of informal interviews. The bulk of my informant data is in the form of more than two hundred open-ended interviews, about three quarters of them on audiotape. Four Nepali co-workers and I conducted these interviews in Nepali, Newari, or English, and sometimes in mixtures of two, or all three, languages. Of the project's four co-workers, two were Kathmandu Newars, one was a Brahman student originally from central Nepal, and one was a Sherpa who had spent most of his life in the city. Each had access to particular social networks and social institutions in the city. Additionally, one of the four was a woman; without her excellent work I would not have a valuable set of exceptionally detailed and candid interviews with women. The interviews we conducted were wide-ranging but generally revolved around the contemporary experience of consuming mass media and/or personal perceptions of changing sociocultural practices. Although each of us went into interview settings with a list of general questions (about consumer habits, likes and dislikes, and so on), our aim was not to fill out a standardized questionnaire but instead to work with the people we met, trying to find the particular experiences and issues that were most meaningful to them.

The project's aim was to interact with a wide variety of people—young, middle-aged, elderly; girls and boys, women and men; Buddhist and Hindu; high-, middle-, and low-caste—though overall the majority of our contacts were with at least minimally educated persons from families involved in some form of tertiary ("service" or nonmanual) labor. Our goal was to interview people from across the social spectrum, "low" to "high," though we aimed to weight our sample between the extremes of poverty and exceptional wealth. The people we interviewed were chosen in a variety of ways: (1) at random (those we engaged in public parks, restaurants, and tea shops, in classrooms, or on street corners), (2) through networks of friends and acquaintances, (3) as representatives or members of social organizations (youth clubs) or businesses (video rental shop owners, beauty parlor proprietors and patrons, etc.), and (4) as individuals with particularly relevant knowledge or authority (filmmakers, television and radio producers, government officials, and so on). Overall, this book's ethnographic material, while not strictly random or "scientific" in its collection, represents a diverse and wide-ranging sample of Kathmandu residents.

Whenever possible, we recorded our interviews on audiotape. Using machines little bigger than a cigarette packet, we were able to record conversations everywhere from parks, stores, and tea shops to homes, offices, and classrooms. By and large we found that the sight of a tape recorder was less novel than the experience of talking one-on-one with a foreigner, or even a fellow Nepali, about one's personal experience. Yet almost all the people we dealt with were willing to offer their time, eager to share their opinions, and intensely concerned about the issues at hand. I am convinced that the benefits of recording semiformal interviews such as these far outweigh the potential drawbacks of interacting in an admittedly artificial setting. Without this approach we would have been unable to compile the hundreds of articulate, detailed, and often impassioned remarks that make up the many voices represented in this book.

Once recorded, each of the interviews was transcribed and translated into English. I worked one-on-one with my co-workers to go through each tape to make the final English transcript. This included my own Nepali interviews, which I made sure to translate with a native speaker so as not to miss nuances in the spoken Nepali. All of the translations were finished while in Nepal and in most cases within hours of the actual interview. The result was hundreds of pages of transcript, based on over one hundred hours of taped interviews.

In our translations we tried to reflect the cadence, style, and grammatical construction of people's remarks, but also to retain the significance of word choice. In particular we were concerned to record those instances of bilingual "code switching"[4] in which people interjected English words and phrases into conversational Nepali. In the ethnographic quotations in this book, words spoken in English in otherwise Nepali speech are designated by the use of a sans serif font. Thus, the common use of English words like "cinema," "real," "inferiority complex," "teen," "make-up," "body," "fashion," "attraction," "self-satisfaction," and many others indicates the degree to which English has become part of everyday middle-class speech. But much more importantly, the use of English words (most of which have Nepali equivalents) indicates how Nepali speakers signal new epistemological codes (new understandings of logic, value, and reality) that are simultaneously acknowledged as foreign (because they are in English) and local (because they are incorporated into a Nepali utterance). Because tensions between contending and often contradictory worlds of meaning are embedded in everyday speech, linguistic practice opens important windows onto the experience of modernity in Kathmandu.

Because it draws on a rich collection of informal interview transcripts, this ethnography is perhaps unusually "voice" oriented: the text is full of people speaking their minds, their stories, and their lives. These transcripts gave me the luxury of considering not just *what* people said but *how* they said it. Indeed, it was in these voices that I began to hear how

[4] Gumperz defines code switching as "a discourse phenomenon in which speakers rely on juxtaposition of grammatically distinct subsystems to generate conversational inferences" (1982:97).

social meaning is produced and circulated in everyday life through the *practice* of language. Working with these transcripts, I came to appreciate the importance of speech as a vehicle for the performance of meaning and the circulation of cultural narratives. Although speech is not the only relevant domain of class practice, it is one of the most important means by which people in Kathmandu actively produce themselves (and others) as class beings. This book is about much more than language, but because of its theoretical focus on class as cultural practice, the discursive production of meaning is a recurring theme.

Because of its emphasis on communicative practice, this book is relatively less oriented toward detailed descriptions of specific microethnographic locales (homes, neighborhoods, classrooms) or social groups (families, clubs, gangs). Readers will find plenty of ethnographic descriptions of everyday life in Kathmandu, but even these underscore the main theme of the book, the construction of social and cultural life in the city. For example, chapter 5 discusses public spaces in Kathmandu but stresses the role of middle-class consumer practice in creating and claiming new kinds of public space (in architecture and urban design) and public practice (through fashion and other class-based consumer practices). Because of its focus on the role of communicative practice in the creation of social and cultural life, this book revolves around the themes of language and consumption as constitutive sociocultural processes.

All Nepali words in this book are written in italics and romanized using Turner's (1931) transliterations. The only exceptions to this rule are proper nouns (names, places), and two or three instances where Turner's Nepali pronunciation differs significantly from current usage, in which case I opt for the latter (for example, *bikās* instead of Turner's *vikāś*).

ACKNOWLEDGMENTS

While it would be impossible to thank everyone who has helped to make this book possible, I will mention at least a few. Sincere thanks to all the following, Ang Tshering Sherpa, Surendra Bajracharya, and especially Ganu Pradhan and Som Raj Ghimire, my co-workers in the research phase of this project; Tirtha Raj Onta and Dilli Ram Dahal for wise advice and dozens of important introductions; Anil Pande, Jagadish Lohani, and Uli Kohler of Youth Vision for their friendship and willingness to broaden my horizons; Deepak Tuladhar and Allen B. Tuladhar for countless cups of tea and seemingly unlimited generosity in sharing their time, knowledge, and insights; Krishna B. Pradhan (of Kathmandu) and Premlata Ghimire, who taught me much more than just Nepali language; Raju Gurung and Anne Kaufman, and Sarita and Pradip Sharma for sharing insights and experiences; Penny Walker and the entire staff of the Kathmandu USEF; Heather Dell, Julia Thompson, Rachel Tolen, and Amy Trubek, as well as Beulah S. Hostetler, who generously read portions of this manuscript and offered critical comments; Arjun Appadurai, Peter van der Veer, Kris Hardin, Carol A. Breckenridge, Richard G. Fox, Ulf Hannerz, and Helena Wulff for their guidance and support; the International Institute for Asian Studies (IIAS) in Leiden, The Netherlands, for a postdoctoral fellowship during which I worked to revise this manuscript; my colleagues at the University of California, Santa Barbara (especially Elvin Hatch and Eve Darian-Smith), and the University of Illinois at Chicago (especially Mike Lieber and Marc Zimmerman) for their help and encouragement; Ray Brod of the UIC Cartography Laboratory for preparing the maps for this volume; Pratyoush Onta, Mary Des Chene, and Lazima Onta-Bhatta (of *Studies in Nepali History and Society*) for encouragement and critical comments; Marjorie S. and Russel A. Liechty for opening up a world of cross-cultural experiences; and Laura Hostetler for believing in me and in this project even at times when I didn't. This book is dedicated to the memory of John S. Oyer (1925–1998) and Atlee Beechy (1914–2000)— teachers, scholars, peacemakers, mentors, friends. "Keep hope alive. Keep the light burning."

Some of the material in this book has been published previously. Parts of chapter 2 appeared in *Studies in Nepali History and Society* 2(1):5– 68, Copyright 1997 by Mandala Book Point, Kathmandu, Nepal. Parts of chapters 3, 4, and 5 appeared in *Selves in Time and Place: Identities, Experiences, and History in Nepal*, edited by Debra Skinner, Alfred Pach, and Dorothy Holland (Lanham, Md.: Rowman and Littlefield, 1998), 131–54, Copyright 1998 by Rowman and Littlefield. Chapter 6 is reprinted in revised form from *Studies in Nepali History and Society* 3(1):87–126, Copyright 1998 by Mandala Book Point, Kathmandu, Nepal. Parts of chapters 8 and 9 appeared in the following: *Youth Cultures: A Cross-Cultural Perspective*, edited by Vered Amit-Talai and Helena Wulff (London: Routledge, 1995), 166–201, Copyright 1995 by Vered Amit-Talai and Helena Wulff; *Geography of Identity*, edited by Patricia Yaeger (Ann Arbor: University of Michigan Press, 1996), 98–130, Copyright 1996 by the University of Michigan.

All photographs are by Usha Tiwari, a Kathmandu-based photographer and photojournalist. Usha Tiwari's photos have been published widely in newspapers and magazines in Nepal and elsewhere in South Asia. Her work has also been exhibited in various parts of South Asia and Europe.

The maps were prepared by the Cartography Laboratory, Department of Anthropology, University of Illinois at Chicago.

PART I

INTRODUCTION

1

MIDDLE-CLASS CONSTRUCTION

> No actual class formation in history is any truer or more real than any
> other, and class defines itself as, in fact, it eventuates. Class, as it even-
> tuated within nineteenth-century industrial capitalist societies, and as
> it then left its imprint upon the heuristic category of class, has in fact
> no claim to universality.
>
> —E. P. Thompson, "Eighteenth-Century English Society"

Performing a Marriage

The wedding took place during the spring of 1991 on the ground
floor of a half-completed concrete home among the seemingly hap-
hazard thickets of similar homes that make up many of Kathmandu's sprawling middle-class suburbs. Above, laundry fluttered like
Tibetan prayer flags from clotheslines attached to the dozens of
twisted steel rods sprouting through the roof from the building's reinforced concrete pillars. Stretching into thin air, anxious for the
day when there would be enough money to add another story, the
metal rods seemed to mimic the family's uneasy straining to maintain the standards of a local middle-class lifestyle and testify to their
part in the ongoing social drama of middle-class construction.

Having been invited by a Nepali friend (a relative of the bride),
I felt privileged to witness the intricacies of an orthodox Hindu wedding and was sure it would be a traditional and authentic event. Yet
before long my happy reverie was shattered by the clamorous arrival of a local video camera crew. As the only "Westerner" in atten-
dance, I felt somehow personally responsible every time the cameramen—to me the embodiments of an intrusive, "alien" modernity—
held up the proceedings: interrupting the Brahman priest's chant-
ing, clumsily rearranging the wedding party, shining bright lights
onto the already distraught bride, and entangling everyone in light
and microphone cords. I was feeling terribly sorry for the group of
dignified women seated to one side—who seemed to be enduring
the almost slapstick proceedings with stoic resignation—until sud-

denly an elderly grandmother tottered to her feet shouting instructions to the wedding party and cameramen to essentially "Redo that last bit!"

In many ways this wedding story is an allegory of life in and for Kathmandu's middle class. The wedding served as a stage on which to perform middle-class culture, a culture that labors to produce itself out of the seemingly contradictory resources of "tradition" and "modernity." The awkward dance of the priest, wedding party, and camera crew is a miniature version of the dance of the middle class in Kathmandu, a dance that brings together a host of competing cultural assets, consumer demands, and media influences into a performance of cultural life that is by its nature complex, halting, unstable, and in periodic need of "redoing"! It is this sense of middle-class culture as practice, production, or performance—along with the anxieties that accompany any act of creation—that I aim to convey in this book. Like the unfinished home where the wedding took place, class culture is always a work-in-progress, a perpetual social construction that is as fundamentally bound to the "concrete" of economic resources as it is to the cultural practices of people who jointly negotiate their social identities.

Although the bride and groom were part of a cultural production shared with their elderly grandparents, the two parties were born on either side of a fundamental turning point in modern Nepali history. In 1951 a popular democratic movement (inspired by the Indian independence movement) put an end to a century of isolationist rule in Nepal. The decades since have seen the Kathmandu valley suddenly awash in a tidal wave of transnational political, economic, and cultural currents that have brought new ideas, new technologies, and ultimately, new ways of being. This book traces some of the sociocultural consequences of Kathmandu's opening to the world. It documents ways in which ever-expanding frames of cultural reference, and spheres of cultural influence, have transformed the lives of people in an ostensibly remote and isolated place.

People in Kathmandu are powerfully aware of living in a radically new era. Whereas the grandparents (and even parents) in this wedding story grew up at a time when communications with the world outside the Kathmandu valley required weeks of grueling overland travel, the bride and groom grew up watching global media events like the Gulf War and the World Cup "live" on television. People born since 1951 have witnessed the world arriving along the first motorable roads into the valley; through telephones and now satellite telecommunications; through electronic entertainment media (cinema, television, video, satellite TV); via air transportation, mass tourism, and a surge of global commodity imports; and through the logics of a new bureaucratic state apparatus, party politics, and large-scale foreign development aid. Technological and social developments that took place over the course of centuries in many parts of the world have in Nepal arrived in the space of the past five decades, and in particular, the last twenty-five years.[1]

In Kathmandu the past and present stand in extraordinarily stark contrast in almost every aspect of daily experience. Seen from the air, Kathmandu resembles a fried egg (map 1): a distinct center marks the old city (once surrounded by a wall), with its densely packed traditional architecture, while the sprawling ring of unplanned post-1950s "development"—rich farmland now covered by commercial districts and middle-class suburbs—stands as testimony to new movements of goods, capital, people, and cultural sensibilities. Similarly, for many urban Nepalis, core social and religious values (often manifest in terms of caste and kin affiliations) are engulfed—and sometimes overwhelmed—by a transformed sociocultural context adrift in new transnational currents: new labor and economic relations, a new universe of material goods, new arenas of public display, and new ideologies of education, progress, and modernity. As Kathmandu residents navigate through a range of built environments with vastly different histories, so also must they negotiate a range of competing and coexisting systems of value and meaning. In Kathmandu the meaning and experience of modernity lies in daily balancing the demands and possibilities of a transforming social and material context against those of a deeply rooted cultural milieu of moral values, systems of prestige, and notions of propriety.

This book has three goals: to describe the cultural contexts and historical processes out of which a new middle-class culture has emerged in Kathmandu; to provide a detailed account of the practices that make up contemporary urban middle-class life; and, drawing on these ethnographic insights, to offer a new approach to conceptualizing middle-class culture. This book argues that *class* best accounts for the new sociocultural patterns that have come to dominate urban life in Kathmandu. Caste, kinship, and ethnicity continue to powerfully inflect sociocultural experience, but the daily lives of people in Kathmandu demonstrate that the "epistemological styles" (Appadurai 1990b) of social life have shifted, leaving class as the framing principle for everyday experience. Within this emerging class society, this study focuses on the local *middle class*, those people carving out a new cultural space which they explicitly locate, in language and material practice, between their class "others" above and below.

[1] As I discuss in chapter 2, the massive changes following Nepal's "opening" in 1951 are due much less to the country's remoteness than to the previous political regime's deliberate policies of social and cultural isolation.

1. Middle-class suburban sprawl encroaching on open lands in Kathmandu's Sankhamul area

In this chapter I introduce some of the study's ethnographic contexts but focus mainly on sketching out the theoretical frame that I will use to make sense of the middle-class cultural life that I describe. This requires an excursion into the politically charged debates over class and cultural practice, debates which reach some of their most arcane and acrimonious levels when trying to theorize the middle class. Drawing from both Marxian and Weberian traditions, this study charts a path toward an anthropology of middle-class culture in Nepal, and elsewhere.

This approach to middle-class culture explicitly incorporates cultural processes of consumption (notably including the consumption of mass media), and the production of "youth culture." Class, consumption, media, and youth have all been subjects of anthropological study, but usually in isolation or in pairs: "youth and media" (Fuglesang 1994), "class and consumption" (Bourdieu 1984), "media and class" (Mankekar 1999), "youth and consumption" (Nava 1992, Sato 1991), and so on. Combining and building on the key insights provided by each of these studies (and many others), this book argues that class, consumption, media, and youth must be seen as not merely *interactive* but *mutually constitutive* cultural processes. In Kathmandu a burgeoning local consumer culture, the growing power of a mass-mediated popular imagination, and the recent emergence of "youth" as a distinct social category are, I suggest, best understood within the context of middle-class cultural life. Cultures of consumerism, media, and youth are not side effects or consequences of middle-class formation. Rather, they are among the most important cultural processes through which an emerging middle class actually creates itself as a sociocultural entity.

Over the past few decades in Kathmandu, an almost entirely new "intermediate" social "stratum" has emerged in the social gap between historically polarized national elites and urban commoners.[2] In the process, members of this middle class have had to construct entirely new forms of cultural practice. This book ethnographically documents the struggles—moral, material, and ideological—that an emerging middle class must undertake to produce a new cultural space where none had been before. The middle class occupies a precarious position along two continua. On the one hand, it is shaped by its self-conscious awareness of its position between "high" and "low" classes. On the other, it is forced to pioneer a space for Nepali national identity somewhere between the global ideological poles of tradition and modernity. People in Kathmandu's middle class are members (and often leaders) of a state with massive ideological and financial stakes in an international economy of "development aid."[3] Yet it is their position on the receiving end of a global development apparatus that defines its targets as undeveloped or "traditional" (Pigg 1992, Escobar 1995) that forces Kathmandu's middle class into the dilemma of reconciling their status as modernity's "traditional" other with their desires to claim a legitimate place within "modernity." Indeed, a great deal of the cultural work described in this book—the work of creating a new middle-class cultural space through processes of consumption, mass mediation, and youth culture—is part of the perhaps impossible project of transforming the idea of "Nepali modernity" from its condition as oxymoron in a global capitalist political economy of places into a legitimate reality in local cultural life.[4]

---

[2] Chapter 2 traces the background and early history of this middle-class formation over the past several centuries in Nepal.

[3] See chapter 2 for a discussion of the role of international development aid in Nepal's national economy generally and Kathmandu's local economy in particular.

[4] It is important to point out that the image of Nepali modernity presented in this study represents the experiences of a certain segment of Nepali society: the urban middle class. In the past decade scholars have begun to document other experiences of, and relations to, modernity in other Nepali communities. These include Jim Fisher's (1990), Vincanne Adams's (1996), Sherry Ortner's (1999b), and Kurt Luger's (2000) accounts of Nepali Sherpas, Laura Ahearn's study of youth, literacy, and concepts of "love" in the hills of west central Nepal (2001), as well as Stacy Pigg's (1992, 1996) and Sudhindra Sharma's (2001) studies of the cultural politics of development "aid" in various communities. Dor Bahadur Bista (1991) offers a provocative critique of Nepal's high-caste national leadership and its struggle/failure to modernize. These studies—along with the present one—document what are

Mirroring the organization of the book itself, the rest of this chapter introduces class, consumption, media, and youth.

CLASS AND CULTURE

Why Class?

Kathmandu might seem an odd choice for a study of class cultural dynamics. Indeed, not long ago a prominent British anthropologist argued in print that *classes* do not exist in Nepal and that *caste* is the only principle of social organization at work (Macfarlane 1994:114–15). While caste remains a strongly determining and self-orienting cultural force, this book shows that in the last decades people in Kathmandu have come to live more and more of their lives in contexts oriented around the social logic of class. From a series of detailed ethnographic perspectives, this book shows that class has increasingly come to be the *framing* paradigm for many people in Kathmandu, encompassing (though by no means eliminating) the social valence of caste. As more and more of everyday life revolves around the social imperatives of the money/market economy, the moral (and economic) logic of caste is subordinated to the economic (and moral) logic of class.

When writing about class, one has two basic options: either treat "class" as a given—a taken-for-granted, natural, universal category or concept that speaks for itself—or attempt to actually explain the word by describing the experience of class in everyday life. It is the latter option, the effort to understand class as cultural life, that poses a challenge to anthropology. But once we take up the challenge of constructing an anthropology of class, we are confronted with a range of problems. First, such an anthropology has to counter the claims that "class" does not exist, or that even if it did at one time, the late-twentieth-century "triumph" of the global capitalist order and its freedoms has made it a moot point. Yet even if we turn our backs on these neoliberal naysayers and side with the true believers, we are often not much farther along in the quest for an anthropology of class. The large social-science literature on class, in which the concept is far more often used than defined, leaves us the daunting task of actually describing and analyzing the relationship between class and culture. Ironically, an anthropology of class has to confront both the myths of classlessness and of class; that is, it has to chal-

---

surely only a few of the many specific social locations from which Nepalis experience modernity.

lenge those who deny the existence of class, even while it attempts to rescue the concept from its static state in social theory.

Out of Sight, Out of Mind

There are many reasons why students of anthropology should be interested in class. Surely one of anthropology's fundamental challenges as it begins a new century is to come to terms—theoretically, methodologically, existentially—with the fact that "the other we study is as modern, or as embedded in conditions of modernity, as we are" (Marcus 1990:5). Indeed, this book will argue that the "conditions of modernity" are even more glaringly prominent on the Third World periphery, in places like Kathmandu, where they stand starkly outlined against memories of earlier, suddenly "traditional," ways of being. Processes of urbanization, market penetration, bureaucratization, industrialization, and class formation play themselves out in ever-changing power relations that bring the local and global together in explosive and unpredictable ways. With fully half of the world's population now living in urban areas increasingly integrated into a world capitalist economy (D. Harvey 1996:403), the complex processes of social life encapsulated in the domains of class relations and practices are realities that anthropologists must confront.

That anthropologists have mainly shied away from the study of class is due only in part to their discipline's "traditional" subject matter. Non-Western, "premodern," "simple" societies were thought to operate around principles of social organization other than class, but then, so were the Western societies that anthropologists called home.[5] Particularly in the United States—an insistently "classless" society in which the vast majority of people self-identify as "middle class" (Roberts 1997)—the idea that "class" (with all of its uncomfortable implications of conflict and inequality) might have something to do with "our" everyday life verges on the antisocial and unpatriotic. In the United States, "we the people" have always been imagined as a classless collectivity in which social inequality must be ideologically subsumed into "one country, indivisible."

But the "we" of "we the people" has also always been an imperfect reflection of the nation, and it is precisely the myth of "the people"—and the nation's "others" that such a myth produces—that lays open the myth

---

[5] As Sherry Ortner puts it, "It is well known that American natives almost never speak of themselves or their society in class terms. In other words, class is not a central category of cultural discourse in America, and the anthropological literature that ignores class in favor of almost any other set of social idioms—ethnicity, race, kinship—is in some ways merely reflecting this fact" (1991:169).

of classlessness. From its very beginnings, America's "classless society" has been precariously maintained through the exploitation of human and natural peripheries. Superabundant North American natural resources (exploited in largely nonsustainable ways) provided an extractive "frontier" that opened the way for social mobility and the vast accumulation of wealth. Over the centuries, slavery, steady influxes of vulnerable immigrant populations, and, more recently, highly productive migrant-labor populations (often criminalized and therefore easily exploitable) have all served as a kind of shifting human extractive frontier (hidden within the nation) that has helped make possible the "classless" middle-class American lifestyle. Finally, late-capitalist economic "globalization" has only helped bolster the North American experience of "classlessness" through a series of new regional and global "free trade" regimes (North American Free Trade Association [NAFTA], World Trade Organization [WTO], etc.) that ever more effectively exile our class others out of sight and out of mind.[6] When the Zapatistas of Mexico's Chiapas region timed the launch of their armed peasant rebellion to coincide with the implementation of the NAFTA agreement on 1 January 1994, they gave clear indication that transnational class antagonisms were alive and well in the "new world order" in spite of the First World's happy, classless rhetoric of freedom, democracy, and "competitive advantage" (N. Harvey 1998:181–82). Middle-class Americans, including anthropologists, may project their imagined classless society onto an "ideal" world of free trade and democracy, but it is a depoliticizing, disempowering myth that finds increasingly fewer takers (Shiva 2000, Escobar 1995, N. Harvey 1998, etc.).

This study of class cultural practice in Nepal does not address the overtly antagonistic, potentially explosive relations between new Third World working classes and transnational capital that some anthropologists have studied (Ferguson 1994, Nash and Fernandez-Kelly 1983, Ong 1987, Weyland 1993). Although it draws from and relates to these and many other studies, this book's theoretical and ethnographic focus is elsewhere. Rather than addressing class theory in general, this book contributes to the specific task of *conceptualizing middle-class cultural practice*. Focusing on the middle class, to the relative exclusion of other class formations with and against which the middle class exists, is not simply a capricious act on my part. Characterizing the middle class as a social and cultural entity has always presented a distinct challenge to class theorists. It is the middle class's extraordinarily complex culture—with its myriad forms of competing cultural capital, its ambiguous and anxiety-inducing relationship with the capitalist market, its intricate systems of dissimula-

---

[6] See Sitton 1996 for an interesting analysis of Wallerstinian world-system theory and transnational class relations.

tion (whereby it hides its class privilege in everyday practice)—along with its increasingly dominant role in cultural process worldwide, that makes it an important and timely subject of anthropological inquiry. Understanding local middle-class cultural processes in world context is no less important than understanding the relations between transnational labor and capital. What is more, understanding the cultural politics of "middleness" in Kathmandu—a place where a new cultural middle ground is still being pioneered, its structures and fault lines not yet obscured by the sediments of time—may shed light on the class-cultural politics of denial whereby we perpetuate our own myth of classlessness.

The "Embarrassment of the Middle Classes"

Despite the fact that "class" has a long and illustrious pedigree in social theory—and is arguably one of modern social science's foundational ideas—it remains an exceedingly difficult concept to pin down. From the very beginnings of modern social science, class has been a category more often invoked than actually theorized. Even Karl Marx and Max Weber, the two seminal theorists of modern capitalist society, never fleshed out systematic, comprehensive theories of class.[7] Although Marx and Weber are often represented as opposing theorists, in what writings they *did* leave on the issue of class, the two are not as far apart as one might suppose. In the last decades neo-Marxist and neo-Weberian class theorists have narrowed the gap even further (Burris 1987:67). Whether this melding represents the "Marxianizing" of Weberian theory (Wright 1997:34) or the fall of Marxist theory to "the Weberian temptation" (Sitton 1996:36)[8] is not the issue here. What is clear is that the strengths of each theoretical tradition have proven to be, at least in part, complementary.

Nowhere has the convergence between Marxian and Weberian class theory been more pronounced than in efforts to theorize the middle class.

---

[7] Tom Bottomore notes that "The concept of class has a central importance in Marxist theory, though neither Marx nor Engels ever expounded it in a systematic form" (1983:74). Similarly, Talcott Parsons—one of Weber's chief disciples and interpreters—observes that, aside from a brief, sketchy, unfinished chapter at the end of Weber's *Economy and Society*, there is "no other part of Weber's published work in which the subject [of class] is systematically developed" (editorial note in Weber 1947:429). Sitton (1996:265) also notes the theoretical inconsistencies in Weber's writing on class.

[8] In one classic exchange, the staunch Weberian Frank Parkin interpreted the partial convergence of Marxist and Weberian class theory as evidence of "the virtues of bourgeois sociology. Inside every neo-Marxist there seems to be a Weberian struggling to get out" (1979:25). In response, the neo-Marxist Erik Olin Wright noted that "One could just as easily say that inside every left-wing Weberian there is a Marxist struggling to stay hidden" (1997:35)!

Marx's failure to anticipate the twentieth-century expansion of middle classes in advanced capitalist societies has been a source of ongoing theoretical crisis for Marxist theorists (Sitton 1996:17). The "embarrassment of the middle classes" (Wright 1985:13) has been the Achilles heel of Marxist class theory. It is no coincidence that Weber's response to Marx's writings on class consists mainly of an elaboration on sociocultural processes within what Weber referred to as the "intermediate strata" or "middle classes." Since that time, "Marxists have drawn heavily upon Weberian concepts in their effort to adapt classical Marxism to the conditions of late twentieth-century capitalism" (Burris 1987:67). An anthropology of middle-class cultural practice needs to unite a Weberian sensitivity to the powerful role of culture in social life with a Marxian commitment to locate different forms of cultural practice in the context of unequal distributions of power and resources in society.[9]

One way to begin this kind of reconciliation is to view Marx and Weber in light of the different historical moments, class experiences, and political concerns that each addressed. In the context of mid-nineteenth-century labor exploitation, unrest, and mobilization, Marx stressed the material underpinnings of class and the historical dynamic of conflict between workers and capitalists. Underdeveloped in Marx's work is an appreciation for the constitutive role of culture in the production and maintenance of class power[10] and a concern for the nature of cultural life within class groups.[11] Marx recognized the link between economic status and ideology; he saw that class privilege produced a privileged (and privileging) ideology. But he did not appreciate how important a role the very *cultures of social privilege* played in actually producing and reproducing the material reality of economic power.

By the early twentieth century, overt struggles between labor and capital had begun to wane, the European and American middle classes were growing rapidly, and a new mass-production–based *consumer society* had

[9] For useful comparative discussions of Marx and Weber on class and culture, see Bottomore 1966, Burris 1987, Elias 1978 [1968], Gerth and Mills 1946, Hall 1997, Robison and Goodman 1996, and Wright 1997:29–33.

[10] Or, as Tom Bottomore puts it, "Marx insisted that the ruling ideas of any society are the ideas of the ruling class. But he did not seriously consider how important the ideas themselves might be in sustaining that rule, or how difficult it would be for the working class to oppose them with its own ideas" (1966:94).

[11] Although Marx rarely used the word "culture," he did occasionally venture into the realms of what we would now recognize as the "cultural." For example, in "The General Relation of Production to Distribution, Exchange, Consumption," which appears in the *Grundrisse* (1973 [1857–58]:88–100), Marx discusses clothing, food, the arts, the constitution of needs, and so on as cultural aspects of consumption intimately tied into the larger unity of the productive cycle as a whole. For Marx the cultural was, ultimately, a product of production. The material was ontologically prior to the cultural.

dawned.[12] Much of Weber's class theory describes the sociocultural conditions of those people I will call "middle-class," even though Weber himself insisted on using only the terms "middle classes" and "intermediate strata,"[13] apparently as a way of registering his opposition to the Marxist practice of collapsing groups of people into class categories based only on their material relations. Although I affirm Weber's contention that the reality of socioeconomic life is much more complex than the materialist class theory of his day could accommodate, I believe it is possible to construct a theory of middle-class cultural practice that acknowledges Weber's concerns for sociocultural complexity while at the same time envisioning a shared sphere of class practice. In this book I will argue that Weber's "intermediate" groups are not just a series of "strata" or stratified "classes" but a "middle class," characterized by a set of class-specific sociocultural processes that Weber himself was among the first to describe.

Weber's writings on class help to correct some of the economic reductionism of the Marxian tradition by introducing what anthropologists would recognize as "culture" into the equation of socioeconomic power. Weber's main qualification of Marxist class theory is his insistence that *class position* (economic power) is distinct from—though often tied to—*social status* (honor or prestige). Weber observed that social status is very frequently related to class position but "is not . . . determined by this alone" (Weber 1947:428). *Class*, for Weber, was a function of a person or group's position in the capitalist market, both in terms of relations of production (capitalist or laborer) and in terms of ability to consume goods and services in the market. Social *status* on the other hand had to do with a person or group's lifestyle; education, training, and socialization; and

---

[12] "This era [c. 1880–1930] sees the emergence of a mass production system of manufacture increasingly dedicated to producing consumer goods (rather than the heavy capital goods, such as steel, machinery and chemicals, which dominated much of the later nineteenth century). . . . Incontrovertibly, it is in this period that all the features which make up consumer culture take on their mature form, but more importantly it is in this period that a modern *norm* emerges concerning how consumer goods are to be produced, sold and assimilated into everyday life" (Slater 1997:13). See also Susman 1984, Simmel 1950 [1903], Veblen 1953 [1899].

[13] In some places Weber speaks of "*the 'middle' classes*" as those groups "who have all sorts of property, or of marketable abilities through training, who are in a position to draw their support from these sources." Later he adds that "independent peasants and craftsmen are [also] to be treated as belonging to the 'middle classes.' This category often includes in addition officials . . . , the liberal professions, and workers with exceptional monopolistic assets or positions" (1947:425, 427). At other times Weber speaks of the same people as constituting the "*intermediate strata*," a "continuum of more or less clearly defined status positions determined by a variety of factors and not simply by property ownership" and characterized by internal "relations of competition and emulation, not of conflict" (Bottomore 1966:25–26).

inherited or occupational prestige. With a critique of Marx in mind, Weber wrote,

> In contrast to the purely economically determined "class situation" we wish to designate as "status situation" every typical component of the life fate of men that is determined by a specific, positive or negative, social estimation of *honor*. This honor may be connected with any quality shared by a plurality, and, of course, it can be knit to a class situation: class distinctions are linked in the most varied ways with status distinctions. Property as such is not always recognized as a status qualification, but in the long run is, and with extraordinary regularity. (Weber 1946:186–87)

Weber never explicitly laid out a mechanism that theorized these links between social status and class situation. Yet by acknowledging that class and status are knit together "with extraordinary regularity," Weber affirmed Marx's equation of property and power, even while insisting that economic dominance is always culturally mediated in patterns of socialization, lifestyles, and discourses of honor and prestige.[14] In effect, Weber maintains that even while power is almost always rooted in economic privilege, it is also always exercised and reproduced culturally. Weber's distinction between class and status helped foreground the role of culture (lifestyle, education, material culture, and so on) in class practice, but by focusing mainly on sociocultural dynamics *within* middle-class groups (a politics of competing status claims), Weber and his followers typically downplay Marxist concerns for ways in which access to economic resources structures relations *between* classes.[15]

This difference between Marx and Weber reflects at least in part the fact that by the time Weber appeared on the European scene a very different class dynamic had emerged, one in which a new abundance of mass-produced consumer goods was beginning to defuse earlier forms of overtly class-based politics by opening up a space for a new middle class. The new middle class did not own the "means of production" (productive assets like factories or plantations), but its members were offered access

---

[14] According to Wright, it should not be surprising to find considerable agreement between Weber and Marx on class since, Wright believes, "Weber's class analysis is deeply indebted to the Marxist legacy which was part of the general intellectual discourse of his time," and "in many ways Weber is speaking in his most Marxian voice when he talks about class" (1997:29, n. 32; 30). The Weberian social theorist John Hall says much the same thing: "The Weber relevant to class analysis is better located within an agenda of political economy deeply shared with Marx" (1997:16).

[15] Class analysis has largely fallen out of mainstream sociological inquiry and has been replaced by models of social hierarchy based on presumably "freely competing" individual status claims.

to other forms of "property": consumer goods, autos, even private homes. The growth of this new middle class reflected both the rapidly increasing bureaucratic, service, and professional labor sectors, and the ability of the new consumer economy to absorb large portions of the old working classes into the middle class by encouraging them to construct their social identities more around the goods and property they *owned* than the kind of *work* they did (cf. Halle 1984).[16] Many social historians have documented this shift in social identification from "you are what you do" to "you are what you have" (e.g., Susman 1984, Lears 1983), but it is perhaps less often noted that the same shift also charts the move, in Western societies, away from a politics of interclass antagonism (analyzed by Marx) toward an increasingly dominant middle-class ethos of intraclass status competition (analyzed by Weber).

The growing cultural and political dominance of the European and American middle classes in the early twentieth century—the "embourgeoisement" of mainstream society—has long been the subject of critical commentary.[17] My own concern is with how emerging middle classes construct themselves as cultural entities, how their cultural life essentially depoliticizes social life (or hides middle-class privilege behind screens of seemingly "natural" cultural practice in the realms of "status"), and what insights we can glean from social theorists like Marx and Weber into the cultural politics and practices of "middle-classness" in other times and places. Drawing on Weber (and other theorists within the Weberian tradition), this book portrays the middle class in Nepal as a domain of *internally competing* cultural strategies, systems of prestige ("status"), and forms of "capital" that are not, strictly speaking, economic (Bourdieu 1985). But, I will argue, this internal cultural dynamic is always also part of a middle-class project to construct itself in *opposition* to its class others, above and below. The middle class is fundamentally situated in a larger class economy in which power and resources are unevenly distributed. This book constantly returns to Marxian concern for the cultural politics of "ruling ideas," or how the cultural practices of the middle class disguise its class privileges (its economic and political powers) behind seemingly noneconomic rhetorics of honor, achievement, and so on. In this book the middle class emerges as a never-ending cultural project that is simultaneously at odds with itself and with its class others. The middle class is a constantly renegotiated cultural space—a space of ideas, values, goods,

---

[16] At that historical moment, Weber notes that, "[F]or the first time mere 'possession' as such emerges as decisive for the fate of the individual" (1946:182–83).

[17] By the likes of Thorstein Veblen (1953 [1899]), Walter Benjamin (Buck-Morss 1991), the Frankfurt School (e.g., Adorno and Horkheimer 1979 [1944]), and Jurgen Habermas (1989 [1962]), to name only a few.

practices, and embodied behaviors—in which the terms of inclusion and exclusion are endlessly tested, negotiated, and affirmed. From this point of view, it is the process, not the product, that constitutes class.

Middle-Class Cultural Practice

Whereas Marx paid scant attention to the role or nature of middle classes (Bottomore 1983:75), Weber focused almost entirely on them. Indeed, one of Weber's main critiques of Marx is that "materialist" theory fails to adequately characterize social dynamics within the middle class.[18] That Weberian theory fails to adequately characterize the politics of *inter*class conflict has already been noted, but Weber did make important contributions to our understandings of middle-class cultural life. Foremost among these are his observations concerning middle-class *relations to the market* and the unstable sociocultural dynamic of *status competition* within the middle class. Weber's discussions of consumption and status rivalry provide very useful insights into the dynamics of middle-class cultural practice in Kathmandu.

One of Weber's key breaks with Marxist or materialist portrayals of class is his observation that the middle class relates to economic or productive processes not primarily as sellers of labor (workers) or owners of capital (the capitalist elite) but as *consumers* of goods in the market place.[19] In other words, the middle class's position is determined less di-

---

[18] A great deal of Weber's work on middle-class values and sociocultural dynamics (e.g., on the "Protestant ethic" [1958 (1904–5)]) is written with the "ghost of Marx" always hovering just out of sight (Giddens 1971:185), usually in the form of critical references to "materialism."

[19] In some places Weber links "class situation" to "market situation":

> It is the most elemental economic fact that the way in which the disposition over material property is distributed among a plurality of people . . . in itself creates specific life chances. . . . "Property" and "lack of property" are, therefore, the basic categories of all class situations. . . . But always this is the generic connotation of the concept of class: that the kind of chance in the *market* is the decisive moment which presents a common condition for the individual's fate. "Class situation" is . . . ultimately "market situation." . . . [F]or the first time mere "possession" as such emerges as decisive for the fate of the individual. (1946:181–83, italics in original)

At other times Weber implies that only "status groups" are determined by consumption and lifestyle, even while insisting that class and status are essentially equivalent:

> With some over-simplification, one might thus say that "classes" are stratified according to their relations to the production and acquisition of goods; whereas "status groups" are stratified according to the principles of the *consumption* of goods as repre-

rectly by its relations to the "means of production" (selling labor or owning capital) than by its relations to the market, that is, by its ability to consume.[20] With its members engaged mainly in "tertiary" labor—professionals, bureaucrats, teachers, retail entrepreneurs, independent artisans, and the like—the middle class is one step removed from the productive processes of capital. Whereas workers earn "wages," and capitalists earn "dividends," members of the middle class earn "salaries," a term that implies a certain *moral* distance from "mere" laboring and "mere" wealth.[21] Instead, the middle class stakes its identity on its accomplishments and refinement, moral discourses that it pursues largely through its privileged access to goods and services (from education to fashions) in the "free" market. Thus, for Weber a group's middle-classness is a function of its place in the capitalist economy, a sheltered space removed both economically and morally from the "vulgarities" of production and enacted through the "democratic freedoms" of the consumer marketplace. Weber's views on how middle-class morality is related to its position within the larger class economy, and how a rhetoric of morality naturalizes and defends middle-class privilege, provide important insights into middle-class cultural practice in Kathmandu.

Weber's other key insight into the nature of middle-classness concerns the way in which a range of different cultural formations, lifestyles, and

---

sented by special "styles of life.". . . The differences between classes and status groups frequently overlap. (1946:193, italics in original).

[20] Weberian social theorists often interpret Weber's insistence that class is a function of a group's "market capacities" as somehow being at odds with a Marxian understanding of class as a function of a group's relations to the "means of production." I, however, agree with Wright (1997:30), who argues that both Marx and Weber saw class as fundamentally a matter of access to "economically relevant assets or resources," and as such, "both are really talking about very similar phenomena."

[21] One of Weber's main objectives in theoretically separating "class" from "status" seems to have been precisely to capture this moral/moralizing tendency of middle-class discourse.

The status order means precisely . . . stratification in terms of "honor" and of styles of life peculiar to status groups as such. If the *mere* economic acquisition and *naked economic power* still bearing the *stigma* of its extra-status origin could bestow upon anyone who has won it the same honor as those who are interested in status by virtue of style of life claim for themselves, the status order would be threatened at its very root. . . . Therefore *all groups having interests in the status order react with special sharpness precisely against the pretensions of purely economic acquisition.* In most cases they react the more vigorously the more they feel themselves threatened. (Weber 1946:192, italics added)

Status "honor" is all about morally distancing oneself from the "stigma" of "mere" economic power, not to mention the stigma of mere labor.

status claims compete *within* the middle class. Precisely because of their ambiguous relationship to the productive economy (as neither workers nor capitalists), members of the middle class live in a relatively unstable socioeconomic space. This instability is mirrored in the constantly contested, highly materialistic, and anxious character of middle-class lives. Forced to market their "skills," "services," and "accomplishments" in the capitalist "free market," members of the middle class are those who must constantly promote and justify their self-worth in the face of competing claims in the market. In many ways the middle class could be said to *absorb into* its own class-cultural practice the antagonisms between labor and capital that have historically been played out *between* the working and capitalist classes (cf. Miller 1995c:49). The anxieties and contradictions of middle-class life might be understood as reflecting this "internalized" class conflict within people who are simultaneously sellers of labor and owners of capital (professional, educational, and so on).

It is interesting that Weber's most detailed discussion of the intensely competitive and anxious nature of middle-class cultural life comes in an account of his visit to the United States, which, he argued, was "undergoing a profound transformation" toward a much more status-oriented and status-conscious society (1946:311). Writing in the early twentieth century, Weber saw the "characteristic form" of "stratification by 'status groups' on the basis of conventional styles of life" emerging "at the present time in the United States" (Weber 1946:188). He stressed how in the United States the neighborhood in which one lived was crucial to claims of "belonging to 'society,' " and "above all," how status claims demanded "strict submission to the fashion that is dominant at a given time in society," a submission that "exists among men in America to a degree unknown in Germany" (ibid.). In the same way that "strict submission" to fashion was a crucial factor in determining one's employment chances, social intercourse, and marriage arrangements in the United States (according to Weber), so also in the 1990s Kathmandu's middle-class culture was characterized by intense social pressures to conform to local consumer fashion standards.[22]

Running parallel with the powerful forces of *emulation* in the United States were equally powerful forces of status *competition*. Weber noted that there were

all sorts of circles setting themselves apart by means of many other characteristics and badges . . . all these elements usurp "status" honor. The development of status is essentially a question of stratifi-

---

[22] Chapters 3 to 5 ethnographically document the strict demands of fashion within Kathmandu's middle class.

cation resting upon usurpation. . . . But the road from this purely conventional situation to legal privilege . . . is easily traveled as soon as a certain stratification of the social order has in fact been "lived in" and has achieved stability by virtue of a stable distribution of economic power. (1946:188)

Here Weber depicts middle-class life as a space of competing status "circles," each trying to "usurp 'status' honor" for its own configuration of "characteristics and badges." But Weber also makes it clear that this game of competing status claims is no cakewalk. For claims to status honor to be more than mere claims, they have to be "lived in" (or "lived out") and converted into "legal privilege" through a cold and ruthless process of valorization "by virtue of . . . economic power." Indeed, it is crucial to see how processes of status emulation ("submission to fashion") and status competition are all fundamentally rooted in the vagaries and instabilities of the market place. Middle-class status is as precarious and fleeting as middle-class fashions, and it is the chronic fickleness of the "fashion system" (Barthes 1983) that perhaps best analogizes the anxious cultural experience of middle-classness. In this book I will argue that the middle class's relations to the capitalist market and productive processes (a position of instability, ambiguity, vulnerability), its distinct internal sociocultural dynamic (of competing lifestyles and consumer paranoia), and the ways in which these lifestyles naturalize economic privilege (by couching it in a language of honor and morality that excludes its class others) are precisely what make up some of the key generative, or constitutive, cultural dynamics of middle-class practice.

How are we to fit contemporary Nepal into this understanding of middle-class culture, a view derived (via Marx and Weber) from the experiences of people in distant times and places? In one way, this study could be read as a contribution to the larger project of chronicling the global social history of bourgeois culture. Many of the cultural processes of capitalism and class formation that this study depicts have occurred—in the broadest sense—elsewhere before,[23] and continue to unfold around the

[23] To give just one example, there are remarkable similarities between the Nepali middle-class discourse of "suitability" (discussed in chapter 3) and what George Mosse (1985) calls the "concept of respectability" that emerged within the nineteenth-century European national middle classes.

The middle classes can only be partially defined by their economic activity and even by their hostility to the aristocracy and the lower classes alike. For side by side with their economic activity it was above all the ideal of respectability which came to characterize their style of life. . . . They perceived their way of life, based as it was upon frugality, devotion to duty, and restraint of the passions, as superior to that of the

world. Yet because many of these processes were palpably new to people in Kathmandu in the 1990s, this ethnographic study is able to capture something of the extraordinarily self-conscious awareness of living in an era of transformation, an experience that fosters overt reflection on the meanings of, and contradictions inherent to, processes of "development" and "modernization." Out of these experiences emerge important insights into how modern consumer subjectivities are created, embodied, and naturalized, how forms of capitalist promotion (media and others) constitute desire in webs of cross-referencing mutual publicity, and how new forms of social identification (for example, "youth") emerge from processes of class formation and commodification. For comparative purposes, this study provides glimpses of a crucial historical "moment" in the development of modern capitalist society.

But it is equally clear that this "moment" in Nepal's cultural history should by no means be understood as the "reliving" of someone else's history, or as the story of Nepal's "catching up with" the West. Middle-class life in Kathmandu is in no way merely derivative or, to quote this chapter's epigraph, less "true" or "real" than the Western experience of class. Though middle-class life in Kathmandu shares some of the key sociocultural dynamics that I have identified above, its meaning, experience, and nature are uniquely Nepali. As I show throughout this book, middle-class life in Kathmandu is mediated by local caste logics and other religiously based notions of propriety and suitability that, in turn, shape middle-class discourses of honor and prestige. Similarly, powerful state-promoted ideologies of "development" intersect with changing consumer market conditions and media exposure to produce uniquely local middle-class experiences of national identity and feelings of cultural marginalization. These and a host of other social, cultural, and economic factors discussed in this book make it abundantly clear that middle-class experience in Kathmandu is *never* a reliving of some Western social past[24] (even if contemporary Nepali cultural life is often represented, and even experienced, in those terms).

Capitalist modernity does not doom the globe to a condition of cultural homogenization, talk of "westernization" and "cultural imperialism" notwithstanding (cf. Tomlinson 1991). If we understand middle-classness as a cultural project or practice—rather than a social category

---

"lazy" lower classes and the profligate aristocracy. Thus, the definition of the bourgeoisie . . . arises out of the growth of respectability itself. (Mosse 1985:4–5)

[24] In chapter 2 I show that processes of class formation in Nepal over the past several centuries are part of the same global historical trends within capitalist modernity that generated class formations around the world. The denial of "coevality" (Fabian 1983) is a popular conceit, but a conceit all the same.

or empirical condition—we can begin to see how the local and the global are brought together in cultural process, not cultural outcome. The ever more globalized condition of capitalist modernity means a world of increasingly shared cultural processes (such as class formation), not shared cultural lives or cultural meanings.

Class as Cultural Process: "Stories That Tell People"

How are we to conceptualize "class as cultural process"? How can an anthropology of class go beyond viewing culture as object, outcome, or product? What alternatives are there for reconceptualizing middle-class culture in processual terms? A number of important steps have already been made in this direction, though ethnographic representations of class practice are few.

For almost a century social theorists have tried to reconceptualize class, in the words of E. P. Thompson, not "as a 'structure,' nor even as a 'category,' but as something which in fact *happens* (and can be shown to have happened) *in human relationships*" (1966 [1963]:9, italics added).[25] Among at least some academics, there has arisen what Patrick Joyce identifies as an increasingly "deeply felt need" to think in "processual ways about the nature of the social" (1997:xi–xii). Yet these efforts to "processualize" class—to think beyond static categories and dualistic "structural" oppositions such as "culture" and "economy"—face a never-ending epistemological battle with the Western predilection toward forcing "object-ness," or stasis, onto all phenomena, even processes (Tyler 1984:27).

Within anthropology this "poststructuralist" turn was marked by the decline of earlier functionalist, "ethnoscience," and interpretive schools in favor of a new trend toward "practice theory" (Ortner 1984, Marcus and Fischer 1986). Pierre Bourdieu's notion of "habitus" (1977, 1980) has been one of the most influential formulations of practice theory within anthropology. Bourdieu's insistence that social science focus on the *ways that culture works* (the "modus operandi") rather than the *outcomes* of cultural labor (the "opus operatum") (1980:52) has helped

---

[25] This is not the place for a detailed history of the efforts social theorists have made to pull a concept of class as cultural process from the teleological and categorical confinements of orthodox Marxist class theory and from political oblivion in Weberian sociology. From the long-ignored writings of Antonio Gramsci (1971) and Norbert Elias (1978 [1935], 1978 [1968]) to the work of the British "cultural Marxists" (Thompson 1966 [1963], Williams 1977) and members of the Birmingham Centre for Contemporary Cultural Studies (Hall et al. 1977, Hall 1986, Willis 1977), efforts to theorize and portray class as cultural practice have been ongoing.

shift culture theory toward processual perspectives.[26] Although not often viewed as an example of "practice theory," Mary Douglas and Baron Isherwood's *The World of Goods* (1979) was one of the first anthropological works on class-cultural process.[27] Since the 1980s anthropologists have looked to other disciplines and theoretical schools for inspiration in efforts to construct more nuanced approaches to culture-as-process. These have ranged from calls for a new process-based anthropological cultural history, building on the work of Gramsci and the British "cultural Marxists" (Fox 1985, 1989, 1991),[28] to phenomenological approaches built around notions of "preobjective," "prereflexive" embodied culture (Csordas 1990:6) and "the making of lived worlds" (Weiss 1996). Drawing on Michel Foucault's poststructuralist theory of power—according to which power is productive or constitutive, rather than simply repressive (Foucault 1979:200ff., 1980:93ff.)—anthropologists have also embraced new process-oriented ideas such as "discursivity" and "governmentality" (e.g., Darian-Smith 1999, Escobar 1995, Ferguson 1994, Yang 1994). Performative nouns like these help us rethink culture away from the image of restrictive "web" and toward an understanding of *the cultural* as that which *produces in day-to-day practice the contours of power*—along the axes of gender, sexual, racial, ethnic, *and* class difference—that constitute social life. But Foucault's radical refusal to locate power in social formations make his ideas like "bio-power" (1980) and "discipline" (1979) difficult to translate from theory to method, spurring social theorists to search for other, less elusive pathways to a view of culture as process.

Theories of "performativity" and "narrativity" are two trends that promise more accessible avenues into the nitty-gritty of cultural process

[26] For all its subtleties, Bourdieu's notion of habitus—even with its emphasis on cultural practice and process—fails to break cleanly with structural, "objective" understandings of culture and class. In Bourdieu's hands, habitus becomes not just a kind of iron cage outside of which creative thought and practice is "unthinkable" (1980:54) but also a kind of black box "generating practices perfectly conforming to its logic and demands" (1980:57). Thus, in *Distinction*, Bourdieu's influential work on French class culture (1984 [1979]), classes remain a priori analytical categories into which cultural traits are simply filed.

[27] By characterizing class groups as spheres of exchange in which people who share certain social and material conditions attempt to synchronize their cultural domains of value (1979:126–27), Douglas and Isherwood insist that classes be understood as sets of cultural processes, rather than predetermined outcomes. Their concept is not unlike Bourdieu's idea of habitus: "Each person is a source of judgements and a subject of judgements; each individual is in the classification scheme whose discriminations he is helping to establish. . . . [A]ny choice between goods is the result of, and contributes to, culture" (Douglas and Isherwood 1979:75–76).

[28] For Fox, culture exists only as it is practiced and, as such, it is "constantly being made, unmade, and remade." Cultural traditions always encode systems of dominance and inequality that are reproduced or abandoned through "active human endeavor" (1989:29).

and practice. This study draws on both of these theoretical perspectives for ways of representing and analyzing facets of middle-class cultural life as cultural process. Often associated with gender studies generally, and the work of Judith Butler in particular,[29] theories of performativity are built around a distinction between deliberate or intentional behaviors ("performance") and behaviors that are enacted and embedded in complex cultural contexts that shape or "script" cultural performances in significant, though not necessarily absolute, ways ("performativity"). As Louisa Schein explains, theories of performativity suggest that "there is no essence, origin, or reality prior to or outside of the enactment of a multiplicity of performances. It is the recurring regularity in performances that makes certain social norms acquire their authority, their aura of inevitability (1999:369)." In the same way that gender could be said to be nonexistent outside of its endlessly repeated sociocultural performance, this book adapts ideas of performativity to class theory to suggest that class also is a reality, but one that exists only in its perpetual sociocultural enactment within a limiting "matrix of intelligibility" (Butler 1990:17).

While the idea of performativity allows one to see class as process, perpetually reenacted and recreated by the bearers of class culture, it is less helpful in opening windows into the "matrix" or context that transforms agentive "performance" into objectifying "performativity." In other words, performativity theory is less successful at conveying the sense of how the historical continuity, or inertia, of cultural life extends from the past into the present, and even projects itself onto the future. Here I feel that a theory of "narrativity" provides a valuable complement to "performativity." The ideas of "narrative" and "narrativity" help us conceptualize, analyze, and ethnographically represent *what it is* that is being performed in sociocultural life, and how the "matrix of intelligibility" is itself culturally produced.[30]

Out of the extensive literature on narrative theory from many disciplines,[31] Margaret Somers's work in historical sociology on processes of class and identity formation (1994a, 1994b, 1997) is particularly relevant to this study. Somers turns to narrativity as a way of escaping classic social-science analytic categories like society, culture, tradition, class, economy, and so on, all of which she rejects as "abstractions, denarrativ-

[29] See Schein 1999:369, 2000 for discussions of the origins of performance/performativity theory.

[30] Performativity theory tends to posit an analytical distinction between performance and context as though the context, like a stage, exists prior to and independently of the performance.

[31] Lewis Hinchman and Sandra Hinchman's edited volume (1997a) is a valuable introduction to the use of narrative theory across a range of scholarly disciplines.

ized and atemporal" (1997:75). For Somers, narratives are "stories that social actors use to make sense of—indeed to act in—their lives" (1997:84). Through stories ("narratives")[32] of honor and shame, heroes and villains, piety and sacrilege, exploitation and resistance, pasts and futures, people construct worlds of cultural meaning, and in turn construct themselves. As such, narratives are not only stories that *people tell*, but "stories that *tell people*."[33] According to Somers, a narrative perspective on social process holds

> that social life is itself *storied* and that narrative is an *ontological condition of social life* . . . ; that people construct identities (however multiple and changing) by locating themselves or being located within a repertoire of emplotted stories; that "experience" is constituted through narratives; that people make sense of what has happened and is happening to them by attempting to assemble or in some way to integrate these happenings within one or more narratives; and that people are guided to act in certain ways, and not others, on the basis of the projections, expectations, and memories derived from a multiplicity [*sic*] but ultimately limited repertoire of available social, public, and cultural narratives. (1994a:613–14, italics in original)

Through cultural narrative people learn who they *are*; through cultural narrativity people learn who they should *become*. It is through narratives and narrativity that groups of people transport ideas about meaning and value from the past into the present, where these stories then stake claims to the futures of those who tell them.

For Somers a crucial aspect of narrativity is its "fundamental trait of relationality": "Narrativity renders understanding only by connecting *parts* (however unstable) to a constructed *configuration* or a *social network* (however incoherent or unrealizable). The connectivity of parts turns (events) into *episodes*, whether or not the sequence of episodes is

---

[32] I use the words "narrative" and "story" more or less interchangeably. Although not all stories are narratives, narratives are stories of a particular kind. Hinchman and Hinchman's definition is a useful starting point: "narratives (stories) . . . [are] discourses with a clear sequential order that connect events in a meaningful way for a definite audience, and thus offer insights about the world and/or people's experiences of it" (1997b:xvi). Similarly, for Seidman, "Narratives tell a story; they are organized around a plot, a linear, sequencing of events, a marked beginning and end, and a tale of good and evil intended to shape social behavior" (1994:205). These definitions capture both the sequential/causative and relational/social aspects of narrative stories.

[33] I borrow the wonderfully evocative phrase "stories that tell people" from the title of Sarah Miller's beautifully written study of high-caste marriage ritual in Kathmandu (1992). Miller's analysis of linguistic "performatives" leads her in some of the same directions as I take here in my use of performativity and narrativity.

presented or experienced in anything resembling chronological order" (1997:82, italics in original). In other words, cultural narratives always exist in relationship both with *other people* and *other times*. Stories constantly circulate through channels of relationships, but they also flow through time (from generation to generation), carrying the momentum of the past into the present and into dreams for the future. In this way narratives serve as powerful carriers of both cultural epistemology and ontology: stories in and of relationality tell people who they are (and are not),[34] but they also place individuals within the flow of cultural time, carrying them along with a tide of cultural inertia that is difficult to resist. It is this cultural inertia of narrativity that, I believe, offers useful insights into the nature of the "matrix" or constraining context of cultural performance and performativity.

This book uses concepts of both performativity and narrativity as ways of understanding the cultural processes of middle-class life in Kathmandu. Performance perspectives help shed light on how people actively produce class culture in ways that with surprising regularity—as in the wedding tale told at the beginning of this chapter—have overtly dramaturgical (and increasingly mass-mediated) overtones. The idea of narrativity, in turn, offers ways of analyzing the "dramas" that are being performed. Through the stories that people *tell* and the stories that people *live out* every day, sociality—including inter and intraclass relations—becomes an ever recreated, reenacted reality.

Such a perspective is particularly well-suited to an analysis of middle-class cultural process because it allows us to capture something of the chaotic interplay of competing, often contradictory, narratives, and the fragmented, nerve-wracking performances that they inspire. This study traces a number of powerful cultural narratives at work within Kathmandu's middle class. As the middle class pioneers a new space of cultural "betweenness"—between high and low, global and local, new and old, "tradition" and "modernity"—as it struggles to produce itself in cultural life, its members must experiment with a host of cultural stories that are by no means necessarily complementary. From the modern consumer logic of "fashion" to long-held understandings of *ijjat*, or prestige, from the state-promoted ideologies of "progress" and "development" to locally circulating stories of cultural decline and resistance, middle-class Nepalis live in an unusually complex world of competing narratives of truth, reality, and value. Each of these stories "tells" the meaning of relationships between people in different ways; each configures the sequence

---

[34] Narrative stories have what Hinchman and Hinchman call "transsubjective truth value" (1997:xvi).

from past to present to future according to its own narrative agenda; each offers its own story of being and becoming, or what it means to be and what a person should become.

While much of the work done in narrative theory consists of detailed analyses of individual spoken or written narratives,[35] this study is more concerned with what have been called "metanarratives," powerful stories of meaning and value that naturalize certain privileged cultural practices. Despite Lyotard's (1984) pronouncement of the end of narrative knowledge in postmodernity, in fact narrative remains a tenacious part of the construction of meaning in everyday life.[36] Some of Lyotard's *grands récits* or "master-narratives" (Science, Religion, orthodox Marxism, etc.) may be struggling in some sectors. Yet the rise of new fundamentalisms, whether religious (Christian, Hindu, Islamic) or secular (neoliberal economics) suggests that new metanarratives have arisen to fill in the gaps. In a country like Nepal, with its "development"-driven state apparatus and (since 1995) rural Maoist insurgency, competing metanarratives have never been more terrifyingly matters of life and death. As I discuss in the chapters to follow, global modernist metanarratives such as progress, achievement, and growth are very much alive in Kathmandu's middle class, where they intermingle with and color other, more local but equally powerful narratives of value, honor, and meaning.

This book documents the almost Herculean task that Kathmandu's middle class faces as it attempts to reconcile a host of narrative forces: new and old, competing and contradictory. If Weber pointed to a sphere of intensely competing "characteristics and badges" (1946:188) as a defining feature of middle-classness, emerging middle-class cultures on the global periphery today are sites of fantastically complex interplay between divergent stories of value and ways of being. Middle-class culture is a veritable economy of circulating and contending narratives of honor, prestige, morality, suitability, and propriety. As these narrative currents disperse, their "sources" become increasingly difficult to locate. Each stream flows in and through the others in ways that "modernize" traditional narratives, localize global stories, devalue stories of value, and valorize narratives of subjection. In this context, performing the cultural narratives of middle-classness becomes a confusing, contradictory, anxiety-inducing, but nevertheless inescapable endeavor. In the remarks that follow, a Kathmandu man defends local tradition in the face of change.

---

[35] See, for example, Mattingly and Garro 2000, Kleinman 1988, Caverero 2000.

[36] Indeed, as Hinchman and Hinchman observe, "the death of narrative may have been 'greatly exaggerated' " (1997:xiii)!

Modernity: "It's just the style."

When an acquaintance wanted to argue that change in Kathmandu was only "superficial," he turned to the subject of weddings:

> Take a marriage ceremony. When it comes to our rituals, we are doing *every* ritual in our *own way*. They aren't getting *any* effect from that [modern forces]. Well, just a little bit. Like in marriage it *was* more of a ceremony. We used to invite them and they would sit [on the ground] and we would distribute food [on leaf plates] and like that. But right now it has changed to the hotel. You know, "buffet style"—that's the thing. But anyway, it's just the *style*.

Anthropologies of Middle-Class Culture

The anthropological study of middle-class groups is in its infancy.[37] Even among the relatively few ethnographic accounts of class, the majority deal with working-class groups, and a few deal with social elites (e.g., Marcus 1983). This "tradition of working around the (class-) edges of . . . society" (Ortner 1991:167) has left the topic of middle-class culture understudied. This book contributes to a small but growing number of ethnographic works on middle-class culture.[38]

The last several years have seen the beginnings of an anthropological literature on non-Western middle-class societies, particularly within the

---

[37] As Sherry Ortner observed, "The first thing that strikes an anthropologist reading the ethnographic literature [on class is] . . . its marginality in anthropological studies." She goes on to note that, within anthropology, "there is a tendency to avoid almost any kind of macrosociological analysis, let alone making class a central category of research" (1991:165–66). For reviews of anthropological literature on class, see Foley 1990: appendix A, Goldschmidt 1950, 1955, Smith 1984, Ortner 1991.

[38] Much of the ethnographically based literature that deals with middle-class culture focuses on educational settings where the middle-class is the main subject or one of several groups studied (Eckert 1989, Foley 1990, Gaines 1990, Holland and Eisenhart 1990, Proweller 1998). This literature mainly addresses socialization and social-reproduction theory, leaving the matter of "middle-classness" more or less unproblematized. Other works consider the plight of middle-class families caught in processes of deindustrialization and "down-sizing" (Newman 1988, 1993, Ehrenreich 1989). To complement a large body of historical works on other middle-class formations (Barry and Brooks 1994, Earle 1989, Hunt 1996, Thompson 1988, to name only a few), we have at least one anthropological history of a national middle class (Frykman and Lofgren 1987). Sherry Ortner's ongoing Weequahic High School project (Ortner 1991, 1994, 1997, 1998, 1999a) is one of very few anthropological studies to, in her words, "take the bull by the horns and tackle both the American white middle class as such, and the complex dynamics that reproduce the Ameri-

booming national economies of East and Southeast Asia. In addition to offering comparative perspectives on the "new middle classes" across the region, these studies document how recent processes of capital accumulation have produced new, intensely consumerist, middle-class cultures (Blanc 1997, PuruShotam 1998), how middle-class cultural practice is gendered (and how gender practice constitutes middle-classness) (Stivens 1998a, 1998b), and how middle-class consumers construct explicitly non-Western, "thoroughly modern 'Asian' "; identities (Blanc 1997; see also PuruShotam 1998, Yang 1997). All of these studies illustrate how, as in Nepal, new middle-class cultures are oriented toward a multicentered (not simply "Western-dominated") global capitalist economy in which competing modernities vie for gender, class, ethnic, and regional affiliation (Ong and Nonini 1997, Robison and Goodman, eds. 1996, Sen and Stivens 1998).

Three other recent studies offer book-length anthropological accounts of emerging middle-class societies in Asia. Patricia Sloane's study (1999) of newly affluent society in Malaysia looks at how young, educated, urban, ethnic Malay entrepreneurs construct new lifestyles and systems of value at the intersection of state, religious, and capitalist market forces.[39] Deborah Gewertz and Frederick Errington's study of "emerging class in Papua New Guinea" focuses on "the social and cultural work of creating new forms of distinction" in a society where new "class-based inequalities" have developed over the past seven decades (1999:8–9).[40]

---

can class structure" (1991:167). To date Ortner has offered only a few glimpses of her findings, but a full account of her project is eagerly awaited.

[39] Although Sloane occasionally uses "middle class" to characterize the "Malay 'haves' " in her study (1999:6), her goal was not to represent or critique class culture per se but rather to ethnographically document and analyze the new culture of entrepreneurship in Malaysia. As such, Sloane's study is framed more as a contribution to understanding alternative cultures of capitalism than as an exploration of class-cultural life. Nevertheless, Sloane's account of how Malay businesspeople weave together narratives of Islamic morality, capitalist modernity, and a highly politicized sense of "Malayness" is an interesting and important comparative study of an emerging middle-class culture.

[40] Gewertz and Errington deal with the topic of middle-class culture extensively, though the class dynamic that they describe is very different from the one in this book. Rather than a middle-class culture emerging from the subjective and structural experience of "betweenness"—the sense of constructing and occupying a cultural space between class others that is evident in the present account of middle-class life and others (Elias 1978 [1935], Eley 1994:320, Frykman and Lofgren 1987:27, 266, Habermas 1989 [1962], Mosse 1985:4–5, Weber 1946:192)—Gewertz and Errington use the terms "elite" and "middle class" interchangeably and describe an essentially two-part class-cultural dynamic between the "grass roots" and the "middle-class elites" (1999:12). Gewertz and Errington promise to provide "fine-grained ethnographic detail" (1999:15), but in the end their short book comes across as mainly anecdotal, a collection of scenes from the expatriates' lives with their class peers at the local Rotary Club, golf course, and so on.

A third recent book, Purnima Mankekar's *Screening Culture, Viewing Politics* (1999), comes closest to this study in both theoretical and regional focus. Subtitled "An Ethnography of Television, Womanhood, and Nation," Mankekar's work situates middle-class culture in north India in the context of state-run Indian television.[41] Perhaps the main difference between Mankekar's study and this one is that for Mankekar, middle-class culture is mainly an ethnographic setting in which to study processes of identity formation and cultural politics, rather than the object of ethnographic inquiry itself. "Middle-classness" is a recurring theme, though it is ultimately framed within other concerns for issues of gender and nationality. My study, by contrast (as I discuss further below), focuses less on the text/reader media dynamic—which Mankekar treats with theoretical subtlety—and more on the place of media consumption within broader patterns of middle-class consumer practice, and how media images, like other consumer goods, find roles in the production of middle-class life.

Consuming "Love"

In the Nepali film *Jivan Yatra*, fashions take on a leading romantic role. Set entirely in rural Nepal, the hero and heroine wear "traditional" village attire from start to finish except during their romantic interludes. For example, in one scene the country hero falls asleep on a mossy bank, dreaming of romance with the heroine. Strangely, in his dream both hero and heroine are attired in modern Western fashions. As dream lovers, the hero and heroine are transformed from rustic village folk into high-fashion urban trendsetters, serenading each other in a luxurious formal garden.

Indeed, in Kathmandu—as in many South Asian films—there is a peculiar logic that links cinema, romance, and fashion. For example, when I asked one young man why Hindi "love stories"[42] had become the most popular commercial film genre in Kathmandu, he responded obliquely: "Look, now we can get all the fashions coming

---

[41] In particular the book explores how middle-class women construct identities as bearers of class, gender, and nationality in the face of powerful ideological forces. Mankekar's ethnographic focus on the intersection between "televisual texts, viewers' interpretations of them, and the viewers' life experiences" (1999:17) offers significant new insights into the politics of mediation and subjectivity in South Asia. Mankekar analyzes Indian national television's role in "the cultural construction of 'middle-classness' through consumerism" (1999:48), the relationship between media consumption, consumer desire, and middle-class status (1999:94ff), and mediated images of middle-class womanhood (1999:113ff.) and offers a range of other perspectives on middle-class life and media consumption.

[42] As discussed in the preface, words spoken in English in otherwise Nepali speech are designated by the use of a sans serif font.

from Hong Kong and Thailand and therefore we young men and women [*keṭākeṭī*] like to go to the theater and watch the love stories." This apparent nonsequitur in fact conveys the logic of an imagined world where media shape and promote youthful romantic longing and then associate this desired relationship with a range of consumer activities, commodities, lifestyles, and objectified body ideals. In the minds of many middle-class Nepali young people, to "do love" one needs "fashions," just as it is "fashion" to "do love."

CLASS, CONSUMPTION, AND MASS MEDIA

Consumption is one of the key cultural dynamics of middle-class life. How class formations relate to goods, and how goods are imbued with social meanings, have been recurring themes in social theories of class from Marx and Weber onward. Significantly, these same concerns have also been at the heart of a new anthropology of consumption that has grown rapidly over the past two decades. In a review essay on consumption studies in anthropology, Daniel Miller (1995a:266) "unambiguously" dates the "birth of the new anthropology of consumption" to the almost simultaneous publication of Douglas and Isherwood's *The World of Goods* (1979) and Bourdieu's *Distinction* (1984 [1979]), both discussed above as ground-breaking anthropological studies of class cultural process. That the anthropology of consumption and the anthropology of class are so intimately connected underscores one of this book's primary contentions; class and consumption have to be seen as mutually constitutive cultural processes, especially when we are trying to conceptualize the nature of middle-class culture.

For class and consumption to be understood as "mutually constitutive," "consumption" needs to be seen as involving much more than simply the act of purchasing some product. To be sure, a person's or group's access to financial resources (money) fundamentally determines their ability to arrive at the "point of purchase": the reality of socioeconomic inequality is the bedrock on which class-based consumer cultures are built. But the act of buying is only one "moment" in the cultural process of consumption.[43] Goods themselves have "social lives" (Appadurai 1986). Who wants what? When do they want it, and why? What do people do

---

[43] Significantly, Marxist-oriented theories of consumption tend to be concerned with capitalist processes of promotion and aestheticization that lead *up to* the point of purchase (Aglietta 1987, Haug 1987, Galbraith 1969, etc.), whereas more Weberian (or Durkheimian) approaches to consumption tend to focus on the social use of consumer goods *after* the point of purchase (Bourdieu 1984 [1979], Douglas and Isherwood 1979).

with the goods they acquire? How do new consumer goods fit into earlier forms of cultural life? How do objects become centers around which new forms of individual and group behaviors form? The anthropology of consumption is less concerned with the objectness of goods[44] than with how goods circulate within groups, or how, as we will see in this study, goods become a kind of social currency that is transacted in middle-class life.

Middle-class culture is uniquely embedded in the social trajectories of things. What things people desire, the meanings they attach to them, the class-cultural practices they construct around them, and thus the very nature of middle-class consumer practice, will vary enormously across time and space.[45] But to the extent that middle-class people share a common orientation to capitalist productive processes as *consumers* of commodities, and to the extent that consumption (with all the social fashioning and practice that the term implies) becomes their primary mode of cultural production, middle-class practice is inescapably consumer practice. Because of their ability to both include and exclude class others, and to both display and conceal class privilege, commodities (and their attendant practices) are the primary currency of middle-class life.

Mass media play a central role in the lives of middle-class people in Kathmandu and are hence one of the dominant themes in this book. But rather than making media its object of ethnographic inquiry,[46] this study situates media consumption within middle-class consumer culture generally: the consumption of commercial entertainment media is inseparable from broader processes of middle-class consumption. By placing assorted media products (TV shows, movies, radio programs, magazines, recorded music, etc.) in the same category as other "consumables" (from fashions to food to education), it is easier to see how commercial media fit into broader patterns of commodity promotion and consumption. Media not only coexist with other cultural commodities but, much more importantly, are in constant "dialogue" with other goods, cross-referencing and mutually promoting each other. An important and recurring theme in this book is how media products constantly intersect with, promote, and naturalize a host of other commodities, helping to create "auras" of meaning that surround other goods with consumer desire. By tracking these "intertextual" linkages in what I call the *media assemblage*, this book examines how the combined forces of commodity promotion synchronize their calls

[44] See Miller 1998 for a collection of studies that focus on the materiality of material culture in consumption.

[45] Consider, for example, the extraordinarily diverse meanings that a McDonald's hamburger can have depending on where it is consumed (Watson 1997).

[46] Anthropologists have begun to make important contributions to "the ethnography of media consumption": Dickey 1993, Fuglesang 1994, Mankekar 1999. See also Manuel 1993.

for consumer identification within an image realm of generalized consumer desire. The synchronized auras of commodified goods and images (mass media) soon cast their shadows onto the minds—and bodies—of local consumers, as in the case of the young male "body builder" described below.

"Just Look at My Body": Media and Imagination

One afternoon in 1991, while waiting in the crowded courtyard of a popular movie theater in Kathmandu, a boy standing next to me observed the mad crush of young men, each struggling to make his way to the ticket window, and sighed: "You know there are no rules here for how to get the tickets. There's no control. So since they're strong and we're not, we can't fight it out. They have body and we don't have body." Speaking in Nepali, he used the English word *body* to describe what he lacked in this context. People who are "strong" and can "fight it out" have "body."

Similarly, a few months later, in the course of an interview, one of my co-workers asked another young man from Kathmandu about his preferences in films. When the young man responded that he preferred "English" films to those made in India or Nepal, my co-worker asked what kind of English films he liked best. At this the young man (a nineteen-year-old college student) paused, and then explained in a somewhat irritated voice: "Well, among English films I like the *Rambo* type of films. I've seen all of them, parts 1, 2, and 3. I mean, just *look* at my body and you can *see* that I'm interested in that kind of film. If you *look*, you can tell what kind of film *I* like."

Here again the speaker chose the English word *body*. Unlike the Nepali word for body, *jiu* (a gender-neutral term), for this young man the English word obviously carried the meaning of a certain physique—a muscular, powerful, and very male physique—firmly associated with the action film hero Rambo. Indeed, in his mediated imagination, the body style he cultivated through a regimen of martial arts and bodybuilding should have communicated visually the fact that he preferred "the Rambo type of films." For him, film preference and body style were so inseparable that either one should have clearly signaled the other.

It is this "mass-mediated imaginary" that Arjun Appadurai identifies as one of the hallmarks of late capitalist modernity (1996:6). Kathmandu's increasingly market-based, media-saturated, and globally inflected cultural economy has begun to transform the ways, the terms, and the means by which individuals come to imagine themselves, others, and their society's meaningful social categories. Mass media, in tandem with other commodities and other forms of commodity promotion, produce a space for the imagination that is increasingly transnational. Whether in cinematic representations of romance, adventure, or luxury; in advertisements for soft drinks or cigarettes; or in shop windows filled with the same consumer goods depicted in films and in advertisements, the world of commodities and media representations forms a cross-referencing, mutually reinforcing realm of images and imagined ways of being.

The anthropological literature on consumption is now sizable,[47] and the anthropology of mass media is growing.[48] Since Tamar Liebes and Elahu Katz's pioneering cross-cultural study of responses to American television dramas (1990), more and more ethnographically based studies of mass media consumption in non-Western societies have appeared.[49] Of these, the studies most comparable to this one are Mankekar's book on television and middle- class women in India (1999; discussed above), Sara Dickey's path-breaking book on cinema and lower-class spectatorship in southern India (1993), and Minou Fuglesang's fine-grained ethnography of media consumption and female youth culture in East Africa (1994). Where this study differs from "ethnographies of media consumption" such as Mankekar's and Dickey's is in its framing of media consumption within broader patterns of middle-class consumer culture. Fuglesang's ethnography relates to this one in several important ways. Like the middle-class Nepali young people in this study (and people in many other parts of the world), Fuglesang's young media consumers are drawn into

[47] For general reviews of the literature, see Miller 1995a, 1995b. Much of the anthropological literature on consumption is either theoretical in nature (Appadurai 1986, Douglas and Isherwood 1979, McCracken 1988, Miller 1987) or in the form of short essays in edited volumes (Appadurai, ed. 1986, Howes 1996, Miller, ed. 1995, 1998, Orlove 1997, Rutz and Orlove 1989). Other edited volumes that speak to issues of consumption from anthropological perspectives include Breckenridge 1995, Cohen et al. 1995, Mitsui and Hosokawa 1998, and Watson 1997. We have several important anthropological studies that chart histories of commodification and consumer subjectivity in colonial and postcolonial settings (e.g., Burke 1996, Tarlo 1996). For notes on the history of commodification and consumer culture in Nepal, see Liechty 1997. There are only a handful of book-length anthropological studies of modern consumer culture in either Western (Bourdieu 1984) or non-Western (Miller 1994, Weiss 1996) settings.

[48] For reviews, see Spitulnik 1993, Sklair 1995:147ff. Ginsburg et al. (forthcoming) is an important contribution to the anthropology of mass media.

[49] Written from a range of disciplinary perspectives and focusing on a variety of media industries and products, monographs include Allison 2000, Armbrust 1996, Dickey 1993, Fuglesang 1994, Gillespie 1995 (on media in the South Asian diaspora), Kottak 1990, Mankekar 1999, Manuel 1993, Michaels 1993, Pinney 1998, Rajagopal 2001, and Tufte 2000. Other studies that pay significant attention to media include Derne 1995, Dwyer 2000, Richards 1996, and Siegel 1986. Edited collections on non-Western media include Babb and Wadley 1995, Brosius and Butcher 1999, and Eickelman and Anderson 1999.

the orbit of the Indian cinematic melodramas. Fuglesang shows how young women derive new ideas of romantic love, female fashions, and commodified beauty practices from Hindi films. But rather than regarding these media-influenced behaviors as possible instances of women's co-option into modern capitalist economic and ideological structures, Fuglesang sees these new perspectives on love, fashion, and beauty as avenues for the release of "repressed and suppressed energies, allowing temporary escape from everyday toil and male dominance, and triggering dreams and visions of alternatives" (1994:12).[50] For Fuglesang, media consumption is about "creating both self-esteem and empowerment" among women (1994:9).[51]

By contrast, this study of mass media, consumerism, and middle-class culture takes a considerably more critical view of capitalist modernity. Where Fuglesang celebrates "a sort of symbolic resistance" in women's cinema-influenced, consumerist fashion practice (1994:144), this study is more likely to see evidence of market interpellation and commercial objectification. The pleasures of consumption, while real, are never far removed from the gut-wrenching anxieties that arise as people attempt to maintain their positions in the middle-class consumer culture. As we will see in chapters 3 to 5, for many in Kathmandu's middle class, the pleasures of commodity consumption are inherently transient, each act wedging the consumer ever deeper into a market-dependent economy of fleeting and vulnerable prestige.

My aim is to present consumer practices not as evidence of passive capitalist victimization but rather as indispensable elements of a larger middle-class cultural project. As I argue throughout this book, middle-class consumption is less about *having* or *possession* than it is about *being* and *belonging*. As such, middle-class consumption is "about" middle-class production; it is in the *practice* of consumer regimens (from "doing fashion" to restaurant going to watching videos) that the middle class *performs* its cultural existence, day by day. That this local class-culture building draws these actors ever deeper into global commodity regimes testifies less to their own victimization at the hands of an external global capitalism than to the fact that Kathmandu's emerging middle class is itself a response to, and active purveyor of, a now globalized capitalist market and commodity regime. Members of Kathmandu's middle class

[50] Fuglesang's interpretive stance is in line with one strand of media and consumer studies that finds potential for resistance and social critique in consumer behaviors (Fiske 1989a, 1989b, Willis 1990, de Certeau 1984).

[51] In her discussion of women's "identity work" and mass-mediated consumerism, Fuglesang celebrates the "freedom of choice gained by today's generation" (1994:88) without critically considering what other "freedoms" and "choices" might have been lost in the bargain (cf. Appadurai 1990b:206, Tomlinson 1991:151).

are precisely those who have hitched their local sociocultural lives to an ever growing world of goods.

"Without Fashion We Can Do Nothing": Youth and Consumption

Noting the stylish ready-made clothes of a seventeen-year-old college student, my research co-worker asked him, "What do you think about fashion?"

"Listen," the student replied, "these days the world has become very modern. So, about fashion, it's like without fashion we can do nothing, there is nothing. Before now, it was a wild, savage age. People used to run around wearing tree bark! Actually, now, in a way, fashion has become a part of our bodies."

"And are you personally interested in fashion?" my co-worker asked.

"That's for sure! Look, I'm a young man, so of course I am really into fashion. Today's young people, we are almost into the twenty-first century . . . so we're interested in fashion, but also films, sports, . . . and the romantic world. We all have interest in these things."

THE MIDDLE CLASS AND YOUTH CULTURE

Occasionally age (or "generation") is added to the standard sociological troika of "race, class, and gender" as one of the main principles that societies use to arrange hierarchies of privilege and power. In other words, along with sexism, racism, and class-based discrimination, "ageism" is one of the ways that societies produce and police authority. But just as we know that race and gender are culturally constructed categories, and that class privilege (or exploitation) is produced in cultural practice, so too the meanings attributed to age are cultural creations. This study considers one such act of cultural creation, the production of a new "youth" identity within Kathmandu's middle class. I argue that in capitalist modernity the constitution of a particular form of "youth" identity or "youth culture" has been an integral part of middle-class formation. The new discourse of "youth" that has emerged in Kathmandu over the past few decades is one of the key facets of the larger process whereby the middle class has struggled to create itself in cultural practice.

The relationships between race and class, and gender and class, have been much theorized,[52] but how the production of age categories might

[52] For viewpoints and reviews of the literature see Burris 1987, Sacks 1989, and Ortner 1991.

be related to class-cultural process has received less attention. In the vast literature on youth and youth culture in sociology, psychology, cultural studies, and education,[53] youth are often represented as the targets of class-based processes of socialization/indoctrination/reproduction (Bourdieu and Passeron 1990 [1970], Freire 1970, Willis 1977), but actual social categories like "youth" and "adolescence" are themselves typically treated as natural, universal, and ahistorical. It has been mainly social historians who have charted and analyzed the sociocultural construction of youth and youth culture in light of shifting class dynamics in the West during the nineteenth and twentieth centuries (Aries 1962, Kett 1977, Palladino 1996, Springhall 1986, Walvin 1982). This study analyzes the specific sociohistorical context out of which new class-based categories of youth and youth culture have emerged in Nepal.

Social categories of "youth" have been brought into being for a variety of class purposes,[54] but perhaps the most enduring cultural process of youth production has been their constitution as bearers of middle-class culture. In capitalist modernity the production of youth has been a central project of the middle classes, with the meaning and nature of "youth culture" perpetually shifting according to the demands of middle-class industrial/consumer society. From the late-nineteenth-century bourgeois "invention of the adolescent" (Kett 1977) at the dawn of the era of industrial mass production[55] to the early-twentieth-century shift in commercial marketing away from adults and toward "youth" as the new "ideal consumers" and fashion leaders,[56] "youth culture" was enlisted to (and co-produced by) the cause of middle-class consumerism. The postwar years saw the creation of the middle-class suburban "teen" consumer through whom "rebellion" was recruited to the cause of consumption (Frank

[53] See Griffin 1993 for a review of "representations of youth and adolescence in Britain and America."

[54] Depending on their locations within new class formations, "youth" have been figured variously as industrial laborers (Perrot 1997), military recruits (Loriga 1997), objects of bourgeois education (Bourdieu and Passeron 1990) and discipline (Foucault 1979), and agents of (often right-wing) political change (Michaud 1997, Passerini 1997), to name a few class-related processes of "youth" production.

[55] According to Kett, "adolescence" was "essentially a conception of behavior imposed on youth, rather than an empirical assessment of the way in which young people actually behaved. The architects of adolescence used biology and psychology . . . to justify the promotion among young people of norms of behavior that were freighted with middle-class values" (1977:243).

Not coincidentally, the same middle-class values that made "ideal youth"—conformity, loyalty, hero worship, anti-intellectuality, body objectification ("fitness," "beauty," etc.)—also made youth ideal consumers.

[56] See Hurlock 1929:165–88 for a particularly revealing contemporary account of this process. See also Ewen and Ewen 1982, Susman 1984.

1997, Palladino 1996). Contemporary post-Fordist ("postmodern") flexible production techniques have led to a vast array of micro-youth markets with manufacturers adroitly manipulating and appropriating inner-city styles for middle-class suburban youth (Spiegler 1996) and allowing young people to "buy into" a seemingly endless menu of youth identities and rebellions.[57] Although young people may have many other (often competing or even contradictory) subject positions or identities available to them, in industrial and late-capitalist societies "youth," as a distinct age-based sociocultural identity, has been largely generated by forces of class-cultural production and reproduction.

Chapters 8 and 9 describe commercial efforts to construct a new "teen" consumer identity in Kathmandu and the heated debate over the meaning of "modern youth" among members of the middle class. These chapters also consider the experiences of young people themselves as they navigate the treacherous narrative currents of "youth," state-sponsored modernism, consumer gratification, and Nepaliness, among others. Creating and debating "youth" is one of the most fundamental cultural projects of Kathmandu's emerging middle class. To the extent that the "modern youth" or "teen" in Kathmandu is constituted and lived as a species of consumer, "youth culture" is almost by definition middle-class culture. As such, youth culture is not simply a by-product of a larger middle-class cultural project; it is in fact the constantly honed tip of the wedge that opens up the cultural space of middleness and constitutes the middle class as a domain of consumerism and consumer subjectivity. Youth act as the vanguard of an emerging middle-class consumer culture. Constituting youth as consumers is the same cultural project as constituting middle-class subjects: producing "youth" *is* producing the middle class.

This book portrays class as a constantly reenacted *cultural project*, emergent at the confluence of processes of consumption, mass mediation, and the production of youth culture. Class is never a "thing" that exists by itself, prior to, or outside of, its actual performance in everyday life. Approaching class as *process* rather than *object* allows me to show how middle-class culture in Kathmandu grows out of cultural practices with both local and translocal roots. The nature and practice of class in Kathmandu is tied to, but does not simply reflect, global patterns of capitalist promotion, distribution, and labor relations. Instead, members of an emerging middle class meld preexisting, local cultural narratives (such as notions of propriety, orthodoxy, and honor) with "modern" logics of

---

[57] It is increasingly difficult to disagree with Alberto Moreiras's assessment that "consumerist globality not only absolutely circumscribes but even produces resistance to itself as yet another possibility of consumption" (1998:92).

value and truth (achievement, progress, development) in their efforts to construct a new sociocultural space and claim legitimacy for their own class values. This study traces the processes whereby people in Kathmandu's social middle strive to speak and act themselves into the joint production of middle-class culture. Following a chapter that lays out the historical and contemporary context of class formation in Kathmandu, the book proceeds through three overlapping ethnographic terrains: class and consumerism, mass media, and youth. The conclusion combines an ethnographic summary with a discussion of the spatial implications of class-cultural practice. I suggest that what class practice *does*—what makes class *a reality*—is its production of cultural space.

2

MODERN NEPALI HISTORY AND THE RISE OF THE MIDDLE CLASS

Nepal is a relatively small country (roughly the size of Florida) covering much of the high-Himalayan region between Asia's two current (and historic) "superpowers," India and China. Acting as a geographic, cultural, and political buffer zone, Nepal has been continuously influenced by these civilizations, though it was never colonized by powers from either the north or south. Nepal's topography made it difficult to penetrate militarily and relatively easy to defend. Even the British colonizers of India chose to leave Nepal an independent state (at times nominally), the only such region in the entire subcontinent by the end of the nineteenth century.

The same topography that Nepali rulers have used to their military advantage for centuries also constitutes one of Nepal's most formidable development obstacles. With roughly one-third of the country at elevations over 4,500 meters (c. 16,000 feet), and another third known as the "hilly region" (full-fledged mountains by North American and European standards!), officials estimate that arable (farmable) land in Nepal amounts to only about 16 percent of Nepal's total area of 147,181 square kilometers.[1] Although Nepal's mountain scenery attracts hundreds of thousands of tourists each year, for most Nepalis—whose experience of space and distance is primarily in the vertical rather than horizontal plane—mountains are often a significant deterrent to meeting daily needs. Even the most basic development projects, such as road building, become monumental and costly undertakings. Nepal is indeed a "poor, landlocked, and under-developed nation," to paraphrase the standard preface to many official descriptions of the country. Even Bangladesh, the poster child of Asian poverty, has higher average-income rates, higher rates of literacy, higher GDP, lower birth rates, and higher life expectancy than Nepal (CBS 1996:303–4).

[1] This is based on the figures given for "total agricultural land" in a recent Government of Nepal statistical handbook (Central Bureau of Statistics [CBS] 1996:57). According to this source, in 1991-92 Nepal had 23,929 square kilometers of "total agricultural land."

This chapter provides a brief historical sketch which situates developments in the Kathmandu valley within the history of the modern Nepali state and its ties to regional and global historical processes. It also outlines the emergence of a proto–middle class in the city during the nineteenth and early twentieth centuries and highlights some of the key economic and social transformations of the last several decades that shed light on emerging patterns of middle-class culture. Kathmandu's position as capital of a modern nation-state—Nepal's gateway (and gatekeeper) to a world of economic and cultural flows—has brought it a degree of economic prosperity, even if these benefits rarely extend beyond the valley rim.

Returning to Kathmandu in the late 1980s after five years spent abroad, one Nepali academic exclaimed, "From what people buy, I just can't believe how much money is floating around! I mean suddenly there is *a lot* of money." Given that in 1993 Nepal's average annual per capita income was only 190 U.S. dollars (CBS 1996:303), it is difficult to understand how the local economy in the Kathmandu valley could have produced the emerging middle-class consumer culture that I describe in this book. How do we account for a growing middle class in the capital of a "least developed country," where over 90 percent of the population is rural and, by most standards, extremely poor? Where did this middle class come from, and how does it relate to earlier logics and configurations of social stratification? Where does the cash that fuels Kathmandu's middle-class economy come from?

KATHMANDU IN MODERN NEPALI HISTORY

Kathmandu is located in a large bowl-shaped valley in Nepal's middle hills at a temperate elevation of around 1,350 meters (c. 4,000 feet). The valley's soil—sediment of a long-gone lake—is some of the most fertile in Asia, making the valley one of the most heavily populated areas in the Himalayan zone. Ties to wider regional, and even global, spheres of influence are by no means merely recent phenomena. Indeed, the founding of modern Nepal in the eighteenth century, with Kathmandu as the nation's capital, has to be seen in the light of political and economic processes under way across Eurasia and around the early modern world (Subrahmanyam 1997). For centuries the city was an important stop on lucrative trans-Himalayan trade routes, and an object of desire for would-be rulers. In the 1760s one such ruler, Prithvi Narayan Shah (1723–75), king of Gorkha, a small hill district west of Kathmandu, began a series

---

Of this agricultural land only 294 square kilometers (or 0.2 percent of Nepal's land) were recorded as "land under permanent crops."

of conquests that eventually brought the Kathmandu valley, and most of the territory of modern Nepal, under his rule (Stiller 1973).

Prithvi Narayan's campaigns across the Himalayas paralleled the steady expansion of British East India Company rule across north India. In the early nineteenth century, the Nepali general Bhim Sen Thapa (ruled 1806–37), alarmed at systematic British expansionism to the south, continued Prithvi Narayan's conquests, extending the country's domains to include a twelve-hundred-kilometer swath of Himalayan territory from Sikkim in the east to Kangra in the west. In 1814 the British, recognizing Bhim Sen as "the only statesman on the subcontinent who truly understood the Company's intentions and methods" (Stiller 1993:50–51), seized territories along Nepal's southern border, provoking Bhim Sen into war. In spite of several important early Nepali victories (which later inspired the British to recruit Nepali "Gurkhas" into the Indian and British armies [Des Chene 1991]), in the end superior numbers and artillery allowed the British to dictate the terms of a cease-fire. In signing the Treaty of Sagauli, which officially ended the Anglo-Nepal war in 1816, Nepal gave up about one-third of its territory (reducing the country to roughly its present size) and agreed to the presence of a British "Resident," or official representative, in Kathmandu.

Kathmandu had long been a major regional political and economic center when Prithvi Narayan Shah took the city in 1768 and made it his capital. Under the Malla kings (roughly fifteenth to eighteenth century), the valley's three independent city states (Kathmandu, Bhaktapur, and Patan) became sophisticated urban areas with highly developed trades and crafts, economic ties with India and Tibet, and extremely complex religious and political cultures (Slusser 1982). For the valley, Prithvi Narayan's conquest marked not just a shift in political rule but also a shift in regional political orientation. In the context of an ever-growing British colonial empire, foreign regions that had once been the source of more or less benign curiosities and various strands of religious/spiritual authority became, by the late eighteenth century, politically significant in unprecedented ways. As the political economy of the subcontinent changed and a new dominant power emerged, Nepal found itself on the periphery of a world colonial power.

Elsewhere I have described Nepal's engagement with the British in terms of "selective exclusion" (Liechty 1997):[2] a process whereby Nepali elites in Kathmandu sought to at once harness the power (political and symbolic) of the region's new paramount rulers, while attempting to keep those powers out of the hands (and minds) of their political subordinates.

---

[2] My discussion here of Nepali-British political and cultural relations in the nineteenth and early twentieth centuries draws on this earlier study.

By the mid-nineteenth century, an implicit British patronage had become a political necessity for anyone who would rule a stable government in Kathmandu, surrounded as they were by an always deeply factionalized court nobility. In Kathmandu ruling elites sought to use British power while making every effort to keep this foreign power foreign. Selective exclusion began as a *foreign* policy, aimed at manipulating the region's dominant power. Yet by the early twentieth century it was becoming an increasingly desperate *domestic* policy, as Nepal's rulers resorted to more and more repressive measures to isolate Nepali citizens from the waves of political and cultural change then sweeping the subcontinent, and threatening to wash over the valley rim.

Although the British Resident posted in Kathmandu at the end of the Anglo-Nepali war in 1816 was not the first non–South Asian foreigner to visit the valley,[3] his presence was a graphic and, for many, humiliating reminder of Nepal's place in an emerging world order. Prithvi Narayan Shah had sought to purge all foreign, and especially British, influence from his realm, seeing Europeans as barbarians steeped in the ultimate depravity of beef eating. But Prithvi Narayan's antiforeign "quasi-ascetic discipline" (Burghart 1984:115) and (speaking anachronistically) almost Gandhian policy that Nepalis use locally produced fabrics and other goods (Stiller 1968) did not last long after his death in 1775. Already by 1793 Nepali leaders were purchasing significant quantities of English woolen "broadcloth" for use in military uniforms (Kirkpatrick 1969 [1811]:212–13).[4]

The thirty-year period (1806–37) during which Bhim Sen Thapa held control of the Nepali government witnessed a significant jump in the quantity of European products consumed in Kathmandu, a rise which traced the nobility's developing taste for foreign goods and styles.[5] Bhim Sen was the first Nepali leader to adopt "purely western dress" (Chaudhuri

---

[3] A few non-South Asian merchants, monks, pilgrims, and explorers had traveled through Kathmandu by the early seventeenth century, when the first Europeans arrived. The first more or less permanent European presence in the valley began in the early 1670s with the arrival of an Italian Capuchin mission. Capuchin presence continued, on and off, until the late 1760s when Father Giuseppe recorded his impressions of Prithvi Narayan Shah's bloody takeover of the valley (Giuseppe 1790), before being expelled, along with other foreigners, by the new king of Nepal. For further details and bibliography, see Liechty 1997.

[4] Imports of British broadcloth for Nepali troops continued throughout the nineteenth century, though eventually the army began purchasing uniforms ready-made from a British tailoring firm in Calcutta (Upadhyaya 1992:140).

[5] This rise is also tied to the flooding of Indian (and by extension, Nepali) markets with European goods following the end of the Napoleonic Wars. After the establishment of the British residency in 1816, the number of Indian merchants in Kathmandu dealing in European goods increased by a third, and local merchants estimated that between 1816 and 1831 trade volume tripled (Hodgson 1972 [1874]ii:92).

1960:214). In portraits he is shown in a European military uniform approximating that of a British general, complete with decorations. In one large equestrian painting, Bhim Sen has even granted himself the insignia of the British Order of the Garter! (See photo in Landon 1928i:83.) Bhim Sen outfitted his army with European-style uniforms and, immediately upon assuming power, adopted the rank designations of the British military (Stiller 1976:92). In 1831 one of the early British Residents in Kathmandu noted that "Within the last fifteen years the gentry of Nepal have become universally horsemen. The court makes large and regular purchases" of horses (Hodgson 1972 [1874]ii:111). Clearly Bhim Sen and the Nepali nobility were embarking on a new style of consumption based more and more on European standards and expectations. It was a transformation that paralleled the emergence of Britain as the region's paramount power.

By the 1830s British Resident Brian H. Hodgson could boast that "The whole of the middle and upper classes are clad in foreign [British-made] cottons" and that English cotton "chintzes" are "much worn in Nepal by the middle and lower orders (1972 [1874]ii:106–7). Only "the poor" still produced most of their own coarse cotton goods, though even among them English-made imitation South Asian textiles were making inroads. What is significant about these new patterns of consumption is the way that foreign goods of various types had begun to mark class divisions, signaling one's position in the social hierarchy. From velvets to chintzes to imitation scarves to homespun, various types of European fabric (or their absence) had become important elements in the language of status and social rank in Kathmandu.

In addition to fabrics, Bhim Sen Thapa and other elites also imported a host of other European goods. From sport rifles, glassware, and crockery to mirrors, plate glass, and lighting devices, Nepali elites were not simply consuming foreign goods but beginning to make significant concessions to foreign cultural practices. Although it is difficult to know precisely how some of these European goods were used, descriptions of Bhim Sen's palace near Kathmandu offer hints. Built on the southern outskirts of the old city, Bhim Sen's grand palace was a combination of north Indian Mughal (domes, minarets) and European architectural styles (P. R. Sharma 1975:121). One contemporary description of Bhim Sen's palace—by the nineteenth-century Nepali poet Yadunath Pokhryal (1966 [c. 1845])—provides some idea of the awe that this structure evoked in its day. Pokhryal's poem describes with special wonder Bhim Sen's "great glass palace" (bhari sismahāl), with its many tall green-glass windows, and the mirror-covered walls before which beautiful women stood to admire themselves. Here "Many are the paintings/portraits [tasbir] of great value. . . . Many are the lanterns and candles. There the night becomes bright like day" (1966:89–91, my translation). Significantly some of the aspects of Bhim Sen's palace most noteworthy (for the poet) resulted from the use of European imports. The European-style portraits and, more important, the mirrors, lighting fixtures, and especially the large amounts of glass seem to have made the structure extremely impressive and distinctive.

What began as experiments with foreign goods and styles (mainly by the Kathmandu elite) in the first half of the nineteenth century became almost an obsession during the era of Rana autocracy. In 1846 a young officer named Jung Bahadur Rana orchestrated a bold and bloody political takeover in Kathmandu (Stiller 1981). Having massacred dozens of political rivals and reduced the Shah king to the position of figurehead, Jung Bahadur and his heirs ruled Nepal as hereditary Rana "prime ministers" for the next one hundred years. In 1850 Jung Bahadur Rana became the first of the South Asian nobility to make the perilous (in terms of ritual pollution) but politically expedient 'pilgrimage' to London (Whelpton 1983). Having paid homage directly to the British throne (thereby bypassing the colonial government in India), Jung Bahadur returned to Nepal eager to pursue a policy that balanced general subservience to British power with a strict insistence that the British deal with Nepal as an officially independent state.

A century of Rana rulers attempted to tread this fine line between anglophilic sycophancy and claims to independence. During the great Indian "Sepoy Rebellion" of 1857 Jung Bahadur sent Nepali troops to aid beleaguered British forces, a decision echoed by two later Rana prime ministers during the world wars of the twentieth century. From Jung Bahadur onward, Rana elites built ever more enormous and lavish European-style palaces in Kathmandu, including the stupendous Singha Durbar, completed in 1903, and said to be the largest structure in all of South and Southeast Asia in its day (P. R. Sharma 1975:120). By the late 1920s the Ranas had constructed an aerial ropeway into the valley, capable of delivering eight tons of freight per hour, "without in any way opening up for passenger traffic the new avenue into the capital" (Landon 1928ii:208). Taking advantage of the increasing scale of mass production in Europe, the Ranas established a "foreign goods department" in Kathmandu and a "buying agency" in Calcutta that mail-ordered goods from European department stores and supply houses for the "domestic requirements" of the elite class (Upadhyaya 1992:128, 253). Porters continued to carry huge items, like massive luxury vehicles[6] and multiton equestrian

[6] One published photo (Proksch 1995:123) shows Kathmandu's "authorized Ford dealer" in Lazimpat in the mid-1930s. Pictured are three new 1935 Ford automobiles, among others. Yet these Fords appear plebeian compared with the huge Packards, Rolls Royces, and other luxury vehicles pictured in the same volume, each "carried over the mountain trails on bamboo cross-poles by teams of 64 porters" (Proksch 1995:122–23).

statues, over the treacherous trails that the Ranas "maintained" in a state of disrepair as a matter of national defense. But the ropeway allowed the Ranas to import countless tons of European luxury goods—from pressed-tin ceiling panels, bath tubs, and decorative statuary to European fashions, fine silver, and liquor. According to one European visitor to Kathmandu in the 1920s, in the stately homes of the prime minister and most of his close relatives, "the comforts and standards of life have . . . been closely approximated to those of Europe" (Landon 1928ii:123).

By the 1920s Nepali commoners too had begun to acquire a taste for imported consumer goods. Already by the mid nineteenth century, shops in Kathmandu sold a variety of basic imported European consumer goods,[7] but demand for foreign wares rose even higher after the First World War, when Nepali servicemen returned with both cash and a desire for some share of the goods that they associated with modernity. Teaming up with Japanese manufacturers in search of new markets for simple consumer goods, the Rana prime minister was able to cash in on this new popular consumer desire. "Nepalese merchants bought, and Japanese manufacturers shipped, practically everything the newly returned servicemen thought represented modern life: shoes, tennis shoes, cotton cloth, umbrellas, and trinkets. . . . Cheap imports from Japan flooded the small market of Nepal," devastating Nepali cottage industries, effectively draining off much of the cash that the servicemen had brought back to Nepal, and enriching the Rana state treasury (Stiller 1993:159–60).

In spite of the consumer "crumbs" that the elites allowed to drop from their loaded banquet tables, during the Rana era the gap between rulers and ruled became a chasm. Having transformed the state treasury into the personal expense account of the prime minister (Stiller 1993:164), Rana elites spent staggering amounts of money and manpower on imported luxury goods and monumental architecture. They further guaranteed their privilege through a variety of sumptuary laws.[8] Foreigners who made it into the valley during the late Rana era repeatedly echo Morris's observation that "The court and the people are two entirely different entities" (1963:26).

Yet between the starkly delineated elites and commoners was, at least from the 1920s onward, a kind of Nepali proto–middle class: non-Rana social groups who (both in Kathmandu and in exile in India) began to

[7] In the early 1850s, the English traveler Francis Egerton noted a variety of British goods for sale in Kathmandu shops, including items "such as needles, tea-pots, empty bottles, powder and shot, &c., &c." (1852i:217).

[8] In the Kathmandu valley commoners were forbidden to ride on horses or elephants (Bishop 1952). Later on, no one but the Rana elites were permitted to ride in motorized vehicles or wear European dress (Leuchtag 1958:63). Only with special permission could one build a stucco house or erect a tile roof (Isaacson 1990:68).

acquire growing economic power and cultural authority. The history of this pre-1950 middle class—and how it sought to reshape the Nepali nation and Nepali modernity in its own image—has only begun to be written. For example, Pratyoush Onta (1994: part 6) offers intriguing insights into how non-Rana civil servants and palace functionaries in Kathmandu ventured into the new domain of consumer modernity during the 1930s and 1940s, using "democratic" technologies such as photography to construct and claim a space of "middle-ness" between the Ranas and the masses. In another article, Onta shows how groups of educated, activist, expatriate Nepalis in India during roughly the same period linked projects of self-consciousness and self-improvement with parallel projects of promoting the Nepali language and patriotic nationalism (1996:39–40). Clearly these projects (of creating a national identity at once Nepali and modern) have much to do with a small but growing middle class's experiments with ideologies and practices of empowerment. The very fact that many of these experiments in Nepali middle-class culture by necessity took place *outside* of Nepal points to the extraordinary efforts the Rana state made to control the political lives of its subjects.

As the anti-British Indian nationalist movement gathered momentum, more and more Nepali activists living in India began to work toward their own country's independence. The Rana regime responded with ever-growing repression; from the 1930s onward, visitors to the Kathmandu valley describe what is almost an armed camp. The streets bristled with soldiers and for decades a strict nighttime curfew was imposed on every citizen. Cannon volleys marked the beginning and end of the curfew, as well as the passage of time through the day (Singh 1990:24–25). The Ranas forbade large public gatherings and were even uneasy about group worship in temples (Leuchtag 1958:63). But try as they might, the Ranas could not seal their country from the influence of the Indian nationalist movement. The political economy of the subcontinent was shifting once again. The Rana dynasty had risen with the aid of the newly dominant British power in the mid-nineteenth century, and fell when the British finally pulled out of India.

The New Middle Class

In 1950 a popular revolution, led by India-based Nepali nationalists, finally ended Rana rule in Nepal. In February 1951 King Tribhuvan (descendant of Prithvi Narayan Shah) was reinstated and a new democratic government installed. At his death in 1955, Tribhuvan was succeeded by King Mahendra, who, after a decade of what he viewed as fruitless parliamentary squabbling between political parties, in 1960 dismissed the elected government and established a system of partyless "Panchayat Democracy," claiming it would "strengthen the voice of the people" (Stiller 1993:202). For three decades the royal family and its entourage ruled in collaboration with an unpopular rubber-stamp parliament. Then, in 1990, Nepalis took to the city streets and mountain trails to demand an end to the king's absolute power in favor of constitutional monarchy and the institution of a popularly elected, multiparty parliament. The *jana andolan*, or Nepali "people's movement," of 1990 ushered in a new era of political participation, though the optimism that democracy would bring long-awaited progress and freedom soured in the 1990s, as successive elected governments proved themselves to be as ineffectual and corrupt as those of the Panchayat era.

The political promises of democracy have been elusive for Nepalis in the last half-century, yet other kinds of "freedoms" have made more tangible inroads, especially in Kathmandu. After 1951 the Nepali state instituted an "open door" policy that meant relatively unregulated commodity imports, the establishment of interstate relations, and the arrival of foreign diplomatic missions in Kathmandu. These in turn set in motion many of the economic and social transformations described in this book: the rapidly growing local economy, the influx of foreign goods and foreigners (tourists), and the shifting registers of social value and prestige. These new processes of modernity are particularly important in the lives of Kathmandu's growing middle class.

Since 1951 the very economic, political, and cultural forces that have drawn Kathmandu into late twentieth-century modernity have also steadily opened up a social space for a middle class between commoners and the elite. Although for centuries Kathmandu has been an important commercial, ceremonial, and political center, agriculture and small-scale craft production were by far the dominant occupational categories in urban Kathmandu until well into the twentieth century. Yet in the decades since 1951, with the growth of government centralization, education, trade, and, more recently, tourism, the most notable development in local labor markets has been the growth and diversification of tertiary activities (service, sales, clerical, professional, technical, administrative, and related occupations). Demographic studies show that the tertiarization of Kathmandu's occupational structure continued through the 1980s, with as much as two-thirds of the local labor force engaged in tertiary activities (Shrestha et al. 1986:89–95, P. Sharma 1989:9–93). This dramatic shift in occupational structures is a key factor in the emergence of a new middle class in Kathmandu since 1951.

Paralleling this rapid increase in wage labor has been enormous growth in the scale of the valley's economy. Kathmandu has become a relatively cash-rich region in an otherwise cash-poor country.[9] One recent study noted that Nepal's per capita income "is among the lowest in the world," and its economy seems to be "going nowhere." "Yet, when a [Kathmandu] commercial bank recently made an initial public offering of shares worth NPR [Nepali rupees] 175 million . . . it was oversubscribed within a week to the tune of NPR 1.4 billion. Nepal, the poorest country in the world, seems to be awash in cash" (Dahal 2000:7).

Where is all this money coming from? The sources have shifted over the past decades, but historically one of the most important channels has been the international aid pipeline. Finding themselves in the middle of several "cold wars" (China/India, United States/USSR), Nepali officials in the 1950s were quick to grasp the financial implications of competing definitions of "progress," and the accompanying offers of "aid." Indeed, the rapid transformation of Nepal's government apparatus—from an instrument of feudal rule to a modern bureaucracy—was often the result of the new need to channel and process various types of foreign aid (Fujikura 1996). Ministries of education, agriculture, urban planning, communications, and so on each developed as variously targeted foreign development monies poured into the national budget.

Because Nepal was one of the few Third World countries in the "post-colonial era" that did not have a colonial past, it became one of the favorite sites for Western experiments with wave after wave of "development" ideologies and programs. Between 1951 and 1997 Nepal received an estimated 3.7 billion USD (U.S. dollars) in grants and loans from foreign countries[10] and international banks (Joshi 1997). By the early 1990s Nepal was servicing a debt of just under 1 billion USD (A. Tiwari 1992). Even though usually intended for rural development, all of this aid money is routed through Kathmandu. By the time the money filters through the maze of centralized bureaucratic bodies and their affiliated nongovernmental organizations (NGOs), often very little remains for projects at the "grass roots."[11] According to one recent reckoning, around 70 percent of Nepal's total annual budget goes simply to running the national government, head quartered in Kathmandu.[12]

---

[9] Indeed, the contrasts between Kathmandu and Nepal's rural hinterlands are often stark. A recent United Nations Development Project (UNDP) report listed the average life expectancy for a child born in Kathmandu as sixty-seven years, whereas life expectancy for a child in Mugu, a remote mountain district, was only thirty-six years (reported in *News From Nepal* 6(3) [May-June 2000]):5–6.

[10] According to U.S. government records, the United States has given Nepal more than 300 million dollars in aid since 1951 (*The Independent* [Kathmandu], 13 July 1994, 5.).

[11] Judith Justice's study (1986) of foreign aid and health development projects in Nepal is an excellent account of this process. See also Blaikie, Cameron, and Seddon 1980.

[12] *The Independent* (Kathmandu), 27 November 1996, 5.

The years between 1975 and 1980 mark an important turning point in the development of Kathmandu's foreign-aid economy. Foreign aid increased steeply after the mid-1970s, when it jumped from an annual growth rate of 16.2 percent (1960 to 1975) to 21.6 percent (1975 to 1990). Significantly, this increase in aid corresponded with a shift away from a preponderance of *bilateral* aid packages to mostly *multilateral* aid. In 1975 bilateral aid (from countries like India, China, the United States, Germany, and Japan) accounted for 65 percent of Nepal's aid budget. By 1991 bilateral aid made up only 39 percent of the aid budget, with over 60% coming from multilateral agencies (World Bank, IMF, Asian Development Bank, etc.). Bilateral aid typically comes in relatively small packages and is directed at a variety of specific and usually rural social-development projects, in such areas as education, public health, or agriculture. Yet the multilateral aid that has dominated the development scene since the late 1970s is more often in the form of massive capital-intensive and centralized projects: hydroelectric, transportation, communications, and the like. Until the late 1960s social-development projects received the largest portion of yearly aid, but through most of the 1980s funding for the social sector remained below 17 percent (A. Tiwari 1992).

With massive amounts of multilateral foreign aid flowing in, one of Kathmandu's growth industries since the early 1980s has been the development of layer upon layer of international and local nongovernmental organizations (INGOs and NGOs). Employing hundreds of expatriate and thousands of Nepali middle-class professionals, these NGOs systematically drain off aid dollars in a complex system of legitimate needs and procedures (feasibility studies, impact assessments, equipment contracts, travel expenses, support personnel, vehicles) and illegal practices (kickbacks, billing scams, etc.).[13] For example, since 1975 (the United Nations' "International Year of the Woman") more than fifty NGOs devoted to "women in development" (WID-NGOs) have sprung up in Kathmandu alone, most of which depend financially on contracts and grants from multilateral agencies and INGOs (M. Aryal 1992). By the late 1980s, Nepal was receiving 5.7 billion NPR (c. 115 million USD) per year in foreign aid (loans and grants) (CBS 1991:461). Even if we disregard the illegal, quasi-legal, or simply wasteful activities attributed to Kathmandu's "development complex," it is clear that legal disbursements alone are enough to channel large amounts of foreign "aid" directly into Kathmandu's local economy.

---

[13] Blaikie et al. argue that the "spectacular growth" of governmental and nongovernmental bureaucracies since 1951 has "served to minimize internal political unrest by absorbing the better educated, and lent credibility to requests for foreign aid by appearing to offer an apparatus for implementation" (1980:3–4).

In addition to development money, in the last two or three decades another of Kathmandu's major sources of cash has been tourism and its offshoot, the handmade carpet industry. From the pseudo-sadhus and faux-fakirs who pose for tourist photos in Kathmandu's Durbar Square to street touts, restaurant boys, casino workers, travel agents, and hotel owners, tens of thousands of people in Kathmandu benefit either directly or indirectly from the city's place at the gateway of Nepal's large tourist industry.[14] By the early 1990s Nepal was earning 70 million USD per year from tourism, and more than fifteen thousand people were employed directly in the tourist trade (in addition to much larger numbers employed in various related service and supply businesses), and the vast majority of the business was focused on the Kathmandu valley (B.L. Shrestha 1992).

Handmade Tibetan/Nepali carpets, originally developed in the 1960s by Tibetan refugees as a handicraft for the tourist souvenir market (Gombo 1985, Forbes 1989), by the 1980s began to find their own international markets (mostly in Western Europe) and by the early 1990s had surpassed tourism as Nepal's number one foreign currency earner. Three times a week giant Lufthansa cargo planes lumbered out of Kathmandu, each loaded with thirty tons of carpets. Between 1988 and 1993 yearly air freight exports from Kathmandu increased from 317,000 kilograms to 3.68 million kilograms, most of which were carpets (Chhetri 1994). By the early 1990s, Kathmandu's carpet industry was bringing in an average of more than 110 million USD per year (Ankerson 1992). Carpet sales in Europe dropped precipitously in the mid-1990s, amid unflattering reports of child labor abuse in the Nepali industry, yet by the end of 1996 orders were again on the rise, after Nepali manufacturers promised to reform their labor practices.[15]

Another major source of cash income in the Kathmandu valley is Nepal's massive remittance economy. Labor migration has been a necessity for many poor Nepali families for centuries (N. R. Shrestha 1990), but a globalized labor market now drives ever more Nepalis to ever more distant work sites. A British development agency study estimated that in 1997 there were around 400,000 Nepalis living abroad who contributed (as remittances) a combined sum of 35 billion NPR per year to the Nepali economy. Of these people, over half (c. 250,000) were working in India,

---

[14] After leveling off during the politically turbulent years of the early 1990s, tourist arrivals have continued to increase steadily at an annual rate of around 11 percent. In 1998 close to half a million tourists visited Kathmandu.

[15] For details on child labor–free carpets and the new "Rugmark" system, see *The Independent* (Kathmandu), 4 December 1996, 5 and 25 December 1996, 3. Because of instability in the carpet industry Kathmandu investors have turned in part to the export garment industry, though this sector too has seen fluctuating fortunes. See *The Independent* (Kathmandu), 18 September 1996, 2.

about 40,000 in the Persian Gulf states, about 44,000 in East and South-east Asia, and only about 15,000 in Europe and North America. Significantly about two-thirds of the total remittances came from East and Southeast Asia, with 14 billion NPR coming from Nepalis working in Hong Kong alone (*The Independent* [Kathmandu], 13 October 1999, 1). A more recent study reported a huge jump in Nepali labor migration to the Gulf (over 200,000 people), estimated the number of Nepalis working in India at around 1 million, and reckoned Nepal's total annual remittances to be a whopping 75 billion NPR per year, a sum just shy of the nation's annual budget for 1999/2000 (Dahal 2000).

Beyond its role of funneling cash into local consumer economies in Nepal, the remittance economy also has important cultural ramifications. Each of these Nepalis living abroad provides a window onto other cultural worlds for their family members and friends back home. Although labor migration figures say nothing conclusive about the relative strength of different foreign cultural influences, they do clearly illustrate how Nepal is positioned in worldwide political and cultural economies that are far more multicentered than standard (uncritically self-congratulatory) "westernization" models can accommodate.

International development aid, tourism, carpet manufacturing, and remittances by no means comprise the entire local economy, yet these four channels (and related activities) do go a long way in accounting for the surprisingly large amounts of cash "floating around" in Kathmandu, especially in recent decades. With several hundred million U.S. dollars funneled into Kathmandu each year, one begins to realize how certain people in certain places may be cash-rich even in a "least developed country" (LDC) whose annual GNP per capita was only 190 USD in 1993. For every person in Kathmandu with his or her hand in one of these cash boxes, many more experience the "trickle down" benefits—even if the trickle rarely reaches beyond the valley rim.

It is this kind of local monetary economy—where cash is relatively plentiful and opportunities for investment limited—that serves as a backdrop for the cultural economies and social formations described in this book. With every generation fewer people in Kathmandu are engaged in primary productive labor, and more depend on exchanging labor for cash, which becomes the basis for subsistence. Cash itself is certainly nothing new in Kathmandu, but the enormous rise in tertiary labor has great implications for changing labor relations and particularly the transformation of Kathmandu's class structure. While the city has long had an active merchant community, based in particular trading castes as well as in groups of resident foreigners (Zivetz 1992), it is only in the past few decades that a significant middle class, engaged in civil service, commerce, and education, has emerged from between the mass of agricultural and craft laborers on the one hand and a tiny national elite on the other. It is this new urban middle class, increasingly submerged in a cash economy with local, regional, and global dimensions, that is the focus of this study.

Submersion in this cash economy by no means implies financial liberation for Kathmandu's middle class. An aura of cash/consumer abundance may permeate every street corner, magazine, and movie, but realizing that abundance always seems to lie just beyond arm's reach. Between the wealthy elite and the urban poor are those people who must constantly renegotiate their positions in a consumer market that both offers them access to the middle class and threatens to drag them into poverty. In the early 1990s a good annual salary for a civil servant was only around 40,000 NPR (less than 1,000 USD) while a new suit of clothes could easily cost 2,000 rupees, and a pair of kid's sneakers 1,200. Faced with mounting consumer demands, fixed incomes, and spiraling inflation, many middle-class families coped by pooling several incomes, (with heads of families often holding down several jobs), renting inherited family property (either locally or in their rural home villages), or engaging in illegal activities (taking bribes, falsifying trade documents, smuggling, etc.). Middle-class families in Kathmandu are, almost by definition, those people caught between state- and business-promulgated images and ideologies of abundance and progress and the reality of fixed (often declining) incomes and an ever more competitive local prestige economy.

Living these contradictions breeds enormous anxiety: in the father who feels dragged into illicit ventures to support his family's growing consumer demands; in the housewife who dreads going to the market where years of double-digit inflation have cut ever deeper into her fixed food budget; in the teenager forced to negotiate the demands of being a "modern youth." This middle-class anxiety becomes particularly acute as members of traditionally low-caste and ethnic groups become successful in the new cash economy, while once-stable forms of social prestige (upper-caste rank, education, government employment) steadily lose ground. It is a fundamental and pervasive fact that Kathmandu's growing cash economy, while greatly expanding the circuits of social, cultural, and economic exchange in the city, also lies at the root of much of the economic hardship, anguish, and despair that colors the lives of so many people represented in this book.

THE URBAN SETTING

Since 1951 the Kathmandu valley has emerged as not only the largest urban center in the Himalayan region but also a transportation and communications hub for the entire subcontinent. Whereas in 1951 the steep rocky trails from the southern plains (Nepal's Tarai region) made Kathmandu inaccessible by any means other than walking, by the 1990s Kathmandu was linked to the rest of Nepal by close to seven thousand kilometers of motorable roads. Along with more roads come more vehicles. From no more than a few dozen cars in the early 1950s, by 1990 the number of moter vehicles in the Kathmandu valley had grown to more than sixty thousand (the number having doubled between 1987 and 1990 alone).[16] In 1958 Royal Nepal Airlines and Air India began commercial service into Kathmandu, which now has direct air links to cities across South Asia, plus direct flights from Western Europe, the Middle East, Russia, East and Southeast Asia. Thanks to foreign aid, Nepal also boasts one of the most advanced national telecommunications systems in South Asia. All of these factors have made Kathmandu a favored site not only for the hundreds of thousands of tourists who descend on the city annually but also for regional offices of various United Nations agencies, and international nongovernmental organizations.

Along with rapid developments in transport communications has come a rapid deterioration in environmental conditions. In a bowl-shaped valley rimmed by mountains, Kathmandu residents suffer from severe air pollution.[17] In August 1993 Kathmandu surpassed Taipei, Hong Kong, Seoul, and even Bangkok to claim the dubious distinction of being Asia's most polluted city.[18]

Many of the valley's soot-spewing vehicles are buses that transport Kathmandu's rapidly growing population. Relatively stable for two centuries (Bjonness 1990:7),[19] the city's population suddenly quadrupled to over 414,000 between 1951 and 1991 (Nepal Administrative Staff College 2048 v.s.:2). As the population swells, congestion grows in the inner city, and more and more of the upper and middle classes flee to the suburbs. Since the 1980s the areas surrounding Kathmandu have witnessed an astonishing building spree (map 1), as city people gobble up more and more of the terraced fields that have for centuries been recognized as perhaps the most productive farm land in South Asia (Hodgson 1847).

[16] For these and more statistics on motor vehicles, see *Himal* 5 (1) (January–February 1992):30.

[17] The valley also suffers from severe water pollution (A. Dixit 1992b:25) and contaminated public water supplies (*Himal* 5 (1)(January-February 1992):30).

[18] A team of American scientists used sensors to measure levels of carbon monoxide, hydrocarbons, and nitrous oxides in vehicle exhaust. Of all the cities measured around the world, Kathmandu was second only to Mexico City in rates of vehicular air pollution (S. Bista 1993).

[19] During the one hundred years of Rana family rule prior to 1951, the ruling elite enforced a deliberate policy of restricting migration into the Kathmandu valley, helping to maintain a relatively stable and homogeneous population (A. Tiwari 1992). For a discussion of recent immigration trends in the Kathmandu valley, see Task Force on Migration 1999.

Shrestha and his colleagues (1986:132) estimate that between 1971 and 1985 over *one-third* of Kathmandu's residents moved from the inner city to the urban periphery. The trend is still much in evidence, prompting one observer to note that the "urban instinct" characteristic of Kathmandu citizens for close to a thousand years is rapidly being replaced by a suburban instinct (K. Dixit 1992:39). The amoebalike sprawl of suburban Kathmandu, along with its overloaded public services and deteriorating environmental conditions, are testimony both to the city's growing incorporation into global economic and cultural processes and to Nepal's continuing position on the global periphery.

The "suburbanization" of Kathmandu also reflects important changes in patterns of domesticity and the sociological makeup of communities. On the domestic front, middle-class migration to the suburbs parallels the growing prevalence of nuclear families. In addition to these, with a population growth rate triple the national average (A. Dixit 1992a:8), Kathmandu is home to a large number of first-generation residents and their children, who make up much of the new middle class.[20] With the growth in opportunities for education and for employment in the government and private sectors, Kathmandu has been, and continues to be, a magnet for persons aspiring to escape the extremely limited opportunities of the hill regions. The extended family—consisting of parents, unmarried children, the families of married sons, and perhaps grandparents—often remains the ideal, for middle-class families like these. But a variety of factors related to physical and socioeconomic mobility have led to the establishment of more and more families composed of a married couple and their children.

In 1950, alongside the small but powerful Hindu Brahman and Chetri communities (including the Rana elites),[21] the large majority of Kathmandu's residents were Newars, the ethnic/linguistic community that has occupied the valley for millenia. (Whether Hindu and/or Buddhist, Newars have historically been divided into ranked endogamous caste/occupational groups [Nepali 1965].) By the 1990s, however, this Newar majority had been significantly diminished by the arrival of immigrants from across Nepal, and beyond. Hill Brahmans and Chetris, groups associated with Tibetan Buddhist culture (Sherpas, Manangis, Tibetan refugees, etc.), ethnic groups from the hill regions (Gurungs, Rais, Magars, Tamangs, and many others), more culturally "Indic" peoples from the Nepal Tarai and northern India—all of these new residents have made the Kathmandu

[20] See Task Force on Migration 1999:6.

[21] In the standard Hindu caste hierarchy, Brahmans are followed by Chetris (Sanskrit, *kṣatriya*); a high (and traditionally dominant) caste group that includes much of Nepal's social and political elite, including the royal family.

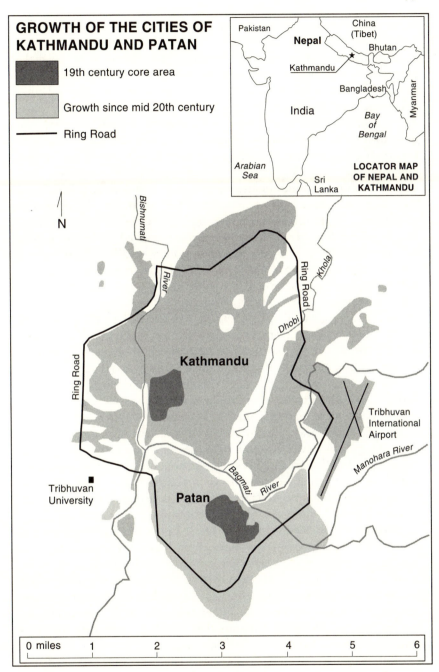

1. Growth of the cities of Kathmandu and Patan.

valley much more socially diverse in terms of ethnic, religious, and caste affiliations.

Kathmandu's new suburbs illustrate most clearly how, over the past few decades, the city's growing diversity has increasingly come to be organized—both spatially and socially—along the lines of class. Whereas residential areas within the walls of the old city were traditionally segregated along the lines of the Newar caste hierarchy (Nepali 1965:55), and have to a considerable extent remained so (Lewis 1984:139), the new suburban settlements are typically much more heterogeneous in caste and ethnicity. The organizing principle in the new suburbs is more likely to be class. From the riverside squatter settlements to middle-class residential areas like Samakhusi, Naya Baneswar, or Sanepa, to the elite residences of Maharajganj, Kathmandu's new suburbs are class communities occupied by people from a range of caste, regional, and ethnic backgrounds.

As I show in the chapters that follow, caste membership remains a relevant factor in the social life of a resident of Kathmandu, yet it does not in any simple way determine his or her social or socioeconomic standing. For example, a 1991 study of extremely poor squatter settlements around Kathmandu (Gallagher 1991:81–82) found that almost one-third of the residents were from high-caste groups (Brahman, Chetri, and upper-caste Newar, including Shresthas), about 40 percent were from various hill communities (Magars, Tamangs, Sherpas, Gurungs, etc.) and the remainder were from low-caste occupational groups (Kami, Damai, Sarki, etc.). At the other socioeconomic extreme, some of Nepal's wealthiest citizens come from traditionally disparaged ethnic communities (Manangis, Tibetans, Sherpas). In between, some members of extremely low-caste groups have been able to successfully adapt their traditional occupational skills to the modern market, enabling them to stake claims in the city's new middle class; palanquin bearers have turned truck and taxi drivers, for example, and metal workers have turned auto mechanics and machinists. My point is not that that traditional caste privilege (or oppression) is suddenly irrelevant: in fact, Nepal's political and economic elite remain disproportionately high-caste (Bista 1991). But caste is becoming less and less likely to *guarantee* (whether by privilege or exclusion) a person's social standing. Indeed, it is precisely the ever growing instability and indeterminacy of caste that makes the project of class-cultural formation all the more imperative. The city's new cash- and market-oriented economy demands that people pioneer new forms of cultural practice, identification, and privilege.

Kathmandu's new "suburban instinct" charts not only shifting demographic patterns but also new class-based experiences, values, and sensibilities. Unlike their great grandparents, today's residents are likely to

2. Squatter settlement along the banks of the Bishnumati River adjacent to middle-class homes near Dallu, Kathmandu

work *individually* to make *money*, not as a family or caste *group* to farm, trade, or make *products*. They are engaged in a monetized economy where their subsistence depends on wage labor and commodity purchases. They spend most of their time away from home and are tied to rigid daily work schedules that do not vary with the seasons. For these reasons and others, a young Kathmandu resident is likely to view urban spaces in very different ways than his/her ancestors did. As the gap grows between work and leisure, personal and group property, self and community, daily life and religious expression, city residents are likely to have very different notions of desirable public and private spaces. The migration to the suburbs, with their single-family dwellings and walled compounds, reflects changing notions of domestic propriety and changing civic values.

One of the most striking indices of shifting labor patterns and social values is the huge rise in the number of educational institutions in the Kathmandu area. Before 1951 there were no more than a handful of schools in the Kathmandu valley (or Nepal for that matter), and formal education was inaccessible to all but the urban elites. By 1983 the number of schools (primary through secondary) in Kathmandu and its adjacent sister city, Patan, had risen to 634. But in the decade between 1983 and 1993 that figure almost tripled, to 1,727 (CBS 1995:250–61). In a later chapter I discuss both the class and labor implications of this education explosion in more detail. For the time being, suffice it to say that the huge rise in the number of schools indicates the centrality of education in the production and reproduction of a new middle-class community in Kathmandu. Although education by no means guarantees success, middle-class parents recognize that without it their children have little chance of thriving in the new labor and prestige market, where earlier forms of social capital (caste, family connections, etc.) no longer represent clear-cut avenues to financial security.

CONCLUSION

Since 1951 Kathmandu's social setting has gone from one in which understandings of self and other were derived from the cultural contrasts found in a relatively stable, local universe of known roles and ways of being to a society whose frames of reference and contrastive awareness are of literally global dimensions. For members of old Kathmandu families, and even more so for the tens of thousands of residents who arrived in the city only in the last decades, a traditional social fabric of caste, occupation, and ritual life is enveloped by layer upon layer of new meaning systems: new patterns of wage labor and new cash economies; new ideologies of education, development, and progress; new arenas of public display and expressive culture; new residential configurations and built environments; and a new universe of material goods. Through repeated enactment and embodiment and their growing presence in daily life, these new systems of meaning form a slowly hardening structure around and within communities in the city, binding people together in new relationships (e.g., class) without necessarily contesting earlier systems of social meaning (e.g., caste). In Kathmandu the fabric of an earlier pattern of sociality still exists, some strands maintaining remarkable strength. Yet other strands slowly disintegrate, leaving the structures of modernity to increasingly bear the weight of social transactions. The chapters that follow open perspectives on the growing salience of class logics in everyday life by exploring various domains in which new cultural processes of class production are at work.

PART TWO

CLASS AND CONSUMERISM

3

MIDDLE-CLASS CONSCIOUSNESS: "HANGING BETWEEN THE HIGH AND THE LOW"

Whoever does not adapt his manner of life to the conditions of capitalistic success must go under, or at least cannot rise.

—MAX WEBER, *The Protestant Ethic and the Spirit of Capitalism*

To be middle-class in Kathmandu is to participate in a social and cultural dialogue about what it means to be a "modern Nepali." But entering this new forum comes at a cost. Participants must be willing (and able) to gamble financial resources in the always shifting game of synchronized public consumption. Even more importantly, they must be willing to walk the fine—and socially unstable—line of "middleness" that cuts not only *between* the poor and the rich but also *through* the categories of "tradition" and "modernity" that a global development ideology associates with this social dichotomy. In Kathmandu the middle class are those people struggling to rescue a socially valid "traditional" Nepali morality from its associations with the provincial vulgarity of the urban poor, while at the same time attempting to define a "suitably" modern-but-still-Nepali lifestyle of moral and material restraint distinct from what they view as corrupt elite lifestyles of foreignness and consumer excess. To be middle-class is to walk this knife's edge between low and high, tradition and modernity, and to be willing to risk the social penalties of falling away from one's social others as they collectively debate and improvise a Nepali modernity. Viewed in this way, the middle class in Kathmandu is less a "thing" to be located in some "objective" social configuration than a new sociocultural project—material and discursive—in which members negotiate the apparent contradictions between what it means to be both modern and Nepali.

CASTE AND CLASS IN KATHMANDU

Before any discussion of class in South Asia can get underway, it is necessary to consider the equally problematic concept of caste,[1] and the relationship between these two experiential frames in local history. Although
caste relations (couched in religious/ritual terms) have until recently been
the dominant social principle in Kathmandu, elements of a materially
based class logic have never been absent. Over the past four decades a
range of socioeconomic processes have produced a shift in cultural idioms
of dominance such that the logic of class has increasingly become the
framing principle in the daily lives of people in Kathmandu. With the
emergence of an increasingly market-oriented economy, new patterns of
political life, and a world of new commoditized goods and activities, more
and more of people's lives transpire in contexts where the language and
practice of class, rather than caste, becomes the most meaningful conceptual and experiential frame. If caste in Kathmandu is "a highly institution-
alized form of social inequality" (Allen 1993:11), class is another form of
social inequality with its own institutions, logics, and practices.

Many ethnographic studies demonstrate that caste identities and
caste relations have been fundamental features of everyday life in the
Kathmandu valley for centuries and remain so today.[2] Yet especially in
Nepal, caste could never be viewed as, in Louis Dumont's (1970) terms,
a purely "religious" institution. Jung Bahadur Rana's famous *Muluki Ain*
(Chief Law) of 1854 is a classic example of political power seeking to
inscribe class privilege in caste terms. In this document the Rana autocrat
inventoried all of Nepal's scattered caste and ethnic communities and then
codified these groups into an overarching system of caste hierarchy (Höfer
1979).[3] It is important that in the late eighteenth century—half a century
before Jung Bahadur's *Ain*—visitors to the Kathmandu valley noted the
relative lack of material ostentation on the part of the Nepali nobility
(Kirkpatrick 1969 [1811]:212–13). In the early Gorhkali state, political
hierarchies were not conspicuously indexed in material terms. Yet during
the Rana era visitors expressed astonishment at the gulf of material privi-

---

[1] "If ever there was a Pandora's box, caste is it" (Quigley 1993:158).

[2] One can trace an emphasis on the experience of caste from Hodgson's early writings
(e.g., 1834) through a host of mid-twentieth-century ethnographic studies (e.g., Rosser
1966) up to recent decades (e.g., Owens 1989, U. Shrestha 1990, Vergati 1995, Gellner and
Quigley 1999).

[3] Just as Jung Bahadur sought to clarify and fix caste ranking in his multiethnic state, at
this time the British in India were carrying out similar programs of caste classification and
regulation (Cohn 1968, 1984). "When the British attempted to pigeonhole castes and tribes
once and for all by means of census reports, the Gorkhalis did the same in Nepal with the
introduction of the . . . *Muluki Ain*" (Quigley 1993:102).

lege that separated Rana elites from a relatively undifferentiated urban mass.[4] At least since the early nineteenth century, relations of dominance could reasonably be characterized in class terms. Moreover (as I discussed briefly in chapter 2, and in detail elsewhere [Liechty 1997]) through the nineteenth and early twentieth centuries class distinctions were constructed increasingly in terms of distinctive material cultures. The logic of class takes hold of imaginations as social distinction is increasingly constructed through patterns of material privilege.

Thus by 1951, even while immersed in the social idiom of caste relations, residents of Kathmandu were fully acquainted with the experience and logic of class relations. In contrast to an earlier, essentially feudal, pattern of class relations between an extractive elite and a surplus-producing (though not homogeneous) mass (M. Regmi 1978, 1988), in the past four decades more complex social relations emerged as capitalist market forces (both local and transnational) were given free rein in the city for the first time. After 1951, in the context of a rapidly expanding cash economy of salaried bureaucrats and service sector employees and wage-earning tradespeople and menial laborers (Shrestha et al. 1986:86–104), it is increasingly legitimate to speak of emerging middle and working classes in Kathmandu alongside the established (though often struggling) traditional elites.

As city residents (especially those from the upper castes) constantly observe, class has emerged as a powerful mode of social logic and paradigm for social mobility. Stories of low-caste taxi drivers with monthly incomes five times that of high-caste government officers abound as people in Kathmandu struggle to reconcile two often conflicting modes of social stratification. While some caste elites successfully translate caste privilege into class privilege, other upper-caste families struggle in vain against the erosion of their traditional cultural capital in the face of a new "democracy of goods." Caste rank is still a good predictor of class rank and lifestyle,[5] yet the radically transformed economic climate of the past

---

[4] Of course, the "urban mass" was not in fact undifferentiated. It was, and to a lesser extent still is, differentiated within the sociomoral idiom of ranked castes. Material culture played a role in distinguishing high from low groups (e.g., Nepali 1965:65). Yet because the range of material goods was limited by import restrictions, and because even those groups of relatively wealthy merchants who could afford distinctive imported goods were denied access to most of them by sumptuary laws and the unlimited rights of appropriation enjoyed by the Rana elites, material culture and consumer goods did not come into their own as a means of constructing status distinction until after the fall of the Rana autocracy in 1951. By that time Kathmandu residents had had over a century of socialization into the world of consumer-based class distinction as practiced by the Ranas.

[5] By the mid-twentieth century much of Nepal's arable land was owned by high-caste families, even if it was often farmed by other people (e.g., Caplan 1970). To the extent that land (both inside and outside the Kathmandu valley) is still in upper-caste hands, and to the extent that land is still one of the few productive assets that Nepalis are likely to have

few decades has lowered (but by no means eliminated) the barriers to economic advancement that had, until recently, excluded those of low birth from any position of social or economic privilege. Social mobility (as easily downward as upward) is a hotly contested, but unavoidable, reality. Today Kathmandu's squalid squatter settlements include Brahman families of the highest ritual ranks (Gallagher 1991), while members of once despised and marginalized ethnic groups preside over vast transnational business empires (Gombo 1985, van Spengen 1987, 2000, Watkins 1996). In the new economic order, social mobility does not occur at the caste level; whole caste communities do not move up or down. Rather, families and (less often) individuals move into positions of greater or lesser sociopolitical power in which the language and practice of class more adequately conveys shared interests and values.[6] As Anup Pahari argues, "The dominant social group in Nepal is increasingly . . . not a *caste*, but a *class*" (1992:54).

THE MIDDLE CLASS IN KATHMANDU

Although the term "middle class" is often used, it is a concept notoriously difficult to "pin down" in objective terms. As detailed in chapter 1, existing studies offer general insights into the composition of middle classes, what kind of values their members hold, how these people relate to processes of production and consumption, and the general roles they play in capitalist societies. But when it comes to actually describing the *experience* of a "middle class"—some sense of *lived middle-classness*, or the way in which class is actually produced and reproduced in practice—descriptive efforts typically fall short. When confronted with the complexity of everyday lives, it becomes clear that "class" as an objective analytical *category* is problematic—resisting, even defying, clear-cut definition (R. Williams 1977:112). Like pointillist paintings, class categories are best, or at least most clearly, seen from a distance. The more closely one looks at a class group, the more its boundaries dissolve and its supposedly distinguishing features blur into a haze of contrasting and conflicting detail. The concept of "class" often belies its origins in social theory by serving as a helpful analytic device, even while proving extremely slippery in "the field."

(whether in terms of agricultural production or simply rent), caste privilege is still often translated into class privilege. However, as their land is divided up or sold off, many once-prosperous upper-caste families struggle to maintain parity between their caste standing and their social prestige.

[6] The main flaw of a recent book on entrepreneurial communities in Nepal (Zivetz 1992) is that it fails to address the current reality of emerging class stratification *within* these communities and deals only with stratification *between* them.

I encountered the same slippage between theory and practice when I tried to talk about class with people in Kathmandu. The concepts of class in general, and of a "middle class" (*madhyam barga*) in particular, were familiar to urban Nepalis. The terms appeared frequently in the local press, in the official verbiage of government policymakers, and in everyday speech. Yet when I asked people to *define* the urban middle class and *describe* its members, the answers were hesitant and often vague. Everyone agreed that a middle class existed, but there was little consensus on what it was.

Urban Nepalis most often focused on material standards of living when trying to define "middle-class." In its most stripped-down version, this definition held simply that middle-class persons were "those who have enough to eat," as one schoolteacher in his late thirties put it. Others had similar, if more elaborate, understandings of what distinguished the middle class. As one twenty-five-year-old college student explained:

> I distinguish people by their way of living. If they have a car and a beautiful bungalow[7] then they're upper-class, no? And then if they have a motor bike, and a house of their own, and, well, if things are going easily, that's middle-class. Lower-class people, they are the ones who if they don't earn today, they don't eat tomorrow.

Like the schoolteacher, this young man contrasted the middle and lower classes by focusing on the fundamental means of survival, food. For both, being in the middle class had to do with being freed from the brutal daily anxieties of basic subsistence. For these two respondents, as for others in Kathmandu, access to at least *some* discretionary income separated a local middle class from the thousands of other city dwellers who lived in grinding poverty.

For this reason it seemed likely that some reckoning of income (wages or salary, individual or family) would be a way of distinguishing class groups. Yet I found that even this was "a very tricky question," in the words of one Nepali economist. He explained that while it was fairly easy to slot the large group of fixed-income government employees into a middle class, anyone who wanted to simply associate certain income scales with certain consumer behaviors would be quickly frustrated. In his own studies this economist had found many families that, by their pooled incomes and assets, could have been ranked in the middle or even upper class. Nevertheless, "Their lifestyle is very simple. They don't raise their standard of living." Conversely, he found other families that, judging from their expenditures on a range of consumer goods, lived middle-class lives yet did so by spending "whatever they earn."

Regardless of these problems, it was clear that disposable income, as indexed in the display of consumer goods, was among the most common

---

[7] Here "bungalow" means a detached suburban house.

means by which people in Kathmandu ascertained class membership. Not surprisingly, in a society where large numbers of people struggle to provide even the most basic elements of subsistence for themselves and their families, a person's clothing is often taken as an indication of class membership. I came upon one somewhat startling example of this association in an interview with a young physician employed in a large government hospital in downtown Kathmandu. This doctor had published a number of epidemiological studies in which one of the data variables was "class." Hoping to have found someone with an "objective" definition of "middle-class," I was surprised to find that he had divided the people in his studies into class groups based almost entirely on the clothing the patient (and those accompanying her/him) wore upon arrival at the emergency ward. If possible, he also collected information on occupation, but, like most people in Kathmandu, the doctor saw no problem with assigning class membership based on apparel. Although at first disappointed at such "subjective" methods of class distinction, I eventually came to realize that, to a much greater degree than in North America (where relatively few persons are on the verge of total destitution), in Kathmandu specific commodities often effectively distinguished class groups, especially the lower from the middle class.

Yet when one began to look more closely, commodity consumption was not always a clear-cut way of defining class membership, especially if one wanted to distinguish "working-class" from "middle-class" based on the distinction between wage and salaried labor.[8] The economic situations of two Kathmandu families illustrate this problem. In the first family, a young man (from a local Newar farming caste) who had not finished high school operated a bicycle-repair business with his father. The young man, his wife and their child lived with his parents and two unmarried siblings in an ancient home that had been in the family for centuries. Here they rented the lower level to a poor family from the hills and enjoyed what could only be called a middle-class life by local standards, with television, indoor plumbing, and basic furnishings. The second family (from a higher caste) was made up of a married couple and their young child. Having completed a master's degree, the husband held a respectable but not very high-paying job in a Kathmandu NGO. This man, who had moved to Kathmandu as a young adult, lived with his family in a rented

[8] Most Nepali government surveys (including censuses) divide urban populations into groups engaged in primary labor (agriculture), secondary labor (tradesmen and factory workers), and tertiary labor (sales, service, clerical, administrative, commercial, professional/technical, educational, etc.) (P. Sharma 1989:92). Thus, studies often divide the urban labor force into two categories—"manufacturing" and "tertiary activities" (e.g., Shrestha, et al. 1986:93)—that would correspond to the basic defining criteria of a working and a middle class.

flat in a middle-class residential area, but they had few of the standard middle-class consumer amenities. It is hard to determine the class rank of either of these two families (so very similar by most demographic standards, including monthly income): the arguably "working-class" family lived a "middle-class" lifestyle as rent takers, while the educated, salaried, "middle-class" family lived as tenants and barely made ends meet. Thus, although people often spoke of the middle class in concrete terms, trying to find objective criteria to characterize a middle class in Kathmandu was like trying to catch clouds with a net.

MIDDLE-CLASS CONSCIOUSNESS: CLAIMING THE MORAL MIDDLE

While struggling to come up with a way to define "the middle class" in Kathmandu, I eventually realized that, rather than try to objectify it in a list of traits and features, I needed to look for its traces in speech and practice. I turned my attention to the ways in which people spoke and thought of themselves and others as class bearers. In this way a concept of *middle-classness* began to emerge, even if an objective definition remained elusive.

What people spoke of was a notion of *middleness*, of occupying a position *between* social others who were characterized by a variety of contrasting values and behaviors. More than a wage category or pattern of consumption, the middle class in Kathmandu is a social space where people negotiate what it means to be both Nepali and modern, a place in which to carry on a dialogue about how to wed the realities of a transformed material and social universe with powerful preexisting cultural values and discursive frames.[9] What constitutes this sense of middle-classness is not necessarily a common lifestyle or a uniform set of values but rather a shared project of locating oneself in a new and legitimate space between two devalued social poles. This space is one separated both from the "vulgar" lives of the national elite, whose distinction lies in their emulation of a foreign modernism, and from a lower class trapped in equally vulgar lifestyles of "tradition" and poverty. The challenge for an emergent middle class is to construct a *between space* that both adopts modernity as a means of distinguishing itself from those below and morally critiques modernity as a means of separating itself from the national elite. The experience of middle-classness lies in this uneasy relationship with "the modern," one of both emulation and distancing.

[9] Like most "modern" spaces, the "freedom" to enter this discursive space is premised on access to material resources, thereby marking it as a zone of class practice and class production.

Much of this middle-class unease seemed to be encapsulated in the remarks of a young Brahman "housewife" in her early thirties (who spoke with one of my female co-workers). Yalina, the mother of two, had some postsecondary education, and was married to a midlevel civil servant. Yalina's remarks help to introduce a number of important strands in the debate concerning what it means to be middle-class in Kathmandu. Among these is the tension between modernity and tradition, a tension that acknowledges the legitimacy of an earlier, simpler lifestyle but also the necessity for engagement with modern goods and practices. Most often this tension is mediated through a sense of moral propriety or acceptability. Through Yalina's comments one begins to see the contours of a space of middleness—the construction of self somewhere between old and new, rich and poor.

> *What kind of differences do you see between your life and your parents' when they were your age?*
>
> Something like the way we dress is one big difference. For example, my father likes simple living. He says that one shouldn't spend too much money on any kind of luxurious things. He thinks of how you will live tomorrow, how you will keep on surviving in the future. As for me, I think one's living standard should be good, with proper food and housing, clean environment. I want some things to show to others, I mean to an acceptable extent.
>
> *Why not this simple living style?*
>
> That simple life was for the time of my parents. At that time life was not expensive, but today life has become so costly. It's hard to keep up with the competition because of the many luxurious things. I mean lives are easier now, because everything has become fast. Today there are various machines, computers, gas stoves, heaters. . . . Daughters-in-law have such comfortable lives. No one has to go far to fetch water.

In Yalina's view, the "simple life" may have been appropriate for an earlier time, but now a changed material context compels her into a different lifestyle than her parents have, in spite of her ambivalence toward these changes.

Later the conversation turned more explicitly to the connections between class and morality, starting with the issue of prostitution.

> *So who gets drawn into this prostitution?*
>
> It's the low-class women who fall into this. They see others eating, wearing clothes of a high standard, and they want to do the same, but they don't have the money so they just get entrapped in this business.

So it's only the low-class women?

No, no. There are also high-ranking people involved in this. They have no social restraints, whereas the middle-class people are tied down in many ways by the social system. But whatever they [the wealthy] do, they are hidden, they are not exposed. And so because of their power, society accepts them, even though they may be involved in some bad business. Yet the middle-class people won't be accepted in this [high] society. So it is the low- and the high-ranking people: they are the two classes of society where you find prostitution. The low class people do it for money, while the high ones do it for self-satisfaction.

Why do the high-ranking people get into this?

They are the ones who watch these blue [pornographic] films. The low people don't have access to this: it's the high ones who have everything satisfied in their lives. They have the free time, they are the ones who seek to find some new recreational things. When they look for greater pleasure, for more bliss in their lives, this is what leads them down the path of destruction.

So the high-ranking people are all doing this bad business?

No, like, I think this smuggling[10] is also being done by some low-class people. I mean, it is the middle-class people who are just busy doing their small businesses, making some money, hanging between the high and the low.

In these comments social distinctions emerge clearly as moral distinctions. Yalina characterizes low-class people as those "entrapped" in immorality by their lack of money. On the other hand, high-class immorality is a more complicated matter. The upper classes have been seduced by the pursuit of pleasure. Their privilege hides them from social view and allows them to indulge in "recreational" sexuality. Middle-class people are those in between, those neither corrupted by deprivation, nor debauched by excess. The middle class is "tied down" by the "restraints" of the social order. For Yalina, like many others, the middle class is a moral community, modern but within "proper" and "acceptable" limits, "hanging between the high and the low."

Morality tales are among the key narratives of middle-classness. Like Yalina, many other people in Kathmandu create themeselves as middle-class subjects through stories that characterize those above and below as

---

[10] Here the English word "smuggling" is used as a cover term for various forms of "shady business."

essentially immoral. One of the most common themes in these middle-class morality stories has to do with the corrupting influence of money. One young man, a midlevel civil servant and father of two elementary-school children, spoke bitterly of upper-class people who "spend money like madmen, without considering the future of their children. It's the children of these families who come to the schools and spread the ideas about '*This is the happiness. . . .*' " Another young woman, a high-caste, master's level student and mother of several children, more explicitly contrasted upper-class excess with middle-class morality.

> They have money and just do whatever they want. That's the kind of situation. They have parties, they go here and there, and since there's a lot of money, there's always a lot of enjoyment. . . . For them, they can have anything. Like money, it's the most important thing, and they have it.
>
> Before, in *our* time, like ten or fifteen years ago, money wasn't so important. Then it was *honesty* [*imāndār*]. That was the main thing. [Then people said] "What is money? People should be honest." But now, honesty is meaningless. Money buys everything. Everybody looks to money now.

From this woman's perspective, once-unquestioned "traditional" values like honesty are now threatened by a degenerate upper class and its money-driven ethic.

More than just a way of labeling those "above" as grasping and unscrupulous, this woman's perception of a recent turn from "honesty" to "money" as a primary value hints at another common characterization of upper-class elites as pretentious nouveaux riches. *Ṭuppa bāṭa palāeko* (something that springs from the top, like a shoot or sprout) is a common expression used to denigrate those whose money is not matched with an appropriate degree of middle-class civility. The phrase captures the notion of rootlessness, impermanence, shallow pretense, and inexperience—everything that is in contrast to a life of honest, middle-class achievement. Another phrase directs many of the same moral critiques at those from the lower class who would attempt to hide their true nature by affecting outward signs of wealth. *Sukul guṇḍā* (literally, "straw-mat ruffian") is a moniker directed at youth who, by implication, sleep on rough mats at night but sport expensive clothing by day, or in other words live beyond their means. Through stories and gossip about those who have gone beyond the bounds of "acceptable" behavior, the middle class perpetually tells the tale of its own moral propriety.

In addition to the corrupting influence of money, another common narrative strategy for producing a middle ground between those above and below revolves around stories of sexual excess and other uncontrolled pleasures. I heard one of these middle-class tales of sexual morality in a conversation with a young (male) upper-caste doctor, who spoke of class and moral value:

> When it comes to things like marriage, middle-class families are more orthodox. But the higher class and the lower class, they are not so orthodox in this way. The lower class, they want to move into a higher class, so they will do anything. So there is no moral value among them. And the higher class, they have the chance to go abroad; they have the chance to meet people. They do not have that cultural and moral value.
>
> You know about AIDS? Well, most of the time, though it's not officially reported, they are high-class people, because they go outside, and they have the contact.

Here again those people below the middle class are represented as desperate, willing to "do anything" to advance socially, and hence intrinsically without "moral value." Conversely, this man (like Yalina) characterizes the "higher class" as being morally corrupted by forces from outside the community. Upper-class people can travel outside of Nepal and are thus not bound by the moral community, which is—as though by definition—local and middle-class. In this story, AIDS is recruited as a symbol of modern sexual immorality that literally marks the upper class.

Especially for women, talking about prostitution was an opportunity to talk about appropriate, moral, middle-class practices. One woman, an unmarried twenty-year-old student, explained what type of people become involved in prostitution:

> I guess it is the uneducated women. They have gotten into this because of some problems they have. It is mostly the low-class people who get into this. This is what I've heard from talking with my friends. Some have been abandoned by their husbands, some have household problems, some have no other way to survive, so they do this.
>
> But part of the problem with this prostitution is that, because these women are involved in that, *other women*, people with good moral character, are also looked upon badly.

Like this person, most middle-class women recognize the societal factors that might lead poorer women into prostitution. Yet at the same time they harbor a kind of unease, bordering on hostility, toward "lower-class" women whose public sexuality threatens to undermine the ideal of female sexual sobriety pursued by the middle class. Middle-class women are aware that the growing incidence of prostitution only "confirms" (in the eyes of males) the common gender stereotype about women's "nature."

They know that their own claims to independence (within the bounds of middle-class propriety) depend on strict adherence to sexual codes of conduct designed to counter the standard South Asian male fantasy of female sexual voracity. Thus, even while women are fully aware of what drives some into prostitution, they also know that the resulting stigma of uncontrolled sexuality threatens to subvert their efforts to construct identities as independent, modern, middle-class women. Ironically, the rise in local prostitution (largely driven by middle-class men) helps bring into relief the conflict of interests between genders within the middle class. In a sense, it is middle-class women who must "pay" for middle-class male consumer sexuality, through constant self-discipline and anxiety over sexual propriety (Liechty 1996b).

Middle-class women perceived similar threats as emanating from the sexual improprieties of the upper class. Middle-class men and women often used the word "prostitute" (*besyā*) in stories of upper-class women whose supposed sexual activity deviated from middle-class standards of acceptability. Here I am less concerned with whether such characterizations are justified than with the narrative devices those who place themselves in the middle class use to voice their condemnations. As many of the remarks above suggest, middle-class notions of propriety are typically rooted in a sense of community: the middle class is a moral community that "restrains" its members in a sphere of "suitable" behaviors. One of the adjectives commonly used to denigrate women (usually young and well-to-do) whose social behavior is deemed unacceptable is *chārā*. Young women who wear "excessive" ("over") makeup and short skirts, who are said to hang out in the tourist areas, or around bars and cinema halls, are called *chārā*. At best *chārā* implies "free-roving," but its main connotation is those who function outside of social controls or norms, people who are dangerous and threatening precisely because they appear to disregard what other people think of them. Scandalous stories of elite *chārā* women help to create and naturalize a sense of middle-classness that is embedded within a self-referencing, encompassing, "restraining" moral community.

Having introduced something of the moral tone of middle-class discourse in Kathmandu—a discourse of honesty, propriety, sobriety, and acceptability—in the following sections I look more closely at some of the main themes in this middle-class project of discursive positioning "between the high and the low." These sections focus particularly on the twin concepts of "suitability" and "necessity," especially as they pertain to middle-class fashion practice and other dimensions of the local consumer culture.

"Somewhere in the Middle": Fashion, Class, and Suitability

Class-cultural practice is about inclusion and exclusion. In Kathmandu much of this cultural work is framed in a discourse of consumption and suitability. Consumer goods (and the economic privilege that they index) are necessary elements of claims to middle-classness, but their uses and meanings are always renegotiated through the lens of "suitability." In stories of everything from food to fashion, middle-class people discuss the promises and pitfalls of consumerism and the need for middle-class restraint. Between "too much" and "too little" they claim "suitable" behavior and the "suitably" fashioned body for themselves, while positioning those class others below and above along a continuum from unsuitable and antipatriotic to vulgar and immoral.

Middle-class suitability is a complex construct, but it begins with the notion of moderation and betweenness. In Kathmandu stories of suitability frequently accompanied discussions of a person's engagements with the consumer economy. For example, one particularly marked sense of middle-class suitability appeared in the remarks of a thirty-five-year-old woman, mother of one and owner of her own small tailoring business.

What do you like to do for fun [majā linu]?

Oh, sometimes we like to go eat at a restaurant and then go to see a movie. We go to the medium-sized restaurants, not the high, or third-class types. We go to a place suitable [suhāune] to our level—a place where we can pay the bill. We like to eat chowmein, tukpa,[11] and that kind of thing.

In fact, we often eat chowmein at our house instead of *dāl bhāt*.[12] Cooking *dāl bhāt* takes a lot of time, and it's very heavy food. We like chowmein because it's lighter.

Even more than Yalina, this woman had a very explicit sense of middleness and suitability. She and her husband stick to those activities "suitable" to their "level." These remarks are like those of one high-caste woman who, no longer able to afford a domestic cook because of declin-

---

[11] A kind of Tibetan noodle soup.

[12] Literally, some kind of cooked legume (beans, lentils, peas) and rice, *dāl bhāt* is the Nepali national meal, usually eaten twice a day (midmorning and evening) and accompanied by curried vegetables, pickles, and other side dishes. Modern work schedules and time demands (especially on women) are making the traditional *dāl bhāt* meal cycle increasingly a thing of the past, or of weekends.

ing family fortunes, made a virtue of her necessity: "I really enjoy cooking and besides, [when I cook it, the food] is always *cokho* [ritually pure]." For many who work to locate themselves in middle-class culture, it is often difficult to distinguish what is *suitable* from what is *necessary*, even if in most cases middle-class choices (or necessities) are cast in tones of moral superiority.

Even more than food, the consumer domain that most frequently elic-ited stories of middle-class suitability was "fashion." This link was appar-ent in the comments of one young married woman. The daughter of a successful Kathmandu shopkeeper, in 1991 she was a part-time college student and hoped to become a college lecturer herself. When asked if she had any interest in "fashion" she replied:

> Well, I'm not *that* interested in it, but naturally these days I like to dress in a moderately fashionable manner.
>
> *How come?*
>
> [Laughter] What can I say? Look at my friends at college: some of them are into makeup, and some aren't at all. I mean, it's not that makeup alone makes someone look good. One should do the makeup that's suitable [*suhāune*] to them. Being too simple isn't good. But being really vulgar isn't good either. So one should be somewhere in the middle, it seems to me.

For this young woman, the "suitable" spot in the fashion spectrum was "somewhere in the middle."

Another way that people spoke about a suitably moderate fashion practice was in terms of *kinds* of fashion. As one young woman explained: "Some people do fashion out of arrogance . . . But I'm not like that. I'm only into one or two kinds of fashion, like hairstyles, saris, things like that. Others I don't like that much." Here, by implication, fashion moder-ation is a matter of not participating in too many domains of stylization. One or two fashion specializations is suitable; beyond this, one enters the region of upper-class and vulgar "arrogance." By this middle-class logic of moderation, suitable fashion practice is not determined by income— *more* fashion is not *better* fashion—but by taste. Thus, even though upper-class elites may have more money, suitable fashion practice is still a matter of *knowing* what is suitable, not simply buying it.

This characterization of elite fashion practice as excess was an ex-tremely common theme in middle-class tales of fashion suitability. Usually excess was not just a sign of elite "arrogance" but of fundamental moral shortcomings. One young woman put it in rather blunt terms.

As for style, if it's good style, I like it, but if it's over style, I think it's disgusting.

What do you mean by over?

I mean like wearing short skirts, or short-sleeved shirts—just looking at them you can tell what type [of person] they are, I mean, whether they're good or bad.

For this woman and others, "over style" meant too close to (what they understood to be) prevailing global high-fashion standards. Since these immodest (immoderate), relatively revealing styles were "bad," and since it was most often the elites who could approximate these international standards of dress, for the middle class "over style" and elite immorality went hand in hand.

If those claiming the social middle could critique elite fashion practice as extreme, arrogant, and immoral, they could also point to it as antipatriotic. Dress is one of a complex collection of elements that middle-class Nepalis (perhaps especially women) balance in their efforts to construct a class identity that is at once modern and Nepali. Dress must be both modern (that is, fashionable and thereby distinctive from the dress of the lower classes) and somehow Nepali, or at least suitable to Nepal (that is, not *too* beholden to international styles). By negotiating and claiming a suitable Nepaliness in dress, and by suggesting that elites—in their fashion practice and the (im)morality it implies—have simply sold out to other centers (and systems) of style and morality, the middle class can, in a sense, claim the nation.

This notion of national or Nepali suitability came through in the remarks of a middle-aged mother of several girls in their late teens. Although she took considerable pride in fostering responsibility and independence in her daughters, "fashion" was one area where she felt she had to exercise parental authority. When asked how she felt her childhood years differed from those of her daughters, she replied:

Now my daughters just sit around and do nothing. We used to sing songs [while working], but I have to ask them even to sing. And now there is more fashion. In our time there were only saris, and maybe *kurtā suruwāl*,[13] but these days there are midis, frocks, pants, and whatever. My daughters don't wear pants.

---

[13] *Kurtā suruwāl* is the term most often used in Kathmandu for a women's outfit that consists of a loose, long-sleeved, knee-length tunic worn over a matching pajama. Known in other parts of the subcontinent as *sarwāl-kamij* or *churidār-kurtā*, this originally North Indian garment is now a pan–South Asian fashion trend (see Nag 1991:106–7, Tarlo 1996).

What? Why not? What do you mean they don't wear pants?

I mean it's *only* pants that aren't OK. Clothes have to be *suitable*. I found that my daughters' structure did not look suitable, so I asked them not to wear pants. They look pretty only in *kurtā suruwāl*, but I've said midi is OK too.

And besides, they are grown up now, and to be in the middle [*bicmā*] in terms of fashion is good. I won't tell them this, but the fact is that in fashion, it should be suitable to one's structure.

It's not that I'm denying them permission to wear something. If the clothes suit and fit them, they can wear it, no problem with me. This is their idea. They are responsible for their future. My only concern is, well, if the fashion doesn't suit her, then, it's useless I think.

A bit later she elaborated further on her ideas of "suitability."

Since our country is poor I think doing fashion is OK up to the point of wearing *kurtā suruwāl*. We shouldn't be doing fashion just for show. That's no good. I like Indian fashion, because they stick to their own style, their own national dress.

If Americans wear American dress, that looks good. If we wear our dress, we look good. In other words, everybody is pretty good-looking in their own dress, not in others'. We should wear what is most suitable to us.

This woman spoke of fashion suitability in terms of "structure"—an idea that on one level had to do with her daughters' particular body morphologies and perhaps also with the fact that they are now "grown up." But at another level it was clear that their body "structure" was less an *individual* than a *national* trait. Her notion of suitability went from something applicable to "them" (her daughters) to "us"; in "our country . . . we should wear what is most suitable to us." Ironically, the "fashion" most suitable for Nepalis is Indian. Thus, for many middle-class women, that which is suitably modern, suitably "in the middle," and suitable for Nepalis, is Indian fashion.

In addition to distinguishing themselves from elites, the notion of suitability also helps those "in the middle" distinguish themselves from those below them in the social scale. While narratives of moderation, suitability, and Nepaliness help separate middle-class consumer practice from that of the elites, "doing fashion" is seen as simply inappropriate for the lower classes. When critiquing those "below" them, people claiming the middle stressed that one should be what one is. To appear to be what you are not—as when lower-class people "do fashion"—is both unsuitable and immoral. One woman in her midthirties—a teacher (with a bachelor's degree) in a local vocational school, whose husband worked in the Kathmandu branch of an international bank—discussed the role of fashion in society:

> I think it's going a little over. If someone does it in a way that's suitable [*suhāune*] to themselves, that's fine, nobody is going to gossip.
>
> Really a person should do fashion according to their education. I mean, a person's fashion should be in line with their education and family financial means. So if a person is uneducated, and if they have nothing to eat in the house, then they shouldn't be out doing fashion. For them fashion is not good, and it's not good for society. There are people like this, who are doing fashion without having anything to eat.

Again, fashion that is suitable to oneself is fine. But here the notion of suitability has another interesting class dimension. For this woman, fashion practice is, or at least should be, an index of educational achievement, just as education is an index of a family's "financial means." Furthermore, it is the uneducated people who "have nothing to eat in the house." In this woman's mind, when poor people "do fashion," they not only deprive themselves of education but in so doing deprive society of the benefits that another educated member would bring. For the poor to "do fashion" is to squander the cash resources with which an individual could achieve *real* personal betterment and thereby advance the collective cause. A poor, uneducated person who "does fashion" is not only vulgar and irresponsible but also immoral, to the extent that her/his actions are antisocial.

Other people expressed similar sentiments in slightly different terms. For example, one woman suggested that laborers had no business "doing fashion." With an intermediate college degree, this woman was active in women's organizations and was married to a businessman. Complaining about price inflation for everything from food to clothing, she remarked, "If you have to work [*kām garnu paryo bhane*], what's the point of doing fashion? It's better to be natural." Here this woman makes the important class distinction between those who "work" (*kām garnu*), and others (such as herself and her husband) engaged in middle-class occupations, which are more often referred to in terms of "doing service" or holding a *jāgir*, or salaried job.[14] By implication, those who "do work" are those engaged in wage labor or other kinds of low-paying, low-class, unskilled and/or menial work. For these people there is no point in "doing fashion." These lower-class people should be what they are; they should be "natural," not fashionable.

---

[14] The Nepali distinction between *jāgir* and *kām* is similar to the class-based distinction between the English words "career" and "job" (Williams 1985:53).

Another way in which people claiming the middle disparaged those whom they felt to be below them socially was to associate lower-class fashion practice with prostitution. By this line of reasoning, poor women who "do fashion" are, almost by definition, prostitutes. Very typical was the response of one twenty-five-year old college student, the unmarried daughter of a local businessman. When asked the "Who?" and "Why?" of prostitution, she replied confidently:

> Those who have nothing but do a lot of makeup and fashion, they are involved in this. I think most of them are from the lower classes. Maybe there are higher-class people too, modern people like the Ranas.[15] But it is the lower-class people who need the money to buy fashion and do makeup. They just go into this business. They have no honor/prestige [*ijjat*]. Some have a compulsion to do this. I have seen one or two cases.

According to this young woman, and many other people, it is "lower-class" women who engage in prostitution in order "to buy fashion and do makeup." They are the ones who, seduced by fashion and having neither money nor honor, succumb to the "compulsion" of selling their bodies for cash.

Other middle-class commentators on prostitution in Kathmandu were a bit more charitable when explaining why some women were drawn into this trade. Yet even these people rarely failed to mention "doing fashion" as one of the primary motivations behind prostitution. For example, one middle-aged woman, active in a well-known women's social service organization, offered these remarks when asked why she thought some women went into prostitution:

> It's just like that. The reason is fashion. They need money for fashion. There are people who, needing money for fashion, will go and do this immediately.
>
> I mean, sure, some do it for food. What else can a woman do if she doesn't have money to buy food? Some have no one to take care of them. Some have parents and siblings to support and they can't get enough money from other kinds of work. To eat they do this.
>
> But still, others do it for fashion. For fashion they need money, so they do this.

Although attuned to the harsh economic conditions that might force women into prostitution, this woman nevertheless *frames* her explanation

---

[15] See chapter 2 for a discussion of the role of the Rana family in Nepali history. While many Ranas are still wealthy and powerful, others have fared less well. Popular stereotypes of the Ranas portray them as rich, modern, and decadent.

of prostitution with strident condemnations of those people who, lacking money but desiring fashion, "immediately" leap into prostitution.

When I first heard stories of women prostituting themselves for fashion, I thought that I had come upon a particularly heinous twist in the saga of Nepal's capitalist modernization. But as the same story was told to me over and over again—"My former neighbor . . . ," "An old classmate of mine . . . ," "A secretary at my office . . . ," "Some of my patients . . . ," "Some students . . . ," "Some nurses . . . ," "Some waitresses . . . ," "Girls from Darjeeling . . ."—I began to see this tale in a different light. I began to wonder if, when people spoke of women who turn to prostitution to satisfy desires for material goods, they were really telling a kind of *morality tale*: a tale less about the morality of the *women* than about the morality of the *goods*. This is not to say that no such cases occur— they probably do—but that for the middle-class person telling such a tale and imagining such a chain of events, the story of the "fashion" prostitute is a way of expressing anxiety over the power of the new world of consumer goods. Through tales such as these, members of the middle class express their fears of a world of alluring but somehow evil fashion goods, a world that threatens to turn daughters and sisters into prostitutes (not to mention sons and brothers into the "teens," "punks," and even "junkies" discussed in later chapters).

By locating the "fashion fall" in classes below and above, people "in the middle" can at once claim the moral high ground and abreact their own middle-class nightmares. Tales of middle-class suitability represent the constant reprocessing of the fundamentally contradictory relationship that the local middle class has with the modern world of goods. The middle class must simultaneously embrace and distance itself from a global consumer culture that offers a status-enhancing modernity but one tinged with immorality. Through tales of suitability and moderation, the middle class attempts to displace this consumer contradiction onto its class others above and below. Yet this narrative sleight-of-hand has to be performed over and over again in efforts to calm middle-class fears over the inherent moral instability of its consumer practice.

"To Look Like You're Good-Looking": The Necessity of Fashion

Along with the notion of *suitability*, people in Kathmandu constructed a space of middle-class culture through stories of consumer *necessity*. People spoke of "doing fashion" for a number of reasons, including for beauty and attraction, but above all they spoke of consumer practice, and "fashion" in particular, in terms of necessity. By speaking of the *necessity* to

3.   Shopping for necklaces in old Kathmandu (Khel Tol).

consume, those who positioned themselves in the social middle could *critique* the new cultural economy of middle-class labor and consumer goods even while minimizing the taint of their own participation in consumer practices such as "fashion."

One subject that highlighted the tensions of consumer necessity was that of middle-class women's labor. For example, office jobs for women are typically thought to demand a certain kind of attire, but jobs for women in travel agencies and hotels are seen as particularly demanding—and potentially compromising—in terms of "fashion." There is an uneasiness about these jobs, in which women assume highly public roles and interact closely with a wide range of (usually male) customers and co-workers. Most men and women harbor suspicions about these "office girls," who are often thought to be "overly" fashionable and promiscuous. Thus, when women spoke of fashion they were often careful to distinguish legitimate practice from the inappropriate extremes. For example, one college student in her early twenties noted that "Fashion is necessary if you need to look smart, like to go to the office. But of course over fashion is not good." For her there is nothing wrong with going to the office and looking "smart" as long as one's dress is within limits. Yet for others, office work compelled women into compromise, both sartorial and moral. Another young woman explained why some women place so much importance on fashion:

> Their interest is to make themselves appear very good-looking for others. But for some people, they have been compelled to do fashion just to feed themselves. Like in the travel agencies, I've heard that they tell the girls, "Ordinary isn't enough!" They are obliged to wear [high-] standard clothing or lose their jobs. They have to look tip-top. That's why the girls who work there have to do fashion whether they can afford it or not. It's for the boss too, you know. They have to be good-looking.

There is a certain discomfort, even among women, about women working in the public realm. Here "ordinary" fashion may not be enough, and women may be driven into uncomfortable and unacceptable situations.

Yet, for the most part, "doing fashion" and "looking good" were perfectly acceptable in other settings, as long as it remained within the bounds of respectability. When asked about *why* they personally enjoyed "doing fashion," women had a variety of answers. One young woman from a low-caste but relatively prosperous family spoke of fashion in terms of *sokh*:[16]

> I've had this *sokh* for a long time. I was doing fashion at my parent's house [before marriage], and I still feel the desire/longing [*rahar*] to wear it when I see others wearing those fashions. It shouldn't matter

---

[16] The Nepali word *sokh* is often translated as "hobby," "pleasure," or "luxury," though these words do not very effectively convey its meaning. In Kathmandu people often talk about an "X-doing *sokh*," which might include something as hobbylike as stamp collecting but just as often refers to some desired way of being, either now or as a future goal. For example, young people spoke of having a "film-acting *sokh*"—a desire to someday act in films—or a "guitar-studying *sokh*," or even a "*sokh* for becoming a doctor." These are less "hobbies" or "luxuries" than desires or longed-for identities. A *sokh* is an innate inclination—part of a person's individual nature—something of more significance than is denoted by the English Word "hobby." Compare Nita Kumar (1988) or Joseph Alter (1992), who translates *shauk* as "hobby" or "infatuation." Alter notes that for some people the term

what you wear; all clothes cover the body. But I see others who look good, so I also have that *sokh*.

Why do you think people usually like fashion?

Each person has their own feeling [*bhāwanā*]. Some think that by doing fashion they'll impress the boys. Some have their own idea that, "If I wear this I'll be good-looking." It just depends. For me, I just enjoy it. It's not for showing off. Who do I need to show off to now [that I'm married]!?

This woman acknowledges that what one wears "shouldn't matter" but ends up defending her own purely personal enjoyment of fashion vis-à-vis others who use fashion to "impress the boys" or "show off."

Another young woman, a teenage student, put the necessity of fashion in slightly different terms:

I don't know why I like fashion. I just like it! But look at me. I'm not *too* [fashionable], am I? I think everyone is doing some fashion, just to make themselves look like they are good-looking and beautiful. Like for me, every few months I go to a salon to have my hair done. But just my hair, nothing else.

For this young woman and many others, the new world of fashion practice allows people to "*look like they are good-looking.*" Through fashion one is "free" to be good-looking. Beauty, like fashion, becomes a material condition that one "does" rather than "is," a commodity aesthetic conveyed and critiqued in the public spaces of the street, the shop window, and the mass media and available in the myriad beauty salons, boutiques, and tailors' shops of Kathmandu.

It is this commodity aesthetic—the commodification of beauty—that lies at the heart of the middle-class necessity to "do fashion." In the words of one college student in her early twenties:

I don't know why but fashion has just become very important. Like, people now think that even an ugly person becomes good-looking with fashion. So there is this competition; everybody wants to be considered good-looking by others. It has really become a necessity these days. So now here, as abroad, there is the same outlook about this.

By this logic the necessity of fashion derives from the fact that it offers a kind of democracy of beauty; "even an ugly person" can become attractive. In the democratic world of middle-class fashion, no one need be

---

implies a kind of frivolous, narcissistic attitude, a lifestyle of desires-out-of-control (1992:327–28).

"ugly," save the poor. For those in the middle, fashion is necessary because its consumer logic equates ugliness with poverty: the absence of fashion means the absence of middle-class standing.

THE *IJJAT* ECONOMY

Another central narrative theme in the moral life of Kathmandu's social middle is *ijjat*, a term that has already surfaced several times in this chapter. Usually translated as "prestige," "dignity," "respectability," or "honor," the notion of ijjat is often the conceptual lens through which people constructing middle-class culture ascertain suitability. Yet ijjat is perhaps best seen, less as a mechanism for discursively producing and naturalizing difference *between* classes, than as a discourse of reciprocity *within* the middle class. Through constantly circulating stories of ijjat people conduct the business of deciding what it means to be middle-class, a debate that is never settled, always in the process of negotiation.

Middle-class ijjat, or honor, is an extremely complex determination, not least because it brings together old and new logics of prestige in competing and often contradictory hierarchies of value. Some of this complexity comes through in the comments of a college student in his early twenties, trying to describe what it means to be in the middle class.

> They are given certain status above the lower castes because they follow certain traditions and values. If they say, "We won't follow these values," they run the risk of losing their ijjat, of being lumped with the lower groups. If they were in the low class, then, in terms of sexual matters and marriage they wouldn't have to be so strict, and they wouldn't have to follow all these [religious] rituals all the time.
>
> They have to do all of this, but it is such a tenuous position. To jump to a higher position they don't have the resources. And if they were low-class, they could just say "Eh, why send the children to school?" But because they are in this class they have to do all these things to maintain ijjat, like spend a certain amount on a wedding, have a TV, send their children to school.

Calculating middle-class ijjat requires an intricate reckoning of caste background and orthodox religious practice as well as consumer prestige, in a host of registers from weddings to education to consumer status symbols. Just how any one person's or family's configuration of ijjat stacks up is difficult to determine, but it is through stories of ijjat that the middle class negotiates its cultural being.

Perhaps more than any other possession, the middle class is built around an economy of ijjat, an economy in which honor or prestige is the central form of capital. Through its constant retelling and renegotiation, ijjat becomes almost tangible: it can be gained or lost, preserved or squandered. In this social economy, sexual propriety, suitable marriages, ritual observances, TVs, and education are not ijjat in and of themselves. Instead, they are things that *give* ijjat (*ijjat dine cij*); they *produce* social capital. Staking claims in this ijjat economy is perhaps the key move in an individual's or family's efforts to negotiate membership in the middle class.

As the young man quoted above indicated, the ijjat economy is never only a *moral* economy or only a *material* economy. It is always both. The construction of middle-classness is always a matter of both upholding the moral canons of sexual and ritual practice, *and* consuming the goods (from fashion to education) that act as recognized material markers of the middle class. By focusing on issues such as sexual sobriety and ritual observance, people in the social middle construct a privileged *moral* high ground which they can claim as their own. In this domain of public morality, the middle class distinguishes itself from the vulgarity of those "below" them. But by laying claim to "traditional" moral values, the middle class also distinguishes itself from those "above" who have sold out to the morally bankrupt lifestyles of affluence, pleasure, and foreignness.

The *material* domain of the ijjat economy is as important as the moral one in generating class distinctions. The wedding celebrations, home furnishings, clothing, and hundreds of other material accoutrements that are required to establish middle-class status effectively distinguish its members from those in poverty. These same goods also signal "modernity"— the middle class's identification with spheres of meaning wider than the strictly local ones in which those below them are trapped. Thus the middle class positions itself in a kind of moral/material modernism. In its moral tempering, this modernism at once critiques the material excesses of elite lifestyles and protects itself from critiques from below by melding its own materialism with a regimen of orthodox practices. In this way the ijjat economy marks out a new middle space between tradition and modernity, between local and foreign, and between high and low. In it people experiment with what it means to be both moral and modern, both Nepali and engaged with a growing world of transnational cultural forms and forces.[17]

---

[17] Of course, this experimentation is never simply a matter of free choice. As I discuss in the following chapters, participation in the middle-class ijjat economy is always predicated on the ability to control and mobilize financial resources. Status within the middle class is part of a complex and shifting calculus determined by parallel and competing hierarchies of value and modes of cultural capital (cf. Bourdieu 1984). Yet it is money that provides access to the middle-class ijjat arena: without it, one "doesn't count."

Stories of social prestige and honor are neither new nor limited to any specific social group in Kathmandu. What *is* new in the local ijjat economy may be its degree or scale: in the modern context of changing urban class formations, vastly increased exposure to transnational cultural forces, and an exploding universe of distinction-producing consumer goods, ijjat becomes almost an obsession for those Nepalis striving to claim a space in the middle class. In this new context of increased social mobility (up and down) and proliferating distinctive resources, the ijjat economy becomes the main arena in which people stake claims to middle-class identities. Ijjat is the narrative idiom in which a new group of urban Nepalis seeks to establish (and constantly reestablish) footholds in the slippery terrain of an emerging middle space produced by shifting labor and economic patterns.

All of this points to the potential for anxiety in the high-stakes gamble of participation in the middle-class ijjat economy. While individuals, families, or groups may pursue different configurations of practice within the moral/material prestige economy, no one can ignore ijjat and hope to maintain a legitimate social identity above the masses of urban poor. Especially for those whose economic resources are limited and whose social status depends on various forms of social and cultural capital (education, caste), ijjat can become an overriding, almost crushing, concern.[18] For most of Kathmandu's middle-class residents—for whom the experience of intense social insecurity is a constant reality—ijjat becomes an almost unbelievably powerful force.

Conclusion

Rather than viewing class as an existential material reality that is ontologically prior to and outside of discourse, this chapter has begun to locate the concept in the historical and cultural terrain out of which class identities and class cultures emerge. In the many ways that they articulate and enact their own interests and privileges, people in Kathmandu's social middle produce the cultural space of class, a space in which specific claims to value, meaning, and reality are lived out and naturalized in everyday practice. Thus, class is never a thing, always a process; like culture itself, class is always "in the making" (Fox 1985).

This chapter has laid out some of the historical and material factors that serve as the backdrop for projects of class production in Kathmandu. But more importantly it has begun to describe the themes and practices

---

[18] The ijjat economy is the domain in which Kathmandu's middle class experiences its own "fear of falling" (Ehrenreich 1989).

around which middle-classness takes shape. Significantly, the language and practice of class does not spring uniformly from what are now globally dispersed patterns of capitalist labor relations (cf. Tagg 1988:27) but instead draws selectively and experimentally on preexisting narratives of status and value that people use to claim and contest social positions. From notions of "honesty" and "suitability" to demands for sexual propriety and religious orthodoxy, the middle class selectively employs a range of distinctly Nepali moral orders in its project of constructing a class culture. But perhaps most important is the middle-class ijjat economy, which explicitly ties a historically validated narrative of prestige to the increasingly vast, unstable, and therefore treacherous realm of material culture. Encompassing both moral and material elements, ijjat is a crucial domain in which people claim and test the boundaries of class membership and experiment with the suitability of modernity in the form of new consumer practices and consumer goods. The following chapters continue the theme of the production of middle class culture by focusing on the language, practice, and motivating force of consumerism in Kathmandu. These chapters suggest ways in which the modern commodity realm, with its rapidly growing and highly commercialized economy of signs, increasingly acts as a critical territory for the social production of class culture.

4

CONSUMER CULTURE IN KATHMANDU: "PLAYING WITH YOUR BRAIN"

> There are so many changes now, even though the old generation still thinks in the same way. But now you have the changes in the fashion of clothes, fashion of people, fashion of food, thousands of kinds of fashions. All you need is money! Compared to before, now everything has changed.
>
> —Twenty-Year-Old Kathmandu Woman

> Modernity has turned every element of the real into a sign, and the sign reads "for sale."
>
> —K. A. Appiah, *Is the Post- in Postmodernism the Post- in Postcolonial?*

Chapter 3 introduced some of the cultural themes around which Kathmandu's middle-class moral consciousness is centered. This chapter considers the role of *goods* in the ongoing process of constructing middle-classness, and particularly how groups of people both construct boundaries around themselves and debate the terms of group membership through commodity consumption and the practices that this consumption entails. In Kathmandu middle-class consciousness is inseparable from a kind of consumer consciousness. Commodities are fundamental components in the middle-class project of constructing itself as a social group. But how is it that goods can be constantly on people's minds? This chapter explores how consumer goods have become a new social currency—a new communicative medium—for Kathmandu's emerging middle class, and how people are drawn into, adopt, or choose to experiment with the logic and values of a new consumer materialism.

THE CONSUMER CONTEXT

Like almost every other Third World capital city, Kathmandu is the center of not only the nation's administrative and cultural life but also its consumer market. From the vast "Hong Kong Bazaar," a tent city of makeshift stalls specializing in low-market consumer goods, mostly from India and China, to the famous "Bishal Bazaar" (literally, "Super Market"), a multistory indoor shopping mall specializing in high-end consumer goods from East Asia and Europe (and boasting the nation's first (and, until recently, only) escalator), Kathmandu is Nepal's consumer mecca. In fact, because Nepal (since 1951) has had liberal import policies, Kathmandu has emerged as one of the subcontinent's leading shopping sites.[1] Kathmandu offers a full array of modern South Asian consumer venues: from glitzy showrooms and fashion boutiques to sidewalk vendors squatting beside small baskets of Chinese hair products, the city has something to incite consumer desire in almost every heart.

Where once people simply saw new goods in shop windows or in other people's homes, now there are more and more organized channels that make it "easy" for people to buy new consumer goods. One of the most common schemes is known as the "*dhukuṭi* [treasury, storehouse, or cash box] system"—a kind of rotating credit club in which groups of acquaintances agree to each contribute a certain amount of money to a kitty every week or month and then either wait their turn or bid to receive the pooled capital. Although *dhukuṭi* credit schemes in Kathmandu are likely as old as cash itself, by the early 1990s their numbers and popularity were rising so precipitously that the commercial banking sector in Nepal actually began to complain of lost business (Uprety 1991). From housewives contributing a few rupees, to business people laying out hundreds of thousands a month,[2] *dhukuṭi* participation was extremely common across a range of ethnic and caste groups in the middle and upper classes. With the funds mobilized through these credit systems, Kathmandu consumers were buying everything from gold and real estate to motorcycles and furniture.

Smaller-scale investors in particular often directed *dhukuṭi* funds into another popular consumer promotion scheme known as an *upahār kārya-*

---

[1] Up until the early 1990s, when India finally scrapped its postindependence import-substitution regime for "economic liberalization" (that is, its markets were opened to foreign imports and capital), wealthy Indians had flocked to Kathmandu's New Road shopping district on weekend charter flights from Delhi and Bombay (Liechty 1996a).

[2] Some wealthy investors join up to ten *dhukuṭi* schemes at a time. By borrowing from one fund at relatively low rates and lending to another at higher rates, savvy investors can make good money playing on the margins—not unlike in a stock or currency trading market.

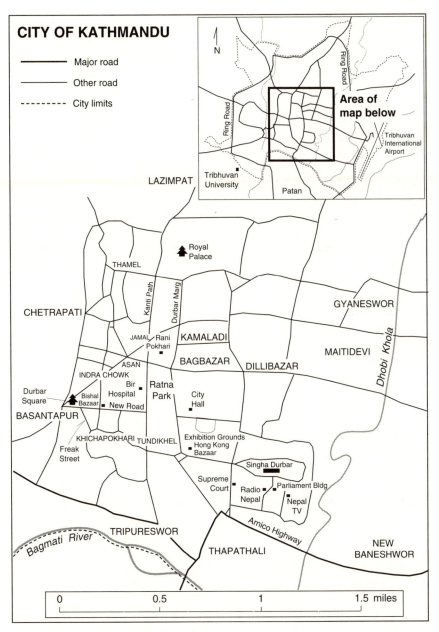

2.   The city of Kathmandu

kram, or "gift program." The "gift program" is a kind of consumer buying scheme that combines advance installment payments with a lottery. For example, someone interested in buying a steel cabinet or sofa set might join a "gift" scheme through which, after twelve fixed monthly payments, s/he is guaranteed delivery of the furniture. "Players" pay their monthly installments, and every month the scheme operators hold a lottery. A certain number of winners then receive their furniture for fewer than twelve payments, while the rest must pay in full. Everyone gets their desired commodity at more or less the market rate, but a few lucky ones get theirs at a discount. "Gift program" schemes help entice hesitant consumers into making purchases by throwing in the element of chance and possible good fortune; at worst, one only pays market price. But for "gift program" organizers, such schemes bring in huge amounts of cash to be invested or loaned at high rates of interest.[3]

Finally, even more common than "gift program" schemes are Kathmandu's ubiquitous consumer lotteries. Although many offer cash, other schemes play directly off people's desires for prestige goods by offering payoffs in the form of popular consumer items ranging from new homes, to cars and motor cycles, to televisions and refrigerators, to furniture and bicycles. Motorcycles were particularly popular lottery items. For a few rupees a lottery player might join the film heroes and urban elites riding about on the city's streets. Entirely unregulated, there were often stories of people being ripped off by lottery scam artists (Upadyaya 1991).

Whether plastered across banners or shouted in megaphones on the streets, blaring from TV or radio, or jumping out in eye-catching adds in local newspapers, consumer buying schemes seem to be everywhere in Kathmandu. Even if many people would have nothing to do with these schemes and scams, the sheer cacophony of images and promotions that assault Kathmandu residents as they move about the city contributes to a general ethos that privileges a material realm of consumer commodities as the domain of *real* value and fulfillment. It is this atmosphere of intense consumer promotion that helps to shape middle-class consumer desire.

"WHAT WOULD YOU DO WITH TWENTY THOUSAND RUPEES?": CONSUMER DESIRE AND "COMMODITY FUTURES"

The contours of this middle-class consumer consciousness emerged in exceptionally clear detail in responses to one question that my co-workers and I often asked: "What would you do if you won twenty thousand

[3] For more on *ḍhukuṭi* and *upahār kāryakram* schemes in the Kathmandu valley, see Rankin and Shrestha 1995.

rupees in a local lottery?"[4] Originally I was simply curious about what kept the hundreds of street-corner and media-based lottery games in operation. But as we accumulated answers to this question, I began to see some unusually vivid social contrasts between long-term Kathmandu residents and recent arrivals in the city. The way people responded illustrated the force of consumer goods in populating the imagination, reconfiguring desire, and structuring visions of the future.

As the location of most of Nepal's institutions of higher education, Kathmandu is host to many thousands of young people from across the country, who come to the city to study at the postsecondary level. Although predominately from higher-caste groups, these students (almost all of them male) are often from cash-poor families and thus work in private schools or shops around the valley while attending classes. Probably the most stark contrast I encountered in all of my research was that between the answers to the lottery question given by some of the many young people in Kathmandu who had come from other areas of Nepal for education and work and those given by young Kathmandu "natives" (those born and raised in the city). The contrast came not only in what they would *do* with a windfall of 20,000 NPR but in their reactions to the very *idea* of such an occurrence.

One of my co-workers, also a student from outside the valley, interviewed a number of his student acquaintances. Among these young men from rural areas, the most typical initial response to the prospect of winning 20,000 NPR was a kind of shock or surprise. For example, one young man, a twenty-year-old studying for his intermediate college degree, when asked what he would do with the money, responded:

> Hah! I don't know . . . , I, I never thought about getting that kind of money, I mean, so unexpectedly. What would I do? Um. . . . Well, maybe I'd buy some good magazines and really good books. . . . Yeah, I'd get books on subjects where I have weaknesses in my studies.

Another young man, a twenty-year-old student from East Nepal, had a similar response:

> Ohhhh! That would be a completely lucky thing! How would I know what to do with that?! I have no plan, I'm not sure. . . . But still, I guess I'd use it for my studies and also maybe for some social-service programs, like clubs. I think that would be my intention, to help where there are problems.

Another student, a twenty-two-year old from Nepal's western Tarai region, responded jokingly with another question: "Why would I want to

[4] In the early 1990s, 20,000 Rs was equivalent to about 400 USD.

win such an unexpected thing?! If I won that kind of money, what would I do with it?!" Eventually this young man suggested that maybe he would give some money to his family, or maybe put it away for an emergency. What seems surprising is that none of these young men had any idea of what they would do with 20,000 NPR. They *simply* had not thought about it; it was totally "unexpected": they had "no plan." Yet when pushed, or given a few moments to think, they all proposed either investing the money in their education, giving some of it away, or putting it in savings.

Some students from rural areas were more quick with answers. For example, a nineteen-year-old economics student from the eastern Tarai replied promptly, "I'd put it into a business plan. In the village area that would be enough to really do something." Similarly another twenty-two-year-old bachelor's-level student in Nepali literature responded without hesitation:

> I'd invest this money in my life, in things which would give me knowledge. Like in Devkota's[5] books and other literature. Actually, many important works [by Devkota] haven't been published. They should be, and maybe I'd invest this money in bringing these to publication. They'd help me too.

Ultimately, the most common theme in the responses of out-of-town young people, assuming they were able to get past the novelty of even *imagining* the possession of 20,000 NPR, had to do with investing the money in "things which would give me knowledge." For these students, life goals revolved around education, the primary mode of "cultural capital" that they sought to accrue.

Young people born and raised in the city had very different responses to the lottery question. Far from the befuddled amazement at the thought of having 20,000 NPR to dispose of, these urban youth had instant answers as to what they would do with the money. They immediately articulated their desires for a fairly limited range of modern consumer goods, as in the response of this eighteen-year-old Kathmandu student from Naksal:

> I'd buy the latest English records. And then I'd take my friends out to some restaurant to celebrate my winning the lottery! Then, I'm also thinking about buying a new mountain bike. Mine is getting pretty beat up.

A nineteen-year-old local student had a somewhat similar response:

---

[5] Laxmi Prasad Devkota (1909–59), one of Nepal's best-known and most-loved litterateurs.

Oh, I'd probably take my girlfriend here and there to restaurants, discos, that kind of place. Plus I'd buy a new mountain bike, shoes—I especially want a pair of those new-style football shoes—and other stuff like that I'd buy.

Another teenage boy, a sixteen-year-old whose father was a fairly high-ranking government official, cut straight to the point:

Hey listen, if I won that kind of money, I'd do nothing else but immediately go out and buy fashions!

One of the more intriguing answers came from a nineteen-year-old Sherpa college student who had spent most of his life in Kathmandu:

Well, first I'd go and buy things that can be bought [*kinnincha jasto cij*], like a mountain bike, some new fashionable clothes, like jeans, shoes. . . . And then I'd just go out and blow some of it on food and stuff for my friends.

For this young man, the lottery question immediately elicited the category of "*things that can be bought*," which was in turn made up of a more or less standard set of desired youth-related consumer goods. In a sense, "things that can be bought" means "commodities," and it is significant that for urban young people the lottery question set off a litany of consumer desires.

What all of these responses from urban youth indicate are minds that are ready, set, and primed for consumption. All of these young men have wants that are clearly defined and waiting at the tips of their tongues. Unlike the students from rural areas of Nepal, for whom education and "things that will bring me knowledge" were identified (after some thought) as their primary desires, for these urban young men visions of material possessions—"things that can be bought"—seemed to be swarming about very near the surface of their waking consciousnesses.

These two sets of answers have important implications for questions concerning future orientation and the "naturalness" (or otherwise) of consumer longing. The question points to significant differences between rural and urban youth, especially in the way the varying answers highlight characteristics of the modern consumer. Clearly the out-of-town young people have their own sense of future orientation; as students they are engaged in the classic bourgeois project of delayed gratification through the slow accumulation of cultural capital that can be mobilized at a later date. Yet although education is a commodity, and many of these young men were working to put themselves through college, few of them thought in terms of "commodity futures." They envisioned futures in terms of effort and achievement: education in the short run and various kinds of professional labor in the long run. By contrast, urban young people seemed to have futures cluttered with commodities. For them the thought of 20,000 NPR quickly brought forth narratives of consumer desires, stories of "what I'd buy" and in what order. In this contrast we begin to see some of the characteristics of the "modern consumer" in Kathmandu. While everyone thinks of the future in some way, the consumer's "commodity future" is a peculiar outlook structured around consumer desire.

These contrasting sets of comments also tell us something about the *nature* of consumer desire. Most strikingly, consumer desire seems to reside in the city. As I will explore in more detail below, consumer desire cannot be separated from the general urban consumer environment of mass media and other forms of commodity promotion. But there is an even more basic set of relationships between consumer desire and the city as the site of intensive commodification. The city is a place where money is likely to be among the dominant registers of social value and therefore consumption among the main cultural dimensions in which need is formulated and desire expressed. Thus, for the urban youth we interviewed, the thought of money activated thoughts of consumer commodities.

A number of these young people also registered an awareness of the link between *having money* and *having needs*. For example an eighteen-year-old upper-caste student from Kathmandu, who drove a taxi part-time to help support his family and his education, responded to our lottery question in this way:

> If I won that much money, the first thing I'd do is take care of my pressing needs. Right now I don't have that many needs. But you know, if you have money, immediately you begin to have other needs! They just spring up! Yeah, I'd probably go out and get a mountain bike and lots of English [music] cassettes.

Functioning with limited financial resources in a fully monetized local cash economy, this young man immediately thought of his "pressing needs," which though few, were clearly on his mind. Yet, with a bit of reflection, he too moved on to a litany of "other needs" that "just spring up," "if you have money."

Along similar lines, one of the most introspective—almost philosophical—answers that we received to our lottery question came from the eighteen-year-old son of a Gurkha in the British Army. This young man had spent most of his life in Kathmandu and had attended a respectable upper-level high school. When asked what he would do with 20,000 NPR, he paused briefly before answering:

> Nowadays people have a lot of needs. Money is the kind of thing that men can't keep forever in a box under lock and key. I mean, if you

have money, money is nothing. So in that case, if I have money, I get the urge to just go out and do something really exciting/titillating [*romācat*]. I mean, this is the feeling that comes. People have *real* needs, but I'm talking about something different.

It's like, if I had twenty thousand rupees, it would be gone in two or four days. So instead, it would be better for me to give it to people who really need it—like the poor guys lying by the side of the street. I'd like to help them. But if there are things I need, I like to get them. Right now there isn't anything I really need, but sometimes I like to go out with my friends and buy food, feed everybody and that kind of thing, so for that I need money. I mean, money is useless unless we have needs.

Like the previous student who contrasted "pressing needs" with "other needs," this young man distinguishes between "*real* needs" (such as the needs of the destitute) and the needs that seem to come with money. He describes the "feeling that comes" when he has money, the urge to go do something "*romācat*," something that gives pleasurable excitement or, literally, something that gives goosebumps, or makes one's hair stand on end.[6] For him, having money in his hands precipitates an urge for titillating excitement, a sense of longing or need, but not "real needs." For this young man and others, consumer longing does not seem to derive so much from *needs* as from simply *having money*. Somehow, money itself excites consumer needs and the longing for consumer "excitements."

Because few families from outside the valley allow their daughters to live on their own in Kathmandu, the young women in the city's high schools and on college campuses are, with few exceptions, from middle-class families living in the valley. The young women my co-workers and I interviewed were from these families. Significantly, unlike the young men from the valley that we interviewed, occasionally some of these young women would express surprise and bewilderment at the prospect of winning 20,000 NPR, as did this one sixteen-year-old student who had just passed her high school certification exams:

Eh, who knows?! I could only say that after having won! Really, I have never even bought a [lottery] ticket, and I've never thought about such a thing.

Yet her response was definitely in the minority. For the most part, young women from the city had the same reflexlike responses as did young men. To a greater extent than the men's, however, women's responses were characterized by a fixation on "fashion"; clothing and makeup dominated

---

[6] The word *romācat* often has strong erotic overtones as well.

their consumer imaginations. Not uncommon was the rather smug answer given by an eighteen-year-old intermediate-level science student
studying at a local campus:

> These days, with twenty thousand rupees [*wrinkles her nose and
> smirks, to indicate that the sum is paltry*]. . . Well, if it's just for me,
> I'd buy fashions, like some nice dresses, shoes. . . . And then I'd buy
> food for my friends, and maybe even give some away to my brothers
> and to my parents.

Another young woman, a twenty-year-old intermediate student, went into
a bit more detail about why she wants "fashions":

> Well, I've never actually even bought a ticket, but [if I had that money]
> I think I would just buy things that I like. You know everybody does
> fashion [*fashion garcha*] these days, to make themselves good-look-
> ing. So I think I would also do the same.

For most middle-class women—and many young men—in Kathmandu,
"fashion" and "doing fashion" loom large among the themes in their consumer consciousnesses.

In total these responses to our lottery question shed some important
light on the little-known processes and role of the imagination in modern
life (Appadurai 1996). The almost spontaneous "commodity futures"
elicited by the prospect of cash suggest that urban youth—those raised in
the highly commercialized and mass-mediated setting of Kathmandu—
have imaginations that are, at least in part, quite literally commercialized.
What sets the urban youth apart from their rural counterparts is not an
orientation toward the future but the way that future is imagined. City
youth had the category of "things that can be bought" firmly and centrally
implanted in their imaginations. For readers from highly commodified
societies (such as North America), this may seem unremarkable, but the
responses of rural Nepali youth—for whom visions of cash and commodities had *not* structured their imaginations—suggest that consumer desire
is not a "natural" component of the imagination. Instead, it emerges in
specific historical/material contexts, where social value is increasingly distributed according to the logic and terms of a cash market economy. In
the modern consumer imagination, desire is not premised on needs but
on knowledge (of "things that can be bought") and, even more fundamentally, on having cash. As several of those quoted above noted, in a consumer society, needs are proportionate to cash: "[I]f you have money,
immediately you have . . . needs."

If answers to our lottery question pointed to a particularly vivid consumer imagination among urban young people in Kathmandu, to what
extent is this consumer materialism something new? Is materialism a

"modern" phenomenon that corresponds with the arrival of monetized economies and consumer markets? In the following section, I suggest that in Kathmandu the meaning and nature of materialism has changed with the commercial transformation of the local material culture.

THE NEW MATERIALISM

One evening during the summer of 1991, Nepal Television aired a drama about an old man whose son-in-law was disrespectful and negligent because the old man had no property to pass on at his death. Then, at the suggestion of friends, the old man started wearing a large key on a string around his neck, and before long his offspring were attending to the old man's every wish.[7] For weeks after the program, the somewhat uneasy joke that floated around town was that the number of savings accounts had suddenly shot up in area banks! Whether or not viewers actually rushed to the bank to open accounts, the drama seemed to prod middle-class, middle-aged city residents into thinking about saving money, not to pass on to future generations, but for their own security in old age. The TV drama highlighted the commonly held perception that values once holding society and family together are breaking down as the role of money increases. While a certain kind of materialism, built around practices of accumulation and property transfer, is surely age-old, people in Kathmandu recognize a new kind of materialism in their midst, one associated with the new highly monetized economy and changing modes of cultural capital.

I was frequently reminded of differences between various modes of materialism. Middle-class adults often spoke of the consumer values practiced by their parents or grandparents, who worked to accumulate land and gold. While earlier generations also wished to live comfortably, they viewed various forms of wealth primarily as something to accumulate in order to propel future generations into more desirable social circumstances. Now, however, patterns of accumulation and forms of patrimony have shifted to better fit the realities of a new social and material logic.

Some spoke of this change in terms of new understandings of parents' obligations to their children, as well as their own rights to personal pleasure. One middle-aged woman, a mother of two, noted that nowadays people believe that parental investment comes in the form of providing education for sons (and increasingly daughters), after which children are expected to more or less take responsibility for themselves. In other words, the woman explained, the transfer of family resources occurs in a

---

[7] The key implied that the old man had a cash box or safe hidden among his possessions.

different manner (in the form of education, not in traditional forms of wealth like land or gold) and at an earlier time (in the child's youth, not at the death of the parent). She said that now parents feel enormous pressure to provide the best possible education for their children and will often actually deplete the family's fixed assets to do so, but once this is done, they feel somewhat less compelled to scrimp and save for their children's sake. Instead, they are more inclined to evaluate their own living standards and pursue the comforts and pleasures they feel are their due. Yet this woman recognized that the standards of comfort her grandparents would have felt to be suitable were to her totally unacceptable. She noted that "comfort" was a completely relative notion, which hinged on an awareness of options and possession of the means to pursue them.

Another man in his early forties, who had grown up in a small town outside of the Kathmandu valley, voiced a similar realization when he said, almost as a complaint, "You know, now there are so many things to enjoy!" He explained the changing nature of materialism in terms of choices. As a child in a rural town, "fun" (*majā*) had been singing, dancing, and eating good food at festival times. He contrasted this with his present life, but even more with the lives of his two children. Now opportunities for enjoyment and entertainment cluttered his daily existence to the point of distraction, and he willingly blamed his son's poor school performance on an excess of *majā*. People typically characterized the shift from old to new forms of materialism in terms of generations, but more particularly in terms of values: the new materialism represented a trend away from the accumulation of wealth, toward the pursuit of enjoyment, even though both forms involve elements of display (whether of gold ornaments or color televisions).

By describing materialism in terms of "old" and "new," I do not mean to imply that one has replaced the other. One young woman, explaining why she saves her money to buy land, said, "Other things, if you eat it, it's finished: if you turn it on, it breaks: if you wear it, it tears. But land can't be exhausted in this way." Many people shared her view, frequently contrasting the permanence of land and gold with the ephemerality of the new goods and pleasures now available in the market. Rather than replacing an earlier consumer ethic of accumulation and permanence with a new materialism of consumer goods and enjoyment, the two coexist in an uneasy combination of logics.

This uneasy coexistence struck me one day while quizzing a friend on what constituted the ideal middle-class sitting room. I asked if this was the room where people would put their most valuable possessions on display. At this he laughed and said, "Of course not. People would never display their gold ornaments in this way!" Instead, he explained, this is where people put their television and often their refrigerator, suitcases (to display their ability to travel), and other modern goods. His remarks pointed to two contrasting though intermingled modes of consumer logic. One is built around conservation and insurance against possible future hardships, while the other communicates participation in a rapidly expanding commoditized regime of value, in which personal status and identity are tied to the control and display of possessions.

The tension between these two consumer logics runs like an undercurrent through popular middle-class consciousness in Kathmandu. It is illustrated by a story I was told so many times[8] that I came to recognize it as a kind of morality tale. Conveyed with a mixture of disgust and reprobation, the story tells of a man who (usually hounded by wife and/or children, depending on who tells the story) sells either gold or land in order to purchase a television, motorbike, or some other high-status consumer item. A variant of this tale recounts the drug-addicted son who, in the ultimate act of filial depravity, exchanges his mother's gold ornaments for a fix. Aside from indicating an awareness of two coexisting, even competing, modes of consumption, the moral tone of these stories points to a kind of ethical ranking of goods. Gold and land are somehow stabilizing and nurturing, tied to notions of permanence and family, while TVs and motorbikes are portrayed as almost hostile intruders into the domestic sphere, extracting resources and, not insignificantly, often associated with addiction.[9]

Again, what is "new" about the new materialism is not some sudden appearance of commodities, much less the association of identity with possessions. Commodities have been at the heart of local economies since Kathmandu's founding as a trading center in the first millennium, and even imported, mass-produced consumer commodities (from textiles to kitchen utensils) have been common in the city at least since the late eighteenth century (Liechty 1997). Rather, what is "new" is the abrupt lifting of import bans, sumptuary laws, and other consumer restrictions in place during the Rana era, the new predominantly cash-based economy, and the subsequent sudden explosion of goods and services in local commodity markets. The transformation is not a matter of essence but of scale; it is tied to an enormous increase in the quantity of commoditized forms and their sudden ubiquity in daily life.

It is this exploding domain of material consumer abundance that forms a powerfully compelling communicative medium both for constructing new modes of middle-class distinction and for carrying on the debate over the meaning of "middleness." As illustrated in the next section, most people in Kathmandu's social middle, even while recognizing

---

[8] Including twice in the first person.

[9] For other critical perspectives linking local consumerism with addiction, see chapter 9.

the intrinsic ephemerality of distinction based on consumer goods (objects which "break," "tear," or are "finished"), feel they have no choice but to transact in the new currency of consumer distinction.

CONSUMER ANXIETY: "PLAYING WITH YOUR BRAIN"

If people in Kathmandu speak disparagingly of the new materialism—if they sometimes characterize modern commodities as almost predatory agents—why is there such enormous pressure to participate in the new consumer culture? What drives people into a consumer economy that they themselves regard as threatening and even immoral? To begin to understand behaviors and motivations, we must keep in mind the almost overwhelming sociocultural flux that many people experience. Over the past two or three decades, many Kathmandu residents have faced a situation of fixed (or declining) resources, not only in terms of income but also in terms of social capital, where entitlements once linked to caste background are less and less assured. Add to this precarious condition the new possibilities for mobility—both spatial (in the forms of migration and suburbanization) and social (in rapidly changing socioeconomic fortunes)—and an enormous increase in the quantity of consumer goods that have become vehicles of marking and claiming distinction, and you have a recipe for intense social anxiety and instability.

To introduce something of what it means for middle-class urban Nepalis to confront a vastly transformed social and cultural order, I recount at some length conversations with two Kathmandu residents. Both of these statements capture the sense of anxiety and the experience of moral dilemma that accompany people as they move further into the new domain of commodities and values. Both statements effectively convey what Fredric Jameson calls "the misery of happiness" (1989:518), or what Arjun Appadurai has referred to as "the agonized drama of leisure" (1991:207). In other words, these people describe the trauma of living the middle-class "good life."

When I spoke with him in 1991, Kedar was already well into middle age, had two teenage children and two occupations: as small-business owner and English teacher. Originally from Nepal's Tarai region and a member of an upper caste, Kedar was proud of his academic achievements (he held a master's degree) but felt financially insecure. In the course of a long conversation, talk turned to the subject of household economics, which Kedar expounded in his characteristically dramatic manner:

> Here the pressure is affecting the housewife especially. Because, well, they need . . . I mean we are not in *need* of a refrigerator, but now it

is a *prestige* issue. Like me, my own TV purchasing. On my street everyone else had a TV antenna sticking out. Even I pretended about that. [I said to my family] "Why do you need that? You're only looking at third-class Nepali programs!"

But my wife and kids, they started to go to the neighbor's house. Every time a good program was coming, they were going and spoiling their education! So I started to wonder, what should I do?

Then I sold my gold—I mean my wife's gold and everything—and then I bought it [a television]. That's right! It was just like a trap. I was in a *trap*! I mean, this is the kind of thing that is happening here! And I, an educated man, was in this trap. Just imagine the others. They can't afford to buy a TV, but now everyone needs a very *good* TV, not some low-class model. They look down on you if you have a black-and-white, or even a Gold Star.[10] They say [*swaggering voice*], "Oh, *I* have a *Sony*!"

At this I asked where such influences were coming from?

Like the *new-rich* people here bought it, everything, right? New-rich people, I mean the Manangi people, with their illegal money,[11] and with that they bought *anything*. And everybody started to see that and they started thinking, "Why not in my home? Why only them?" [They said to themselves] "You are educated and you can't buy this. Look at him. He's only tenth-class. And he did like this, and he doesn't have *this*. [*pointing to his head*] Use this *brain*!"

Look, I'm a good person. But what's the use of your image if you can't earn money? Yeah, it happened to *me*! That's why I sold off that gold. That's why. . . . I'm thinking, "Hey, I'm an educated person in Nepal. Its affecting *me*—then, what for others?" Well, you can imagine! They will have an inferiority complex, and from that complex you can't survive for long. [They have to say to their families] "Oh, I can't give you good food. I can't give you a fridge. I can't even give you a *fan*!" Even if you have something, you are always lacking something. You can't fulfill everything, you know.

[10] Gold Star color televisions are assembled in Nepal from Korean components and are slightly less expensive than most imported models.

[11] Manang is a mountainous region of West-Central Nepal whose residents have for centuries been involved in long-distance trans-Himalayan trade. In the decades following Nepal's opening, they were able to use their trading networks and expertise to capitalize on a number of legal, quasi-legal, and illegal business opportunities. In the process, members of the community were able to amass enormous personal fortunes (see van Spengen 1987, 2000, Watkins 1996). The combination of their Tibetan ethnic background and their great wealth makes the Manangi community a "natural" whipping boy for upper-caste members of Kathmandu's middle class, who view Manangis as a threat to their traditional forms of cultural capital.

When I asked if it was really the Manangis who were causing people to feel these anxieties, Kedar admitted that it was not so simple as that.

> All around are things that make you think, "Oh, I wish that I could have that one also!" I mean, it's always playing with your brain. And whenever you get the chance, any chance—like for taking bribe money—you leave your values, and that's not a good thing. But the whole thing is coming there. [Everybody says] "Oh, my wife was pressing me on this thing, on that thing. Oh, if I only had that money."
>
> Like my relatives: one is a customs officer,[12] and right now he has everything. My wife and my children are saying [to me] now, "See there, he's a less experienced, less famous man than you, but he has a carpet, he has a refrigerator, he has a TV. He has *everything*! He has ornaments, he has gold, and whatever he likes, he can do that."
>
> But I told my wife, well, he's only arranging for the family. But he, look at the very cheap-class watch he's wearing. And the cheap-class clothes he's wearing. Because the government will suspect him. Got what I mean? He can't expose what he's earning [i.e., in bribes]. And *I know* what is his mental state. You don't know that. *I* know that. Always suspicion, suspicion. . . . In this way he will die, always having boozing, and this and that.
>
> Me? I'm doing my body building.[13] I don't have any pressure. I'm free to do anything. Which life do you like?

From his earlier statements about feeling "trapped," it would seem that Kedar was not in fact "free" of pressures to conform. Yet by drawing a sharp line of distinction between himself and his corrupted relative, Kedar clearly tied the life of consumer abundance to a life of moral compromise. There is almost a Faustian contract in Kedar's account of the customs officer driven to corruption in order to acquire consumer goods for himself and his family, and now destined to die a paranoid and "boozing" death. For Kedar consumer goods are "all around," always "playing with your brain," and challenging your sense of self-worth. "I'm a good person," "I'm an educated person"—so why are these other people better off than me? One question seemed to sum up the dilemmas Kedar faced: "[W]hat's the use of your image if you can't earn money?" Kedar finds himself in a "trap" in part because the forms of cultural and social capital he holds (especially family background and education) are losing value,

---

[12] In Nepal customs officers are widely believed to be corrupt and able to make big money through bribes, smuggling, and kickbacks. Stories abound of families "investing" large sums in order to acquire a job in the customs service for a son or nephew.
[13] Kedar followed a daily regimen of calisthenics.

or at least being outpaced by a new index of value based on an economy of possessions. Kedar's comments clearly illustrate the enormous seductive powers of the new domain of consumer goods and the moral and economic dilemmas that this domain poses. But his words also contain a powerful critical dimension. The love-hate ambivalence toward the modern consumer economy that Kedar conveys in his stories of commodity desire and entrapment is a central theme in the discursive construction of middle-classness in Kathmandu.

If Kedar represents a male's point of view, how do women experience and deal with the pressures of the new middle-class consumer economy? While Kedar (and other men) frequently blamed wives and children for the pressures to succumb to consumer demands, what are the factors that compel women to enter the new world of goods?

Some answers to these questions emerge in the remarks of a young high-caste woman interviewed by one of my female Nepali co-workers. In 1991 Gita was in her early thirties, identified herself as a "housewife" (though she was still officially a student, working on incomplete exams), and was the mother of two sons, ages three and seven. Gita's comments very effectively capture the precariousness of daily existence for many people struggling to maintain their stakes in Kathmandu's middle-class culture. By local standards her extended family—some members of which occupy high positions in the civil service or live abroad—would be seen as relatively well-to-do. Yet what the family could claim in social capital and prestige was constantly threatened by the limited economic resources it could muster. Gita's anxiety focused precisely on how, as wife and mother, to maintain what she called a "standard of living" in the face of severe economic shortages.

After touching on problems that parents have disciplining their children, the conversation took an interesting reflective turn.

> A decade ago the situation of children was different. Today there's less control. I feel that now the standard of living is rising. Maybe that's because people are earning more. But for us, we still have problems, troubles, hardships in living, not enough money for food. Well, [at least] we are a family, and everybody brings in a little, but still we feel hardships.
>
> What I see now is that even lower-level people are wearing clothes the same as people in the middle class [madhyam barga]. Or the high-class families are wearing expensive, high-quality clothes, and the middle-class people are wearing the same things.
>
> How are they doing this? *That's what I want to know!* It's very surprising. *How are they coming up with the money?* You see some

soldier on the street wearing pants that cost three or four hundred rupees. That's the same as his officer is wearing!

So, how does this happen?

It's hard to say how they can maintain this. Maybe they have some part-time job, or business, or wear such nice clothes only once a year.

But there's one thing that people from *our* level do. For instance, if I buy clothes for the children, they wear those only when they go out [of the house]. And then when they come back, I wash them if they are dirty. Otherwise I just put them back on the hanger, and then I have them put on other clothes that are only used when they're around the house. This is what we must do these days.

For Gita, rises in the society's "standard of living" are intimately tied to changes in consumer patterns as they relate to class. When soldiers are appearing on the streets wearing the same clothing as their officers, "people from *our* level" resort to new strategies to improve living standards, or at least put forward the appearance of having done so. Gita elaborated on the theme of maintaining public appearances by suggesting that things nowadays are different than before:

I don't think the previous generation had it like this. They just didn't care so much about clothes. They could go out [of the house] wearing any kind of clothes. At that time fashion wasn't so common, but now, now the mothers are educated, they like cleanliness, they want their children to be clean, they put them in special schools. . . . Because of all this, the changes have come. This is the reason for the changes in the standard of living. People are now willing to eat less, in order to show themselves to be of a high standard.

For Gita, education and a concern for "fashion" and "cleanliness" are all inseparable parts of being a modern woman and a modern mother. Because of these things "the changes have come," even to the point where people are willing to sacrifice food for public prestige.

How can it be that people think that wearing is more important than eating?

Well, wearing *isn't* more important than eating. We all need nutritious food. I mean, I'm not one of those who thinks spending more money on food is not good. One should eat properly, with a balanced diet, as long as it is within the budget, not going over the expenditure limit, and, if possible, having some savings.

I usually don't spend extra money. My husband does, a little. I don't go outside much, and that way I can save some money, like what would have been spent on a taxi or something. For example, if I go outside and see a restaurant, I feel like eating! So I just try not to go out that much. That way I can save money which later can be spent on constructive things.

Like, I don't buy the cheap cotton bedsheets, because they are not colorfast. Yet, these are the cheapest ones, only one hundred rupees. So if my husband gives me two hundred rupees for buying sheets, I wait for one more month and add another hundred rupees and buy the teri-cotton, the better-quality ones, and then just do the sewing myself. I like the teri-cotton sheets; they give you a better standard of living. When they are seen, they look nice, and also they last longer, at least eight years. I feel that if I invest my money like this, I get a long time duration. In this way we can maintain a good standard of living.

In these sentences Gita suddenly launches into the language of classic economic rationalism. With budgets, limits, and savings; with investments, calculations of duration, and delayed purchasing, Gita is a housewife who has very consciously embraced economic-maximization strategies in order to "maintain a good standard of living."

Why do you think people want to show off this standard of living?

It's because . . . Now European society has come here. Everywhere there is talk about high thinking, clean environment, high standard of living. Everybody wants a comfortable life. The older generation used to just light a fire, but now [we use] gas stoves or heaters [electric cooking elements]. The main reason for wanting a modern life is so that you can have a comfortable life.

And now people are sending their children off to school. There's competition in this too. Here people are sending their children. . . . They don't want their children to have some inferiority complex. So people are trying to send [their children to school] even if they don't have the [financial] capacity to do it.

So now, in the boarding school, you'll find children from all levels of the society—high, middle, and low are all there. I was thinking that my children wouldn't have any problems if their friends were from wealthy families, but they [my children] feel poor. So for this reason, they are always suffering from this inferiority complex. They are afraid to talk to other children! So I just don't want my children to have this inferiority complex, and if we can increase our standard of living little by little, they won't have it.

Like, suppose if we don't have a cassette player and our children don't know anything about this. And then they see some other person's cassette player and we say to them, "Hey, don't touch that! You shouldn't play with that." [If we say that] Then they're going to fear these things, and they may never learn how to use something like that.

But as for my son, *he knows* how to turn on the television, and the deck [VCR], even though I fear that he might break something in the process.

In these comments Gita begins by equating "modern life" with the comforts of modern consumer goods as well as disciplines like cleanliness. Yet these ideas are closely tied to her own class consciousness, and she soon returns to her feelings of anxiety, especially as they relate to her children, who have been thrown into the "competition" of an expensive private school. Here she admits that whereas she had thought it would be good to have her children in school with children from "wealthy families," in fact they were now suffering from an "inferiority complex" and have trouble talking with the other children. In order to save her children from feeling inferior and underprivileged, she wants desperately to raise the family's living standards. For Gita it is her parental duty not just to *own* modern consumer goods but to make sure her children know how to *use* them. She can be proud that *her* seven-year-old knows how to use a TV and a VCR.

For both Kedar and Gita, the problem is how to construct and maintain a middle-class material existence in the face of constantly upward-spiraling standards on the one hand and extremely limited resources on the other. Like a card game where the stakes are constantly being raised, it takes more and more cash outlay for people in Kathmandu to stay at, as Gita put it, "*our* level." For Kedar this had meant selling off some of his wife's gold in order to buy a TV and thereby avoid the humiliation of having his family members troop off to the neighbor's sitting room every evening. Compared with Gita, Kedar was more willing to portray the forces of consumerism as immoral. In his opinion, some people may appear to be living high, but they do so only by lowering themselves to a state of moral baseness. For Gita, however, moralizing does little to change the (perceived) reality of children stigmatized for not consuming at certain material standards. As a wife (in charge of a household) and mother (in charge of children), Gita asks, "How are [other people] coming up with the money?" Ultimately much of the burden of projecting an appropriate living standard falls on her, whether by making sure the children are changed into good clothing whenever they leave the house, resisting frivolous purchases and maximizing her returns when she does "invest" in things like bedsheets, or doing whatever she can to save a rupee here and there. As a modern middle-class woman, it is her duty to "increase [her family's] standard of living little by little," whether she wants to or not.

"Just Like a Plant": Fashion Consciousness in Kathmandu

Perhaps the ultimate question confronting anyone who tries to describe the process of shifting cultural logics in a place like Kathmandu is, Why? Why are people "compelled" or "lured" into the consumer economy? In the comments of Kedar and Gita we have seen the beginnings of an answer to these questions. In their remarks Kedar and Gita described something of the sociology of middle-class consumerism in Kathmandu. They emphasized the competition between different groups, each of which brings a different configuration of social and economic resources into the arena of middle-class discourse. They stressed the demands and moral compromises inherent in the struggle to remain at "our level" as the criteria for determining social standing become increasingly tied to consumer modes of distinction.

But another way of exploring the question of motivation—of *why* people enter the consumer economy—is to move beyond a strictly interpersonal or intergroup perspective. Are there other means, motivations, or avenues by which a consumer logic takes hold of middle-class imaginations? Some of Gita's comments suggest that there are. For example, her fixation on clothing and, to an even greater extent, her repeated references to cleanliness, hygiene, nutrition, and comfort point to narrative components of consumer consciousness that are not simply matters of social competition but cut more deeply, to core conceptions of the *body* and even of *being*. With these signs of a new understanding of body and being, we begin to catch sight of a new consumer logic that is not just sociological but epistemological in its implications. The new cultural practice being pioneered by Kathmandu's middle class is not simply about using things to create social distinction but about reimagining what it means to be social, or about being social in new ways.

In later remarks in the same conversation, Gita provided a variety of other important glimpses into this new middle-class epistemology. Many of her thoughts on new modes of body and being were woven into stories of modernity and fashion. Having discussed the problems inherent in trying to maintain a family's standard of living in the face of inflation and declining resources, the conversation between Gita and my co-worker turned to the recent upsurge in concern for "fashion."

Are you also interested in fashion?

Sure, I'm interested in it: fashion is necessary, especially for women.

How so?

After marriage a girl's physical structure becomes a little messed up and doing fashion helps to maintain it. This is necessary. It doesn't make any difference when you're young, but after you're thirty, you should maintain your skin, your hair, your body, by doing fashion. This is for self-satisfaction and also for attraction of one's husband.

Plus, I mean these days, the children of this generation, they don't even like to walk on the streets with their parents because their parents and their own fashion are in such contrast! Today's fashion is very modern. My parents' fashion is a little bit less than that. So we don't really like to walk outside [the house] together. But if we walk outside wearing nice fashions—looking tip-top—then our children won't have that feeling.

So for older women, keeping the hair styled, either cut or keeping it long but nice, washing it with good shampoo or soap, that's good, and it's more healthy too. And makeup, and cutting and trimming, these are all necessary things. All the parts of the body, like your skin, must be taken care of, especially after you're thirty. It's just like a plant: it also needs cutting and trimming to keep it looking good.

For Gita fashion is, first and foremost, a necessity. While Gita is ashamed to walk on the streets with her own parents, she feels that by conscientiously "doing fashion" her children will be spared such embarrassment. For her the body is "just like a plant," but not just any plant. This plant must be "maintained" and "taken care of." It must be cut, trimmed, made up, washed, attired in "fashions," and kept healthy, all in order to "keep it looking good." Significantly, "doing fashion" extends far beyond clothing and makeup to encompass the treatment and presentation of the entire body. For Gita "doing fashion" is a necessity that involves an almost total self-objectification: a transformation of the body into a visual platform upon which "all parts" are turned into sites for improvement. In contrast to her parents', Gita's fashion is "very modern."

Gita went on to elaborate on her comments regarding "self-satisfaction" and "attraction."

Fashion is done for self-satisfaction and attraction, but I guess especially for attraction. I mean, women like it when someone comes and gives them a compliment. Like "Oh, your sari!" or "Your shawl, how beautiful!" Hearing that, I get a lot of pleasure. I feel bliss! Everybody feels happy when they are complimented. But if one is wearing old, mended clothes, they are always thinking about that, always worrying.

Thus, for Gita, "attraction" has to do with winning the attention and admiration of others. Likewise, "self-satisfaction" does not come from fashion in and of itself but from the compliments paid to the fashioned body. Indeed, in this kind of "self-satisfaction" the fashioned body seems to become a surrogate for the self. Earlier in the conversation, Gita had noted that "the earlier generation" was very different.

> They just didn't care so much about clothes. They could go out [of the house] wearing any old kind of clothes. At that time fashion wasn't so common.

Now, on the other hand, when one wears old or mended clothing, one is prey to constant uneasiness, constant "worrying."

The conversation next turned to questions of where one learns about fashion.

> *Where do you learn about how to take care of your skin, hair, and all these things?*

> Oh, I read about all this in *Grihashoba, Manorama*, you know, these Hindi [women's] magazines. They tell you how to make up the face, how you can do this or that at home by yourself.

Earlier in the interview Gita had noted that she likes to read Hindi women's magazines and often buys them when out shopping. From them she learns about cooking, home decorating, and health care, in addition to makeup and clothing. She also enjoys Hindi "art films" and estimated that she has watched one thousand of them in the five years since her husband bought a VCR. According to Gita, "Indian fashion is good enough for us. I think, for fashion, if we just look at India, we don't need to look any further."

The conversation next turned to the topic of "suitability," that is, what fashion is enough, what is too much, and why. After noting that there can be competition when it comes to fashion, Gita went on to explain:

> Too much of anything is bad. So fashion isn't a bad thing, if one does it according to one's own capacity. Like, foreign cream is not a must for applying to one's face. One can use local things, like potato, or lime, or cucumber. Doing fashion doesn't mean that you have to spend a whole lot or spend just a little. The point is that it should be suitable, it should suit oneself.

> I mean, people shouldn't overdo fashion. Using lots of lipstick doesn't mean fashion. Or wearing a three-thousand-rupee sari doesn't mean fashion. Fashion is your style of wearing, how you match up clothes, match hairstyles, match makeup, *this* is fashion.

For Gita good fashion is not a matter of quantity. It takes money to "do fashion," but simply having lots of money does not mean that one is automatically fashionable.

This leads Gita to her second line of reasoning; "suitable" (*suhāune*) fashion requires *knowledge*—of a particularly embodied kind. In order to "do fashion," one must know how to "match up": how to fit together clothes, hairstyles, cosmetics, and every other component of the fashioned body. It requires that one learn how to view and present the body in such a way that all of its parts are blended, balanced, "fashioned." Fashions require money, but fashion *sense*—the knowledge of how to be fashioned—is something that must be acquired and cultivated. According to Gita, "*this* is fashion." As discussed in the previous chapter, this notion of fashion "suitability" is a characteristically middle-class sensibility. That it requires some disposable cash excludes those below the middle class, but the fact that fashion knowledge is acquired and embodied helps to naturalize middle-class privilege and ensures that fashion is not only the province of the rich.

At the broadest level, the meanings attached to, or conveyed through, any particular commodity are less important than the simple fact of "doing fashion." Different women "do fashion" differently, and often to a far lesser degree than Gita. Yet it is the *practice* of fashion—and the acknowledgment of commercially mediated standards of value—that is most significant. The practice of fashion opens up new ways of imagining oneself and one's community in commodity terms. In short, fashion is less about having than doing. Fashion ("doing fashion") is not a thing but a performance, and the thing performed is class.

Indeed, one of the most important channels through which regional and global fashion systems enter into local social practice is via processes of class formation. The global capitalist fashion episteme is characterized less by messages that tell people *what* to be—the battle over "suitability" is always fought locally—than by messages that suggest *how*, or by what *means*, one should be. The content and meaning of any local fashion system is always different, but the methods by which one achieves the fashioned self are broadly the same. The attraction of consumer materialism for the middle class is not simply material; it is not simply about *having* something distinctive but about *doing and being* something distinctive. For the middle class in Kathmandu, an important part of the motivational power of consumerism is that it offers not just new things but new embodied behaviors and, ultimately, a new reality. It is this new reality—the material and embodied logic of a capitalist consumer episteme—that people in Kathmandu harness to their project of naturalizing their own collective interests and constructing a middle-class space.

Prestige Inflation, Cash Compulsion

Another way of viewing the "allure" of new forms of consumer material-ism is to consider the implications of local commercial and prestige econo-mies in which cash has become an increasingly inescapable organizing factor. While cash economies are nothing new in Kathmandu, the com-mercialization of an ever expanding range of ritual and social functions means that the failure to generate cash now often means the failure to maintain social status and parity. When faced with the possibility of social extinction, many in Kathmandu have little choice but to embrace the com-mercial/consumer realm and its logics.

A popular rhyme often recited by Kathmandu locals goes like this: "While Brahmans are ruined by greed, and Chetris are ruined by pleasure, Newars are ruined by feasting!"[14] As many accounts of Newar social life in Kathmandu have documented, patterns of sociality often revolve around the festivals and feast days that fill the community's ritual calen-dar. At many of these events, families or individuals take turns bearing the responsibility for feeding others in their neighborhood and/or caste group and/or *guṭhi*.[15] Because these are extremely important occasions, at which social status is claimed or maintained, sponsors will go to great lengths to ensure that their obligations are carried out in an acceptable manner. Indeed, for many people, failure to meet these obligations is tan-tamount to abandoning any claims to respectability in the eyes of the community.

While for many people in Kathmandu these ritual events remain im-portant points in the annual cycle, my aim was less to study or describe them than to inquire as to how they have changed in the context of the new economic patterns, social dynamics, and material culture of contem-porary Kathmandu. While Kathmandu's prestige economy is nothing new, what *is* new is a kind of rapid inflationary effect brought about by increased cash flow and the influx of new material goods (and commercial services). In this new economy, even once-unquestioned forms of prestige, such as caste status, have to be backed up by the display of goods, as those able to adopt new consumer lifestyles threaten to subvert traditional systems of prestige altogether.

---

[14] In Nepali, *bāhun bigryo lobhle, chetri bigryo mojle, newār bigryo bhojle*! See also Lewis 1984:337.

[15] "A Newari word which means approximately a social structure or organization or establishment which is in charge of certain religious property or charitable funds. The Guthi system divides the Newars into various social groups based on religion, kin, and caste" (Hedrick and Hedrick 1972:57).

4.   Passing time in Kathmandu's Ratna Park.

I met Sano Raj Shrestha in Kathmandu's Ratna Park one sunny spring afternoon in 1991. A Newar from an old Kathmandu family, Sano Raj had been born within a stone's throw of where we sat and, at age forty, was still living nearby, married, and the father of three children. Sano Raj and a friend were smoking marijuana and passing time in the park while they waited to meet two Italian tourists who had agreed to purchase airplane tickets from them. Sano Raj worked as a "broker" for a local travel agency and was paid on a commission basis for bringing in business. From this job his monthly earnings were about 1,200 NPR (about 25 USD), which he supplemented with occasional income from acting as a guide for foreign tourists and from the illegal sale of ganga and hashish. He confided that life was tough and that drinking alcohol or smoking pot "brings bliss" (ānanda lāgyo) when he is "feeling down" (bor lāgyo). From his somewhat ragged clothing, generally disheveled demeanor, and public use of marijuana, it was fairly clear that Sano Raj was among those in Kathmandu in the process of falling out of the social middle and being left behind in modernity's wake.

When I asked how he could support his family on such a small income, Sano Raj shook his head and explained, "Before, things were cheap and money was valuable, but now goods are expensive and money is worthless." For example, he complained, now a Western-style suit costs 2,000 NPR and a person can no longer wear simple shoes but instead must buy leather shoes. Before long the conversation turned to the subject of Newar festivals. Sano Raj complained that community ceremonies were getting out of hand, dragging common people into poverty and poor people into deeper poverty. Things are bad, he said, and getting worse.

For example, one was previously obliged to invite only one's nearby relatives for most feast occasions, but now one was expected to send invitations to relatives scattered out across the valley and even beyond. With public transportation and communications devices like telephones, the number of relatives that might show up had become almost limitless! Even worse, a host could no longer provide "simple food," like beaten rice and meat dishes prepared by women in the family and served on leaf plates to guests sitting outside. Now a "respectable" or "prestigious" (*ijjatdāri*) host must serve his guests "buffet-style," that is, have the meal catered by some local restaurant that serves fancy fare and charges high rental fees for crockery, cutlery, folding chairs, tents, etc. In other words, the respectable host can no longer stage a feast by mobilizing family labor and acquiring ordinary foodstuffs either from his own land or in the local markets, where commodity transactions might be made in kind. Instead, he must mobilize *cash*, and large amounts of it.

In the same vein, a wealthy Tibetan businessman complained to me of how one of his Newar subcontractors had come to him pleading for a 40,000 NPR cash advance—an amount equivalent to a full year's salary for a well-paid government civil servant—because it was his turn to feed the people in his local *guṭhi* association. When the businessman asked "Can you afford it?" the man blurted out, "It is not a matter of affording!" In other words, like Sano Raj, this man was in a position where his social survival depended on his ability to generate cash and thereby keep his stake in his community's prestige economy.[16] While Sano Raj had already essentially slid out of this economy, to live a life of substance abuse and shame, this Newar man was still fighting to maintain his family's place in a local prestige system that threatened to destroy him. As local prestige economies become not only increasingly cash-based but more and more extravagant in their demands, Kathmandu residents experience extraordinary pressures to embrace the wage/market economy (and the social logic of class), or risk sinking into social oblivion.

What becomes clear from these stories is that the intense commercial compulsions felt by members of Kathmandu's middle class exert their

---

[16] Writing of the Kathmandu Newar community, Declan Quigley notes: "To be excluded from [one's *guṭhi*] association is tantamount to being casteless, which is an option that few Newars are prepared to consider. To be casteless means to be without potential marriage partners. . . . This is the ultimate force in the obligation to conform to the demands of . . . *guthis*. Not to do so is to jeopardize the future of one's offspring" (1993:108).

power less through their ability to somehow "brainwash" consumers than through their proficiency in feeding off of, or capitalizing on, the *social imperatives* that people face in their daily lives. Consumer goods become necessary to the extent that they become part of the social currency, narrative resources, and cultural performances that make up projects of class formation in Kathmandu. Not everyone participates with the same intensity, and even those heavily invested in the local middle-class consumer economy often articulate a sense of moral compromise as they embrace a new form of materialism. But regardless of the ambiguity in their relationships with the new material culture, all Kathmandu residents share in an experience in which personal or corporate (usually family) prestige (ijjat) is increasingly tied to the acquisition and display of consumer goods. Like the man who flatly insisted that "It is not a matter of affording!" everyone in Kathmandu struggles to maintain parity with those in their social communities.

Conclusion: Consumption and Communication

One of the most common themes in this chapter has been the anxiety that arises from, if not a new, then a heightened sense of social "competition"—a competition often played out in the commodity realm, thereby driving more and more people deeper and deeper into the cash economy. What I have called a kind of "prestige inflation" in Kathmandu is related to a large and rapidly growing consumer field. Even if we cannot say that "culture" is on the increase, we can certainly say that material culture is now far more diverse and conspicuous, as is a kind of "culture of the material" embedded in a host of new ideologies, ranging from "development" to "education," and embodied practices such as "fashion." As one man quoted above put it, "now we want so many *other* things." Yet as another lamented, "Even if you have something, you are always lacking something." With every new consumer delight comes another consumer anguish—a tension reflected in the deeply ambivalent attitudes toward goods in middle-class stories and practices of consumption.

Along with the increased availability and variety of material goods in the local economy come increased opportunities for consumption aimed at producing or claiming distinction. From televisions to bedsheets to "buffet-style" banquets, as more and more distinctive commodities enter a social setting there are ever greater opportunities for persons to harness these goods to their own projects of individual or group distinction. In Kathmandu a rapid influx of distinctive commodities has severely disrupted established codes of display, thereby opening up avenues for persons and groups to either stake claims in higher social categories or, more often, raise the stakes for maintaining membership in groups to which they already belong.

These inflationary trends are especially strong when new cultural goods enter an already volatile social setting characterized by an influx of new people, a huge increase in local cash flow, and new, permeable and shifting social formations emerging out of once relatively stable and closed (endogamous) caste hierarchies. For example, in Kathmandu successful immigrant groups (or portions of them) that have arrived in the city over the past few decades—such as the Tibetans, Manangis, Darjeeling Nepalis, and Sherpas—have adopted modern material lifestyles, converting newfound cash resources into the cultural capital of modern consumer materialism. These groups pursue a relatively unadulterated strain of class/consumer politics. Yet on the other hand, the stories of Kedar, Gita, and Sano Raj illustrate how, for the majority of people in Kathmandu, more long-standing social identities linked to caste and kin remain highly relevant (to the extent that they can be used to legitimize claims to social superiority), even as these groups increasingly confront the modern pressures of class differentiation. In previous generations, a variety of leveling devices and a broad sense of corporate identity (often based on a shared mode of labor) tended to keep members of a particular caste and kin grouping at a more or less shared standard of living. But now most caste/kin groups in Kathmandu are beginning to show signs of cracking along class lines. While Kedar and Gita have been relatively successful in maintaining ties with their caste fellows within a broad space of middle-classness, it has been only with considerable difficulty. Sano Raj, on the other hand, has fallen victim to the increased costs of maintaining cultural parity with his one-time social equals.

Middle-class competition is real; it is about making and defending claims to power. But while the competition may produce "losers" (like Sano Raj), it does not really produce "winners." In other words, the middle class is a kind of performative space characterized by constant alignment and realignment with class others, and where goods play active roles. Because many different configurations of cultural capital can become the group's basis of an individual's or group's claim to status—combinations of education, job status, political power, cash wealth, business assets, caste, or what Weber called the competing "characteristics and badges" of middle-class culture (1946:188)—ranking is almost impossible. A person's rank within the middle class shifts with context (depending on where and when one's particular constellation of cultural capital is most valuable) and is subject to never-ending debate. Ultimately, middle-class membership is not about fixing rank but about *claiming* and *maintaining* a place in the ongoing debate.

Here again the *language* of class and consumerism is important. When people speak of "fashion," they most often speak of it not as a *thing* but as a *practice*. Typically, the English noun is linked to the Nepali verb, as in fashion *garnu*, "to *do* fashion." That fashion is less often a possession than a practice—that its importance is less in the *having* than in the *doing*—underlines the central role of consumer practice in the ongoing collective performance of middle-class culture. Hence, the consumer desire associated with "doing fashion"—and all the anxiety that it creates— is less about things, actual material objects, than about another kind of desire. Consumer desire is ultimately a desire to keep open the channels of dialogue with one's class others, to be acknowledged as a participant in the joint production of class practice. The word "fashion" marks those consumer goods with currency in the ongoing middle-class cultural economy, but as fashions come and go, *maintaining one's place* in that economy is the real consumer desire.

Thus, the inflationary consumer "competition" that people speak of is not intended to set "winners" *apart* from their social reference group and into some "higher" social category (à la Veblen). Rather, the necessity of consumerism is the necessity of preserving the social capillaries that link members of a social group. Here I agree with Mary Douglas and Baron Isherwood, who argue that consumption is at least as much a matter of intragroup reciprocity as of intergroup competition. By "keeping up with the Joneses," people are not necessarily trying to *outdo* each other but may be simply "trying not to be excluded" (Douglas and Isherwood 1979:126). The consumer anxiety that people speak of in Kathmandu is typically less a matter of competition aimed at surpassing others and more a matter of synchronizing the categories of value within groups who share similar social and material conditions. To "win" in this competition is to maintain social parity within the space of the middle class. To "lose"— as Sano Raj and thousands of others in Kathmandu have experienced— is to be left behind, unable to meet the changing demands for membership as one's social reference group transforms its identity standards. In this way the material performances of class (the consumer imperatives and behaviors discussed in this chapter) merge with the moral narratives of class (the stories of "honesty," "suitability," and ijjat discussed in the previous chapter) in a larger cultural project whereby Kathmandu's middle class seeks to order society in its own class terms. In this middle-class project, *property* sets the standards of *propriety*.

5

"DOING FASHION" IN KATHMANDU: CLASS AND THE CONSUMER PUBLIC

> There is a prior and pervasive kind of reasoning that scans a scene and sizes it up, packing into one instant's survey a process of matching, classifying, and comparing.
>
> —MARY DOUGLAS AND BARON ISHERWOOD, *The World of Goods*

> Now even babies are wearing foreign clothing! You really can't even compare then and now, there are such differences.
>
> —TWENTY-TWO-YEAR-OLD KATHMANDU WOMAN

> There is no way out of the game of culture.
>
> —PIERRE BOURDIEU, *Distinction*

The two previous chapters described how middle-classness is constructed through a range of narrative practices and how consumer behaviors take center stage in the cultural performances through which people enact the new realities of a local commercial culture. This chapter shifts focus to consider middle-class culture as *public* practice. Through the language, practice, and materiality of a local universe of fashion, the middle class in Kathmandu lays claim to new public spaces and uses these as zones in which to perform, naturalize, and literally embody its own class privileges.

PUBLIC PATRONAGE IN THE RELIGIOUS IDIOM

Mounted on the wall in the courtyard of one of Patan's most magnificent multitiered "pagoda-style" temples is a peculiar inscription.[1] Among the

---

[1] Patan is Kathmandu's adjacent sister city.

most recent additions to a series of inscriptions that record pious donations to the temple by generations of wealthy benefactors, this inscription
is unusual not in its content but because it is in English, not the formal
Nepali or Sanskritized Newari most often used for temple records. Although undated, the inscription records a donation probably made some-
time in the first half of the twentieth century. Because it was in English,
and its location on the wall seemed to indicate that it was among the last
donations memorialized in this manner, this inscription struck me as a
particularly interesting historical artifact. The gifts of the proud patrons
hark back to a tradition of public giving rooted in centuries of local practice, but the language employed seemed to signal an uneasy recognition
that new modes of public discourse and prestige were on the horizon.
Now more or less dilapidated, and maintained precariously through donations from UNESCO and the German government, the temple stands
surrounded by carpet factories and multistoried concrete homes, the new
monuments of local prestige.

The indologist Jan Pieper noted that in Kathmandu "The Newar consume communally whatever wealth they have been able to accumulate. . . . Newar cities are so rich in temples and public resting places
(*patti*) and votive structures, for the construction and maintenance cost
was raised from [public] contributions" (1975:68). Even if these practices
were no longer in place when Pieper wrote of them, there is nevertheless
a wealth of inscriptional and other historical evidence to support Todd
Lewis's contention that "Formerly the characteristic way to spend excess
wealth was through the conspicuous patronage traditions" (1984:588).
The wealth of medieval and early-modern religious architecture documented so meticulously by scholars[2] bears witness to centuries of public
patronage.

This built environment points to a mode of social existence in which
religion was the primary idiom or arena for public life. This is not to
suggest that social process was propelled by some set of benevolent, pure
religious motives, but rather that religion formed the conceptual frame in
which other domains of life were articulated. For example, Kathmandu
businessmen today speak of a time when their grandfathers pursued business objectives similar to their own but through different means. In those
days entrepreneurs were expected to take active roles in community ceremonial events as sponsors, hosts, and participants. Similarly, the community expected businessmen to register both their merit and their social
standing through public donations ranging from gold butter lamps to temple repairs to gifts for priests. Businessmen now speak of how, in earlier
days, anyone who chose *not* to participate in this public religious arena

---

[2] See, for example, Slusser 1982, and Levy and Rajopadhyaya 1991.

was likely to become more or less invisible in the community, have little opportunity to forge or maintain business contacts, and have few avenues available for social or political advancement. In this society religious values and practice formed the medium within which practically all forms of social transaction—including trade and finance—transpired. As the temple inscriptions illustrate, religious piety (in the form of donations) was a mode of public display and a means of converting economic into cultural capital.

While in past centuries the modes and means of public life in Kathmandu were performed in a religious idiom, the basic logic of that practice was not so different from that of today. One way to illustrate this point is to dig deeper into the details of Rana-era public practice. As introduced in chapter 2, and discussed in detail elsewhere (Liechty 1997), over the past several centuries Kathmandu's political isolation by no means implied total cultural isolation. This suggests that neither public consumption patterns nor local business practices in nineteenth-century Kathmandu should be seen as "pure" or autochthonous expressions of "local culture." For example, long before Nepal's "opening" to the world in 1951, people in Kathmandu were well aware of a range of modern mass-produced commodities. European and Indian textiles and other consumer goods had been imported into Nepal for centuries. By the early twentieth century, commercial interests were actively promoting tea consumption throughout the hill region, and Nepali soldiers returning from two world wars brought with them tea-drinking habits, as well as a hankering for such basic consumer commodities as soap and tooth powder. But far in excess of their own firsthand experience as consumers of modern commodities, Kathmandu residents also had for centuries been observing what the Rana and royal families desired as consumers. From luxury autos to Paris fashions, people in Kathmandu were fully aware of a universe of consumer goods that existed beyond their reach.

For the most part these consumer goods were kept in the hands of the ruling elite. Through a combination of travel and import restrictions, as well as sweeping sumptuary laws, the elite ensured that public and private consumer behaviors were tightly regulated. Many Kathmandu residents still remember when even the few commoners who could afford to acquire Western-style clothing were forbidden to do so. Others recall that few would have been foolish enough to wear such clothing even if allowed, for fear of attracting the "evil eye" (as one acquaintance sarcastically put it) of the Ranas. Because the Rana elite recognized no distinction between state and private resources, members of ruling families were free to confiscate property, and even women, from local families (Lewis 1984:42). Throughout the nineteenth century and into the early part of the twentieth, a number of Kathmandu Newar families amassed fortunes transporting commodities between Calcutta and Lhasa via Kathmandu (Lewis 1993), but lived in constant fear of having their resources levied, impounded, or simply appropriated.[3] Wealthy merchants appeared before the Ranas in simple clothing and lived in relatively modest homes, even though they often controlled valuable real estate in Calcutta and Lhasa.

While on the surface Kathmandu may have appeared to be a proto-, even pre, capitalist society, with a noncommercial consumer culture, in fact this state of affairs was anything but natural. The Rana state's extractive authority helped to minimize the potential for unimpeded local capital accumulation and transformations in consumer practices, even though some in Kathmandu were able to amass capital outside of Nepal.[4] The religious ethos that pervaded Kathmandu's local economy into the early twentieth century, and its relatively simple commodity culture, were "real" to the extent that they reflected a certain mode of sociality and a certain set of community-oriented values. But by the end of the Rana regime, the sociocultural context of Kathmandu was already deeply influenced by competing consumer values and logics of prestige. While the ruling elite pursued social strategies based on an almost hyperdisplay of distinctive consumer goods (Liechty 1997), the mass of Kathmandu's commoners were restricted by decree and necessity to a prestige economy that maintained earlier patterns of public charity. The early-twentieth-century votive inscription rendered in English captures some of this tension by both continuing a community- and state-sanctioned mode of public consumption and hinting at new but forbidden modes of distinction.

FASHION: ADORNMENT AND ARTIFICE

Although modern consumer fashion practice in Kathmandu has its roots in nineteenth-century elite patterns of public consumption and display (see chapter 2), it is only after 1951, with the unimpeded growth of a local

[3] One businessman from a long-established Newar trading family maintained that Jung Bahadur's visit to England in 1850 (Whelpton 1983) was funded by a special tax extracted from Kathmandu Newar merchants, as was the construction of Chandra Shamsher's magnificent Singha Durbar. I have been unable to directly confirm this in published accounts, though P. S. Rana describes the palace as having been built largely by pressed labor and using appropriated materials (1995:162).

[4] When the Lhasa-Calcutta trade collapsed after the Chinese invasion of Tibet, a number of Kathmandu trading families were able to transfer capital resources in Calcutta in the direction of new business opportunities, including tourism, in Kathmandu. In the nineteenth and early-twentieth centuries, Calcutta was the heart of the South Asian tourist industry, and after the fall of Tibet, several Kathmandu families were able to segue into the tourist trade in Kathmandu via already established Calcutta holdings and business contacts.

middle class, that fashion has become the public practice par excellence in Kathmandu. The emergence of fashion as a narrative and performative force is an important trend in the ongoing development and shifting logics of public practice in Kathmandu. Through talking about and "doing fashion"—fashioning selves and bodies in dialogue with their class others— the middle class constructs a new "outside," or public, domain and claims this new public space and publicness as its own.

The challenge of dealing with the concept of "fashion" lies in distinguishing what is new from what is not. How can we describe "modern" fashion practice in Kathmandu without implying that various forms of stylization and bodily objectification have not existed for millennia? One way is to use Georg Simmel's notion of "adornment" as a common thread from past to present, while asking how the qualities of that thread may change with time.[5] The question becomes, How does the nature and meaning of adornment change?

Simmel stresses both the personal and social dimensions of adornment.

> Adornment intensifies or enlarges the impression of the personality by operating as a sort of radiation emanating from it. . . . The radiations of adornment, the sensuous attention it provokes, supply the personality with such an enlargement or intensification of its sphere: the personality, so to speak, *is* more when it is adorned. [Adornment allows] the mere *having* of the person to become a visible quality of its *being*. (1950:339–40, italics in original)

Thus, it is in commanding "sensuous attention" and in enlarging and intensifying the personality's "sphere" that adornment becomes a means of communication. Adornment is social practice; it is the "being-for-the-other which returns to the subject as the enlargement of his own sphere of significance" (Simmel 1950:432). The adorned body is the social body ("the being-for-the-other"), though the *social meaning* of adornment practice is historically contingent.

Like identity, adornment is simultaneously about distinction and identification; it is used to set individuals and groups *apart* from some and to signal *sameness* with others. For centuries Nepali elites have appropriated foreign clothing styles (often with accompanying sumptuary prohibitions on the general populace) (Liechty 1997) in efforts to display their "distinctive" power. By the early nineteenth century, Nepali men of the elite class were beginning to adopt Western-style clothing; paintings and photographs from the beginning to the end of the Rana era depict

---

[5] Like Simmel I use the term "adornment" in its broadest sense, to include not just jewelry and body markings but also all items of apparel.

men in heavily westernized costume, while women's attire was most often North Indian,[6] though occasionally showing European influences.[7]

The adornment practices associated with Kathmandu's non-elites—until recently, largely the urban Newar community—while also distinctive, are perhaps more fruitfully seen as communicating identification *within* groups than as promoting distinction *between* them. Bronwen Bledsoe's work on "jewelry and personal adornment among the Newars" (1984) is a valuable introduction to the "social implications of adornment" in Newar communities around the Kathmandu valley. Bledsoe discusses the uses and meanings of jewelry or ornaments (*gahanā*) as well as practices of decoration or beautification (*siṅār*, n.; *siṅārnu*, v.t.), or marking (*laksyan*, n.). Although Bledsoe's account of Newar adornment practice would no longer describe many urban Newar women (not to mention women of other caste/ethnic backgrounds), it nevertheless serves as a useful ethnographic "benchmark" against which to gage contemporary practice.

At the risk of minimizing the aesthetic and affective dimensions of adornment practice, for my purposes I will focus briefly on the more functional elements of Bledsoe's account. In her analysis Bledsoe stresses both the dimension of male control over women through adornment and the role of adornment in signaling transformations through different stages in life. In particular I am interested in highlighting Bledsoe's suggestion that "traditional" adornment is largely "a token of women's standing in proper relationship to husband and society at large" (1984:87). In the traditional cycle of life stages and transforming rituals—from adolescence to old age—adornment often signifies a woman's relationship with men, whether fathers, husbands, or sons. For example, widows abandon all jewelry, although with time they may resume wearing simple pieces and even "a fair amount of gold . . . if one has sons" (Bledsoe 1984:67). Again, leaving aside adornment's role in displaying economic standing, its religious meaning, and the sensual pleasures it may bring its wearers, the point here is that adornment has been an important element in signaling a woman's social status vis-à-vis her family and the broader society.

In Kathmandu in the early 1990s, women also spoke of adornment's role in designating *types* of women, though often in the context of describing how earlier forms of differentiation were now made with less frequency. For example, one twenty-year-old woman spoke of how she felt "fashion" practice had changed from earlier generations:

---

[6] See, for example, the photo in White (1920:279).

[7] For example, plate V in Wright (1972 [1877]:28,29), entitled "A Rani or Nepalese Lady of High Rank," depicts a Rana woman wearing a sari *over* a billowing hoop skirt. Other outstanding collections of photographs (mostly portraiture) from the Rana era include Landon 1928, P. P. Shrestha 1986, Sever 1993, and von der Heide 1997.

They had a lot of fashion back then too, I think. Like, my grand-mother always says that today's people can't do makeup as the old generation used to. They had their fashion at that time. They said you should put *koṭhi* [beauty marks] here and there. They could make *alak* [curled hair], even though beauty parlors didn't exist at that time. They learned about it themselves, and the clever ones learned it easily.

Yes, they used to do all kinds of makeup. But now, what's the difference between married and unmarried [women]? They both use exactly the same kind of makeup! There's no difference.

What is significant about this young woman's remarks is that she recognizes that "makeup" itself is nothing new, although its meaning has changed; the social function it once had of distinguishing married from unmarried women is gone. Another woman, in her late twenties, had some related comments:

Before, people used to wear lots of ornaments [*gahanā*], but today people have more clothes, do more makeup. I mean, before, people used to pass through the years with one or two sets of clothes. But now we have so much fashion.

In this woman's opinion, the emphasis of adornment practice has shifted from gold ornaments toward clothing and "makeup," which she equated with "fashion". Significantly, for her "fashion" implies not just a *kind* of clothing or "makeup" but an *amount*: before, people had mere clothing, but now they have "so much fashion."

Her remark that people previously would have had relatively few sets of clothes corresponds with ethnographic observations from the 1950s that describe attire in Kathmandu as relatively uniformlike. For example, G. S. Nepali notes that dress was "a mark of distinction" both between different ethnic groups and between different "social and economic strata" within the Newar community. But Nepali stresses that "distinction is made not by the variation in the items of garments [which were relatively uniform], but by their mode of use and colour" (1965:65). In other words, distinction was not signaled by different styles or cuts or items of clothing but in relatively subtle (though meaningful) variations in the fabric and trim of similar garments. Even setting aside economic factors that would have limited how much clothing a person owned, in this cultural milieu the wide variety of clothing styles that characterize contemporary "fashion" would have made no sense.

In addition to describing trends away from relatively elaborate orna-mentation and uniform clothing toward more emphasis on "makeup" and clothing variety or quantity ("fashion"), Kathmandu women in the early 1990s also spoke of changes in the sexual/erotic meaning of clothing. As discussed in more detail below, questions of decency and "suitability" are very much alive today, especially in regard to women and Western clothing. Yet this is by no means new. The advent of more "revealing" styles in clothing, especially women's clothing, has been an issue for decades. For example, as the Indian-style sari became more and more common in non-elite circles, it brought new problems with it. One Chetri woman in her late forties described her experiences as a young woman with changing styles in sari blouses:

> At that time we used to wear a uniform at school, but at home we wore saris. Of course, we would always wear a full blouse, at least up until I was about fourteen or fifteen. About that time the three-quarter blouse[8] started coming in, and I liked it, so I made one. But I couldn't even bring myself to come down to the courtyard [of my own home] because of shyness [*lāj*]! I got used to it; but then, four or five years later, the *half*-blouse came in, and that too I wore, but for many days I was too embarrassed to even leave my house!
>
> So gradually this has all changed. It just depends on one's own opinion. There are some who even today can't wear that kind of blouse. But I feel that we have to keep pace with today's fashion.

Whereas G. S. Nepali could say that among Kathmandu Newars during the late 1950s "The principle involved in the wearing of [women's] dress seems to be to cover the body completely" (1965:66), this "principle" was already beginning to change in the face of "fashion," at least *outside* of the Newar community.

This woman's experience with changing styles in sari blouses points to another common theme in the comments of women and men who contrasted contemporary fashion with what they understood to be earlier adornment practices. Changes, and even cyclical changes, in style were often associated with "fashion." When describing how things were different now than they had been when she was a child, one woman in her thirties noted:

> For one thing, at that time there was not much fashion. I mean, at that time fashion wasn't so expensive. Now it has become very expensive. And now you see the fashion is returning; it is going in circles. Take pointed shoes, for example; they had those fifty years back, and now again you are finding them in the market. I think every generation has their fashion, but it's not the same. Like now, actually, fashion is always moving around into many different styles.

---

[8] When speaking of sari blouses, "full," "three-quarter," and "half" refer to the amount of midriff coverage.

This woman acknowledges that "every generation has their fashion" but still insists that something unique is going on today. The main difference has to do with quantity and therefore expense. While using the same word—"fashion"—to describe styles of the past and present, this woman suggests that the very nature of fashion practice has changed greatly in recent times.

Another factor contributing to changes in adornment practice is law. Along with the fall of the Rana regime in the early 1950s came the abandonment of sumptuary laws that had guaranteed the Ranas exclusive rights to certain clothing styles, especially Western fashions. Memories of these restrictive laws are still alive even in the minds of people too young to have had personal experience of them. Women in particular often associate "fashion" with "freedom." For example, one thirty-year-old married woman noted:

> Today people want to show that they are free. Before, they couldn't. They weren't so free. At that time, maybe the Ranas had fashion, but they didn't let anyone else show it [dekhāunu]. Today everyone has the freedom to show fashion, so we see it everywhere.

In Kathmandu, the classic middle-class construal of "freedom" as "freedom to consume" takes on a different meaning; modern consumer practice has to be seen in light of a past in which even those with resources were simply not "free" to consume. Against this background, the consumption of "fashion" becomes, at least potentially, a quasi-political act.

These brief glimpses into the history of local adornment practice suggest that adornment is a theme that links past with present, but its *meaning* is always changing. An earlier system of adornment served to position individuals within family and society. The emphasis on ornamentation and particular kinds of marking helped locate a person within a local universe of meaning, to signal his or her sexual/marital status, social standing, ethnicity, or place of residence. As commodities, ornaments made of precious metals also signaled the *amount* of wealth a person or family possessed.

What these women describe as contemporary adornment is also about *amount*, although in modern fashion practice the commodities being accumulated are very different. While gold is rapidly converted into other material resources, a modern commodity associated with fashion loses its value not only with use but as fashions change. Both the commodity itself and its meaning are eminently perishable. The new mode of adornment is a part of a new mode of commodity consumption tied more closely to mass production and cash economies. In the European context, Roland Barthes distinguishes premodern adornment from the modern "fashion system" by noting that at one time "the length of [a dress's] train exactly signaled a social condition." Clothing was "an ensemble of signs" such that "in former ages, costume did not connive at function, it displayed the artifice of its correspondences" (1983:268). Similarly, with the arrival of "fashion" in Kathmandu, we witness a shift away from clothing-as-fetishized-object toward clothing-as-fetishized-commodity.

In other words, clothing (and other adornment) is increasingly less about the explicit marking of social categories (livery, royal garb, sumptuary restrictions, ethnic, marital, or caste indicators) and more about a new regime of commercial signification that denies any clear-cut social function for clothing in favor of a consumer aesthetic of newness, pleasure, and even progress. As argued below, the modern "fashion system" in Kathmandu still signals "social condition," but these social meanings are often hidden behind reasons and rationalizations that mask fashion's "infidelity" (Barthes 1983:273). In Kathmandu, as the *overt* social meanings of adornment—perhaps best embodied in Rana-era sumptuary laws—disappear, adornment practice is more and more couched in other rationales. From the imperatives of "modernization" (*bikās*) that justify women's "keeping pace with today's fashion," to the middle-class values of equality and individual achievement ("now everyone has the freedom to show fashion"), contemporary adornment practice in Kathmandu is increasingly embedded in the artifice of new, thoroughly "modern" values and discursive systems. It is through this artifice that the structures for a new form of "natural" public practice take shape.

FILM AND FASHION

How do shifts in public adornment practice like these come about? Where does a new "fashion consciousness" come from? Surely the most frequently cited culprit is film.[9] Already by the late 1950s, G. S. Nepali could point to the "introduction of the cinema [as] one of the contributory factors for bringing about a new trend in the style of dress in Nepal" (1965:68). Likewise, the people that my co-workers and I interviewed almost unanimously spoke of the film industry (whether approvingly or otherwise) as the source of fashion inspiration. Not surprisingly, film also figured prominently in the accounts people gave of changing practice in recent decades. Indeed, film and fashion are so intimately linked in people's minds that it is worth laying out some of the most common themes in this association.

---

[9] Chapter 7 considers the roles of other media (radio, television, magazines) in these processes.

For many people the arrival of cinema in Kathmandu marked the starting point for modern fashion practice. One of the most detailed accounts I heard came from Hari, a man in his late forties. Though born in the Tarai, Hari has lived in Kathmandu since the mid-1960s, when he came to the city to study. Having grown up next door to a cinema hall in Biratnagar, Hari was an avid movie fan and, as a boy, consciously styled his life after what he saw in the films. All of this made for quite a shock when he arrived in Kathmandu, where cinema-going was still in its infancy.[10]

> At that time—I mean, when I came from my home town to here—the people were very innocent. They didn't know anything about what is the fashion. Especially here in the valley, the Newars—oh! they were so-o-o innocent! They were ashamed even to look at us, because we were proud [of how we looked], and they knew that we were influenced some from India. At that time everybody I met was very simple: no pickpockets, no thieves, none of that.
>
> But slowly, like when I went to see a movie here . . . Well, at that time only the Rana people were doing the fashion, because they had good money. And so they would come with all this fashion to see this lousy cinema hall. Because there was no other entertainment, and the public thing, you know. They were coming all this fashion this and that, and they were staying up in the balcony, and we were seeing them from below. Oooooo! [*Looks up with a face of fawning admiration*] And they were claiming that they were not copying fashion from Bombay [as we were]. "We are copying this fashion from *Paris*!" [they said].

Ironically, at this time the cinema hall was a place where one could see fashion both on the screen and on the bodies of the wealthy Rana socialites ensconced in the balcony. More than in the 1990s, Kathmandu cinema halls were at that time places to see and be seen, places to see other places and other classes.

But there was more to popular fashion education than just going to the cinema. According to Hari, before the "jean revolution" there was only a "very slow change." Yet "when the jeans came," things started to pick up. In Kathmandu the "jean revolution" coincides with the arrival of tourists, and especially young tourists in the late 1960s and early 1970s. Up to that point, the few Western tourists in Kathmandu were mostly late-middle-aged, wealthy, and comfortably sequestered in one or two relatively posh hotels.[11] Yet with the arrival of younger tourists, including the so-called hippies, more and more foreigners began to hit the

---

[10] See chapter 6 for a brief history of cinema and cinemagoing in Kathmandu.
[11] See Peissel 1966 for an account of the early hotel trade in Kathmandu.

streets. A whole new sector of "budget-class" tourist businesses sprang up which in turn began to spread tourist dollars to a much wider segment of the local economy.[12] As Hari explained:

> From that time [on] people had money, and afterward there was no [one] class to do the fashion. Everybody can do the fashion; everybody can wear jeans.
>
> Before this, people worried about their dress only during some festivals or some marriage ceremonies. They needed the very good or very clean clothes. But they didn't know what is the teri-cotton, what is the gaberdine, what is the really good-quality cloth.
>
> But it is from *that* period, when the jeans came, that they got fashion. And movies, that was one of the things. Like in Indian movies, they are doing, like the hero always wearing the fashionable things, and *they* are giving the fashions here for the middle class, and the lower-middle. Like *what* Amitabh Bachchan is wearing, *what* Mithun Chakraborty is wearing[13] . . . The youngsters over here, they want to do *here*.
>
> So first was the Hindi [cinema], and *still* it's affecting. For everything from talk, to manner, the way [*strikes several chic poses*], and like this. Otherwise [before cinema], it was completely village-type, these people here. At that time, the tourists were appreciating this place very much, the Kathmandu valley.

Although Hari feels that cinema is the main factor in transforming dress and fashion, the story is incomplete without mention of tourism: "when the jeans came"—both the clothes and the tourists who wore them—cash flow and the availability of new commodities increased.

Another way that people in Kathmandu link media with fashion is in terms of the media-induced fads or fashion phases that wash over the city at periodic intervals. By chance my second visit to Kathmandu—in the late 1970s—coincided with what people identified as the first non–South Asian fashion wave. Up to that point, aside from a few elites and other marginal types, most fashion-minded people in Kathmandu took their cues from the styles portrayed in Hindi films.[14] By the time of my visit,

---

[12] See Liechty 1996a for more on the development of budget tourism.

[13] Bachchan and Chakraborty are Hindi film stars.

[14] By most accounts, aside from introducing blue jeans, Western tourists in Kathmandu during the 1970s did not have a very wide impact on popular styles in the city. Very few Nepalis entered into the full "freak" lifestyle or wore fashions associated with the young tourists. Of those that did, some were actually Nepalis from Darjeeling who were already very cosmopolitan and had themselves been attracted by Kathmandu's tourist scene. For more on relations between Nepalis and tourists in Kathmandu, see Liechty 1994:193–98 and Liechty 1996a.

however, video film technology had arrived in the form of American "disco" films, and "Saturday night fever" had already reached epidemic proportions. As in the United States, flowing hair, "bell-bots," and enormous platform shoes were de rigueur for many young men in Kathmandu.

What is significant about Kathmandu's "disco wave" is the fact that it was closely tied to the arrival of video technology. With "video parlors" sprouting like mushrooms in the late 1970s (see chapter 6), for the first time a broad cross-section of Kathmandu residents had access to Western films. By all accounts, the initial demand for these Western films—along with Indian and East Asian ("kung-fu") films also available on video—was enormous. School children cut classes to see them, and fortunes were made overnight, before government regulations and the spread of VCRs into private homes cut into the "video parlor" trade. When video arrived, Kathmandu residents had already been exposed to waves of young Western tourists, but it was only with general access to Western mass media that the first Western youth fashions took hold.

This link between media consumption and clothing fads suggests that the meaning and allure of modern fashion is intimately tied to the mode of its presentation and representation. Fashion becomes meaningful—and thereby potentially attractive and emulative—primarily in the mediated contexts (here cinema) *in which* it is represented. Commercial media render fashions meaningful by situating them in image worlds into which the viewer can project the fashioned self and others. By the late 1970s people in Kathmandu had seen at least a decade of Western youth fashions—ranging from the "mod" to the hippie-esque—that were, from the Nepali perspective, no more inherently bizarre than the disco fashions of John Travolta. What disco films provided, that resident westerners did not, was an entire sphere of signification within which a certain fashion fit. Clothing became the material signifier for a whole range of referents from disco music (also commoditized) and youth identities to particular styles of sexuality, gender display, and freedom. With disco films (and disco cassettes) came a new imaginary space (which took its place alongside those produced by Indian films and their associated fashion commodities) in which people could experiment with other ways of being.

These observations have important implications for understanding how media consumption is tied to the consumer imagination. The story of disco films and disco fashions in Kathmandu points to ways in which commercial media construct spheres of signification around commodities (here "fashions"). These are complex auras of meaning that bring together a range of identities, ideas, behaviors, and commodities—for example, youth, freedom, dance, fashions, and music—that are conflated to form an imaginary unity. Western clothing styles themselves, though frequently worn by young tourists on Kathmandu streets, did not "capture the imaginations" of local young people nearly so much as cinematic representations of these same fashions were able to do. Although earlier fashion practice in the city had been inspired by Indian cinema, Kathmandu's "disco wave" provides a particularly clear illustration of the power of media representations, by showing how the mere presence of consumer goods is not enough to inspire consumer desire: to generate demand, fashion goods require auras of meaning that transcend their mere functionality, and the media are crucial channels for this modern consumer signification.

Following the "disco fever" fashion phase came a succession of other clothing styles influenced by Western movies. Acquaintances described a "Western wear" phase that followed on the heals of disco in the early 1980s. Denim jackets, bandannas, and boots became popular as young men fixated on heroes like Clint Eastwood and others in the "cowboy" film genre. Next came the Michael Jackson "Thriller" wave, with zipper-bedecked jackets, wet-curl perms, and "break dancing." Other pop stars, like Boy George and Madonna, also passed through the local image scene—becoming more and more unrecognizable with every graphic redeployment on clothing, posters, and stickers, until their images show up as blurry blobs on the sweaty T-shirts of poor day laborers and are identifiable only by their English captions.

While it is easy to link Indian, Western, and East Asian films to certain broad patterns of fashion practice, simply citing these links does little or nothing to answer questions of how and why they are forged. The sections that follow turn to these questions of how people participate in fashion and the implications these practices have for the construction of new public spaces and the privileging of a new class culture.

"Fashion Happens": Means, Motivations, and Media

One question my co-workers and I asked whenever conversations turned to the subject of fashion was, "Why do people do fashion?" Most responses followed the basic lines of this one, given by twenty-four-year-old woman:

> If one person does fashion and others see it, they think [to themselves], "Oh, how nice I'd look doing it too!" So they say, "Yes, I'll do it too!" In this way, fashion happens.

With money, and personal interest, "fashion happens." But how?

Part of the answer is tied to how and where people learn about fashion. Like the woman above, many people learn about it just from seeing others. "Whatever's going around, that's what I wear. Like, I used to wear [skirts] above the knee, but now, below; it's today's fashion," remarked one eighteen-year-old student. Another woman, married and in her mid-thirties, remarked, "I don't go searching for new fashions [in shops]. I just have made [by a tailor] what I see on the streets, what I see others wearing. But even so, I don't like these new fancy-style kurtā-suruwāls. They make me look like a real slob [bhyātlaka]!"

Although there are more and more ready-made clothing stores in Kathmandu, items there tend to be priced out of the reach of all but tourists, expatriates, and local elites. Middle-class women and men are more likely to have their clothing made at any of the hundreds of tailor shops scattered across the city and its suburbs. The ready-made shops more often provide the prototypes for less costly tailor-made garments.

Women occasionally spoke of making their own clothing but they almost always made a distinction between "clothing for inside" (i.e., the house), which they made by themselves, and "clothing for outside," which they had tailor-made. One twenty-year-old student brought up this topic while listing some of her favorite pastimes:

> Well, I like things like cooking, knitting, sewing clothes. . . . I mean clothes for *outside* [the house] I have made *outside* [by a tailor], but the clothes I wear here in the house I make myself.
>
> *How do you choose what kinds of clothes to have made?*
>
> I learn about these things from, like, the "filmfares,"[15] [other] magazines, and just from seeing what other people are wearing.

Thus, clothing for wearing *in public* is often explicitly distinguished from clothing for "in the house." Public clothing is more likely to be made "outside" and to be modeled explicitly after images in the public realm: images from mass media and designs seen on the street. On the other hand, clothing worn at home is often strictly for that space alone and may be homemade. The tailoring and fashion trade in Kathmandu is intimately linked to this sense of an "outside" or public domain, in which public images are often mass-mediated.

Certainly the most important channels through which fashion consciousness moves are the mass media. When talking about films and film magazines, people repeatedly brought up the subject of fashion. For example, in a discussion of popular films, my co-worker asked one nineteen-year-old Newar student, "What makes a film good?" She replied thoughtfully:

---

[15] *Filmfare*, published in English and a variety of Indian languages, is one of India's oldest and most popular film magazines. However, at least in Nepal, "*filmfare*" has become a generic term for practically all film magazines. For more on film magazines, see chapter 7.

Well, there's singing, dialogue, acting, and dressing; these things make a film good.

What do you mean, dressing?

I mean I have a special interest in dress. I like mostly the simple kind of dress. I don't like to look over [too fashionable]. [I like] things like the jean-pants of the Western style and *kurtā suruwāl* of India.

For her the clothing styles conveyed in films ranked as one of the key factors in what made a film "good." Fashion was among the prime attractions of the cinema. Similarly, another unmarried Newar woman in her early twenties described why she liked to read *Filmfare*:

I read it because it's my *sokh*.[16] I look for new clothing designs, and fashions in this [magazine]. I basically want to see it to find out if there's anything new in there!

For this woman, reading (or at least looking at) film magazines is part of her *sokh*—a kind of elemental desire—for keeping up with "new clothing designs, and fashions." From conversations like these, it seemed that for many people in Kathmandu it was almost impossible to disengage interests in film, film magazines, and fashion. The boundaries of each seemed to blur into the others so as to make an interest in one inseparable from interests in the rest.

This connection between films, film images, and fashions was one that seamstresses also made frequently. Indeed, the tailoring trade in Kathmandu seemed to be intimately tied into the world of filmic fashions. Women in particular often spoke of going to tailor's shops where they would peruse collections of posters and postcardlike pictures of Indian film heroines as well as stacks of fashion catalogues from India, Europe, and North America.[17] Said one woman, "At Namuna [a popular New Road tailoring establishment] they have catalogues and we can just look for the styles we want and take them from the catalogues." Just as often, seamstresses spoke of clients bringing in their own fashion pictures. One self-employed seamstress in her late twenties said of her customers:

They'll bring a catalogue or magazine to show, or a photo card of some film heroine and show that. I had one woman come in here a while back who had four or five kids, and even *she* had this photo of

---

[16] See chapter 3, note 16, for a discussion of "sokh."

[17] These catalogues were sometimes fashion collections put out by particular designers, though the European and American catalogues often consisted of a more or less random collection of mail-order brochures, ranging from old Sears catalogues to brand new books from upscale French and Italian department stores.

5. Seamstresses at work in a women's clothing shop, Thapathali, Kathmandu.

a film heroine. She asked me to make her a dress just like that one. Even *she* wanted to copy the heroine!

According to seamstresses, the magazines that women bring to their shops include not only film magazines but also a range of glossy Indian magazines aimed at women: *Mayapuri, Grihashobha, Femina,* and *Manorama,* among others.

While seamstresses often assist their slightly older clients in negotiating the maze of stylistic differences arrayed in catalogues and film-star cards, children and younger women and men are more likely to have very clear ideas about fashion and to demand that the tailor or seamstress replicate these. This trend comes through clearly in the comments of Nirmala, a middle-aged seamstress who had been making clothes in Kathmandu for more than a decade. Her remarks summarize many of the recent trends in fashion practice and highlight her perceptions of how it has changed over the years.

It's mostly the sixteen- to twenty-year-old girls who like the new designs in clothing. They make up most of my customers. I get a lot of girls with a lot of money.

The sixteen- to twenty-year-olds, these are the ones who determine the new designs and styles. I mean, as soon as they see a new design, they'll come in and ask me to make it. It doesn't matter how much it costs. They only care about wearing the new designs, not about the money.

Like, if they see a heroine in a film with some kind of new dress, immediately they want a dress like that. In fact, they don't care much for the catalogues I've got in the shop. They watch the films! As for me, I don't even have to go to the films to know the new styles! They come and tell me, and that's enough. From that I can make it!

Like right now [1991], the most common dress [that girls ask for] is from the film *Maine Pyar Kiya*.[18] Also these days, a lot of girls are wearing the loose, umbrella-cut *kurtā-suruwāl*. And then of course, the Punjabi-style *kurtā-suruwāl* never goes out of style. It's always the same, evergreen.

For both Nirmala and her clients, new fashions and mass media seemed to live a kind of symbiotic existence:

After watching a film, people know the new styles automatically. And of course educated people can also learn this from magazines, ones like *Manorama* and *Grihashobha*, these Hindi magazines. New things are given in them. I also watch these magazines for new fashion.

For many in Kathmandu, films and magazines are essentially the exclusive channels for the creation of "fashion," the apparent means by which "fashion" is both produced and disseminated.

Continuing on the theme of her largely youthful clientele, Nirmala also made a number of interesting observations about how fashion consciousness had developed since the time of her childhood.

There are many differences! Twenty years ago boys wore any old kind of clothes. They didn't even know what fashion was! But now, even little kids come into my shop saying, "Sew me a punk-style shirt!" or "Make me a big [baggy]-style shirt!" I mean, really little boys are in here saying, "No, this isn't what I want. Make the pocket *here*, make *this* style of cuff, make *this* collar!" I mean, there is *this much* difference between then and now!

The older generation used to just follow along with the clothes they always had, with what was always common. They could not have cared less [*matlab chaina*] about it! But now even little girls will come asking for some special *kurtā-suruwāl* of this or that design. I guess they need all these different designs now . . . [*Shrugs.*]

---

[18] A 1989 Hindi film with a title that translates to "I have Fallen in Love." For details see Rajadhyaksha and Willemen 1999:490.

> Of course then, also, before, they [young people] didn't go walk-
> ing around [outside the house] all the time. But now you see them
> walking around, group after group, going to films, going to restau-
> rants, to shops. I mean, before, they didn't even know what things
> were eaten![19]

Even allowing room for exaggeration, this is a powerful account of perceived change. A generation ago, people could not have "cared less
about" fashion; now, even young boys and girls come to her shop preoc-
cupied with the stylistic subtleties of cuffs and collars. Earlier generations
wished to have what "they always had," what was "always common."
But now, for some reason, young people seem to "need all these different
designs." Nirmala proposes that perhaps this new "need" has something
to do with the fact that the young people are out on the streets, "group
after group," going to films, restaurants, and shops. Indeed, it is in the
new public spaces of the shopping districts, cinemas, campuses, and restaurants that "doing fashion" becomes a need. For Kathmandu's middle-
class, public space is the space of fashion, and film (in tandem with other
allied commercial media and commodities) is a key component in the
formation of a public fashion consciousness.

FASHION PRACTICE: CLASS CULTURE

For members of Kathmandu's middle class, "doing fashion" is not a luxury but a necessity. Indeed, attention to, or even a preoccupation with,
fashion was almost a defining feature of the middle class. In the city's
streets, campuses, and offices, people were almost hyperattentive to dress
and demeanor, which were read as an index of an individual's "home"
or "family condition" (gharko sthiti). In different ways, the equation of
fashion practice with class practice is a common theme that runs through
hundreds of the interviews my co-workers and I conducted.

A teacher at one of Kathmandu's postsecondary campuses explained
how he distinguished children of "higher families" from the majority of
middle-class students.

> You can see, even among the youngsters at campus, there is a part—
> there is a different class. If you go there, you can see that. Some are
> there in cheap clothes, just throwing something on, like the Americans
> do. [They say,] "Eh! Who cares?!" Because they know the fashion.

---

[19] She means that, before, young people did not even know what foods were the fashionable or "in" things to eat.

But then there are the others [who boast], "Oh yeah, I *just* got it, you know. My father brought it from [the] *States*," and on and on like this. Big deal, right? Well, these middle and lower families, they try their level best to buy *good* clothes. They want to look very nice, to have a good personality, and all this.

For this teacher, what distinguishes upper-class students from the bulk of middle-class students is a certain (perhaps cultivated) indifference, a kind of lackadaisical disdain for appearances. These students "*know* the fashion"—they have nothing to prove—and their families' financial security allows them to "just throw something on." On the other hand, the rest of the students try hard to look good. The *in*security of middle-classness breeds a kind of focused earnestness about dress and the need to boast about new acquisitions. For them, proper clothing is a "big deal" and constitutes an important part of their claims to membership in the urban middle class.

Some who practiced fashion celebrated the role it played in their lives, as did this young married woman:

Fashion is a necessary thing. It's a must! One shouldn't just sit and do nothing with fashion. You should be active! I mean, fashion isn't only makeup. Fashion is needed to complement your natural strengths. And besides, even little things have now become fashion, wouldn't you say?

Now that just about every thing has caught the fashion bug—has become the object of fashioning—fashion has become a necessity. She chose to actively appropriate fashion and use it to "complement" her "natural strengths."

Others claimants to middle-classness welcomed the fashioning of life with less enthusiasm. For most people the necessity of fashion was a new fact of life: a new, and often unwelcome, reality that could not be avoided. One young woman compared modern fashion with traditional ornamentation.

It is like a new kind of ornament [*gahanā*] these days—for the girls. They say that it is a must these days. If you wear worn clothing, people will call you crazy! People say that fashion introduces the person, says who the person is. Being well dressed is a sign of being civilized [*sabhya*]. I think that's why people want to do fashion.

Although adornment has probably always functioned to say "who the person is," now people scorn the new commercial, and "civilizing," discipline of ever-changing fashion only at the risk of being called "crazy."

Other women spoke of modern fashions much less favorably as compared with styles from the past. One young married woman complained that complying with the dictates of fashion made her feel like a prostitute.

According to our religion [*dharmako anusār*], it's written that women shouldn't be prostitutes, dancers, and all this. But just for society I have to wear makeup: lip stick, eye makeup, fancy clothes, . . . or else they'll all say, "Eh! What a hillbilly [*pākhe*] she is! She doesn't even know how to properly use the things she has!" So for society's sake I have to look *cute* [*ciṭikka pārera*] whenever I go out walking.

Before, women didn't care about this and any decent clothing was acceptable. Then, even patched clothes were all right for going out. But in our time, now we can't even wear something a little worn, because we're afraid of what people will say about us.

Even my husband notices this, so you can be sure others will notice too. He's worrying about his prestige [*ijjat*]; so if I don't do all this stuff, he'll lose his prestige.

Though she feels uncomfortable (even sinful) getting made up and dressed up every time she leaves her house, nevertheless, "for society's sake" and in order to preserve or enhance her husband's social prestige, this woman bears the burden of making herself "look cute" through fashion.[20] Before, "any decent clothing was acceptable," but now she must dress up, for fear of "what people will say."

In the interviews we conducted it was also very common for people to preface their remarks on fashion practice with some acknowledgment that such behavior was frivolous or inappropriate in the Nepali context. But these comments were almost always followed by some qualifier to the effect that, in spite of its frivolity, doing fashion was a social necessity. Speaking of what he thought about fashion, one twenty-year-old college student said:

Let me recite one quotation from Gandhi: "Plain living, high thinking." Well, even though I have this kind of feeling from Gandhiji, still, in these days we have to live according to the times. This [fashion] is our obligation [*kartabya*]. If I don't do it, I won't be able to fit [*namilne*] into society.

"Plain living" may have been good enough for Gandhiji, but now one is "obliged" to "live according to the times."

Another young man, an eighteen-year-old, was extremely ambivalent about fashion, although acknowledging it, as one of his strongest personal interests (*sokh*):

Yes, I really have a lot of *sokh* for fashion. But when I talk about fashion in a place like Nepal, there are problems, because when some-

---

[20] See Ewen and Ewen 1982:105–7 on middle-class women as "vicarious consumers," or a woman's obligation to publicly demonstrate her husband's "ability to pay."

thing, in the name of fashion, goes ahead of everything else, it just disguises other things. I mean, having fashion go ahead of real needs is simply foolish. And we have that condition now. Here, day by day, we are bending more toward Europe.

So I personally like fashion, but behind this *sokh* we have very poor economic conditions. Compared to Europe, our condition is very backward, valueless. On the one hand, I'm really attracted to new fashions, but on the other hand, in my mind, I get an uncomfortable feeling about this fashion because of our economic condition.

Here, if a person goes to another's house, the first thing they look for is what the person is wearing, and they immediately base their respect on this. Only later, after talking, maybe they'll learn about the person's practices and behavior, and maybe they'll base their respect on that. This is what I mean about why we now have to respect, or pay attention to, fashion.

These days an ordinary person—even a peon—if they go somewhere suited and booted, with a tweed coat and tie, if he goes to the [government] minister's office, even *he* will be immediately respected. But if the same person goes without this, he'll be stopped at the door. I mean, this is why so much depends on fashion. Fashion is like this.

There is almost anguish in this young man's account of fashion. He feels viscerally the fundamental contradiction between the reality of Nepal's crushing national poverty and the insistent demands of a local middle-class consumer culture. The consumer excess embodied in fashion practice is as unconscionable as it is unavoidable. As *many* others did in our interviews, he recounts the tale of the peon, "suited and booted," at the minister's office to illustrate why nowadays in Kathmandu no one with aspirations to social standing can afford to ignore fashion's dictates.

The same kind of distress was apparent in the comments of a young woman, an intermediate-level student in her late teens. From films and film magazines the conversation turned to the topic of fashion.

So, what about this fashion? What do you think about it?

Look, Nepal is a poor country, with no raw materials. Everything has to be brought in from the outside, and now everything is becoming more and more dear. So now, in this situation, people are doing all this fashion! But what can we do? In some ways, fashion has become necessary. I mean, *even your own relatives* will ignore you, or pretend they don't know you, if you're not looking fashionable! These days, if you do fashion, even though there's no money and nothing to eat in your house, people will consider you to be a rich person.

Yes, that's right! People just want to show off by doing fashion. Being arrogant, some people go abroad and bring back all this stuff from foreign countries. There are people who import all these things from overseas. I think the whole system should be eliminated.

Again, for this young woman, fashion is inappropriate for Nepal, but socially "necessary" nonetheless. But there is an interesting class dimension as well. Part of the problem with fashion, she complains, is that even a person with "no money and nothing to eat" might be mistaken for "a rich person." Through fashion even the poor can impersonate the rich. On the other hand, she hints that it is the elites—those "arrogant" people who "go abroad" and bring back foreign goods—who are responsible for the "whole system," which seems to threaten stable hierarchies with a new democracy of consumer goods. The fashion system creates an anxiety that leaves those in the social middle with no choice but to follow its demands.

Having indicated earlier in the interview that she herself pursued certain kinds of fashion, the same young woman defended herself when asked why she participated in a system that she personally thought should be "eliminated."

As for me, I don't do *real* fashion. All I do is try to be about equal with my friends, since they are all doing fashion. Really, this is how most everyone is doing fashion.

Here perhaps is the central reason for why many people "do fashion." Unlike a few who might be said to, in this woman's words, "do *real* fashion," most people in Kathmandu, rather grudgingly and with various degrees of anger and anxiety, try to maintain cultural parity with their friends. In this sense, fashion practice—as a communicative mode—is class practice; it is a new performative medium through which people attempt to synchronize their lives with those of others. In this way fashion integrates the new middle class, less around a set of agreed-upon goods or styles than around a shared practice or mode of consumption.

Fashion was also a very important part of how middle-class people in Kathmandu imagined themselves as members of a larger, even global, movement. Through fashion people could imagine themselves as members of a transnational fashioned class, while distinguishing themselves from their lower-class compatriots, urban or rural. For example, one young man, a twenty-year-old college student with relatives in the British army, when giving his opinion about "fashion," noted:

I like it because it's really according to fashion that people are able to move [*calnu*], to get on with their lives. Without it they're looked at with contempt. As in other big cities, we have a lot of concern for fashion here in Kathmandu, I mean, compared with the rest of Nepal.

For this young man it was fashion that simultaneously linked him to the modern world—the "other big cities"—and separated him from "the rest of Nepal." Through fashion he could identify both with other fashionable people in the city and with a transnational urban fashion scene. For him fashion linked the local middle class with a global culture of modernity.

How to "Count" in Kathmandu

If "fashion" is a social necessity for the Kathmandu middle class, what is the fate of the unfashioned in the city? One of the more telling epithets that I heard in Kathmandu was *tyo mānche gandaina*. Directed at a porter, construction worker, hill villager, or sidewalk hawker, the phrase means literally, "That person doesn't count" and has connotations very similar to the English expression. When a person "doesn't count," s/he is out of the game, beyond the purview of the rules and expectations that apply to those who "do count." In Kathmandu the phrase designated someone so peripheral and plebeian that they did not have to be dealt with in a serious manner. These people "didn't count" because they had not (or could not) enter their stakes in the local game of middle-class status negotiation. Unlike those who *did* count, they were nonentities in the urban "prestige" (ijjat) economy.

In the eyes of the middle class, many of Kathmandu's residents fall into the category of those who "don't count." Typically these are people from outside of Kathmandu who have come to the city to find work or pursue education. They rent rooms or squat on public lands, while trying to subsist at the bottom of the city's meager wage economy. Others who "don't count" may belong to one of the extremely low-caste groups that have lived on the city's periphery (both socially and geographically) for centuries. Leather workers, butchers, sweepers, and others of "low" occupational-caste origins still, as a rule, encounter enormous barriers to social advancement.

When it comes to determining who counts and who does not, fashion is the name of the game. In the display and negotiation of status and prestige, fashion—and the consumer lifestyle generally—is the most alluring and ubiquitous contest in the city. At the most basic level, "doing fashion" serves as a kind of gatekeeping device for the middle class. Without a certain disposable income, many in Kathmandu are unable to stake a claim to middle-class membership, because they are unable to display a fashioned self.

Perhaps not surprisingly, members of these lower or socially peripheral groups looked at fashion with contempt and/or longing. For example,
one young man, a poor (though upper-caste) twenty-year-old student
from a rural hill village, did not mince words when commenting on the
fashion trends among his fellow students:

> I really hate the fashion situation here in Kathmandu. Yes, I know,
> I'm from the village, but that's my opinion. I guess every person has
> their own ideas.

For others fashion is, more or less, a nonissue. In one interview an unmarried twenty-five-year-old woman described how she spends her money.
Originally from an extremely poor hill district north of Kathmandu, she
came to the city looking for work. In 1991 she worked as a cleaning
woman in a one-star tourist hotel and lived with an aunt in a poor, low-
caste neighborhood. Her monthly salary was less than 25 USD. When
asked what her money goes for, she replied:

> I have to eat, ride the bus, and buy clothes. With that the money just
> disappears. But I like different fruits a lot, and sometimes I buy some
> momos [Tibetan dumplings] in a restaurant.

> *What kind of clothes do you buy?*

> I usually just wear this Punjabi style *kurtā-suruwāl*, just the ordinary
> one. Of course, I like to look in the catalogue, but I like to wear the
> simple ones.

> *What about decoration* [siṅārne] *or makeup?*

> I don't put anything on my face. Well, I *do* have one lipstick that I
> sometimes use. I paid eight rupees for it. And I've never had anything
> done to my hair.

For this woman "the money just disappears," and what little discretionary income she has typically goes for special foods. She likes to look at
fashions in the tailor's catalogues but prefers the "ordinary" and "simple"
styles. As for the single cosmetic item she owns, she knows exactly what
she paid for it and rarely uses it.

Most poorer men and women are aware of fashion but recognize
clearly what excludes them from it. For example, one eighteen-year-old
woman from the ritually low Newar barber caste, spoke of the connection
between fashion and money. After her mother died, her father had remar-
ried and left the city, leaving her and several siblings dependent on aging
grandparents. She dropped out of school and in 1991 divided her time
between housekeeping and garment piecework from which she earned
seven or eight hundred rupees (about 18 USD) per month. Having talked

about how she enjoys films and film magazines, she was asked what she thought about "fashion."

> Actually, fashion doesn't make any difference to me. I just wear what I have. To do fashion, I would need more money. I don't have that kind of money. When I need a new outfit, I spend maybe two or three hundred rupees.

> *Why do people think fashion is so important?*

> Maybe to make themselves look beautiful: maybe that's why they stress this.

> *Do you have any desire to do fashion?*

> Sure, I have the desire to do it, but I have to think of my situation. If I had piles of money, of course I'd spend it on fashion, on clothes.

For this young woman fashion was simply irrelevant. She was fully aware of its presence around her and wished to take part in it, but recognized that for someone in her "situation" fashion just "doesn't make any difference." Like the previous woman, she is mainly focused on basic survival.

While the lives of most young women from poorer families revolve around the home (whether by custom or necessity), young men from the lower class are much more likely to spend their time outside: working, looking for work, or just hanging out. For them the pressures to conform to group standards, especially in terms of dress, seem to be greater than for poor women. One such young man was a twenty-four-year-old from a Newar farming family on the outskirts of the valley. A former heroin addict and street hustler in Kathmandu's tourist district, his parents had married him off in hopes that new responsibilities would bring him down to earth. Now the proprietor of a tiny vegetable shop, he had given up heroin for hard alcohol, lived in a rented room in Kathmandu, and occasionally sent money back to his wife and child, who still lived in the outlying village from which he had come. Part of his problem was regularly seeing his old friends on the streets, a subject that came up when he was asked what he thought of fashions in Kathmandu.

> Yeah, sure I'm interested in all that [fashion stuff]. I like to be at the same standard [level] as my friends, like with clothes and all that. Like, if you're wearing something—pants, coat, or whatever—then I also want to wear it. But it should be within my capacity. If it's not, how can I do it? If I have money, sure I'll wear it.

> *So how do you do fashion?*

> Hah! I live in a rented room. How am I supposed to do fashion?!

6. Shoppers and vendors in the heart of old Kathmandu (Asan Tol).

In many ways this man's last comments say a great deal about who "counts" and who doesn't in Kathmandu. The divide between those who pay rent and those who do not often closely approximates the line between the middle class and those below, who "don't count" in the game of fashion and prestige. Few people have the financial resources to both pay rent and buy fashions.

When talking about fashion practice as delineating some "line" between classes, we must remember that fashion—as a means of embodying class—is more than clothing, shoes, makeup, and hairstyles. As Gita (chapter 4) observed, "all parts of the body" are subject to fashion. Or, in the words of another woman quoted above, "now everything has become a fashion"; all dimensions of life are capable of being fashioned. Being fashionable is about more than simply *what* you have; it is also about *how* you use it, how you carry it off. Demeanor, comportment, and manners are also clear indicators of whether or not an individual "counts."

This lesson was reinforced for me one afternoon while sitting on the steps of a temple overlooking a crowded street in the heart of old Kathmandu. From this vantage point, a Nepali friend and I were scrutinizing passersby, he trying to educate me in a few of the more elementary rules of distinguishing social types by clothing and comportment. Having been informed that for men the "safari suit" was a very "*ijjat rāckne*" (prestigious or prestige-ascribing) outfit, I pointed to a man in a safari suit walking down the street and asked if he would be considered a "prestigious" (*ijjatdāri*) person. At this my friend rolled his eyes. No: because of the way this man walked (shoulders forward, slightly hunched over) and the *ṭopi* (Nepali cap) on his head, he was obviously someone of recent rural extraction. As the man came nearer, we realized that he wore rubber sandals on his feet—a dead giveaway of someone living in poverty. Footwear, my friend explained, is one of the clearest indicators of a person's *gharko sthiti*, his home or family condition. Anyone leaving his home without proper shoes and socks probably did not care about, nor deserve any, ijjat. As for safari suits, it was not just the clothing but the total effect that counted. With the right shoes, comportment, hairstyle, and accessories, such as a briefcase or, better yet, a motorcycle, a safari suit could be *very "ijjat dine"* (prestige-giving).

By the end of the afternoon I realized that a Kathmandu native could recognize the stiff-legged shuffle of an Indian (or Tarai Nepali) or the bent-knee strut of a person from the hills, from a distance of a hundred meters. The way a woman moved her arms while walking or a man carried packages on the street might indicate either city or rural origins. One's speech—volume, vocabulary, accent—and hand gestures gave hints about one's education, caste, regional origins, and general degree of urbanity. Finally, the cut, fit, and fabric of one's clothes, not to mention how up-to-date the styles were, were also taken into account almost instantaneously by my Nepali acquaintances. As one of the young men quoted above lamented, in Kathmandu "the first thing they look for is what the person is wearing, and they immediately base their respect on this." Comportment and demeanor were equally important for determining middle-class status. Indeed, these embodied features of class practice—"the imperceptible cues of body *hexis*," in Bourdieu's terms (1977:82)—make social barriers difficult to transcend, even though fashion seems to offer prestige for cash.

Perhaps, then, it is not surprising that "finishing schools" have begun to sprout up around the valley, offering students (mostly women between the ages of fifteen and thirty) lessons in walking, talking, and etiquette, in addition to beauty advice (clothing and makeup). One school offers to "develop social graces, etiquette and personality, dancing and exercising prowess and also improve [students'] communicational abilities." "No more embarrassment, no more holding back, the price is rupees 5,000.[21] Worth it, if you want a new YOU!" In short, if you "want to make yourself more presentable . . . the Finishing School is your choice."[22]

[21] A sum equal to roughly half of Nepal's average annual per capita income.
[22] Quotations taken from an "institutional profile" of Kathmandu's New Era Finishing School published in *Teens* (Kathmandu) 1(7) (December 1991):28–29.

7. Street children and middle-class pedestrians eye each other on a Kathmandu sidewalk.

While some are willing to commoditize middle-class knowledge by selling fashioned selves in the market, others bitterly resent these commercial inroads. Selling embodied social graces is perhaps most threatening to those people in Kathmandu's middle class who lack significant social and economic capital beyond their own middle-class bodies. For most, though, pursuing and presenting a fashioned self is an inescapable fact of modern life, a new channel in which people play out what is surely an age-old desire to "be about equal with [one's] friends."

CONCLUSION: THE MIDDLE CLASS, FASHION, AND THE PUBLIC SPHERE

In Kathmandu, as in other late-twentieth-century modern places, fashion is a distinctly public phenomenon. Fashion practice aids the middle class in its efforts to stake out its own cultural territory, a consumer space of commodified objects, services, and information that largely corresponds to new forms of public space. Fashion clothes the public persona while in public spaces: on the streets, in shops and restaurants, in schools and on campuses. People in Kathmandu's middle class constantly speak of fashion as something for *outside* the house (*ghar bāhira*), a space that the unfashioned body enters at the risk of being counted among those that "don't count." In this new public space, one finds both public goods (commodities that all are "free" to consume) and public bodies: bodies produced, or fashioned, through consumption for public display. By transforming public space into a commoditized zone, and then claiming legitimate (moral, modern, honorable, patriotic) consumer practice for itself, the middle class claims public space as its own legitimate class domain.

Kathmandu's "New Road" (Nayā Saṭak) is a new public space par excellence. Laid out along a line of destruction, where the city was literally rent apart by the great earthquake of 1934 (B.J. Rana 1935), New Road is the only wide, multilane thoroughfare in old Kathmandu. Lined with four-or five-storied buildings housing mostly upscale retail shops, New Road is a highly visual and visible modern canyon (sun-filled by day, neon-illuminated by night) cutting through the bedrock of old Kathmandu that lies behind New Road's fashionable commercial facade, a large area of dimly lit, narrow alleyways, tiny, dark shops, and multistory homes enclosing hidden courtyards.

From the outset, New Road was designed to be the city's modern commercial center. New Road hosted the city's first public cinema hall (now demolished), some of its first hotels and restaurants, and its first indoor shopping mall. New Road, with a few adjoining streets, still constitutes Kathmandu's major commercial district, housing most of the city's businesses that specialize in consumer electronics, prerecorded video- and audiocassettes, imported clothing and shoes, upscale custom tailoring, camera equipment and photo developing, and a host of other modern consumer goods and services. The sidewalks are crowded with well-dressed Nepali shoppers, Indian tourists in the city for shopping excursions, beggars, and hawkers. Poor Nepalis in from the hills or the Tarai come to New Road to ogle the tall buildings, colorful lights, and busy traffic, or to cluster around shop windows displaying electronic goods or photo-developing machines, set up so as to provide a public spectacle. New Road is a public space designed for the display and consumption of modern commodities.

While New Road is a new kind of public space, other public spaces have been a feature of Kathmandu's urban landscape for millennia. Neighborhoods are typically centered around public squares that feature market spaces, shops, and public buildings such as temples and shrines. Veranda-like public rest houses called *pāṭis*—constructed in generations past as pious acts of public charity and now mostly in advanced states of disrepair—abound throughout the city. These old public spaces and buildings frequently serve as venues for the religious processions, festivals, and public rituals that dot the annual calendar. These spaces were, and still are, also used communally for drying grain, washing clothes, bathing, playing, chatting, and engaging in various types of small-scale local craft production, such as producing and drying ceramic wares.

To the extent that these old venues still exist in Kathmandu, there remains a sense of public space as communal space. These communal spaces are largely *productive* spaces: spaces for the production of day-to-day life (at public water taps, vegetable markets, rest houses, and temples) and, in a sense, spaces for the production of community, through everything from gossip to formal ritual. This is the kind of public space to which people in Kathmandu refer when they talk about how formerly one could go about publicly wearing just about anything.

By contrast, the new public spaces are largely spaces of and for *consumption*: like New Road, they are spaces for consumption of consumer displays and display of consumer goods. Here one's body becomes a public body, open to the scrutiny of passersby, who plot its position on the fashion axes of suitability and moderation. As one recently married woman put it:

> Before we decide on what clothes to wear, we have to look at the neighborhood. I mean, it depends on the place I am. You have to look to see what people are wearing. Around here everyone is so competitive [*ek-se-ek*] that you wouldn't even know anymore that most of us are daughters-in-law![23] So it's according to the place.

The new public spaces dictate what kind of clothing one wears, or at least *should* wear; those who fail to conform "don't count." Similarly, high school and college students complain about classmates who now come to campus "dressed as if they were going to a party or something." Whether in offices, schools, hotels, restaurants, or shopping arcades, the new public spaces are commercial, or commercialized, spaces for the consumption or display of commodities.

Indeed, the new public spaces are the spaces of the new middle class: the expansion of one parallels that of the other. The new public spaces are spaces of, by, and for the new middle class. To the extent that the middle class is removed from productive processes, it adopts consumption as its mode of identity production. For the middle class, the new public spaces are spaces for the display and negotiation of claims to middle-class membership, and the consumption of "fashioned" commodities is a key element of this practice. In a sense, "fashioning" or "doing fashion" *is* the productive work of the middle class. In "doing fashion," the middle class

---

[23] Previously, a young, recently married woman would have been expected (or required) to wear very simple, inconspicuous clothing, befitting her low status within her husband's extended family.

produces itself and its cultural existence from the raw materials of consumer goods.

Earlier modes of adornment practice in Kathmandu signaled linkages between individuals in the local social realm; adornment practice oriented individuals and groups within a local public. Yet significantly, even though contemporary fashion is a local practice—part of a local project of class formation—its resources, whether material or imagined, are often not local products. Thus, while the class-building project and its meaning are local, its orientation is translocal. Indeed, Kathmandu's middle class often produces its own local consumer public in terms of a translocal, usually mass-mediated consumer culture. Compared with an earlier form of largely productive and locally referencing public culture and public space, Kathmandu's new middle-class publicness is a more universal, and indeed *universalizing*, public domain. Its significant social "others" are no longer only others of local difference (as in a local ethnic/caste hierarchy) but others of imagined universal sameness (within a now global commodity realm and consumer class). Within Kathmandu's middle class, fashion consciousness and practice are not simply parts of an identity of local differentiation but also gestures or signs of global identification.

Thus, Kathmandu's middle-class public is local even as it draws on translocal resources to ideologically and materially construct itself. But if commodity consumption links class production in Nepal to larger transnational forces, it does so less via *transferred meanings* than shared *cultural practice*. From a transnational perspective, fashion practice in Kathmandu is not about "foreign influence" as much as it is the expression of a global cultural logic that harnesses goods to the interests of an emerging local middle class. In this light fashion is less about "westernization" than about class production. In the culture of fashion in Kathmandu, the links with structures of transnational capital are less at the level of shared meanings and more at the level of shared practices through which a new local middle class imagines itself.

PART THREE

MEDIA CONSUMPTION IN KATHMANDU

6

THE SOCIAL PRACTICE OF CINEMA
AND VIDEO VIEWING IN KATHMANDU

> Most people who write about the media's power to present notions of
> society emphasize that it takes place through the telling of stories in
> one form or another. . . . The power of stories is not that all people in-
> terpret media images in the same way, for they often do not. Rather,
> the tales direct attention toward certain concerns and away from oth-
> ers. Stories tell audiences what civilization out there is like, how they
> fit in, what others think of people like them, and what people "like
> themselves" think of others.
>
> —JOSEPH TUROW, *Breaking Up America*

A study of popular music conducted in Kathmandu in the mid-1970s
concluded that "Nepal is still largely a pre–mass media society in which
people perform to entertain themselves" (Anderson and Mitchell
1978:256). Yet only fifteen years later, by the early 1990s, Kathmandu
had unmistakably entered the mass-media age. With the widespread availability of audiocassette players, a booming local cassette recording industry, and direct links to the major pirate cassette mills of Singapore and
Bangkok, by the early 1990s the valley was permeated with commercially
recorded music ranging from Hindi film songs, Nepali pop, and traditional Newar folk music to Elvis, Stan Getz, Beastie Boys, and King Sunny
Adé. Along with this flood of commercial music, film hoardings touting
the latest Hindi and Nepali cinematic offerings cluttered the city's skyline,
and hundreds of videocassette rental shops provided a steady stream of
mass-mediated entertainment from around the world for Kathmandu's
middle-class homes. In the 1990s many people in Kathmandu increasingly
interpreted their lives, locations, and systems of value through the ever
expanding frames of reference offered them in television and print media,
cinema, international music, and the new realm of commodities from
around the world.

This chapter outlines the history and sociology of mass-media consumption in Kathmandu. Focusing on electronic visual mass media—commercial cinema and video—it explores the changing class and gender dynamics of electronic-media consumption in the city: Who watches what? In what settings? Why? How have these patterns developed over time?

As in many peripheral (in geographic and/or economic terms) areas of the globe, in Kathmandu private entrepreneurs used relatively low-capital video technology to bring a global array of cinematic (as opposed to televisual) media products to urban markets before the Nepali state was able to establish television broadcasting.[1] Thus, the fact that this book pays less attention to television than to cinema or video is due in part to television's relatively recent arrival on the Kathmandu scene.[2] But just as important is the fact that at the time when most of the research for this book was conducted (1988–91), video viewing still made up a larger part of people's media diet than TV viewing.[3] With the arrival of pan-Asian satellite television in late 1991 (Melkote et al 1998), that equation began to change, and the steep drop in the number of video rental shops in Kathmandu between 1991 and 1996 suggests that urban Nepali consumers no longer treat their television sets—once referred to as "screens"—merely as appendages of their VCRs. Though Nepal has a slowly growing media industry (producing films and television programming), the majority of mass-media products consumed in Nepal are foreign, mostly from India but also from East Asia, Europe, and North America. This chapter provides some sense of the experience of cinema and video viewing in a society where video predates television, where cinematic modes of narrative development and representation are more popular than the conventions typically associated with television, where state control of mass media is relatively low, and where most of the media products consumed are foreign. Even while participating in some of the

---

[1] As a place where video predates television, Kathmandu provides an important contrastive case to Conrad Kottak's study of television viewership in Brazil (1990). Kottak proposes five stages of viewership, from the introduction of television (stage one), to the eventual arrival of VCR technology (stage five). My aim is not to dispute Kottak's stages but simply to point out that in Kathmandu stage five predates stage one! The differences between Brazil and Nepal underline the importance of rooting media studies in local historical and ethnographic contexts.

[2] Whereas the first commercial cinema hall opened in the early 1950s, and video viewing was widespread by the late 1970s, it was only in December 1985 that Nepal Television (NTV) began regular broadcasting. For a more detailed discussion of television broadcasting in Nepal, see chapter 7.

[3] This is an impression shared by other media researchers: see, for example, Baral 1990:67–68.

archetypically *modern* technologies and transnational commercial processes of the twentieth century, this unique mix suggests that Nepal's
media culture cannot be easily subsumed under some uniform "master
narrative" of modernity.

Cinema in Kathmandu

In an article published in *National Geographic* in 1935, Penelope Chetwode paints a romantic picture of Kathmandu as the capital of a "sequestered kingdom" characterized by a "curious mixture of new and old."
Alongside ancient, exotic, and fantastically ornamented temples and palaces, one finds "severely practical barracks, schools, colleges, hospitals,
and prisons built in the 'European style,' " as well as "immense 'modern'
palaces" designed by European architects. Speaking of the then-reigning
Rana autocrat Juddha Shamsher, Chetwode enthuses: "The Prime Minister is modern and enlightened in his outlook and anxious to introduce
any new invention which may benefit his country, but prohibits importa-
tion of certain Western creations. Foremost among these is the cinema.
He believes that to show vivid scenes of intimate occidental life has a
demoralizing effect on the spectators" (1935:328). Indeed, Juddha
Shamsher, like his brother Chandra Shamsher before him (see Landon
1928ii:2), was both "anxious" to introduce Western disciplinary technologies ("barracks, schools, colleges, hospitals, and prisons") and "anxious" about maintaining tight control over foreign representations, and
representations of foreigners.[4] Recognizing that their own authority depended on the maintenance of British power in India, the Rana elite kept
tight control over all information about, and representations of, the world
beyond the Kathmandu valley. Their efforts ranged from all but prohib-
iting the movement of Nepalis or foreigners in and out of the valley to
banning or tightly controlling books and newspapers. The particular "demoralizing effect" that Juddha Shamsher feared most from cinema was
the emergence of an awareness of the outside world no longer dictated,
or "mediated," by the Nepali elite.

Juddha Shamsher almost certainly had film-viewing experiences, both
in Kathmandu and while traveling abroad, long before he constructed
Nepal's first cinema hall around 1943 (Joshi 2045 v.s.:35).[5] But Juddha's

---

[4] For a more detailed discussion of this anxiety—which I call "selective exclusion"—see
Liechty 1997.

[5] In fact, Rana elites had probably been viewing cinema in Kathmandu from as early as
the turn of the twentieth century. P. S. Rana (1978:109) notes that during the celebrations
marking Dev Shamsher's ascension to the position of prime minister in 1901, public film

cinema, built on the grounds of his palace, was a private hall, reserved for the viewing pleasures of the Rana and royal elites alone. By the time the first public cinema was opened in Kathmandu during the final chaotic years of the regime, the Ranas were already going the way of the British in India. Around 1949 the Janasevā ("Public Service") cinema opened on a prime spot in Kathmandu's New Road commercial district (Baniya 2045 v.s.:51). The Rana government kept tight control over the Janasevā's public cinematic offerings, apparently favoring conservative, pious Hindi religious films ("theologicals") over more racy fare. The Janasevā's first publicly shown film was entitled *Rām Vivāha*, or "Ram's Wedding." Prayag Raj Joshi writes that "In the Janasevā hall, when "Ram's Wedding" was being shown, the audience thought that Lord Ram himself had actually come to the hall. Even people with balcony tickets crowded to the front of the hall, hoping to get the direct blessing [*darśan*] of Lord Ram" (2045 v.s.:37). In an interview, Joshi recalled how cinemagoers threw rice, coins, and flowers at the screen, as they would have at a temple image of Ram.

For decades prior to the opening of the Janasevā hall, Kathmandu residents had heard tales of the cinema from people returning from business trips or pilgrimages to India, and were eager to experience these forbidden cinematic wonders themselves. For young and old, cinema became one of India's primary attractions. One elderly Nepali gentleman from a long-established Newar trading family recalled how, as a boy (in the 1930s), he would eagerly await the return of trading parties from India. Three or four times a year family members would return from the south and "The first thing they would talk about was the films they had seen in India." He and his cousins were enthralled by the stories of how, in India, one could see horses running, people fighting, vehicles driving—all "on a piece of cloth." "I was amazed! How could all these things be happening on a piece of cloth?!"

But cinema viewing was only one of a host of social, political, and economic liberties denied to citizens by the Nepali government. Thus, with the end of the Rana regime in 1951, people in Kathmandu reacted to a century of repression and isolation by establishing a democratic polity and flinging open the borders to more or less unregulated traffic of people and goods. A number of private cinema halls sprang up and by the mid-1970s the valley boasted five film venues (Anderson and Mitchell 1978:250), screening mostly Hindi films and the occasional Nepali or English production.

---

exhibitions were held on Kathmandu's Thundi Khel parade ground. Surely Dev's decision to show films to the masses only contributed to his reputation as a dangerous liberal. Dev Shamsher was deposed by his brother Chandra after only three months in office.

In the memories of many city residents the 1970s were something of a "golden era" for cinemagoing in Kathmandu. Young adults from middle- and upper-middle-class families recalled how, as children, going to the cinema was a major social event. One Newar businessman described how the whole family—including cousins, aunts, and uncles—would attend the cinema together on Saturdays. Everything was organized; some people were sent to buy tickets, while others prepared food. On special occasions, such as when his father wrapped up a particularly profitable business venture, his family would celebrate midweek by going to see a movie. Another young man, the son of a high-ranking civil servant, recalled that "when I was a kid" in the mid-1970s, going to the cinema "was like going to a party!"

> If you were going to a film, it was like going to the theater! People got all dressed up, and they would go and have a show. Even my family, my mother dressed up, and my father, and we'd get in a car and go see a film.

Others too described how in earlier days it was common to see cinema courtyards crowded with the cars of wealthy moviegoers. The most common film fare in the 1960s and 1970s was Hindi cinema, but many Kathmandu residents recall that during these years, more so than in the 1990s, English-language films were also occasionally featured in local halls.

In the 1960s and 1970s Kathmandu's cinema halls hosted the full gamut of local society, from rickshaw pullers to top government officials. The same young man who described moviegoing as being "like a party" noted how it brought together high and low:

> At that time everybody in the city used to go to the movie theater at the same time, from the top to the bottom of the society. But now it's very uncommon for people of different economic backgrounds to come together like that.

> *But even then, people weren't actually all sitting together, were they?*

> No, but they were all consuming the same thing, the same product, and there were indirect relations. I mean, they felt each other's presence. And they also—like, how were people sitting down below *reacting* to films? Normally—I don't know how they do it now—but from the balcony there was absolutely no reaction. But from the lower section there was whistling and clapping when the hero comes and fights. There was just a lot of reaction, but none from the balcony.

During these decades Kathmandu's cinema halls were like microcosms of the local class universe. Upper and lower classes occupied high and low spaces in the theater, where, even while separated, "they felt each other's presence." In this setting, the price of one's ticket was inversely proportional to the bodily affect that one displayed. While those below whistled and clapped, those above displayed their class distinction in the classic mode of self-control (cf. Elias 1978 [1935]). Yet, as this man pointed out, even while upholding class difference, the cinema hall at this time was a place where all of local society shared a common consumer space and a common consumer object. All of this changed dramatically with the arrival of video technology in the late 1970s and the video boom of the early 1980s.

THE VIDEO BOOM

In the late 1970s there was a massive surge in video consumption in Kathmandu. In 1978 government trade regulations shifted, allowing people to import (and own) video technology for the first time.[6] One acquaintance of mine reported the rumor that members of the royal family were the first to acquire import privileges and made huge profits during the first year. Whatever the case, Todd Lewis, who personally "observed the coming of the video boom to Kathmandu," reports that almost overnight 150 VCRs hit the local market. "Entrepreneurs opened up video salons that were packed night and day for almost ten months" (1984:580). In the rush to stake claims in this entertainment gold mine, those with cash or convertible resources invested up to one hundred thousand rupees in video equipment. During the first few months of the video boom, by packing fifty or more people in a room, at up to fifteen rupees per head, for up to seven or eight shows a day, Kathmandu's video entrepreneurs could earn thirty thousand rupees or more (several times the average annual income) in a single week.

The video salons or "parlors" were little more than converted storerooms and living spaces in private homes. The original parlors were famed for being cramped, dark, smelly, hot, unventilated rooms, where people sat on straw mats. Electric fans, if present, were more likely to be keeping the VCR, rather than patrons, from burning up! With time some entrepreneurs tried to capture a more upscale clientele by offering more comfortable seating, snacks, and limited admission, for a price.

With dozens and dozens of video parlors, each offering a different film, Kathmandu residents could suddenly choose from an enormous selection of media products. No longer limited to the slow-to-change offerings of the cinema halls, film fans could select from dozens of Hindi films

---

[6] I have been unable to find the official documentation pertaining to this shift in import regulations.

and, for the first time, a wide variety of English-language and East Asian films. Clint Eastwood, John Travolta, and Bruce Lee took their places alongside Hindi film stars in the estimation of Kathmandu youth. Those who were schoolboys at the time remember cutting class to watch video films. Stories abound of the embarrassment that ensued when the lights went up at the end of a video session to reveal teachers, parents, neighbors, and relatives who had also been watching the same (sometimes questionable) film!

Young people in particular had an almost unlimited appetite for films. One young man (the son of a prosperous merchant) who grew up in the heart of the old city, where most of the parlors were located, remembered that

> At the beginning, when [video] first came, I used to watch every day. At that time you could watch three films for twenty-five rupees, all night long. Sometimes I'd watch all day, sometimes all night. Anyway, I used to watch a lot!

Businessmen and office workers also recall how they would take three-hour "lunch breaks" to watch films in the middle of the day. Many people pointed out to me that in Kathmandu video technology made film viewing a truly mass phenomenon. Cinema halls had long been popular, but video parlors were located in private homes, so for the first time everyone, from infant to grandmother, was watching an international smorgasbord of commercial cinema.

From the outset, one popular dish in this cinematic banquet was the "blue," or pornographic, film (Liechty 1994:439ff., 2001). But ultimately it was a political, rather than a moral, threat that spurred the government to regain some of the control over media consumption that it had lost with the coming of video. The Hindi film *Krānti* ("Revolution") hit the Kathmandu video scene soon after its cinematic release in 1981 (cf. Rajadhyaksha and Willemen 1999:133). This big-budget allegorical depiction of the Indian struggle for independence from Great Britian caught the attention of the Nepali government, who saw it as a threat to the country's one-party "Panchayat Democracy." Since the then-banned Nepali Congress Party had close ties to the Indian nationalist movement, leaders of Nepal's "Panchayat Raj" banned the exhibition of *Krānti*. In the short run, the ban did little more than to increase the demand for the film. People with *Krānti* cassettes charged up to twenty-five hundred rupees for three hours and accompanied their cassettes to secret screenings to make sure that no copies were made. But eventually the *Krānti* incident led to a government crackdown on public video showing. A series of nebulous regulations, taxes, and licensing procedures were established, so that running a video parlor soon became far more complicated and far less profitable. For a few years small, private video halls flourished at Kathmandu's exhibition grounds (Brikhuti Mandap), where their offerings could be controlled by the government. These too eventually succumbed to a government regulation that only Nepali films could be shown on the premises.

Video parlors continued to operate more or less clandestinely into the mid-1980s (and a few, mostly specializing in pornography, continued into the 1990s), but what government regulation had weakened, lessening of demand has nearly eliminated. Through the 1980s more and more middle-class families acquired VCRs, allowing them to screen their own choice of films with far more comfort and convenience. Indeed, as more and more VCRs entered private homes for private use, the next video-related "boom" (an echo of the first) swept the valley. Through the mid- and late 1980s videocassette rental shops opened up, their numbers increasing exponentially. At first confined mostly to the New Road commercial district, shops began appearing to the north, in the Chetrapati and Thamel areas, before showing up in almost every residential area across the Kathmandu valley. By the early 1990s supply seemed to have met (or exceeded) demand, and some of the once-thriving cassette rental shops either folded up or were forced to diversify.

HALL VS. HOME: CLASS DISTINCTION AND TECHNOLOGY

As a result of Kathmandu's "video boom" and the subsequent arrival of VCRs into middle-class homes, by the early 1990s most middle-class adults had not set foot in a movie hall for close to a decade. Once regular patrons of cinema halls featuring Hindi films, most businessmen, civil servants, professionals, and their families now watched the same Hindi films (plus a variety of others) at home. Unlike the large numbers of seasonal and permanent laborers who make up the urban working poor, members of the urban middle class are far more likely to have access to a VCR, either their own or that of a relative or neighbor. In most middle-class neighborhoods VCRs are so common that access is not a problem. "Before, I used to go to the cinema a lot. But now everyone has a deck, so why go?" asked a married man in his mid-thirties. Viewing the same trend from another perspective, one Nepali film producer lamented, "Classy people don't go to the [movie] theater anymore."

Except to view Nepali feature films (which are not available on video-cassette), most middle-class city residents have indeed almost no reason to go to a commercial cinema hall. Practically all Hindi films, as well as films from outside the subcontinent, are readily available in local video shops, often on (or even before) their official release date. Kathmandu is an important node in the South Asian distribution network for pirated videocassettes; couriers vie with each other to get prints of the latest Bombay films onto the international market. Kathmandu's larger cassette merchants have banks of VCRs capable of high-speed dubbing ready to crank out copies of Hindi films so that hundreds of local fans can enjoy the latest offerings, often on the same day that the film is released in Indian cinemas. Major American films show up in Kathmandu shops long before they are officially released on video and sometimes even before their cinematic release (as in the case of *Batman* in 1989). "Why should I go to the hall?" asked the twenty-four-year-old wife of a local businessman. "All the new ones come to our house too. They're brought from India and, like, if it's released today [in India], we can see it today immediately."

Kathmandu's commercial cinema halls run mostly popular Hindi films. Of the almost one thousand feature films produced in India in an average year (Nandy 1998:1), only the more successful productions reach Kathmandu movie theaters, usually arriving some months after their Indian release. Thus, contrary to the experience of most video film viewers in the West, by the time, a popular film arrives in Kathmandu theaters, most middle-class cinema buffs have already seen it, perhaps many times, on video. One eighteen-year-old girl told us, "A while ago some friends asked me to go see [the very popular Hindi film] *Dil* in the hall, but I'd already seen it three or four times here at home, so I didn't go." Furthermore, by the time a Hindi film arrives in Kathmandu, people are already familiar with the film's songs from listening to Nepali and Indian radio and have probably read about the film in Hindi film magazines available on every street corner. In another peculiarly South Asian twist, a few people mentioned that they will go see a Hindi film in the theater if, after seeing the video many times, they decide they really like the songs and action.[7]

Thus, for middle-class viewers there are at least *some* occasions when they might see a Hindi film at the cinema. Many people who almost never watched Hindi films in theaters admitted that the excitement of the "big screen" experience could not be reproduced at home. Others complained that the video prints available in Kathmandu are sometimes of such poor quality or so cluttered with on-screen advertising that it is difficult to enjoy the film. But even so, most preferred home to hall, as did this twenty-two-year-old Newar woman, married to a factory manager:

> There's a big difference between seeing a film in the hall or on video, big screen or little. But still I prefer watching at home. Once you've gone to the hall, you just have to sit there and watch. But with the video, you can select and choose how you want to watch.

[7] The same is true of film fans in India (see Akela 1991).

Being able to control the viewing experience is one important reason for preferring home to hall.

Yet beyond the common assertions that cinema halls are too stuffy, hot, crowded, noisy, and generally uncomfortable, potential middle-class cinema patrons complain that going to the movies is simply inconvenient. Because the halls have no system of advanced ticket booking, anyone who goes to the cinema has to stand in long lines, only to be jostled by all kinds of "unruly riffraff." Moreover, except on weekends, when halls are truly mobbed, it is difficult to fit a trip to the cinema into a middle-class working schedule. Office workers who might consider catching a six o'clock show know that by the time the film ends at nine there will be few taxis,[8] not to mention buses, available. For those Kathmandu residents whose lives are structured around office or business hours, the inconvenience associated with cinemagoing is more than enough to keep them at home in front of their own VCRs.

The exception to this rule is in the case of Nepali feature films. Time and again women and men said that they, in the words of one twenty-five-year-old Newar woman, "never go to the cinema hall except to see Nepali films." Nepali films are simply unavailable on videocassette; film producers know full well that any video pirating of their work would spell financial disaster in an already limited consumer market. To protect their investments, film producers vigilantly guard their prints against any reproduction, guaranteeing that anyone who wants to see a Nepali-language production *must* catch the film during its sometimes brief run in the commercial halls.

It is not surprising, then, that in the early 1990s Kathmandu's cinema halls often had a distinctly different atmosphere on those occasions when a Nepali feature film replaced the standard Hindi fare. In general, when Nepali films were showing, cinemagoers tended to be better dressed, there were more women in the audience, and the average age of those present was somewhat older. In particular, Nepali films brought out groups of well-dressed married Newar and Brahman-Chetri women, often with children, who would come for one of the late-morning or early-afternoon shows. But these shows also brought out far more of the smartly dressed teenage and young-adult men and women, who would normally not set foot in a commercial theater.

Even though middle-class people in Kathmandu often disparage Nepali-language productions as being "not as good as Hindi films" or, as others see it, "just as bad as Hindi films," these same people will often go out of their way to see a Nepali production. For example, when a well-

---

[8] Most South Asian commercial films are between two and a half and three hours long, with an intermission.

8. Film viewers disperse after midweek showing of the Nepali film *Yo Māyāko Sāgar* [This Ocean of Love] at Kathmandu's Bishwa Jyoti cinema hall.

educated journalist in his late thirties mentioned that the only time he goes to the cinema is to see Nepali films, I asked why.

> Like, if I go see a Nepali movie, well, I'll see it for certain reasons. One could be, well, it's Nepali! I want to know how these films are coming along. And then another reason could be, "Hey, come on, let's go see this for a change." Or it might be that I want to go see how the hero or heroine in my neighborhood has acted!

In other words, Nepali films attract middle-class men and women to the cinema halls for many more reasons than simple entertainment. In a local market dominated for the past fifty years by the Hindi film industry, Nepali audiences are interested in local productions for their novelty appeal, but also have a stake in their "Nepaliness" and want to see how they compare with Indian films.

If most of middle-class Kathmandu only goes to the cinema to see Nepali films, who then makes up the audience for the much more common Hindi films?[9] In the words of the same Nepali film producer who bemoaned the lack of "classy people" in local theaters, since the arrival

---

[9] According to one local film industry insider that I interviewed, cinema halls in Kathmandu screen one Nepali film for every six Hindi films.

of video, "The audience is basically the lower strata, and I notice that now almost no one over thirty goes to the cinema any more." He confirmed my own impression that the large majority of those people who attend Hindi film shows in Kathmandu are lower-class teenage males. Because of over-population and economic deterioration in much of rural Nepal, the Kath-mandu valley—one of very few significant urban centers in the hill re-gion—attracts thousands of people from the hills, the Tarai (Nepal's southern lowlands), and even from India, in search of permanent or sea-sonal employment. These people fill the swelling squatter settlements (Gallagher 1991, Yami and Mikesell 1990) and tenement houses around Kathmandu as they seek work as day laborers, domestics, construction-, garment-, or carpet-industry workers, office peons, and street vendors. Along with a large student population from rural Nepal, this is the group—mostly young, male, and financially strapped—that makes up the bulk of those who attend commercial screenings of Hindi films.

For landless and/or low-caste Nepalis in the hill regions, labor migra-tion has been a necessary domestic strategy for centuries (N. R. Shrestha 1990). Young men leave their villages headed for employment in India and sometimes Kathmandu. For example, one young man that I inter-viewed was from a low occupational-caste group in a rural area to the northwest of Kathmandu. When I met him, Shiva was working as a ven-dor, selling Chinese costume jewelry, hair ornaments, and Tiger Balm from a wicker basket on the crowded sidewalk next to Kathmandu's Rani Pokhari. Then in his mid-twenties, Shiva had first come to Kathmandu as a teenager and worked there for a short time before going on to India, where he lived for five years. He came back to Kathmandu with some savings and, in collaboration with some village friends, got into the busi-ness of buying Chinese goods from Tibetan traders and then selling them direct to the public. Shiva told me that on a good day he can make a profit of up to one hundred rupees. When I asked him if he planned to save money to return to his village, Shiva said no.

How come?

Because in the village, even if you have money, there's nothing to buy that you really want; there's nothing enjoyable to buy. Plus in the village, it's always work, troubles, and misery [*dukha*]. There you can find nothing enjoyable [*ramāilo*] to do.

For Shiva and many others from rural backgrounds living in the city, one of Kathmandu's main attractions—what made it an "enjoyable" place—was the cinema. Having lived in India, Shiva not only understood and spoke Hindi but had become very fond of Hindi films. Two or three times a month, he packed up his goods and took in a Hindi film with a group of friends from the village with whom he shared a rented room. The Hindi film star Govinda was Shiva's favorite actor, "because he can sing, dance, fight, and do everything very well." He especially liked the "action" and "*dandan-dundun*" (rowdy, thrilling, chaotic) type of films. Shiva's experiences are similar to those described in Phanindreshwar Paudel's study (1990) of Nepali menial laborers working in Bombay. Paudel notes that the only "specifically urban characteristic" of these men's lives as city residents was "viewing the cinema" (1990:64). Outside of their family's basic needs, films were the only thing they spent money on. For people like Shiva and the men described by Paudel, marginalized by their places of origin and economic status, cinemagoing is one way of being a part *of* the city and not just *in* it.

Indeed, for the past few decades, one of Kathmandu's primary points of attraction has been the cinema. Stories abound of people being drawn to the city to watch films: stories of astonishment, delight, even terror. One man—a Chetri originally from east Nepal, in his early forties, and now a teacher in Kathmandu—reminisced about his first filmgoing experience:

> The first time I saw a film, I was eight years old. I'd gone to my uncle's house in Kathmandu. It was my first one, and I've remembered it ever since. In fact, I still do. I remember how in this movie there was one scene with a big tiger. I was so frightened that I wanted to get up and run away! But my uncle grabbed me and said, "Don't worry, it will stay on the screen. It's not going to come out." So I stayed, but some others in the hall actually got up and ran out![10]
>
> People coming from this condition, like me, we *heard* about cinema, we *heard* about cars. When we were young, people would come to the village and talk about this and that. From this we had a strong desire to see these things for ourselves. Like bicycles, the first time I saw one, some guy had ridden it home from work [to my uncle's], and there it was. I had heard that bicycles had two wheels and went whizzing along, but when I saw it that night, how wonderful it was! I was amazed at how it could go without falling down.[11]
>
> This kind of curiosity was the same I had for cinema, cars, and all kinds of other things. In the hills we heard lots of things, because there were lots of soldiers who had been in the British Army and they told lots of stories. And others, after the rice is harvested, would go to the plains and come back with goods and stories. From these people we'd get a long, detailed description of every film that they saw.

[10] Nacify (1989:52) records a similar film-going incident in Iran.

[11] In most of Nepal's rural hill regions, the terrain makes any kind of wheeled vehicle useless, even the most "low-tech."

For this reason, we kids, as soon as we got to a town, we'd go straight for the cinema!"

I asked him if he could describe what it is that attracts rural people to the cinema.

In cinema we see things we've never seen before. For example, in our society, where people come from the hills to the city, they see a woman dancing on the screen without many clothes. This you could never see in the village! [I was thinking] "What is this? Where am I? What is happening?" This is what is going through people's heads when they see this stuff. It's like another world. They don't know if they're dreaming or not. So for these reasons also, people like to stay in the city. Like for me, when I saw my first film, I still remember only the really strange or amazing scenes—the rest I've all forgotten!"

For this man, and likely for other arrivals from rural Nepal, the cinema, like the city itself, is like a bizarre dream, "like another world." Along with cars, bicycles, and other marvels, such as electric lights, the cinema is part of what makes the city modern. But unlike these other things, the cinema is also a place to revel in the dreams of modernity, to play at the borders between "dreaming or not."

For many recent arrivals in the city, attending the cinema is almost unavoidable, like a fact of life. For example, when one young man, a twenty-year-old Brahman student from east Nepal, mentioned that he liked Hindi films, I asked how he had gotten interested. He answered in a tone that suggested my question was silly and naive:

Actually, it's mostly just a matter of the environment of Kathmandu. I mean, it's not like someone has to come and force you to go! [Cinemas] are all over the place. Signs are everywhere on the street. So why not go? After the first time, I just kept going by myself.

Another young man, also a twenty-year-old student but from north of Kathmandu, had a similar answer:

Look, it's not a question of who got me into this. It's a fact that in Kathmandu there are so many halls that one is automatically interested in films if one lives here. That's the environment—I got interested by myself.

For these people the cinema is a fundamental part of the urban environment. Halls and hoardings are everywhere you look, and interest is "automatic." No one has to "force you to go."

But the automatic attractions and pleasures of cinemagoing are about more than exploring the frontiers of "another world." For people who frequent Hindi film shows in Kathmandu, there are also pleasures near at hand, the pleasures of the group, of being surrounded by hundreds of others with whom you share an experience. When I asked one young man, a Brahman student from central Nepal in his early twenties, why he enjoyed going to Hindi films he replied:

> There is much enjoyment in doing something like this in a big group. The people watching there with you are part of the attraction. Like, if you're watching a social [*sāmājik*] film, then you are there crying along with *everyone* in the hall. This way of doing is *most* enjoyable! And then when the good part comes, we all clap our hands, or shout at the slow parts.[12]

Another young man echoed these sentiments:

> Once you get inside [the cinema], you are sitting there with hundreds of people, all arm to arm. There is real feeling [*bhāwanā*] in the hall! When there is a funny part, everyone laughs. When sad, everyone cries. There is strong emotion there, not like other places. It is like going to a fair [*melā*]; there is real satisfaction [*santuṣṭi*].

Often, for the rural-born, poor, working-class patrons of Hindi films, the "satisfaction" and "enjoyment" of cinemagoing derives largely from the experience of shared emotion: of laughing, crying, and shouting in the company of hundreds of others who, in that instant, perfectly share your own strong feelings of pathos, fear, joy, and anger. The "real satisfaction" of cinema lies in people affirming one another's understandings and experiences of pleasure.

In a very real sense this is "mass entertainment": the mass-as-entertainment, the pursuit of entertainment in mass settings, or the necessity of the mass in order to be entertained. For many of Kathmandu's cinema hall patrons it is precisely the experience of being en masse that brings pleasure. The cinema brings together those who delight in the experience of oneness with the group, those who celebrate the experience of losing themselves not so much in the mediated images before them as in the social body around them.

Perhaps not surprisingly, many of the experiences that regular cinema attenders crave are precisely what many in Kathmandu's middle class find abhorrent. The crowds, the noise, the group affect that is supremely satisfying to some, are supremely threatening to others. Even ensconced in their higher-priced balcony seating (as they were in earlier decades), the "upper"

---

[12] Nacify's account (1989:41) of cinemagoing in Iran during the 1950s describes a similarly raucous atmosphere of catcalling, running commentary, cheering, booing, etc. See also Thomas (1985:128–30), who describes this atmosphere as the South Asian norm.

classes feel the affront of the "mass audience" below, whose powerful emotional synergy threatens to drag them "down" into the social strata they wish to escape. Significantly, cinematic entertainment for the middle class is not a "mass" experience. Whether watching video films alone or with small groups of family or friends, these people shun the mass emotions of the cinema hall in favor of the more individualistic freedoms and conveniences of home viewing. In a sense the "move" from lower- to middle-class conditions of entertainment is the shift from *inclusion* to *exclusion*: while the Hindi film viewers in the cinema halls seek the inclusive pleasures of oneness, the middle-class video viewers seek the exclusive pleasures of separation, individuation, and freedom—*from* "the masses."[13]

The shift from the cinema audience of the 1960s and 1970s (where different social strata shared a mutual, if somewhat uneasy, viewing experience) to the audience of the 1980s and 1990s (dominated by the lower social strata) was brought about largely by the introduction of a new modern consumer technology, the VCR. Although its effects are perhaps more dramatic than other consumer goods, the VCR is little different from a host of other modern commodities that—through the social practices that revolve around them—serve to isolate and individuate the middle class even while the middle class uses these goods as marks of distinction. In the case of the VCR (and its companion, television), the arrival of this single commodity into the home guarantees a continuous flow of other commodities, both in the form of video films, and eventually, as in Kathmandu, televised commercial images and messages. This consumer strategy at once allows the middle class to distinguish itself from the mass; begins to transform the middle class into a group of "free," individuated, isolated consumers; transforms the middle-class home into a consumer space; and eventually reproduces itself, as young people are socialized in a class ethos in which the work of class production is consumer consumption. In a very real sense commodity consumption is about class production, the production of a class of "free" and individuated consumers.

Film Preference: Gender, Class, Age

Like any other film industry, Hindi productions span the gamut from those aimed at the international film festival circuit to splashy, big-budget extravaganzas, "B-grade" action pictures, and back-room pornography.

---

[13] The middle-class freedoms of consumerism—in which material privilege provides access to the "open market"—are freedoms predicated on the denial of, or limited access to, commodity markets by those without economic means. Thus, in a sense the freedoms *of* consumerism are freedoms *from* the masses.

Not surprisingly, then, most people in Kathmandu had very definite ideas about film categories and film quality. Middle-class viewers in particular divided films into many different genres: "art," "social," "action," "love," and "blue" (not to mention a range of Western and East Asian films).[14] This section explores how stated film preferences correspond to gender and age categories within the middle class.

So far this chapter has implied that people from the lower and middle classes watch essentially the same films, only in different settings, whether hall or home. Yet cinema owners know that a middle-class audience will only be lured into the theater when a real blockbuster arrives, and even among blockbusters it is only those that appeal to middle-class young people (those with time to go to the halls) that might attract "classy" viewers. Much more likely to draw a crowd—even if it is a lower-class crowd—is a certain kind of thrilling, action-packed Hindi film that features excitement, romance, music, and spectacle, all in one cinematic package. Hindi film stars like Govinda, who, in the words of Shiva (the street merchant introduced above), "can sing, dance, fight, and do everything very well," are the heroes that play well to the average cinemagoer in Kathmandu. Thus, middle-class film fans can point to the standard fare in the local halls and complain that the films shown are vulgar and deplorable.

What, then, are middle-class Hindi film fans watching on their VCRs? And who are these viewers? For the most part, middle-class Hindi film viewers are women, both young and middle-aged, who watch video films at home. As I discuss in more detail later in this chapter, middle-class men and boys also watch these films, though they rarely express a preference for them, and when they do, it is with more or less elaborate qualifications.

The entrance of VCRs into middle-class homes in Kathmandu is only one of many factors at work to radically change the nature of women's domestic experience. With increased education levels among women; increased cash flow in middle-class families; easily available, low-cost domestic menial labor; improved transportation, and the arrival of various mediated entertainments (radio, video, television) into the home, young and middle-aged women live lives far removed (in terms of ease and luxury) from those of even their own mothers. While the changing middle-class domestic lifestyle deserves an entire study in and of itself, here I consider only one facet of that experience: the experience of video film viewing at home.

For many women in middle-class homes—where husbands and fathers are at work and children at school during much of the day—video

---

[14] For more technical discussions of genre in South Asian cinema, see Thomas 1985:120, Vasudevan 1989:30, and Chakravarty 1993.

viewing has become a regular feature of their daily routines. If not every day, then several times during the week, one of the family's young men will be commandeered to go to the video shop to pick up a new Hindi film. People listen for word of new arrivals and are willing to pay a premium for a copy of the "latest" Hindi film. While the family may watch a film together in the evening, just as often groups of women watch together during the slow hours of the early afternoon.[15]

One young woman, an eighteen-year-old Chetri who had just acquired her high school diploma and was preparing to attend Kathmandu's all-women college, described the film-viewing patterns around her home. After noting that she watches three or four video films per week, she explained that these days she doesn't even go to the cinema hall to watch Nepali films. "Why bother?" she asked. "I can see and hear the song sequences on the *Gitanjali* program on [Nepal] TV, and if I want to hear the dialogue, I can go buy the cassette."[16] As for seeing Hindi films in the theater, she observed, "There's always a big crowd there—and why go if I can watch them here regularly?" Speaking for herself and the other women in the household, she went on to explain how video viewing fits into the daily routine:

> After eleven, when we're finished with the morning cleanup and other jobs, one of my *didis*[17] will come over and invite me to see a film, so I just go and watch. We just watch them for entertainment, to pass the time. Otherwise, I just take a nap.
>
> So after eating in the morning, we start a video at maybe eleven or twelve, and the time passes quickly. By the time the video is finished, it's already time for tiffin! After having tea, I might listen to some songs on the radio before getting ready for the evening meal.

What is striking about these (and related) comments is how video viewing helps to stem the boredom of day-to-day existence in many urban middle-class homes. Unlike women in rural farming areas, whose chores are never ending, or lower-class women in the city, who either must work outside the home or cannot afford servants, the lives of urban middle-class women can often be ones of more or less housebound monotony.[18]

---

[15] In her study of "audio-visual culture" among South Asian families in London, Marie Gillespie (1989) describes a similar situation in which women (young and old) have a "generally greater engagement with popular Hindi videos" than do boys and men (229).

[16] Film soundtracks available on cassette usually include at least some of the dialogue in addition to songs.

[17] Literally, "older sister"; *didi* is also often used as an honorific for any older female.

[18] This is often the case in multigenerational, extended-family households, though of course this pattern does not hold for educated middle-class women who work outside the home or for middle-class, single-family households in which both parents work.

Women in joint families may have each other for company, but with the arrival of the VCR, what they share is often video viewing, during which "time passes quickly."[19] Video technology thus serves as both a marker of middle-class homes, and—in the creation of daily routines—a focal point around which middle-class experience is constructed.

While not all middle-class women agreed on what films were best, all had discriminating tastes that served to separate their ideas of acceptability from others'. For these women, all Hindi films are *not* created equal. For example, one Newar woman in her forties compared the experience of going to the cinema hall now to the experiences of going twenty years ago.

> At that time, no matter what film was in the hall we'd just say, "Let's go and see a movie!" But now people are interested in some certain kind of film, like social, or art, or whatever. But before, any film that was shown, people would go see it.

The way that women talk about film preference is important for what it says about how people in Kathmandu articulate their class values or taste. I was particularly struck by the way women used words such as "realism" and "realistic" (sometimes in English) to distinguish the kinds of Hindi films that they preferred from others. Different women disagreed on which Hindi film genre was most realistic, but most explained their own preference in terms of a particular genre's degree of realism. For example, one young woman, a twenty-year-old unmarried Newar college student, described her favorite films in this way:

> I like the love story films mostly, and the social type also. There are also the fight-type films, but I don't really like those. I mean it never actually happens like that in society. They show things like smuggling, and all that, in a very exaggerated way, and it's not realistic [*bāstabik*] at all. It's this kind of unrealistic film that I don't like.

This basic three-part division of Hindi films into the categories of "love," "social," and "fight" films was, with a few minor variations, a very common system of classification among middle-class Hindi film viewers. Significantly, what separates the films this young woman likes—"love" and "social"—from the "fight" films that she dislikes is realism. Another young woman, a twenty-four-year-old Newar married and living with her in-laws, expressed a similar view:

> I like the more realistic films, ones that are similar to my own experience. Sometimes they show impossible films, things that could never happen, or bore-type, very slow films—these also I don't like.

[19] Compare with Fuglesang's account of women and video viewing in urban, middle-class Kenyan homes (1994).

Indeed, many women echoed the opinion that good films were ones that showed scenes "similar to [their] own experience." One woman defended her preference for "social" and "familial" (*ghar parivārik*) films thus:

> Because they're similar to our own situation and environment. There are so many similar [*milne*] things that you can see! They show things that really happen [*bhayeko kurā*] that especially go with life. Like wives being abused [*helā garnu*] by their mothers-in-law and things like that.

Is that like your experience?

> Well, no. But, like, the other day I saw a film where the mother-in-law discriminates against the daughter-in-law, and it's true that in society we find this kind of thing going on.

Thus films that are "real" or "similar" to women's lives are ones that include scenes that "show true things that . . . go with life," even if women do not actually share in the experiences depicted. To be realistic, a film should be plausible and touch on issues in women's lives.

Of course, not everyone agrees on what is "realistic." For example, younger women often included "love stories" among realistic films whereas older, usually married women were more likely to lump the Hindi "love" films into a broad category that went by a range of disparaging names from "*hāwā*" (airy or empty) to "today's teenagers' films," to "*bāhu*" (rambunctious, delinquent), to "formula films." One thing that younger and older women agreed upon was the general characterization of Nepali language films as "social," and thus relatively realistic and free from gratuitous "fights."[20] Said one woman of Nepali films:

> They're of the more social, sad [*dukha*], or religious variety, not this *hāwā* type, with nothing but fights. Usually it's the boys who like the fights, not the girls. They give me a headache.

In the opinion of many women, it is "the boys"—most often those who frequent the cinema halls—that "like the fights." These boys, like these films, need to be avoided. What gives pleasure to some gives headaches to others.

One of the most important corollaries of middle-class women's preference for films that are realistic is the idea that *these* are films from which one can *learn something of value*. Women repeatedly backed up their insistence that good films were realistic films with the explanation that if films dealt with "things that really happen" (*bhayeko kurā*), then people

[20] Which is not to say that many of the most recent Nepali films do not have plenty of stylized violence.

can learn from them. Speaking for herself and her husband, one thirty-five-year-old teacher explained that:

> We don't like all these "fight-sight"[21] films. We look for something practical, like the social films, so we can learn something. To make a movie good, it should be oriented to increase a person's knowledge. It should be practical and realistic. It shouldn't be just baseless.

Another woman explained why she liked social films that show *dukha* or "sadness." "In these films," she said, "you can learn about what to do if something happens. We learn, like, if this happens, that should be done, and so on like that." One other woman explained that a good film can teach about morality.

> It should be real. In a good film there are lots of events, both moral and immoral, and we can learn something from this. Also, if people are doing bad things, and they see the punishment in the films, they may not have the courage to do it again.

All in all, good films are films that are "real," films from which one "can learn something." For these women, a "good film," in its realistic portrayal of life, is both practical for the self, and capable of instilling a proper sense of morality in others.[22]

The subject of men's viewership of Hindi films can be dealt with more briefly than that of women's, largely because men were far less likely to claim a preference for Hindi films. When they did talk about watching a Hindi film, men tended to downplay its importance. This is not to say that middle-class men do not watch Hindi films. In fact, in most homes where families watch videos together, the standard fare is Hindi film. Because Hindi films are deemed suitable for general consumption by young and old, female and male, and because video viewing is often a family activity, unless they actively shun them, all family members, including men, are likely to get a steady diet. But though men frequently watch Hindi films, they rarely claim to prefer them over other media products.

---

[21] The expression "fight-sight" is an example of a typical Nepali colloquialism or play on words in which a word is spoken twice but beginning with an *s* sound the second time. The meaning is something like "X and all that goes with it" and assumes that the listener already knows all the meanings associated with that word.

[22] The fact that these women often justify their film preferences in terms of practical gains or being able to "learn from film" is similar to the kinds of attitudes described by several other media researchers. For example, the Brazilian informants in Conrad Kottak's study "again and again made the point that TV brings knowledge (*conhecimento*) of the outside world" (1990:142). Janice Radway's work on women and romance novel reading in the United States (1984, 1991) offers another comparative perspective on the Nepali scene. Americans too tended to rationalize their consumer practices in terms of acquiring practical knowledge (Radway 1991:480).

One of the few educated urban young men that acknowledged a taste
for Hindi films, an eighteen-year-old graduate of one of the city's top high
schools, did so only by going to some lengths to qualify his interests.

> Well, I like the recent ones, but not *that* much. I mean, like the love
> stories, they're OK. Actually, it's the songs, they're the most entertain-
> ing part: that's what brings real pleasure [*ānanda*]. So when I hear
> that a film has good songs, well, I'll try to see it.

Similarly, another young man, a twenty-year-old college student from
Kathmandu, admitted that he likes Hindi movies, "but really only after
English films. I guess I like the love tragedies the best." As for many of
their male peers, for these young men any interest in Hindi film had to be
couched in layers of qualification.

Adult middle-class men also sometimes spoke of watching Hindi
films, although they too seemed often to be more skeptical or choosy than
women. Most of the men in their thirties or forties that my co-workers
and I spoke with noted that they had grown up watching Hindi films.
Some continued by pointing out that now they are more selective than
before. One man, a college-educated Brahman business man in his mid-
forties, made this point clearly:

> I was always watching Hindi movies since my childhood. It was part
> of my life, and I can speak very good Hindi *due* to those movies. That
> means I am very influenced by that culture.
>
>   But now I am choosing. Like, if there is a good artist, a good
> director. . . . Now there are two kinds of movies: there are art movies,
> and there are commercial movies. Nowadays I would like to see the
> art movies.

Like many of the women quoted above, this man divides genres and states
preferences, though his distinctions are more blunt. Hindi films come in
two varieties: "art," which he "would like to see," and "commercial,"
which includes everything (and everyone) else. For him art and commerce
are antithetical. Whereas "art movies"—refined and tasteful by their very
nature—are his kind of film, "commercial movies" are for those incapable
of appreciating the qualities of art.

Rather than divide current Hindi films into good and bad, many middle-class men were inclined to simply dismiss them all. Instead of searching out Hindi films that they might like, these men (usually relying on
their children to make selections at the video shop) tended to look at what
was playing on the family VCR and reject it as stupid or offensive, often
in comparison with films from their childhood, when "things were better." One man, a Newar office worker in his forties, complained that
whereas films used to be of the more "social" or "religious" (*dharmik*)

types, now films have nothing but "singing and dancing" and "*bāhu garne*" (ruffianlike behavior).

> Today's films have nothing to do with reality. I can't understand the themes in these new films, the reasons why they do things, or what is happening. They're too unreal.

Unlike the many middle-class women who used the criterion of realism to distinguish good Hindi films from bad, this man, like many other middle-class men, was more inclined to discard the entire Hindi film industry as "too unreal." The following section on English film viewing points to some of the reasons for this male rhetorical rejection of Hindi cinema.

ENGLISH FILM VIEWING

While most middle-class women in Kathmandu, young and adult, stated a preference for Hindi films of one kind or another, middle-class men, especially young men, frequently named "English" films as their favorites. In this regard a remarkably stark contrast emerged between urban teenage and young-adult males and their age mates from rural backgrounds also living in the city. With few exceptions place of birth (or at least place of primary and secondary education) correlated closely with film preference for young men. Those from a rural background preferred Hindi or Nepali films, while urban, educated, middle-class young men were avid consumers of "English" films—a broad category that included essentially all locally available non–South Asian films, often including East Asian martial-arts action pictures, as well as assorted Western music and sports videos and pornography.

For many middle-class young men, watching videos is part of their daily routines. Typically, these young men are in an educational limbo, waiting to either take (or retake) some exam or to pass on to the next level of study.[23] Even those people currently enrolled in some sort of post-secondary education have vast amounts of time on their hands, since many choose not to attend classes but instead cram from textbooks prior to exams. In the meantime, middle-class attitudes toward any manual or menial labor guarantee that these young men will be un- or underemployed. A few volunteer in various social-service organizations while others, with sufficient motivation and cash, enroll in private schools and institutes to receive training in foreign languages or computer science. But for the most part, young men from middle-class families have plenty of time to kill.

---

[23] For more on youth and education in Kathmandu, see part 4 (especially chapter 8).

Videos are often the time-killers of choice. Many of the young men we interviewed typically consumed one or more English videos a day. Parents often told the same story, though usually as a complaint. Walking in Kathmandu's New Road commercial district—home of the city's most popular video rental shops—one often saw young men on multigeared "mountain bikes" with stacks of videotapes strapped to their fender racks.

Hanging out in a downtown ice cream shop, a seventeen-year-old student noted that he had "sokh" for watching English films; in other words, he had a kind of passionate interest in theme films.

How often do you watch?

I watch a lot. I'd say daily I watch video. I see them at a close friend's house, or sometimes I'll rent one and take it home.

Do you watch with family or alone?

It depends on the film. Like if we've got a blue film, we'll never watch it in front of the family, only with a group of friends. But if it's social, or historical—I mean, like some kind of subject or theme film—we'll watch it with the family.

Indeed, for most young men, watching English films often called for careful planning so as to escape parental detection. A nineteen-year-old student said, "If I'm home alone and I don't think anyone will come, I bring home a cassette and call my friends. Otherwise, I go to a friend's house." Another teenager explained that:

If its a good picture, we watch together with the family, if there aren't any indecent [*ashlil*] scenes. But if it has that kind of scene, then we have to arrange a time, like when mother and father have gone to the office, or have gone out.

With more and more single-family homes in the suburban areas, and more and more working parents, it is usually not difficult for at least one out of a group of friends to have a safe spot to watch even the most risqué "English" films.

When it came to the subject of genre preference within the broad category of "English" films, most young men's interests clustered around a few general types. Most identified "action" as among their favorite types, though some separated "military action" from "martial arts" and other varieties of action films. Some preferred "cowboy" films, and others singled out English "love stories," like *Pretty Woman*. Still others cited English music videos as their favorites, and some even favored locally available Western sports videos that featured weight lifting and boxing competitions.

When it came to the question of *why* young men preferred "English" films to others, a more consistent series of answers emerged. One was very pragmatic and harks back to my earlier discussion of "learning from films"; several young men pointed out that one could learn the English language from watching English films. One of the schoolboys quoted above went on to explain his (and his friends') preference for "English" films in terms of their educational value:

> Usually now, in this modern age, we need English. To improve our English, we try to watch as many English films as we possibly can.

Another student from a well-known Kathmandu high school elaborated on this theme of modernization:

> The thing is that we Nepalis all want to learn English. We have that desire [*rahar*]. By the influence of this desire, it seems to me that every time we watch an English film, we can learn at least two or four new words! And in our Nepali society, we are bending toward the European civilization; I mean the willingness to do this is increasing. By this I mean if a man sees, rather than just hearing or reading, it's much more effective. There's more change that comes from seeing. So I like to see English films often.

For this young man, watching English films was about more than just learning the English language. In an elegant manner he argues that by *seeing*, not just "hearing or reading" about, "the European civilization," one can learn more than just language. Compared with books or radio, "There's more change that comes from seeing."

The second, and most common, reason young men gave for favoring "English" films was their realism. Again, like the middle-class women who favored some Hindi films over others because they were "more real," men too felt that the degree of realism determined a film's value. But while women rejected only some Hindi films as unrealistic, many middle-class young men gave all South Asian films a low ranking on verisimilitude. For these men "English" films excelled all others because of their superior realism.

One young man, a twenty-seven-year old resident of one of Kathmandu's northern suburbs, had a system for ranking a film's realism. He said he had little interest in either Hindi or Nepali films but, when pressed, acknowledged that some Hindi films were better than others: "I like to see the social [*sāmājik*] films because there's reality in them, I don't mean 100 percent real, maybe about 75 percent." "English" films, on the other hand, were the most real. He recalled the first such film he had seen:

> I remember, it was called *Good, Bad, and Ugly*—a cowboy film. I liked it a lot, because everything in that film looks so real [*sācikai jastai dekincha*].

Since that time he has preferred the English "action" films, "because, as I said, everything seems real, and they spend a lot of money making them." A sixteen-year-old high school student from Kathmandu's pricey Maharajganj suburb voiced a similar set of criteria for movie preference. His favorite films, he said, were "kung-fu" films, such as *Blood Fight*.

> I like these English films because when you watch them, they're so real. Like when they kill someone, it looks exactly real. I mean, that's why I usually like these English films.

For these two young men what makes "English" films enjoyable, and preferable to other films, is that everything "looks exactly real." While the best Hindi films might be about 75 percent real, "English" films were pushing the 100 percent mark.

How it could be that the violent "action" of "cowboy" and "kung-fu" films could look "exactly real" to young Nepali men, whose own experiences of reality must surely be very different, is a matter I will consider at the end of this chapter. At this point, however, it is important to recall that even while many middle-class young men point to "English" films as their favorites, and indeed consume these films in quantity, this does not mean that they are not also watching Hindi and Nepali films. Indeed, I sensed that most young men tended to segregate South Asian from "English" films in the manner of apples from oranges; both were enjoyable but for different reasons. For example, an eighteen-year-old student, after claiming a preference for "English" films, explained that South Asian films were not in danger of being superseded by products from outside the subcontinent. "Both of them have their own styles and separate existences. They're both going to be popular. People will watch both." Young men might chose to align themselves with "English" films, but this is not to say that they *necessarily* abandon all interest in South Asian films based on new non–South Asian evaluative criteria.

The question then remains, Why do young middle-class men consistently claim "English" films as their favorites? Part of the answer is that, for young men, watching "English" films is an important means of establishing and maintaining privilege in terms of class distinction. As for women, the rhetoric of "learning from film" and film "realism" helps to position middle-class viewers above others who are unable to understand the "value" of certain films (even if they had the financial resources needed to consume them).

But beyond the role of English film viewing in helping to produce class distinction, male film preferences are also tied to the production of gender distinction. English film viewing *within* Kathmandu's middle class is perhaps most important for how it mirrors, and helps to reproduce, gender privilege.

The role of "English" films in helping to structure gender difference in the daily routines of middle-class Kathmandu families came through most clearly in the comments women made about their experiences with these non–South Asian films. The women that my co-workers and I spoke with confirmed my strong impression that, in the domestic setting, males were far heavier consumers of electronic media than females. Women might find special times for video viewing during the day, but young men in the family—unemployed and usually minimally occupied with school-work—usually dominated the TV set and VCR. Compared with married and unmarried women, young men are often given few responsibilities and have more time for mediated entertainment.

But beyond simply having more time for viewing media, males in the household typically act as censors or gatekeepers, determining who can watch what in the family. In the course of my research, it soon became clear that men determined if and when women can watch "English" films.[24] One twenty-four-year-old married woman complained:

> They don't let us watch, so who knows about that? I'd like to also watch that [English] kind of film, but what can I do with my desire [icchā]? Only the boys are sitting there, and they won't let us in. They say it's like Hindi, but that we shouldn't watch. [They say] "Only those who are very brave can watch this, but your hearts are weak!"

Unmarried women complain of the same prohibition. One young high school girl described the difference between what her brothers watched and what she was allowed to see.

> My brothers? Well, they're boys, so they can watch everything. Like, they bring the English films here and watch them with their other friends. But we girls aren't allowed to go in and watch them. In fact, whenever there's an English film, they won't let us see them.

While these women implied that the men in their households keep them from ever seeing "English" films, more typical were homes where men allowed women to see a few carefully selected films. In the words of a married women in her mid-thirties:

> It's said that in the English films there are some scenes that are not good. So we watch the English films only after the men have watched them and say that they are OK. My husband's younger brother, he was educated abroad and watches a lot of English movies, but we don't watch that much.

---

[24] With the arrival of satellite television in the early 1990s, it is likely that women now have increasing access to various media products without the supervision of men.

In other families it is not simply "the men" who control women's access to "English" films but parents-in-law in particular. Said another married woman in her early twenties:

> Once in a while I get the chance to see an "English" film. If the film isn't of that bad kind—the kind that makes you feel uneasy when watching it—then that's the kind we like to see. Since the TV and deck are in my parents-in-law's room, we only watch the kinds of film that are suitable for the whole family.

The kinds of films that are likely to get past a family's male censors are those without "that bad kind" of scene. For example, women often spoke of having seen children's cartoons and slapstick comedy films like *Home Alone*. In 1991 several women spoke of having seen an English "love story" film about "ghosts" [*bhut*]. Probably the American film *Ghost* (no one could remember the title), one woman described it like this:

> In this film the boy dies, but his spirit [*ātmā*] protects the girl. Who knows?—it could be true and we just haven't seen it. I mean, true or not, because it's a love story, that's why I liked it.

Another woman described an English film about a "robot" that she had seen. "When I saw this film," she said, "I felt that there was nothing in the world that humans couldn't do."

For the most part, women—even if they have "the desire" to see English films—shy away from them in order to avoid the "uneasy" feeling that comes when watching "that bad kind" of scene. Just as it is socially suspect (and potentially damaging to her reputation) for a woman to move about in public spaces unaccompanied by a male relative (or at least a senior woman),[25] it is also seen as dangerous for a woman to view English films without men present. In mixed company women not only risk feeling "uneasy" at viewing sexually explicit scenes but also risk losing social prestige through association with that type of behavior. Indeed, for most women the "uneasy" feeling comes less from embarrassment or shyness than from fear of being labeled as loose or vulgar. As one female college student remarked, "If we girls want to watch English movies, we have to be a lot more careful than the boys."

If men tend to rank English films as more realistic than South Asian films, it seems that they judge that "reality" to be more than the women in their own households can handle. Even though middle-class women and men share in a class-defining rhetoric of realism, men claim the ultimate privilege of consuming "reality" (or the privilege of consuming the ultimate reality) for themselves. Like the Rana patriarchs described at the

---

[25] For a discussion of women's freedom in public spaces, see Liechty 1996b.

beginning of this chapter, middle-class men seem to fear that "vivid scenes of intimate occidental life" might have a "demoralizing effect" on *their* women. If there is power in realism, certain groups, whether classes or genders, will seek to limit its circulation.

Conclusion: "Realization" of the Middle Class

> Television is a centralized system of storytelling. . . . In fact, most of what we know, or think we know, is a mixture of all the stories we have absorbed.
>
> —Gerbner et. al., *Growing Up with Television*

Why this middle-class fixation on some notion of "realism," or realistic portrayal in film? Why do middle-class viewers insist that "reality" is what makes a good film good? How is it that middle-class teenage boys in Kathmandu can view "spaghetti westerns" and incredibly violent and bloody "kung-fu" action pictures, and then announce that what they see looks "exactly real"? How do these commercial fantasy worlds begin to "look just like reality"?

Clearly the answer is not that Nepalis lack the critical ability to distinguish reality from fiction—though many of the Nepali intellectuals I spoke with claimed this to be the case. According to them, people in Kathmandu (especially young people) "can't separate the true from the false," or "They take all those things shown [in films] for dramatic purposes as normal life, as real." In contrast to these views, I hold that (to paraphrase Sudhir Kakar [1989:28]) no sane Nepali believes that films depict the world realistically, even if they (like the rest of us) might enjoy indulging in fantasy. For example, people I spoke with in Kathmandu knew full well that to make a film look realistic required a great deal of money, which was one reason why non–South Asian films looked more real. Even when middle-class viewers in Kathmandu said that some film looked "exactly real," I do not feel that they were mistaking *realism* for *reality*, either their own or someone else's.

But what is "realism"? At the most basic level, one could make a crude distinction between a nonrealistic mode of representation (in which the meaning of an image lies outside of itself, in its symbolic reference to some real or ideal world) and a realistic mode (in which meaning purports to reside in the image itself). For example, a religious icon symbolically points to a greater external reality, while a police "mug shot" carries the burden of reality in and of itself. In semiotic terms, nonrealist modes of signification privilege the *signified*, while realist modes privilege the actual signifier or medium of representation (Abercrombie et al.

1992:118–19). Nonrealistic modes of representation refer to symbolic meanings beyond the image at hand, while realism is self-referential.

This self-referencing quality of realism is important, because it helps to analytically distinguish *realism* as an effect from *reality* as lived experience. In film, realism is an effect produced by a variety of cinematic and narrative techniques that knit together a range of spatial and temporal fictions into a mutually referencing whole. But in addition to simply assembling images in narrative sequence, "The illusion of a single space-time continuum . . . is created by the many converging codes of representation: linear perspective, camera ubiquity, camera movement, eyeline matching, continuity editing, and so on" (L. Williams 1989:65). In short, film realism is an effect produced by the skillful inter-referencing and interlocking of a host of pictorial/narrative sequences and representational codes to create a unified diegetic field. In this way a cinematic production is "realistic" to the extent that a spectator acknowledges its *plausibility* (its self-referential coherence) rather than its identity with her or his lived reality.

Although some theorists portray realism as a condition in which "fictions . . . do not present themselves as fictions" (Abercrombie et al. 1992:121), it is perhaps more reasonable to suggest that media realism does not claim to represent reality (that is, it does not try to *deny* its own fictitiousness) but simply constructs a sense of plausibility. For example, a science fiction film can be "realistic" not because we think the action has happened but because we accept that it *could* happen. (Even the most surreal content can be made realistic if it is organized into a tightly inter-referencing whole.) The power of film realism lies in convincing people not that filmic representations are *real* but that they are interreferentially *possible*. What realism constructs as "true" is not some representation of "reality" but a representation of plausibility.

What *kind* of plausibility is created in cinematic realism? A systematic ideological critique of the "cinematic apparatus" is far beyond the objectives of this book,[26] yet it is important to recognize how cinematic representations privilege certain constructions of plausibility over others. As a visual enterprise, media realism privileges the eye, privileges the material as real, and privileges the communication of meaning and value in the visual domain. In the visual/material mode, objects are made to bear a heavy burden of representation. Commercial films typically deploy an array of objects (fashions, vehicles, and other consumer goods) to index character traits and lifestyles. Furthermore, narrative conventions in cinema privilege modes of cause and effect that construct individuals (rather

---

[26] See Rodowick 1988 for an introduction to "criticism and ideology in contemporary film theory."

than groups or institutions) as actors who through time live out stories for which they are individually rewarded or punished. Indeed, Haque claims that South Asian commercial cinema—with its fixation on the hero/heroine/villain—converts "all political, sociological and economic dilemmas into personal dramas" that are "inevitably" resolved via "individual solutions" (1992:60). In South Asia (as elsewhere), cinematic realism has the power to construct (imagine) the individuality (and individual agency) of the hero, or star, in a way that the eye cannot. The simultaneous privileging of consumer materiality and a moral economy based on individual agency, achievement, and punishment are only two instances of how cinema realism participates in a discursive project that has played a fundamental role in representing and naturalizing bourgeois sensibilities and values for the last century (cf. Kellner 1990, Susman 1984, Tagg 1988). Arguably, what film realism helps to make plausible is less some new concrete image of reality than a set of new understandings in the realms of being and knowing.

What middle-class media consumers in Kathmandu identify as realistic in films, and the lessons they consciously seek to learn and affirm from those films, have to do with these new epistemic understandings. These are people interested in seeing and learning other modes of plausibility, or new worlds of possibility, that can be harnessed to their own goals of producing distinctive practice. When people demand that films be "practical and realistic," and that films teach "what to do when something happens," they have begun to experiment with new understandings of themselves and their social lives.

This shift in orientation toward media is related to what media researchers have called the "cultivation effect" (Gerbner and Gross 1976, Gerbner et al. 1994). According to cultivation theory, the more time people spend consuming mass media, the more they will tend "to hold specific and distinct conceptions of reality, conceptions that are congruent with the most consistent and pervasive images and values of the medium" (Shanahan and Morgan 1999:2). Or, to put it another way, "The more time people spend watching television, the more they perceive the real world as being similar to that of television" (Kottak 1990:52). This somewhat counterintuitive "effect" is one in which, rather than seeing the images depicted in media as more and more "real," people begin to understand their own lived experience as essentially more and more "like in the movies," that is, more and more mediated by, or filtered through, the structurizing, ideological lens of media. Commercial media products become the interpretive frames within which one makes sense of everyday life, rather than vice versa.

At the most basic level this "realizing" effect relates to the now well-established point that people use shared media consumption experiences to construct group identities (Caughey 1984, Lipsitz 1990, Meyrowitz 1985). As Dyuti Baral (1990) notes, the programs that middle-class school children in Kathmandu watched the night before are often the basis for conversations the following day. But shared media experiences do more than determine what people will think about; they begin to shape the dimensions of what is considered possible, or thinkable. As George Custen (1987) argues, when groups of people watch the same movie, rather than talking about the movie itself, they use the shared movie experience to talk about their own everyday experiences. Film becomes a source of frames, or mirrors, that people can use to evaluate or interpret their lives. This interpretive transformation lies at the heart of the "cultivation effect." As people's daily lives become more and more deeply invested in media consumption, the narratives, narrative logics, and images of media serve more and more as interpretive resources for life, ways to make sense out of life, and eventually methods to interpret and even represent life. This is the power of media realism: it does not make media images real but makes lived reality an increasingly mediated experience.

Why then this middle-class investment in a rhetoric of realism? Part of the answer lies in how talk of realism signals taste. Stressing the educational and self-help dimensions of their own film-viewing practice allows the middle class to claim a utilitarian justification beyond simple escapism, frivolous entertainment, or pleasure. But middle-class investment in realism is about more than self-justification. The emphasis on realism among middle-class film viewers is part of a dual process in which they are at once "realizing" their own lives and attempting to "naturalize" a certain middle-class culture of "reality." By "realizing" their lives I refer to the "cultivation effect" in which middle-class lives begin to follow more and more closely the ideological and experiential contours of a mediated realism. At the same time, as their lives become more and more "realized," members of the middle class seek to elevate their new, partially mediated, lifestyle—their new culture of realism—to a privileged position. Middle-class "realization" is about naturalizing the cultural practice and values of the middle class: the material and "realist" logics of consumerism, labor, democracy, freedom, individual achievement, and responsibility. In a sense, the middle-class project is the project of realism, an effort to naturalize a set of class values built upon certain visual/material systems of value, and certain narrative understandings of causation privileging an ideology of achievement and personal responsibility. This chapter has shown how media and media consumption help to produce and reproduce relations of class and gender dominance by privileging and naturalizing an ideologically charged epistemic mode from which others can be excluded.

7

MEDIA CULTURES: THE GLOBAL IN THE LOCAL

Having considered something of the history and contemporary practice of film and video viewing in Kathmandu, this chapter turns to other portions of Nepal's mass media spectrum. Providing a comprehensive account of mass media in Kathmandu is beyond the scope of this book, but the three case studies presented in this chapter—on television, print media, and popular music, respectively—highlight specific ways in which mass media relate to, and help to produce, emerging class and commodity cultures in Kathmandu. These case studies are neither histories nor detailed accounts of these industries per se, but rather focus on how peculiarly local circumstances of production and distribution lead to equally unique consumer experiences and consumer cultures.

This chapter also introduces the idea of the *media assemblage*, a term I use to describe how various commercial media interact with and cross-reference each other. These case studies illustrate not only how individual media industries are intimately interrelated but also how, as an assemblage, they engage media consumers simultaneously on many fronts. Furthermore, these examples illustrate how local or state-run media enterprises are never fully independent of transnational commercial forces even when they try to be.

Nepal Television: Programming the Nation

In his annual address to the nation in 1980, Nepal's King Birendra ordered a feasibility study for the introduction of television in Nepal. By early 1982, with the help of the French government, a study had been concluded, and on 13 February of that year, Nepali government officials signed a memorandum authorizing the establishment of the Nepal Television Project (Khatri 1983:20–22). The project's director, Nir Shaha (an experienced Nepali film actor and producer), set out to operationalize the king's directives and, with help from the Worldview International Foundation, proceeded to train a full team of television production experts in everything from camera work to program production, editing, and sound. NTV's inaugural transmission occurred on 26 December 1985, when, during the king's state visit to Australia, NTV produced daily half-hour programs for viewing at eleven locales scattered about Kathmandu. By the early 1990s Nepal TV was broadcasting four and a half hours daily (divided between morning and evening), with an extra two hours on Saturday afternoons.[1]

From the outset Nepal TV was seen as a means of producing a Nepali *national* identity. While national unification has been one of the Nepali state's main projects since the eighteenth century (Burghart 1984), the arrival of electronic media on the subcontinent changed the rules, and raised the stakes, for creating and controlling the national consciousness of a far-flung and diverse population. Particularly troubling for Nepal's government was that the Indian state television network, Doordarshan, had been easily available all across Nepal's southern flank since at least the early 1980s. Because most Nepalis live closer to India than to Kathmandu, by the mid-1980s it was apparent to Nepali government officials that something had to be done to combat the inroads of Indian state media, especially into the Nepal Tarai.[2] Said one NTV official:

> At that time, if you would ask a man or woman [living in the Tarai], "Who is the prime minister of Nepal?" they would answer, "Rajiv Gandhi"! This is because they didn't have any access to the Nepal Television. They could not see who is the king, who is the prime minister, who are the other people. So that is the reason why we decided to come into transmission.

With the goal of helping to shore up national awareness among the citizenry, NTV set out to provide Nepali viewers with a steady diet of Nepali-language programming. For NTV the challenge was not only to produce programming but to produce products that could compete with Doordarshan. Before the arrival of the huge pan-Asian satellite networks in 1991, people in Kathmandu could choose between NTV and Doordar-

---

[1] For more on Nepal Television, see *Kamana* (Kathmandu) 50 (2047 v.s.):93–95.

[2] Spurred by the phenomenal viewer interest in the televised 1982 Asian Games in Delhi, the Indian government, under Indira Gandhi, invested heavily in increased television transmission facilities prior to the 1984 national elections. "Within one year beginning in 1983, potential coverage [television viewership] was increased from 23% to 70% of the population" of India (Farmer 1994:3). Between 1983 and 1984 Doordarshan installed six new transmitters in Bihar and eighteen in Uttar Pradesh, the two Indian states flanking Nepal's southern border (Audience Research 1989:62, 69–70). By 1985 Doordarshan had developed a nationwide delivery system through advanced communication-satellite technology (Pendakur 1990:245).

shan; simply having Nepali programming did not mean that people would watch. But it is almost impossible for NTV to compete with Indian state television. With its highly developed media industry, India is far ahead of Nepal in production capabilities. Furthermore, like the major American television networks, Doordarshan actually produces very little of its programming. Aside from news programs, Doordarshan buys most of its offerings from private Indian production houses. Nepal TV on the other hand, must itself produce all of the Nepali-language programming it offers.[3] Whereas Doordarshan makes money selling advertising time, in the early 1990s NTV was lucky to attract any advertisers at all, let alone at a rate that would cover their investment in production expenses. With an annual subsidy of only 2 million NPR (cut to 1.6 million in 1990) (Bhattarai 1992), NTV struggled to make ends meet. Speaking of advertisers, one NTV production manager lamented, "If somebody comes, luckily, then we accept it. Otherwise, it's just spending, spending, spending."[4]

From the outset Nepal TV was committed to producing and airing its own programs. During its first years 90 percent of NTV programming was in Nepali, with the remaining 10 percent divided among various foreign-language products (Hindi, English, Urdu). As is typical of fledgling industries, limitations in equipment and other resources restricted the first programs to simple indoor dramas or single-set talk shows and current-events features (cf. Lyons 1990:426). This type of program still predominates, but NTV also produces its own serials and telefilms. Unfortunately, before long the percentage of Nepali programming began to slip. The NTV production manager I spoke with explained:

> As time went by, the equipment started being less dependable. We do not have the ability to repair the equipment. So, once the equipment is, . . . well, when something has gone wrong with that, it is just put in the storeroom. We don't have the skilled manpower to maintain it.

As its production hardware—originally a gift of the Japanese government—ceased to function, NTV's output began to dwindle accordingly.

---

[3] In this respect NTV is like the Brazilian national television network, Globo, which "makes much of what it shows, including virtually everything in prime time" (Kottak 1990:44).

[4] In 1991 there were several private video production houses in Kathmandu, but aside from some commercials made for TV, almost none of their products were aired on NTV. Privately made video productions were too expensive for NTV to purchase and were instead being made for display in video cinema halls. Part of the reason why private video productions were so expensive was that Nepal's government imposed a 235 percent import tax on all production equipment and stock, thereby guaranteeing that finished products were artificially expensive.

The nearest authorized Sony repair shop was in Hong Kong, and NTV's storeroom began to fill up with hi-tech Japanese electronics that it could not afford to even have serviced. Through the late 1980s, with less equipment and shrinking government subsidies, the amount of Nepali-language programming slipped to 60, then 40, and at times as low as 25 percent. This decline underlines the fact that the actual ability of a state-run media enterprise to produce its own local programming hinges on a host of factors above and beyond the level of official government intent and policy commitments.

In the Nepali year 2047 v.s. (1990–91), despite budget cuts and equipment shortages, NTV managed to produce forty-two full-length telefilms, as well as hundreds of hours of other Nepali-language programming (Mathema 2047 v.s.). Yet even at this level of output, they struggled to meet, and often fell short of, their goal of maintaining a level of 40 percent local programming. During the same year NTV also aired seven English and six Pakistani serials, as well as four Hindi serials, including the enormous, ninety-one-episode Hindi cinematic version of the *Mahabharata*[5] (on which NTV spent close to 20 percent of its annual budget) (Mathema 2047 v.s.). Thus, although they do air programs from India, NTV recognized early on that one way to compete with Doordarshan is to broadcast programming *unavailable* on Indian TV. The NTV production manager told me, "We buy soap operas and [other] English [serials] like *Night Rider* and *Street Hawk* and things like that from the outside, because Doordarshan doesn't *show* these types of films." Foreign programming, like these American TV serials, helps NTV improve its market share against Indian programming, which is more sophisticated than anything that can be produced locally (given NTV's financial constraints).

Furthermore, hour for hour, it actually costs *less* to air an English television serial than to produce a Nepali drama.[6] Working with American and British distributors like MCA and Thames Television, NTV managers ask for "top programs" that are "within our budget." NTV looks for programs that cost between three and four hundred U.S. dollars per hour. Every year distributors send out fifteen or twenty preview cassettes in this price range, and NTV makes its selections. The officials I spoke with told me that, in English programs, NTV wants "action." As one man explained:

The main thing is that most people can't understand English properly, you know. So we try to get something with action, then people will

[5] For more on the social and political implications of televised religious epics in South Asia, see van der Veer 1994 (especially 175–78), Lutgendorf 1990 and Rajagopal 2001.

[6] The same is true in Europe, where "buying second-hand American television programmes costs 10 percent of the price of new, European-originated material," much to the dismay of European media producers (Taynbee 1996).

understand what it is. Even the man who doesn't follow, he can understand the action. That is the main thing here.

At this point another official entered the conversation to note that the right kind of "action" was not always so easy to find:

> Two years ago we asked for *Miami Vice*, and we got it. It was in our price range, but the problem was, it was of the wrong sort—all "B" scenes. We cannot, in our country, we cannot show nude, topless, . . . we cannot show. So sometimes one episode would be cut down by thirty-five minutes! Edited!
>
> So now we tell them [the foreign suppliers] this thing also: we don't want sex, and we don't want violence. Now they know pretty much what Nepal TV wants.

"Action" can include fistfights, shooting, car chases, and all kinds of thrills, as long as there is not too much blood, skin, or sex. In addition to "action" programs, NTV regularly airs American and European children's cartoons, sports, nature programs, and other fare that does not depend heavily on language comprehension for enjoyment. Indeed, one study (Baral 1990) of television viewing among 205 middle-class children in Kathmandu between the ages of five and twelve found that characters from *The Smerfs* and *The A-Team* were among the most popular and recognized of all television figures, even though the children understood little English. "Watching 'The A-Team' hardly required any analysis or conceptualization as the program was one of sheer entertainment" (Baral 1990:72).

English programming was popular not only with viewers like these, and with NTV executives looking to stretch their budgets, but with advertisers as well. One of the main reasons why more and more foreign programming finds its way into Nepal Television is that the only shows that consistently attract commercial sponsors are foreign, English-language, most often American serials. Spared the expense of producing these shows, NTV is also rewarded for airing them by being able to defray their purchase cost. According to one journalist, the "sponsor bias" of Nepali advertisers guarantees that "Almost all foreign programmes are . . . about five times cheaper [to air] than locally produced shows" (Bhattarai 1992). From instant-noodle and rubber-footwear manufacturers to beer and cigarette companies, Nepali business interests want their products associated with the glitz, glamour, and "action" of foreign programs.

Emphasizing the high percentage of foreign programming on Nepal Television is not to say that Nepali viewers are becoming "Indianized" or "westernized" by what they see on TV. Watching *Bonanza* reruns and Hindi sitcoms is not likely to make viewers "less Nepali," even though media consumption might influence understandings of self and other. Much more significant, and ironic, is the way modern communications technology originally introduced in order to raise national identification among a culturally diverse citizenry has now taken on a life of its own. Instead of beaming a state-mediated Nepali consciousness into towns and villages, national television is transformed—due to NTV's financial constraints and the advertising agendas of local and transnational business interests—into a showcase for foreign media products, as NTV officials look on in despair.

Initiated by the state with specific nation-building objectives, in the 1990s television emerges as more than just another expensive "development" white elephant (like a silted-up hydroelectric project or an ecologically disastrous road). Instead, local and global market forces seem to wrest control of the medium from its state masters by creating a context where (to remain economically viable) television, designed to foster the nation, can only feed its viewers more and more foreign products. Strangely, in Nepal even the ownership of broadcasting technology does not guarantee control over the contents of those broadcasts. While some "developing" nations (e.g., "semi-peripheral" countries [Wallerstein 1974] like India and Brazil) have been more or less successful in constructing state-controlled, nation-building media empires, for "least developed countries" like Nepal, experimenting with mass media has been like playing with fire, and getting burned.

FILM MAGAZINES: KEEPING THE STARS IN MOTION

A visit to any of the hundreds of storefront or open-air newsstands in Kathmandu brings one face to face with an amazing array of newspapers and magazines representing every political viewpoint, a variety of languages, a wide range of print quality (from glossy to shabby), and a host of different interests and target audiences (sports, crime, romance, fashion, children, women). In this dramatic medley of reading materials, film magazines play a leading role. At any one time it is not hard to find dozens of different Indian film magazines (in Hindi and English), as well as four or five different Nepali-language film magazines dealing with the Hindi and Nepali film industries respectively.

While the Indian film industry is one of the oldest and largest in the world (Pendakur 1990, Rajadhyaksha and Willemen 1999), its Nepali counterpart is small but growing rapidly. Between 1965 and 1990, only about fifty Nepali films were made, and of these only about half were actually made and produced by Nepalis in Nepal (*Kamana* 50 [2047 v.s.]:

25–57).[7] Before the early 1980s, Nepali film releases averaged fewer than one per year. Starting around the mid-1980s, releases increased to four or five per year. However, since 1990 Nepali film production has swelled; over ten new Nepali feature films enter the market every year.[8]

With so few Nepali films produced over the past few decades, it is easy to understand why Nepali film-magazine publishing has not been a very successful business. With only a handful of movies and stars, grist for a film magazine's mill was difficult to find. Even so, by the time Nepal's longest-running and best-selling film magazine, *Kamana*, was founded in the mid-1980s, there had already been a number of short-lived (usually single-issue) attempts to launch a Nepali film magazine. By the early 1990s news stands had seen eleven different Nepali film magazines. Of these most had disappeared soon after their inception, and a few published only sporadically. Of the few that managed to publish regularly, *Kamana* was the only one that had developed a reputation such that its future looked secure.

It is not coincidental that *Kamana* was launched in the same year (2041 v.s.) that the Nepali film industry saw a burst in its annual production from less than one film per year to six. Film magazines need films. Without them there *are* no film stars, no film news, and no film fans. By entering the market when it did, *Kamana* caught the wave of increased film production and rode it.

Just as important as what films do for film magazines is what these magazines can do for the film industry. Because both depend on the same set of consumers, each party promotes itself when it promotes the other. For example, in an article describing *Kamana*'s first six years in business[9] the magazine's publisher recounts how various film stars and film producers helped make the magazine a success. The publisher describes how even though some actors were hesitant at first to become involved with the magazine, others quickly recognized the significance of such a venture and were forthcoming with interviews and stories. Several famous actors and musicians even went so far as to volunteer their time to write columns fielding questions from readers. In addition, the names listed as official advisors to the magazine read like a "Who's Who" of the Nepali film

[7] Actually, the first Nepali-language film was made in the early 1950s, though like many that came later, it was made in India. A few other Nepali films have been joint productions with other South Asian countries, such as Pakistan or Bangladesh (see *Kamana* 50 [2047 v.s.]:25–57 and Nepal Chalchitra Sang *Rajat Jayanti: 2045*, 73–77).

[8] This spurt in production is due in large part to changes in government taxation policy intended to make film production more profitable. For more information see *Gorkhapatra* September 30, 1991, 4; *The Rising Nepal*, 1 April 1989, 1, 7.

[9] Entitled *Kāmanāle malāi dhani banāeko cha* ("*Kamana* Made Me Rich") (P.L. Shrestha 2047).

industry, including famous actors, producers, and music personalities. Over the years *Kamana* also sponsored a number of gala, live-entertainment events in auditoriums around Kathmandu that helped publicize actors, singers, and the magazine itself.[10] In an interview I conducted, the publisher of *Kamana* described his relationship with film actors:

> My magazine is the only one. I mean, it is the largest of the film magazines. So naturally the artists depend on this magazine, because there are no other sources encouraging them—certainly not the government. My aim is, how to encourage them. If they have any problem, I telephone them, or I personally meet them and talk about their problems. Sometimes I suggest them what to do, how to improve. We discuss about the problems.

Perhaps even more so than in India, where close to one thousand films are produced each year and where actors are constantly in the public eye, in Nepal, where the films themselves are still relatively few and far between, film magazines play an important role in promoting the film industry by keeping the stars in motion even when their films are not. Films and film magazines are companion commodities, like two strings in harmonic convergence: vibrations in either one help keep the other alive.

The question remains, though, How is it that film magazines can capture the public imagination? What do film magazines in Nepal contain, and how do they engage their readers? What do people actually think of these magazines? Who reads them?

The only available published data on film magazine readership is a survey conducted by *Kamana* in 1987 (see *Kamana* 28 [2044 v.s.]:29). Some of the most salient points of this survey are as follows. Of all *Kamana* readers who responded:

- two out of three are male.
- 75 percent are between the ages of fifteen and twenty-five.
- 40 percent are "students," and another 35 percent are either employees or "businessmen."
- 60 percent report no personal income.
- over 60 percent are high school graduates.

Furthermore, according to the publisher, in the early 1990s more than one-third of *Kamana*'s monthly press run was consumed *within* the Kathmandu valley. Judging by this survey, the "average" *Kamana* reader is young, male, educated, urban, and unemployed. My own research indi-

[10] *Kamana* has also sponsored charity soccer matches in which teams of celebrities compete in order to raise money for causes such as earthquake relief.

cates that women of a similar demographic profile are just as (if not more) likely to read film magazines, which leads me to suspect that fewer women than men responded to *Kamana's* voluntary survey. But male or female, the combination of education, unemployment, and disposable income strongly suggests that "average" *Kamana* readers are middle-class youth.

Another interesting feature of the *Kamana* reader survey is the finding that on average thirteen people read any one copy of the magazine. This confirms my own strong impression that in Kathmandu far more people flip through film magazines they find lying about than actually go out and buy them. For example, one teenage boy, the son of a civil servant, described how he started reading film magazines:

> When I was a kid, I used to read lots of comic books,[11] and then with my friends I'd trade them back and forth. And then I started trading some of them for film magazines, and like, now I like to read *Kamana* now and then.[12]

Similarly, a twenty-year-old woman, a student from a prosperous business family, described how often she read magazines:

> I don't read [magazines] that much. Maybe one or two in a month. Like, I read the Nepali magazine *Kamana* to learn about our Nepali heroes and heroines. Even though I have no real interest in being a heroine, I like to hear about their character and read about their lives.

Since many people view Nepali films as (at best) inferior versions of Hindi films (see chapter 6), showing too much interest in local productions is in slightly bad taste. Some justify their interests by giving them a nationalist slant, like the woman above who wants to keep track of "our Nepali heroes and heroines." For others reading film magazines is just an extension of reading habits established as children. At a certain point film magazines take the place of comic books in helping to consume a middle-class young person's free time. Indeed, as they are traded from person to person, family to family, magazines such as these literally become part of the currency of a middle-class culture for both youth and young adults.

What is in film magazines, and how do they attract people's interests? A brief synopsis of one issue helps to give some feeling for the content and style of Nepali film magazines. In the interest of diversity, I have chosen an issue of *Chalchitra* rather than *Kamana*. Also published in Kathmandu, by 1991 *Chalchitra* ("Motion Picture") had published its

[11] Indian, British, and American comic books abound in Kathmandu book and magazine shops.

[12] At ten to fifteen rupees per copy, Nepali film magazines are *not* insignificant purchases for most people.

thirteenth issue, although it appeared on the newsstands fairly irregularly. On the cover of the thirteenth issue is a sultry picture (in color) of the Nepali actress Mausami Malla, with the quotation "I believe in karma."[13] Rather than give a page-by-page account, I will describe the magazine's contents by categorizing different types of material.

This issue of *Chalchitra* offers readers articles about, or interviews with, five different film-related figures. One main article is an interview with the Nepali film star and play-back singer Udit Narayan Jha (a figure also famous in India as a successful film-music recording artist). Another features the cover girl Mausami Malla, who has appeared in several popular Nepali films. Among other things, Ms. Malla describes the beauty parlor she owns and operates on Kathmandu's New Road. (For Nepali film actors and actresses in the early 1990s, earning a living from films alone was usually almost impossible.) The other three articles are on lesser-known figures: an actor, director, and musician, respectively.

Issue 13 also includes three feature articles on various film-related themes. One traces the development of music in Nepali films through the careers of various singers and composers. A second article is entitled "Fights [*dunda*] in Nepali Cinema: Their Introduction and Evolution." Noting that these days "a film without a fight is like eating vegetables without salt," the article examines when the first fight scenes appeared in Nepali films and names some of the industry's most well-known fight directors. The third article, "Cinema and Politics: For Peace, Freedom, and Democracy," considers the future of the Nepali film industry after the fall of the one-party Panchayat government in 1990. There are also two general-interest feature articles. One, under the heading "Sports World" is on the Brazilian soccer star Pelé and the possibility of his running for political office. The other article, headed "Health Description" and entitled "Facial Paralysis and Acupuncture Treatment," is written by a doctor and features "before" and "after" photos of patients.

From write-ups on film stars to film-related features to general interest articles on sports and health, *Chalchitra* provides readers with a number of full-length articles on a variety of subjects. But there are also short columns and features. These include short articles under headings like "Movie News" and "Miscellaneous News," a center-spread color "blowup" of a popular actress, pages of camera stills from recent and upcoming films, reviews of recent cassette recordings, and a column entitled "Musical Composition." In issue 13 this feature includes the words and music (including chord notations) of a popular song from the Nepali film *Chino*.

This last feature, in particular, begins to point to some of the ways in which film magazines work with other media to engage their readers.

---

[13] "*Ma karmamā vishvās rāckchu.*"

For most readers, the song from *Chino* would have already been familiar because of the regular air play it received on Radio Nepal, and because many people purchased the sound track on audiocassette even before the film's actual release. Here, on this page, readers can see the lyrics and, if they can read the chords, even learn to strum along on the guitar. By including features like song lyrics and music, film magazines build bridges not just to films but also to other mass media, like radio and other commoditized entertainment forms like cassette-recorded music. By casting its net broadly, a film magazine can engage its readers' interests and imagination on a variety of fronts.

The interactive overtones of *Chalchitra*'s "Musical Composition" page point to a final content category. The last ten pages of the magazine are devoted to pages and columns that feature readers themselves. One page, headed "Editors Answer," includes brief letters from readers across the country asking film-related questions such as, Who appeared in a particular film? How many pictures has a certain director made? and so on. Another page, headed "Readers Say," features letters from around the country, almost all of which gush about how wonderful the magazine is and how much they enjoy reading it. Each letter is accompanied by the name and address of the writer. One letter in issue 13, however, is in a different tone. In this letter the writer complains that some time ago he had sent in his picture, along with thirty rupees, in order to have it published in *Chalchitra*'s "New Talent" (*ākurā*, literally "sprouts") column. The editor assures him he will be next in line for publication.

The "New Talent" column offers readers the opportunity (for a fee) to have their photo published, along with their name, age, height, address, the film role they would like to play, and their experience. In issue 13, one of two featured "Sprouts" is Dilip Shrestha, age eighteen, height 5'5", from Chitwan, who seeks a "main role" in a film and has "limited experience." Finally, one last page is headed "Pen Pals" (*patra mitratā*) and features notices submitted by twenty-seven readers from the Kathmandu valley and across Nepal, ranging in age from twelve to twenty-two. In addition to name, age, and address, each entry notes the individual's interests. Aside from being pen pals, these interests include reading magazines, listening to the radio, being in dramas, singing songs, aspiring to be an actor, and a variety of sports.

One of the most important things that these interactive pages and features do is to coalesce widely dispersed individuals into groups that share certain interests and dreams (a phenomenon considered in more detail in chapter nine). They give readers a forum in which they can see themselves (even their own photos), or at least see their own names in print. With their names and photos in these pages, readers can interact with the editors and sometimes even the stars themselves. Speaking of the

Indonesian popular media, James Siegel argues that magazines such as these set into motion new "circuits of exchange" between stars and fans (1986:231). But one could go one step further: media, especially in the case of film magazines, not only *link* stars and fans but actually *produce* them. If the interviews, film stories, and feature articles in magazines like *Chalchitra* help to produce the modern category of the "star" or "celebrity," the same magazine's interactive pages, question-and-answer pages, and "Readers Say" columns help to produce the "fans." In building bridges, or "circuits," between the two, film magazines help to constitute both sides of the star/fan equation.[14]

One of the characteristics of the fan/star relationship in Nepal is that, in most cases, the fan dreams of being a star. Rather than quote the scores of women and men who spoke to me and my co-workers of their wishes to break into film or to become famous singers, I conclude this discussion of film magazines with two brief stories that relate this widespread desire to some of the themes developed above. The first anecdote ties in with *Chalchitra*'s "New Talent" or "Sprouts" column and was told to me by a junior editor for Nepal's government-run English-language daily *The Rising Nepal* (*TRN*). Far from unique, these new-talent columns are in fact regular features of magazines around the world. Not surprisingly, when *TRN* decided, in the late 1980s, to inaugurate a weekly entertainment supplement, they included a column in which they printed the photos, names, and interests of people wishing to be in films. Said the *TRN* editor:

> So we had started that column, and suddenly we were flooded with so-o-o-o many of these people who wanted to be printed that we had to cut the feature! We just could not manage to cope with all those people!

Completely unaware of how thousands of people (mostly teenagers and young adults) longed to break into films, *TRN* staffers quickly ended the feature, realizing that what they had originally intended as a service to readers was actually a disservice, in that it falsely raised their hopes of making it in the world of film.

The second story relates to the full-page advertisement that appears inside the back cover of *Chalchitra*'s thirteenth issue. In Nepali and English the ad's banner announces the newly opened "Academy of Performing Arts, Film Acting and Western Music School" in Kathmandu. The ad's main text, under the heading "Acting course," is translated as follows:

---

[14] The politically oriented "fan clubs" that Sara Dickey describes in her ethnography of cinema and the urban poor in South India (1993:148–72) are absent in Nepal, where media figures are far less likely to be engaged in campaign politics.

Are you interested in acting in the movies? Now you don't have to go through the hassle of going to Pune, Bombay, or Delhi. Now in Kathmandu you can study with famous producers and directors from the Nepali film world. We'll be glad to send you information.

1. Study the Stanislavsky method of acting, just like in Pune or Bombay.
2. Teachers trained in the Film & Television Institute of India in Pune and also from Bombay.
3. Special guest film stars.
4. Study acting aids like yoga, speech, and diction as well as special dance movements.
5. Seat numbers are limited and each batch has only 10–15 students.
6. Entrance candidates are chosen only after difficult tests and screenings.
7. After their training student actors will be evaluated through the use of short video film productions.
8. Students who pass the acting school course will surely be give suitable roles in Nepali films by famous Nepali directors and producers.

Curious about the film-acting school that sought students among the readers of *Chalchitra*, I followed the map printed on the advertisement and found it housed in several large rooms on the second floor of a commercial building in Kathmandu's busy Kamaladi district. The director and founder of the Academy of Performing Arts (APA) was a man with previous experience in both film acting and directing: he had even once tried his hand at film-magazine publishing. Sensing the degree of interest in film acting around Nepal, the owner had "high hopes" of attracting twenty to twenty-five serious candidates from which to choose ten or fifteen students for his first class. Unfortunately, out of the many hundreds of inquiries that had rolled in from across the country, only a tiny handful could afford the six-thousand-rupee entrance fee[15] for the four-month crash course. Rather than choosing the ten most talented applicants, the school accepted all eight of the upper-middle-class young men who could pay the tuition. As for female applicants, when I visited the school there had been none. Even a well-publicized offer to provide *free* training and *guaranteed* roles in upcoming films to two qualified (good-looking, somewhat talented) young women garnered not a single inquiry, let alone application. "What the Nepali film industry needs," confided the APA's director, "is not *better* actors, but *more* actors, especially women. The audience gets bored."

That Nepal's film industry was in need of revitalization was an opinion shared by the Academy of Performing Arts' five other principal coinvestors:

---

[15] One hundred and twenty dollars in 1991, a whopping amount by local standards.

- two well-known and successful film producers,
- the owner of Nepal's Coca-Cola bottling company,
- the owner of Nepal's largest photo processing establishment, and
- the owner of Nepal's most successful pop and film song recording studio and cassette music business.

What these men have in common is a commitment to making money via a set of intricately intertwined media businesses and commodified representations of glamour, pleasure, and leisure. What is intriguing is how all of them have united in a plan to promote the Nepali film industry by bringing in a new generation of actors. These men recognize the crucial links between media consumption and consumerism—links that emerged clearly in the previous chapters on middle-class culture in Kathmandu—and are willing to invest in them. They know that a healthy local media culture means a healthy local consumer culture.

Western Pop Music in Kathmandu: Variations on a Global Theme

Pop icons like Madonna and Michael Jackson are usually the stuff of which tales of Western "cultural imperialism" are made (cf. Tomlinson 1991). In Kathmandu too, if a poor street vendor knows of an American singer, it is likely to be Jackson, and the interior decor of many taxicabs is built around a recurring Madonna sticker motif. Yet there is much more to the Western music scene in Kathmandu than just these stale stereotypes. In fact, the story of "rock" music in Kathmandu is incredibly complex; an amazing variety of transnational forces have combined to produce a local history, and a contemporary scene, that are at once uniquely modern and uniquely Nepali.

By the time I arrived at the soccer stadium in one of Kathmandu's western suburbs on a Saturday morning in the winter of 1991, the day's "Rock and Roll Music Festival" was already underway. The opening act, a rock band from Kathmandu, had already finished, and one of the show's featured attractions was just taking the stage. The "Hell Riders" were one of the most popular bands from Darjeeling—the Nepali-speaking hill region of India to the east of Nepal—and as they started belting out classic hits, it was clear that they were an accomplished group of musicians. Tunes by the Doors, the Rolling Stones, Steppenwolf, and Grand Funk Railroad followed one after the other, but it was soon apparent that the local crowd was not getting into the groove. While the Hell Riders played a tune by Deep Purple, people in the crowd started shouting out "AC/DC!" "Anthrax!" and "Bon Jovi!" Finally, after an impromptu huddle between band members, the Hell Riders launched into a rendition of a currently popular Bon Jovi hit. The crowd got to its feet, roared in approval, and started singing along with the tune. Closing out their set with contemporary numbers by the likes of Guns & Roses and Gary Moore, the Hell Riders managed to salvage what could have been a disastrous showing.

Made up mostly of young men in their late teens and twenties, this Kathmandu crowd illustrated how, for the most part, middle-class young people's tastes in rock music are closely tied to the latest trends in mass marketed pop music. Fed by the pirated-cassette mills of Singapore and Bangkok,[16] music shops in Kathmandu stock the latest mass-market releases from around the world. By the early 1990s, the "lag time" between an album's release in Los Angeles or New York and its arrival in Kathmandu shops was not much different from that experienced by medium-sized towns in the United States. But the same cassette shops that featured the "latest hits" by groups ranging from Nirvana to New Kids on the Block also did a brisk trade in "evergreen" classics like the ones with which the Hell Riders opened their set. These were favored by an older generation of rock music fans, people whose experience with Western pop music has been completely different from that of their juniors.

Rather than watching music videos on their VCRs, or MTV on the new pan-Asian "Star TV" satellite channel, these older listeners were in some cases part of the very scene that generated the psychedelic rock of the hippie era. What was so remarkable about the pop-music scene in Kathmandu during the 1960s and early 1970s was the fact that the young Western tourists who flocked to the city were among the trend setters or tastemakers for a radically new form of music.[17] To the extent that Nepali young people participated in this scene, they too were close to the cutting edge of a new musical form.[18] Although the hippie counterculture was obviously a "foreign" domain, those Nepalis who joined in, or just watched (or listened) from the sidelines, were close to the heart of things.

---

[16] For more on cassette piracy in Bangkok, see Wong 1995:43.

[17] Sherry Ortner goes so far as to suggest that the global youth "counterculture" movement developed in Nepal *before* it emerged in the West:

> The 1970s saw the birth of the vast popular movement in the United States and Europe that came to be known as "the counterculture." As part of this, *starting in the late 1960s, Nepal became probably the single biggest magnet in the world for the countercultural lifestyle.* Hippies from virtually every nation flocked there for the cheap living, "Eastern religion," and legal marijuana. (Ortner 1999b:186, italics added)

[18] See Liechty 1994: ch. five for a more detailed discussion of hippie tourism and the Kathmandu music scene, including interactions between tourists and young Nepalis in Kathmandu, and Liechty 1996a on the relationship between mass media and mass tourism in Nepal.

These young Nepalis got a fairly "pure fix" of the new music, relatively unmediated by middlemen, international distributors, import agents, and government censors. The bizarre happenstance that made the city a hippie hangout (Liechty 1996a) meant that young Nepalis in Kathmandu were listening to the likes of Frank Zappa long before his music hit comparably sized towns in the United States, and decades before it would ever have reached Nepal via commercial channels.

If, during the 1960s and early 1970s, Kathmandu's pop-music scene was close to the heart of an emerging global youth counterculture, during the late 1970s and the 1980s Western music came to Kathmandu through more and more conventional, commercially mediated, transnational channels. Thus, the "generation gap" between a forty-year-old Santana fan in Kathmandu and his twenty-year-old cousin who adores Jon Bon Jovi is more than just a matter of taste. Much more importantly it is a difference in what might be called the *mode of mediation*. Tastes in Western music among young men in Kathmandu in the early 1990s were, compared with their elders, far more likely to be aligned with the international commercial pop mainstream—to favor artists like New Kids on the Block, Madonna, AC/DC, or U2. Compared with twenty years earlier, local Nepali tastes in Western music now had almost nothing to do with tourists' tastes but instead looked to other commercially mediated sources for inspiration.

Perhaps the first commercial wave of Western pop music to roll into Kathmandu was disco in the mid- to late-1970s. Through films like *Saturday Night Fever* and in internationally marketed bands like Modern Talking, Abba, and Boney M, disco was probably the first truly global pop music form, taking root in local markets around the world. That disco was (arguably) the first globally marketed musical style is probably attributable much less to the genre's inherent musical qualities than to the fact that its popularity coincided with the emergence and global spread of audiocassette technology.[19] Cassette technology revolutionized the world of recorded music, making music much more affordable and transportable, as well as easier to pirate (cf. Manuel 1993).

As air links opened up with East Asia, and as Kathmandu became an increasingly important destination for legal (and illegal) consumer commodity imports in the 1970s (van Spengen 1987), disco music tapes were among the most common items to appear in local import shops. Before long, shops dealing in imported cassettes from Hong Kong, Singapore, and Bangkok opened in Kathmandu's New Road commercial district, of-

---

[19] The fact that *video*cassette technology was also making powerful inroads into local consumer markets during the late 1970s and early 1980s (as discussed in chapters 5 and 6) also contributed to the emergence of disco as a global musical phenomenon, via the worldwide popularity of Western disco films.

fering disco and other mainstream Western pop styles illegally produced in Asian pirated cassette mills. For many middle-class families that bought their first cassette player in the late 1970s or early 1980s, a few Western disco cassettes were more or less standard equipment, alongside the more popular Hindi film songs.[20] Even if its popularity was limited, far more people in Kathmandu listened to pirated Western disco cassettes than had earlier followed the musical tastes of tourists.

Although the global disco wave's arrival raised the level of consumption of Western music in Kathmandu, the mid-1980s saw a far bigger jump. Several of the cassette importers/dealers I spoke with in Kathmandu noted that in the mid-1980s the consumption of English music greatly increased as young people began giving up disco and turning instead to a wide variety of pop music. One New Road dealer told me in 1991.

> In the last six or seven years I've found a big difference. Before, people didn't buy that many English cassettes. But now, with Nepal TV and Sunday Pop—after that, young people really started buying English tapes. They see a really good group on Sunday Pop and come in and start saying, "Give me this cassette! Give me that cassette!" That's the way it is now, not like before. There's a big change from before. Maybe ten or fifteen years ago people would have listened to Boney M. But now people usually like pop more than disco.

Although other dealers had reported the same surge in interest in English music, it was only after speaking with this shopkeeper that I realized the link between the advent of television and the increased consumption of Western music. The one-hour weekly program called Sunday Pop was, in the early 1990s, probably the single most popular show on NTV. Consisting of mainstream (mass-market) Western pop-music videos presented in an MTV format, the program was de rigueur viewing for middle-class young people in Kathmandu. One shopkeeper enthusiastically described the link between consumer demand and Sunday Pop:

> These days there's Sunday Pop on the TV. And from this has come a really big influence. Each Sunday they see this. Like, now there's someone called "Mona." After seeing her on TV, demand got huge and now you can't find the cassettes; they're sold out. The demand is huge! You can't buy it!

Another New Road cassette dealer elaborated on the changes he had seen since the mid-1980s:

[20] Disco also had a profound effect on Indian commercial film songs. Indeed, by the 1990s many people in Kathmandu associated "disco" more with Indian cinema than with the West.

Its not like before, now we have TV—I mean our own, not Indian—and there's Sunday Pop. And now every imaginable magazine is coming here. In those you find the ten tops; and whatever is released, you can read about it in the magazines. Again, this is not like it used to be. I mean nowadays, as soon as something is released in Europe or America, we get people walking in here asking for it!

Which magazines are they looking at?

Lots of Indian ones, about films and music, and even foreign ones you can get here, even though they're expensive. I don't know which ones, but I remember seeing the lists of popular songs. There's *Sun* magazine also from India, in there, too, they tell about music. And now, in *Rising Nepal*,[21] on Saturday or Sunday they give the ten tops. So they get lots from those places, and also from the latest Western videos that come in. Lots of stuff comes.

While young people have started learning about Western pop music from television, they are also getting information from a host of other sources. Western video films (including concert videos and compilations of music videos) are available in hundreds of shops around the valley and offer access to recent music.

Perhaps more important in influencing consumer choices in Kathmandu are the lists of "ten tops," or Western music top-tens, published in Indian and local magazines and newspapers. In some cases these top-ten lists come straight from the centers of power in the Western music industry, through some rather surprising channels. One middle-aged proprietor of another New Road cassette shop explained to me how people find out about the "latest" songs.

Like, here, we go [just down the street] to the American Library[22] and get the charts from *Rolling Stone*. We send someone there to photocopy and bring it back. These songs are very popular, and people look there for what they like. That's why they look there. [*Pulls out a clipboard full of charts xeroxed from Rolling Stone.*] We have the charts here and we show them [customers] the chart. They choose just according to the chart. They look at this [*Rolling Stone* list] and this [*Rising Nepal* list], and then they choose. . . . The choice here is just like in America. American pop—people go for it immediately [*ṭhyākkai milcha*]!

These days people are listening to music *a lot* more than they used to. Before, they used to listen to a lot of disco, ten or fifteen years

[21] The English-language daily published by the Nepali government.
[22] Run by the United States Information Service (USIS).

ago. But now disco hardly sells at all. Only a little bit. Only a few buy it.

Another cassette merchant explained to me that he in fact bases his whole-sale orders on the *Rolling Stone* top-ten lists, which he too acquires cour-tesy of the United States government. Perhaps I was naive to be surprised to find Nepali shopkeepers basing their orders on *Rolling Stone* hit lists and then posting these charts as a service to their customers.[23] But what this demonstrates clearly is that the consumption of Western music in Kathmandu by the early 1990s had become firmly plugged into high-power transnational promotion and marketing circuits, even if in this case it was the pirated-cassette manufacturers in Bangkok who were raking in the money, not the Euro-American recording industry. The arrival (in 1991) of twenty-four-hour-a-day MTV broadcasts on the new satellite "Star TV" (Melkote et al. 1998) only secured Kathmandu's direct line into the heart of the Western music megabusiness. Watching MTV via satellite, local Nepali pop-music fans are now consuming in "real time" (cf. Wilk 1992:86–88), sharing the same mediated "cyber space" with millions of others around the globe.

While most cassette dealers pointed to things like "top ten" lists, Nepal TV, and *Sunday Pop* as factors behind the phenomenal rise in inter-est in "English" music in the mid-1980s, they did not mention an equally important catalyst that arrived on the local middle-class youth scene at about the same time. In the mid-1980s Radio Nepal began experimenting with commercial sponsorship in order to lower its dependence on state subsidies. To attract advertisers, Radio Nepal decided to upgrade its not-so-popular half-hour Western music show[24] to a one-hour program, in English, during the prime Saturday noon-to-one-o'clock time slot. For their English-speaking host, Radio Nepal enlisted the services of a young Nepali "disk jockey" with several years of professional radio experience in Europe. In this way Radio Nepal's *Musical Hour* was launched primar-ily as a vehicle to attract revenue from beer and cigarette manufacturers looking for avenues into the growing middle-class market.

In an interview I conducted with the host of the *Musical Hour,* he described how during the first several months of the program he had filled

[23] Local retailers in Singapore also use American and European hit charts in determining what titles to stock and promote (Wells and Lee 1995:31–33).

[24] Although it is officially mandated to promote Nepali music and thereby a Nepali na-tional consciousness, Radio Nepal has, at least since the 1970s, included small amounts of Western pop music in its programming. Writing of the early 1970s, Anderson and Mitchell noted that "Until recently, three or four English or American hit tunes were played each day. This was reduced to what can be performed in a single half-hour show each Friday evening" (1978:252).

up air time with selections from his own tape collection, brought back from Europe. Realizing that this could not go on forever, and that Radio Nepal was not interested in buying Western music recordings, he soon came up with a solution to his problem.

> Something hit my mind. How about approaching the listeners directly and requesting them to send the cassettes and in return we are going to then have their names broadcast and we are going to mention about their likes and dislikes; their choice of songs will be played. That's when we started the "title holder" business, that means the participants—we call them "title holders." Half an hour to one "title holder," half an hour to the other.
> Well, that became very popular. So popular that now I am fully— well let's use the word "equipped"—equipped with music for another ten years!

In this scheme listeners send in cassette tapes with a half-hour mix of their favorite Western pop songs, and if their submission is accepted, they become one of that week's "title holders." Participants also include their mailing addresses (and usually phone numbers), requesting that other listeners contact them. According to the program's host, many local young people have established links, even friendships, through listening to the *Musical Hour*.

In 1985, during the first seven or eight months of the "title holder" system, "disco numbers were very popular," said the show's host.

> But all of a sudden I started receiving complaints that, "Why is the *Musical Hour* just playing disco songs?" And then I also suddenly found a change in, well, regarding the contributions they make; and in the lists, well, I started seeing some rock numbers coming up. And after some time it was heavy-metal numbers. Since then it's been some rap, some reggae, and on and on. So you see, it's like you start with one thing and you end up with something else! And so now, the most popular star among Nepalese youngsters is Jon Bon Jovi. At least once a fortnight he is there. As for Michael Jackson, he just disappeared!

Indeed, the program's play lists show a surprising shift from requests for disco hits and "evergreen" singers, like Elvis and Mick Jagger, to very contemporary numbers by groups like the Beastie Boys, REM, and Simple Minds. With growing access (on the part of local middle-class listeners) to Western music videos, top-ten columns, and mass-market recordings, Radio Nepal's *Musical Hour* soon became a showcase for the latest mainstream commercial rock and roll.

Even though *Musical Hour* was largely listener-driven, it would be inaccurate to say that the music simply reflected the tastes of the program's audience. On early Saturday afternoons the same song by Twisted Sister floated on the breeze in mountain hamlets and Tarai villages across Nepal, and fans wrote in from as far afield as Darjeeling and Uttar Pradesh in India. Yet the show's "title holders" were almost invariably upper-middle-class teenage boys and young men from Kathmandu. Because of "postal problems," the program's host explained, cassette contributions just about had to be hand-delivered, making it next to impossible for anyone from outside of Kathmandu to participate.

While locality is one limiting factor, language is another. From the outset *Musical Hour* was conducted in English, as was the correspondence from would-be "title holders." The program's host explained:

> When you are talking about an English [music] program, then I think you must have a presenter who *does* the program in English too. Of course one could have done that program in Nepali, but taking that rock number, or rap number, or punk, or whatever it is, and it becomes extremely difficult to present those songs in Nepali because the word power is not there, the vocabulary is not too powerful. And the way you just present in Nepali—I mean, it's too idle, it sounds too idle and too lazy. Whereas when you're playing an English song, why not English? Why not talk in English? And then that becomes even more, let's say, "smarter," even more powerful.
>
> What I'm talking about here is the power of words, you see, and the way you present it. And actually you cannot do that when you are doing a program like that in Nepali. It becomes totally impossible.

Indeed, "the power of words" was crucial to determining who participated in *Musical Hour* as a "title holder." Those who command English are "smarter" and "more powerful." Judging from listeners' letters, practically all "title holders" were enrolled in a group of about eight or ten upper-middle-class English-medium high schools or were recent graduates. What unites these persons (of often diverse caste and ethnic backgrounds) is class membership, as indicated by how and where they were educated. But just as important is the role of Western music itself. Young people use this music (access to which is limited by education and wealth) to stake their claims to middle-class membership. Perusing the "top-ten" lists, collecting the "latest" pop music, and participating in the *Musical Hour* are all activities that illustrate how young people meld consumer practice and class practice in an ongoing, always emerging, middle-class culture. For middle-class youth, music is an important consumer domain through which the project of class membership is forwarded. By having their names and selections announced on national radio, these young people in Kathmandu both create a node around which class identities can be formed and effectively project (broadcast) their own class privilege, in the form of taste, to the nation. In establishing this interactive radio format, Radio Nepal provided a relatively small group of Kathmandu youth the chance to naturalize its class privilege by making its distinctive tastes in Western music serve as the national standard.

CONCLUSION

This chapter traces some of the complex channels of communication that link Nepal, the "First World" (East and West), and an increasingly global sphere of consumer commodities that can no longer be tied to place. Mass media (and other forms of mass communication, such as tourism) transcend local boundaries, moving images, goods, and people through space with often unforeseen consequences. While other chapters have considered the local *meanings* of transnational objects and images, this chapter has shown *how* an ostensibly isolated spot like Kathmandu is tied in intricate ways to a new world of commercially mediated identity resources.

Beyond simply illustrating the transnational character of modern mass media, this chapter also emphasized how no single form of commercial media can be realistically isolated from others. From television, to video, to cinema, to film magazines, to film songs, to radio, to music videos, to satellite communications, to MTV, to pop songs, to audiocassettes, back and forth and on and on, each media platform not only helps to *produce* others but ultimately *depends* on the others for solidifying and expanding its own market. By playing off of and constantly referring to each other, this complex *media assemblage* forms a tangled web of linkages that promote and channel consumer desires in never-ending circuits from one media product to the next.

Understanding the cross-referencing powers of the media assemblage also sheds light on commercial media's ability to engage consumers' imaginations, either overtly (in the interactive strategies found in film magazine question-and-answer pages or in Radio Nepal's "title holder" scheme) or through the more subtle effect of building a virtual reality within a mutually validating commercial sphere. While assisting in the construction of consumer imaginations, "mass" media also help to naturalize individuating ideologies and categories ("stars," "fans," etc.) by publicly disseminating names, addresses, photos, likes and dislikes. In this way consumer practice produces new patterns of sociality by opening new ways of constituting groups ("fans," "title holders," etc.). In turn each of these groups becomes a location in which people seek to either claim or naturalize privilege through an idiom of taste and distinction.

Finally, in this chapter we see many different levels of state and private interests interacting with regional, and ultimately global, multinational capitalist forces. Because of limited production capabilities, huge media distributors like MCA help to determine what Nepalis see on TV. Coca-cola money finds its way into the local Nepali film scene, where investments in leisure products and images promise payoffs in the proliferating elements of a local consumer culture and ethos. In the Western pop music scene, one finds the growing presence of powerful marketing forces operating through likely channels, such as *Rolling Stone*, and unlikely ones, such as the United States Information Service. While none of these transnational interests can be said to be *driving* local consumption, neither can it be said that the local scene is free of their influences. Often the interests of the Nepali state and local businesses were at odds, as when local commercial interests favored foreign programming over nation-producing, locally made, Nepali-language programming. Similarly, these stories show how the public does not always live up to business's expectations, as in the case of the film acting school (financed by high-power businessmen) that could not recruit paying students. From the three case studies in this chapter emerges a picture of "popular" or "mass-mediated" culture in Kathmandu that is unmistakably implicated in a host of forces associated with the global cultural economy, but also unmistakably Nepali, in that local historical and cultural contingencies form the ground from which a particular contemporary experience emerges.

PART IV

YOUTH AND THE EXPERIENCE OF MODERNITY

8

CONSTRUCTING THE MODERN YOUTH

Does not the true character of each epoch come alive in the nature of
its children?

—KARL MARX, *Grundrisse*

Many of the dilemmas and compromises of modernity in Kathmandu
come to a focus in the category of middle-class "modern youth." "Youth"
and "youth culture" are particularly important sociocultural constructions because they show in stark terms the contending forces at work
in any project of claiming middle-class modernity. A host of state and
commercial forces compete with middle-class adults and young people
themselves in a high-stakes game to define the cultural territory of the
"modern youth." With "youth" an essentially *new* social category—
emerging from prolonged middle-class educational expectations, new
media and commercial forces, and a severe shortage of "suitable" employment—what is at stake in the struggle to constitute the "modern youth"
is nothing short of the future of middle-class culture in Kathmandu.

In light of the middle-class love/hate relationship with consumer culture described in previous chapters, it is not surprising that the debate
over "modern youth" brings out the full range of contradictions that characterize middle-class culture generally. The same forces at work in constituting middle-class culture as a consumer culture are also at work in the
constitution of the "new youth" as a category of consumers. Thus, the
same patterns of embrace and rejection that we have already seen in middle-class attitudes toward modernity are extended to the new category of
"teens," who literally come to embody the middle class's consumer hopes
and fears. Middle-class young people are left to live these contradictions.
They must pioneer a new social identity that forces them to reconcile
images of themselves and their futures according to state and commercial
narratives of progress and abundance on the one hand, with the real
world of scarcity and precarious claims to social standing on the other.
This chapter and the next describe the *struggle for*, and the *struggle of*,
the modern youth.

As in many other non-Western societies, the study of "youth culture" in Nepal has rarely gone beyond the standard ethnographic consideration of transition rites (cf. Fuglesang 1994:39). A variety of works provide valuable accounts of male and female life-cycle rituals that, as Lynn Bennett says, mark "the transition to adulthood" (1983:52). To the extent that these rites are currently performed in urban Kathmandu, they remain an important part of the social production of young adults. But there are new modes of cultural production in place that increasingly shape the experience and meaning of youth. Many contemporary cultural forces are now less involved in producing "adults" than a new "in-between" category of "youth."

Regardless of whether we view "adolescence" as a natural "intermediate" human developmental phase or a modern historical cultural construct,[1] it is undeniable that the experience of adolescence has been radically transformed in the cultural context of capitalism, and especially consumer capitalism (Kett 1977). Unlike most social theory—including much educational and modernization theory—that unproblematically views the condition of modernity as requiring "that manhood be *delayed* while youth prepares for its tasks and responsibilities" (Rudolph and Rudolph 1967:3–4 n, emphasis added), I focus on the *constructedness* of such taken-for-granted categories as "youth" and "teen" and the general concept of "adolescence." What does it really *mean* for "manhood" (not to mention "womanhood"[2]) to be "delayed"? What interests strive to initiate, dominate, and perpetuate this "delay"? Like all culturally constructed social categories, the modern concept of "youth" has a history tied to particular socioeconomic processes. "Modern" middle-class "youth," like middle-class culture itself, is a volatile cultural experience marked by powerful state and commercial forces that compete with powerful local critiques and dissent to create the unique configuration of Nepali modernity.

THE SOCIAL CONTEXT OF YOUTH

The fact that more and more middle-class young people are engaged in longer and longer periods of education points to a series of profound

---

[1] See Schlegel and Barry 1991 for a discussion of differing interpretations of "adolescence."

[2] In chapter 9 I discuss the gender politics of "youth culture." The fact is that, even in the middle class, womanhood (and its responsibilities) is indeed less likely to be "delayed" than manhood. In other words, the age-segregating cultural processes of "youth" formation (e.g., education) are more likely to target (and privilege) young men than young women. The experience of "youth" as an "in-between" stage is, I would suggest, less distinct for women than for men, though this is likely to change.

shifts in economic, demographic, and political patterns in the Kathmandu valley. Because entrance into the "officer" level of the civil service and most government and private corporations requires a bachelor's degree, most middle-class young men (and their parents) consider it essential to have achieved at least a college diploma. Similarly, employment in business, management, or nongovernmental "development" work increasingly calls for at least some college-level training. Since middle-class family lifestyles often cannot be sustained without more than one income, women too are increasingly expected to engage in professional labor, though at levels that demand fewer years of higher education. In contrast to earlier generations, children of the middle class are now often in their mid-twenties before completing their schooling.

Sadly, however, even then, for most middle-class young people it is almost impossible to find acceptable employment in the already bloated tertiary economy. In Kathmandu, middle-class youth are almost by definition educated and un- or underemployed. Many thousands of young people, upon finishing high school classes around age sixteen, spend year after year in a kind of limbo: taking and retaking college exams, waiting for test results, working on "back papers," and sitting out vacations and student strikes. Indeed, many pursue postsecondary education less because they clearly perceive a link between education and personal advancement than because there is simply little else to do.

Compared with previous generations, young people in Kathmandu enter meaningful employment later and later in life, and since marriage is usually delayed until the groom has a job, the average age of marriage for men and women is also rising. A young man may spend many upaid hours behind the counter of some relative's already overstaffed retail establishment, but in most cases his marriage will be postponed until he has found some way to contribute to the family's earning power. Young men especially are aware that marriage without a decently paying job means just one more mouth for their parents and/or older siblings to feed at home.

The picture that emerges is of a new group of urban young people confronted with a host of "modern" problems. They are trapped in the role of representing and fulfilling the hopes and dreams of middle-class families. They are tied to a precarious wage/cash economy where inflation always threatens to outstrip a family's hard-won financial gains. They are torn between the supposed benefits of education and the reality of a stagnant market for middle-class employment. And they feel increasingly frustrated by the contradiction between a market economy that plies them with more and more titillating, sexually explicit print and electronic media and socioeconomic realities that postpone the age of acceptable sexual expression. The experience of middle-class youth in Kathmandu is not one of "manhood delayed while youth prepares for its tasks and

responsibilities" (to again quote the Rudolphs), much less a phase in preparation for life in some future "modern" society. Rather, it is the experience of modernity itself. The lives of middle-class young people in Kathmandu—lives that for many are full of frustration, anxiety, confusion,
desperation, and rage—are the lived expressions of modernity on the periphery of the world stage.

EDUCATION AND SOCIALIZATION

Education, as a market-supplied commodity with the potential to both
raise social standing and provide doors to the world beyond Nepal, has
become one of the primary institutions around which new class-based
communities are formed in Kathmandu. It is perhaps not surprising that
the decline of the extended family and caste community as settings for
middle-class youth socialization should be mirrored by the rise of state
and commercial educational institutions.[3] The same socioeconomic forces
that promote greater and greater incorporation into the labor-for-cash
economy also promote education as a means of socialization. The state
benefits from education in that it provides a privileged site from which to
construct—through standardized curricula, examination systems, etc.—
national identities for youth in opposition to local, regional, ethnic, or
caste identities (Onta 1996, Pigg 1992). Yet the mushrooming growth of
private, usually boarding, schools in the Kathmandu area in the late
1980s and early 1990s attests to the enormous potential for commercial
gain available to anyone able to sell education. Education is both the
business of the state and near the forefront of the current state of business.
Yet ironically, while the state wishes to produce subjects with a homogeneous, unifying sense of national identity, commercial education both re-
sponds to and reinforces sentiments in which individuals and groups are
defined in terms of their access to power and financial resources, or more
simply, in terms of their class.

   Primary and secondary education in Kathmandu is available in public
(government-run) or private (commercial or parochial) schools. The latter
are distinguished by their relatively high (sometimes extremely high) tuition fees, reputation for higher academic standards, and, above all, their
emphasis on the English language as the medium of instruction. Children
in the public schools also study English from an early age, but middle-
class and wealthy parents are willing to pay large amounts for school

---

[3] See chapter 2 for a brief discussion of the huge proliferation of schools in the Kathmandu valley, as well as the increasing numbers of nuclear families living in relatively homogeneous class-segregated neighborhoods in and around the city.

environments where their children hear and use English as much as possible. Thus, even if almost every school child knows *some* English, the extent to which s/he is actually able to function in an English-speaking environment depends largely on the school s/he attends. As a rule of thumb, the higher the tuition fees, the better the quality of English instruction. For more and more people in Kathmandu, English proficiency is simultaneously the key to a better future, an index of social capital, and a part of the purchase price for a ticket out of Nepal.

Those who benefit from the national emphasis on education and the concentration of resources in Kathmandu are not necessarily from one caste or ethnic community. What unites them is their ability to participate in a market economy that distinguishes groups based on their access to financial resources. Education, and especially English proficiency, has been commoditized such that, for the most part, consumers get what they can pay for. In Kathmandu, what people increasingly want, and are willing to pay for, is recognized class membership, and for many, education is among the primary commodities by which class membership is asserted or imposed.

Aside from bringing children into far more frequent contact with age peers, Kathmandu's market-based education system also has implications for the social composition of those groups. The peer groups formed in private schools are more and more likely to be class groups rather than groups based on ethnicity or caste. Again, no one could suggest that schooling obliterates notions of caste or ethnic identity. Yet the fact remains that the school a family's children attend is one of the clearest indices of its *economic* standing. Schools at most levels bring together children from a range of caste, ethnic, and regional backgrounds, uniting them into peer groups based on class. Even if within these groups a child may at times gravitate toward persons with a similar family background, they learn that their larger social reference group consists of people who share similar financial conditions. The child knows too that others of his/her caste/ethnic background are in either more or less prestigious schools because of their greater or lesser financial resources.

In these new school-based peer groups, children come to see themselves less as representatives of one ethnic or caste community and more as indices of their own family's economic standing. In other words, schools become spaces in which people are encouraged to imagine themselves in terms of economic class. Other identities rarely lose their relevance (even when individuals wish they would) but instead take their place alongside some form of class identity. In the same midlevel, moderately expensive Kathmandu boarding school, one might find a relatively low-caste, local Newar boy whose family sold land in order to pay his tuition, a Brahman girl whose parents are first-generation residents employed as fixed-income, midlevel civil servants, and a boy from one of Nepal's indigenous ethnic communities whose father is employed in the Indian Army. Whether or not they perceive their class identities to be more or less desirable than other forms of social identity, these children will nevertheless grow up with daily reminders that their economic standing, for better or worse, is a powerful factor in communicating who they are, and who they are not.

One of the most important implications of these new class-based peer groups is that young people begin to consider themselves and others increasingly in material terms. Of course, the idea that material possessions index social rank is nothing new. For example, dress has for generations, if not centuries, served to mark distinctions between socioeconomic strata in Kathmandu's Newar community (Nepali 1965:65). Yet in the past several decades these socioeconomic strata have become far more permeable and fluid, more open to movement up and slippage down.

It is precisely this sense of mobility—whether regarded with hope or terror—combined with a more and more powerful awareness of class and the need to communicate one's social standing in material terms, that begins to convey some idea of the experience of middle-class youth in Kathmandu. Members of Kathmandu's middle class face the daily challenge of holding themselves precariously between high and low, struggling to convert often extremely limited (even declining) resources into middle-class lives, and constantly reorienting themselves toward the shifting currents of the middle-class cultural mainstream. Young people are acutely conscious of these struggles. They are fully aware that their positions within class-based peer groups are always tenuous and need to be constantly reaffirmed and resubstantiated.

It is this often intense, deep sense of economic and social insecurity that begins to account for the kind of powerful materialistic peer pressure often found among middle-class young people in Kathmandu. As described in the next chapter, youth are often engaged in a subtle, slow-motion dance with their peers, vying with one another both to conceal and display their social and economic resources. Especially for young people whose sense of economic and class insecurity are compounded by instability at home—parental substance abuse (usually alcohol), loss of a parent, a father bringing in new wives, or simply parental abuse—the attachment to peers and the norms of the peer group can become almost slavish. This attachment was most often expressed by conformity to group standards, usually in dress and types of entertainment. Thus, the experience of youth among peers is very often an intensely materialistic one, made all the more compelling by the constant awareness of one's ethereal claims to class membership.

"EDUCATION CULTURE," OR EDUCATION AS MIDDLE-CLASS IDEOLOGY

If Kathmandu's elite, as well as many intellectuals, see education as a means of opening avenues to the *outside*, the bulk of the city's middle class remains oriented to lives *within* Nepal. Indeed, what often distinguished the elite from Kathmandu's middle class was not an emphasis on education, but rather their dreams for the future. While the elite construct their dreams around imagined lives in distant global culture/power centers, for the middle class, perceptions of the future are still very much centered on Kathmandu. But even if middle-class persons perceive their future lives to be *Nepali* lives, the nature of those lives is, for many, almost unimaginable. Unlike the elites who, via travelers' tales, videos, and magazines, can dream of modern lives at the metropole, for the middle class committed to modern lives in Kathmandu, the future is unknown. Members of the middle class are those who have staked their very identities and values in a modern future whose contours lie in a grey zone of uncertainty. It is precisely within this space of anxiety and hope that *education* lodges—an abstract, almost mystical commodity that represents the only avenue to a modern future that middle-class parents can imagine for their children.

One young professor I spoke with summed up many of these feelings. Born and raised in a high-caste Kathmandu home, educated in Nepal and abroad, and now the often exasperated father of two young children, he himself was intimately familiar with the anxieties of middle-class parents.

> The transition that Kathmandu entered into in, oh, around the 1970s, and which has been moving at a greater and greater speed, is something which parents and children just can't forecast. Where we will be in the next ten years, next twenty years, no one can imagine. I mean, parents are at a loss to know how to guide their children. Some children have failed their parents, in the sense that they have not been able to compete at school or in their occupations. The rest of us look at these children who have just been left behind by the system and worry about our own children.
>
> It used to be, before the seventies, well, one pretty much had an idea what he would be doing in the next twenty years—like how much money he would earn, what kind of household he would be able to afford, this kind of thing. But now, who can say? We are charting into a very uncertain future.

These comments capture well the sentiments of thousands of other middle-class parents in Kathmandu who recognize that their children's ability to maintain the family's social status (let alone advance it) nowadays depends less and less on some transfer of authority and resources and more and more on a child's (especially a son's) ability to play a new game. While the rules of the new game are unclear, all perceive education as mandatory preparation. For middle-class families—especially those who by virtue of upper-caste background or inherited property currently command certain fixed resources—the threat of rampant inflation and competing systems of social status combine to make education one of the only reliable points of reference in an otherwise twisting landscape. Education is the mantra that middle-class parents repeat in hopes of propitiating the vagaries of an unknowable "modern" future.

But if parents have visions of their children's futures as successful workers and wage earners, other interests are at work to prepare these same children for futures as consumers.

"Teens" in Kathmandu: "Somewhere in Between"

Part of my daily routine in Kathmandu was to peruse the offerings at several of the hundreds of sidewalk magazine vendors and storefront bookshops that I encountered on my rounds about the city. These dealers offer hundreds of publications to the reading public, ranging from Hindi murder mystery/detective magazines and dozens of film magazines in Hindi, English, and Nepali to specialty magazines for women, children, and sportsmen. Dozens of newspapers—from government- and privately produced Nepali and English dailies to a proliferation of vernacular weeklies—represent all the shades of Nepal's vibrant political spectrum. On one such day I noticed a title I had never before seen. Because it was printed on rather low-grade stock and had a simple two-color cover, I guessed that *Teens* magazine, although in English, was probably a local publication.

That evening I read the premier issue of *Teens* cover to cover and realized that the magazine's contents, commercial backers, and target audience brought into particularly sharp focus the ways in which local, regional, and global market forces intersected in the construction/imagination of the modern youth-as-consumer in Kathmandu. The magazine took a strong stance in the local debate over the meaning of the words "teen" and "teenager," English terms that have entered colloquial Nepali and that designate a new cultural space of "modern youth" still hotly contested between young people, parents, state, and commercial interests.

A few days after I read its first issue, I had the first of several long talks with the two editor-owners of *Teens*. Diane and Gopal were a married couple in early middle age. Both were from ethnic communities with roots in Nepal, though they themselves had grown up in India and South-

9. Shopping for magazines at a New Road sidewalk newsstand.

east Asia, where their Nepali "Gurkha" fathers were stationed with the British army. Both had master's degrees from foreign universities and had "returned" to Nepal as adults to build careers. Their first publishing venture had been a nonprofit monthly devoted to development issues in Nepal. Before long their hopes were frustrated by the fact that while enough people were willing to contribute material to the new magazine, few were willing to pay the subscription fee needed to buy print stock and pay a small staff. Eventually they turned to soliciting advertisements to help defer production costs. Yet their struggle to get a handful of local businesses to put up money for ads was only greeted with criticism by readers who accused them of commercializing the magazine.

Still hoping to keep the magazine alive, Diane and Gopal hit upon a novel marketing scheme. They offered businesspeople free advertising space in their magazine if they would agree to provide sales discounts to magazine subscribers. The idea was to encourage people to subscribe by offering them reduced rates on a variety of goods and services, including restaurant meals, plane tickets, drugstore items, and dry cleaning, furniture, and groceries. Much to the editors' surprise, within months subscription levels had soared, even though relatively few new members were actually interested in the technical, development-related content of the magazine! Diane and Gopal realized they had stumbled upon a very promising commercial opportunity and by early 1991 were considering phasing out the development magazine to focus completely on a consumer's club scheme. As Gopal exclaimed, "Our marketing strategy is stronger than the product itself!"

Not long after their development journal's subscription rates had begun to climb, Diane and Gopal heard that subscribers' sons and daughters were also using the magazine's membership/discount cards. Gradually they conceived of a whole new marketing and publishing thrust that would target a particular youth market via a new subscription magazine for young people. The magazine would link local youth with a range of local businesses that had particular interests in a youthful clientele. In this way *Teens* magazine was conceived of as first and foremost a marketing scheme aimed at upper-middle-class youth and designed to move them onto a track leading eventually to membership in the adult consumer club.

Before launching their new youth magazine, the publishers researched the market and targeted an audience. "Who is our customer? was the main question," explained Gopal. They decided to focus on upper-middle-class youth in their late teens. "They haven't left the school, and haven't entered into work. They're somewhere in between," Gopal said. Diane went on to explain their target audience in more specific terms:

> Our target group is teenagers coming from boarding schools, English boarding schools.[4] Nowadays, Hindi is fast fading, except for public school teenagers—maybe they still like to see it. But boarding school kids, if they want to *be English*, they have to *read* English magazines, *listen* to English music, *watch* English videos, I mean, *everything*. That's who we're going for.

When I asked why the English boarding school students were singled out, Diane replied, "They are the ones who have the purchasing power, or at least their parents do." Diane and Gopal estimated the market to be about six thousand young people between the ages of ten and twenty-one. The publishers had identified an audience of upper-middle-class youth who were pioneering the category of "teen," the newly opened modern space between child and adult. Their aim was to also move into this "between" space of "teen" ambiguity with a product that would provide youth with answers to questions about what it means to be modern, or "to be English." From the outset they envisioned a magazine that would provide youth with a blueprint for what it means to be a "teen."

---

[4] Many of Kathmandu's private, and relatively pricey, "boarding schools" in fact have many local day scholars. Additionally, it is not uncommon to have students in boarding who are actually from the Kathmandu valley.

As with their earlier adult-oriented development magazine, *Teens* made money by publishing free advertisements and collecting subscription fees in return for a card which entitled members to discounts at a growing number of local "member establishments." Diane explained:

> When we chose our member establishments, we took into account, like, what are the facilities that our teen members would like to use. So we said, like, they'll go to teen joints, they'll go for physical fitness, to, say, stationary [greeting card and poster] shops, ice cream shops, jeans places, all this kind of thing. We just asked which is the best place for these kinds of things.

The first issue of *Teens* included advertisements for twenty-eight local businesses hoping to cater to upper-middle-class youth. These included audiocassette shops and video rental stores, beauty parlors and body building clubs, computer and foreign-language training schools, photo studios and sporting goods stores, stationers and bookshops, yoga centers and discos, and a range of snack and fast-food restaurants. Six months later the number of advertising "member establishments" had risen to fifty-two, now including a driving school, a pharmacy, and the music and acting school (described in chapter 7) that encouraged readers to "Be A Film Star! Be an accomplished musician!" Each of these establishments offered *Teens* members discounts on a range of products and services for "teens."

Because it brings together a host of business ventures all interested in creating and servicing a youth market, *Teens* magazine is an ideal window onto a new local commercial "youth culture." The youth culture promoted in the ads and articles of *Teens* is an "ideal world" of youth, leisure, and goods presented as naturally desirable and waiting to be consumed, embodied, enacted. Yet perhaps more important than the actual components of this universe is the way in which the components interact. From restaurants to driving schools, beauty parlors to fitness clubs, photo studios and tailors to video and cassette shops, *Teens* member establishments form a mutually reinforcing, cross-referencing sphere in which leisure activities, commercial images, and public appearances are constantly promoted. Although diverse, the "parts" of this world share a common logic of public display, the display a public, material "self" through consumption. In its constant references to transnational consumer modernity in the forms of film, video, pop music, stars, and fashion, *Teens* participates in a kind of global, intertextual *media assemblage* that constructs its own privileged world of reality-in-images. It is onto this transnational public sphere, the media-assembled space of imagination, that local merchants project their dreams of a local "youth culture."

Although conceived of as a marketing vehicle, *Teens* magazine offered its readers more than just advertisements. The magazine offered prize competitions, comic strips, Nepali folktales and Greek mythology, short stories, popular-science articles, "believe-it-or-not" features, puzzles, contests, and games. Yet from the first issue on, there was a second category of article that fell somewhere between entertainment and advertisement. This category ranged from articles on sports heroes like Pelé, Diego Maradona, and Gabriela Sabatini ("the glamour doll of tennis"), which could be seen as promoting certain mediated spectator sports or commoditized sporting activities, to more explicitly consumption-oriented articles. From the first issue, *Teens* carried pages devoted to pop-song heroes and heroines (from Debbie Gibson and New Kids on the Block to Jim Morrison and Robert Plant), including bio-data and lyrics to popular songs. Starting with the second issue, the music pages were accompanied by a listing of the "top ten [English] albums of the month," provided "courtesy of" a *Teens* member establishment dealing in imported pop cassettes.[5] Recent English video releases were also featured from the first issue on, and by issue 5 the magazine included a "video top ten" column "courtesy of" a member video rental store. Although the publishers did not view these music and video features as advertisements, these examples and many others[6] often blurred the fine line between entertainment and consumer promotion.[7]

The same link between information/entertainment and commercial interests also existed on a more programmatic level. One of the most consistent consumer themes in *Teens* magazine had to do with fashion and the promotion of a fashion consciousness. From the first issue, *Teens* featured a regular column entitled "Kathmandu Goes the Fashion Way," provided courtesy of a local "fashion wear" boutique. In the first issue, readers were informed that "each individual has a personality + a style of their own." Women are then advised that "this summer" certain items of clothing give "an extra chic look," such as culottes, which are "so very in." For men, "the look" includes baggy trousers, but they are warned that "collars this season are slightly broader" and "Ties also are preferred a little wider." In the second issue, "Young Fashion Steals the Spotlight," while in the third

---

[5] For more on the commercial music scene in Kathmandu, see chapter 7.

[6] Perhaps less overtly, the "ten-minute exercise" pages (featuring "muscle-toning" calisthenics for women "to slim down those 'critical' areas") and the regular "discovering-computer" features also helped to promote "member establishments" specializing in yoga/physical fitness and computer training.

[7] *Teens* magazine provides a print media example of what Raymond Williams calls television "flow": that is, the entertainment and advertising relate as "a sequence in which the advertisements are integral rather than as a program interrupted by advertisements" (1974:69).

the writer concludes with the admonishment, "So youngsters, don't wait for that heady feeling of confidence which comes from knowing that you're looking great. Go for it!! and be a real head turner."

The fashion feature in the fifth issue, entitled "Clothing—The Silent Language," told readers:

Appearance says a great deal about a person before a word is spoken. When you look at someone, 80 to 90 percent of what you see is the persons apparel. It is the most important signal that attracts or warns people away in an initial contact. Does putting this much emphasis on dressing strike you as shallow?. . . Well, that's the way of our hep world. Clothing and grooming draws an instant reaction because it demands speedy conclusions. "Eat what you want, but dress up for others" is the motto of the modern time.

Furthermore, readers are told to "deal with the realities of your face and figure," and "learn to recognize your short-comings and learn to minimize them." After all, "Fashion can be fun and is not something to resist." The article concludes with a reassuring synopsis:

Consciously dressing to gain positive reaction of others is not a dishonest action. It is a way to encourage people to regard you with interest. It is an invitation to explore the interesting and dynamic person that is behind a well presented visual image.

All of these fashion articles contain a number of underlying themes. First is the insistent association of reality with materiality: one's "face and figure" are "realities" with "short-comings" that must be "dealt with"; a person *is* what you *see*; *feeling good* is the result of *looking good*. Significantly, the writers are always aware that their local readers will likely see such equations as "shallow" or even "dishonest" but repeatedly soothe reader apprehensions through assurances that such behavior is "hep," "modern," and unavoidable and will encourage people to "regard you with interest." All of these fashion articles construct modernity as a discourse that privileges the material as real and equates persons with objects and pleasure/emotion with material conditions. Readers are instructed that this new type of *common sense* is "not something to resist."

A second theme is the tension between messages that fashion is about personal style and expresses characteristics unique to the presumably unchanging essence of the individual and messages describing the constant changes in hemlines, collars, patterns, and other aspects of what it means to be young, confident and "in." According to Roland Barthes, commercial interests in capitalist society simultaneously promote the pursuit of two dreams: the "dream of identity," in other words, "to be *oneself*, and to have this self recognized by others," and the "dream of otherness," to be transformed, via some act of consumption, into a desired other (1983:255–56). In promoting these contradictory dreams—the longing to be valued for what you are, and the longing to become some desired other—consumer forces such as *Teens* magazine capitalize on the heightened experience of ambiguity in "modern societies" by using the anxious energy of insecurity as the driving force in a circular process whereby identity formation is tied to the pursuit of two fundamentally irreconcilable "dreams."

A third theme is "clothing as language," which echoes a concern found in Western social and cultural theory starting as far back as Georg Simmel's 1903 essay "The Metropolis and Mental Life." According to Simmel, because the metropolitan "modern man" lives in an intensely monetized, cash-based socioeconomic setting, he must constantly fight the tendency by which his personal essence is reduced to a quantitative, monetary value. This he does by seizing upon the "qualitative differentiation" offered him in commoditized forms of adornment, dress, and bodily disposition. No longer able to enjoy the "frequent and prolonged association [which] assures the personality of an unambiguous image of himself in the eyes of others," the modern man must "appear 'to the point,' to appear concentrated and strikingly characteristic . . . [within the] brief metropolitan contacts" that make-up his daily relations (Simmel 1950:420–21). The *Teens* article on clothing as language takes a Simmelesque world of consumer alienation as given and celebrates the "modern" necessity of "dressing to gain positive reaction."

In many ways the "silent language" being taught by *Teens* and its commercial backers is less a language that people speak than one which speaks people, or at least a certain kind of person. It is a language that turns people into things (at least "80 or 90 percent"), bodies into "realities" in need of fashioning, and modernity into materiality. It is a language that turns "shallowness" and "dishonesty" into "motto[s] of the modern time." It is a language that draws the performance of self into the logic of the market through the endless pursuit of "fashion."

Teens magazine had a variety of ways by which it sought to interpellate young people, or to encourage them to use its language to speak themselves into a new kind of being. Often this involved recruitment into the category of the "teen." This summoning of a "teen" identification started in the first issue with the announcement of the "Mr. Teen & Teen Queen" contest. Opposite the fashion page was the following message:

> Hey Gorgeous Gals and Great-Looking Guys!! Ever Won A Prize Just For Looking Great? Just Give A Try. Send Us Your Photo (B/W, P.p. size) Along With Personal Details And Win Special Prizes As Our Mr. Teen & Teen Queen.

That subsequent issues featured photos of that month's "Mr. Teen & Teen Queen" is perhaps less important than the fact that *Teens* regularly invited its readers to imagine themselves as bearers of images—images constructed from fashion purchases and fixed in photography.

But the meaning of the word "teen" constructed in the pages of *Teens* magazine goes beyond appearances. In *Teens* "teen" is a "natural" category, desirable and of unquestioned value. Inside the front cover of the first issue is a cartoon of a young boy lying on his stomach, his head propped up in his hands. Above his pensive visage appears a bubble caption with the words, "God, when am I going to be a teenager?" Scattered about the cartoon boy, as though appearing in his mind, are a range of images: boys playing tennis and soccer, a guitar player, people laughing, a cartoon cowboy with a gun, attractive girls, mystery gift packages, jet planes and planets, and boys and girls sitting around a canopied table at an outside restaurant. When I asked Diane what they intended these images to convey, she replied:

> Oh, on the first page we show that every child who's ten wants to be a teen. And anyone who's twenty-four still wants to be called a teen. You know, they don't want to say that they are old already! Twenty-one, twenty-two, twenty-three, they still want to be teenagers!

Diane's remarks seem to sum up much of the intended meaning of *Teens* magazine. The aim is to constitute "teenage" not so much as an age category but as a kind of desired condition, a way of life that can be achieved through the adoption of a range of consumer behaviors. In these pages "teen" is an identity waiting to be subscribed to (pun intended), embodied, and lived out in a series of commercial transactions.

Another important technique that *Teens* used to constitute "teens" was through regularly featured, self-administered tests of *teenness* and articles on the nature of "teens." The "take a test" pages of the first issue helped readers determine what *type* of "teen" they are. An article in the second issue discusses "Why Teens Are Emotional" and describes the "in-between years" as characterized by "moodiness, sulkiness, temper tantrums and a tendency to cry at the least provocation." "Teens," readers are informed, suffer from occasional "emotional instability" and frequently dwell on "the all important issue of romance." The third issue lets readers answer the question "How Reckless Are You?" and in the fifth, a test asks "Are You Sunny, or Moony, or Both?" In these and other features, *Teens* encourages young people to imagine themselves within a constellation of taken-for-granted "teen" traits, ranging from emotional instability and recklessness to consumer desires and a longing for romance. *Teens* never asks "*Are* you a teen?" but instead encourages readers to assume the givenness of the category in the constantly repeated question "What kind of teen are you?"

In her book on fashion and modernity, Elizabeth Wilson (1985) describes how in Europe and North America popular women's magazines in the 1940s and 1950s promoted a certain typology of women by regularly printing quizzes and tests encouraging readers to identify themselves in the choices offered, and then "Dress to your type" (1985:124–25). As with *Teens*, these magazines offered people the satisfaction of "belonging" to a type, but only at the expense of conforming to the consumer demands of that category. As Wilson says, "There's a strange psychological reassurance in the idea that one *can* be categorized, the thrill of self-recognition in saying 'I'm . . . typical' " (1985:145). Offering them an image for self-identification, *Teens* magazine constantly encourages readers to ask, "What is a teen?" and then provides explicit and implicit answers to its own questions. As a marketing vehicle out to create a market, *Teens* helps teens to imagine themselves as "teens."

To what extent is it fair to say the publishers of *Teens* explicitly intended to create a group of young consumers? Although perhaps rare in the degree of calculation that it displays, *Teens* is only a more overt example of other similar commercial processes. From the outset, Diane and Gopal viewed *Teens* membership as a kind of apprenticeship for future participation in their adult consumer club. As Gopal explained, the magazine was only the "first stage" in a "big huge plan." Diane and Gopal intended to use the profits from the magazine memberships to finance a series of future commercial ventures. In the short run, they planned to sponsor music festivals and rock-and-roll concerts in Kathmandu to promote *Teens* memberships and raise money. Further down the road, they intended to open a country club for upper-middle-class families, with an emphasis on facilities for youth and activities like bowling, swimming, and roller skating. The point is that the publishers of *Teens* had a clear vision of a range of products and services, as well as a potentially lucrative youth market. The goal of the magazine, as a "first stage," was to shape this potential market by offering it the terms of a group identity; a sense of groupness within the domain of commoditized leisure and consumer goods that the publishers (and their supporters) wished to advance.

By dwelling at some length on *Teens*, I do not mean to suggest that this magazine is somehow single-handedly creating a group of youthful middle-class consumers. There are also a host of other commercial interests at work in Kathmandu hoping to produce (and reproduce) "teens" as a specific consumer "public." These include (as I discussed in chapter 7) interactive radio shows where youth submit favorite "hit" songs, commercially sponsored sporting events and rock-and-roll concerts, MTV-style video shows on Nepal Television sponsored by manufacturers hoping to capture youth markets, and each of the hundreds of local businesses that, like the *Teens* "member establishments," seek to create a clientele for whom their goods or services make up a part of the very identity of modern youth. Yet *Teens* is a particularly enlightening window onto an emerging consumer culture in which entrepreneurs, peddling a whole new universe of mass-produced consumer goods, come together to create an "ideal" category of "youthful" consumers.

In this way *Teens* magazine exemplifies what I call the media assemblage: an apparently seamless and mutually promoting sphere of commercial media forms (from pop music and television to video and cinema), as well as a host of other consumer goods from professional sports to fashion. In *Teens* all of these consumer domains are invoked and then linked to the dozens of local "member establishments" whose goods and services bask in the aura of this "star"-studded commercial firmament. The common project of commodity promotion binds together everything from Hindi film stars to beauty parlors to rock music into the transnational sphere of the media assemblage.

But what about the *Teens* target group, those six thousand upper-middle-class boarding school youth? During my last meeting with Diane and Gopal, I found that things were not going as their membership projections had predicted. About half a year into their new venture, the publishers were coming to the unsettling conclusion that even though membership numbers looked good, they might in fact be missing their target audience. As Gopal explained, it was becoming clear that a sizable number of readers and subscribers were *not* upper-middle-class youth. Rather, these were middle-middle- and even lower-middle-class kids: their photos (clothing, demeanor, etc.), their level of proficiency in English, and the schools they attended gave them away as less than the type of reader/member the publishers had hoped to attract. The intention had been for *Teens* to take root among the upper strata, and then spread down. "But if *Teens* gets associated with these lower groups, we'll never have the upper ones," lamented Gopal.[8]

Although unfortunate for the publishers of *Teens*, the fact that the magazine attracted youth from across the middle class is significant for two reasons. First, it indicates that a wide variety of young people are attracted to the concept of teenness. The publishers had guessed correctly that youth in this "in-between" space—between childhood and adulthood, high and low class, desire and fulfillment—were looking for an-

---

[8] For a more focused discussion of youth magazine readership and reader reaction, see chapter 7.

swers to the questions about meaning and identity that their ambiguous positions pushed to the fore. Yet they misjudged how deeply—how far "down" into the middle class—these anxious feelings of ambiguity and longing for certainty extended.

Second, judging by names on the long lists of game and contest winners published in the magazine, *Teens* readers form a *self-associating group* (through their common consumption of, and participation in, *Teens*) that could never have been imagined in Nepal even a generation ago. From Brahmans, Chetris, and high-caste Hindu and Buddhist Newars, through a range of mid- and low-level Newar caste members, to a variety of ethnic communities, including Tibetans, Sherpas, Rais, and Gurungs, and even a smattering of Euro-American expatriates, *Teens* readers are young people brought together by an incredibly complex, thoroughly modern, set of factors. A concatenation of local, national and transnational forces have led to the contemporary urban experience of emerging class formations and new cultural logics.[9]

It is this turbulent mix of people and forces, and the new class culture that they are producing, that a product such as *Teens* seeks to capture and mold into its own image. In *Teens* we see an effort by dozens of local businesses to channel this social current into the profit-generating streams of consumer identities.[10] *Teens* aims to unite youth from the new middle class in the common experience of a consumer public, but also offers them a new *language*: in the words of the *Teens* fashion article, a "silent language" of images, consumer goods and services, a language that *speaks its readers* into a new identity as "teen." This is a language that speaks new forms of identification into being even if those "modern" identities remain out of reach. The popularity of *Teens* among "lower groups" attests to the fact that the magazine speaks at least as much to the *desire* for identification with "modernity" than to its *possibility*. The "silent language" of *Teens* magazine constructs consumer identities for youth, even if for many young people this new identity is only a space of longing, a sense of deprivation, or an unfulfillable "dream of otherness."

---

[9] These forces include Nepal's new place in global commodity markets (as consumers/importers and as producers of cash commodities such as handmade carpets); the country's past and current role as a source of transnational military labor; global mass tourism; mass poverty and international development aid; and the rise of a centralized state apparatus in Kathmandu.

[10] *Teens* readers resemble the *remaja*, or Indonesian "teenage" readers of a popular youth-directed fan/fashion magazine called *Topchords*, described by James Siegel (1986: ch. 8). Siegel shows how print media can set into motion new "circuits of exchange" between "stars" and audiences and how commercial forces can capitalize on these new relations by defining the terms of exchange in an idiom of taste, fashion, and consumer goods.

"Teen" as Youth-Category

One remark that I heard early on in my research struck me as particularly significant and often returned to my mind as I spent more time with young people in Kathmandu. In the course of a conversation an upper-caste man in his early fifties who owned a small business described his experiences as the father of three sons, two of whom were still in their teens. He spoke of how so often these days children will pressure their parents into making a wide variety of purchases. Wanting to probe his sense of how things had changed, I asked "Is this something different from thirty years ago?"

> Oh, yes! In those days children were not that much provocative. They could not expect much, even from their parents. I mean that then their interests were very much limited. They didn't know about so many things, and even if they did, they had no influence over their parents.

When I asked "What has changed?" he replied:

> Twenty or thirty years ago there was no idea of this middle group, these teenagers. I mean, then they went from being boys to being adults. In between there was not this type of stage.[11]

With time I realized that this man's use of the word "teenager" to denote a new "in between" stage was significant. Some youthful "in between" experience was probably not totally unfamiliar to him, but the nature of that experience had changed, and it was to some new type of "middle group" that he attached the word "teenage."

I found that, like this man, many other Kathmandu residents used the English word "teenager" (whether speaking in English or Nepali) to designate a new category of youth. Although the meaning of "teen" or "teenager" was not entirely fixed, uniformly the words were used to distinguish one type or group of youth from other young people, not youth as an age category from other age groups. Also, "teenagers" were always *modern consumers*: of drugs and pornography for some, of legitimate goods and services for others. It is these mixed, often intensely negative,

---

[11] These changes seem to parallel historical shifts in North America documented by Joseph Kett (1977). Kett writes that until the middle of the nineteenth century Americans noted no intermediate "adolescent" phase between childhood and adulthood. Children entered the work force at age seven, with "full" incorporation for a male at around puberty (Kett 1977:17). For more on the origins of "teens" in North America, see Palladino 1996, Wilson 1985:173.

meanings associated with the word "teen" that stand in such sharp contrast to meanings promoted in commercial media.

To my surprise, few of the scores of young men my co-workers and I interviewed used the English word "teenager" to describe themselves. More typically they used the Nepali terms "boy" [keṭā] or the more inclusive "boys and girls" [keṭākeṭīharu]. However, one eighteen-year-old college student, a long-time resident of Kathmandu, did describe himself as a "teenager," and in a most interesting way. In an interview conducted by a co-worker, this young man explained why he liked Hindi "love story" films the best:

> Listen, our age is teenage, isn't that right? In this age we're usually interested in doing love [love garne]. These are the things [we're into], no? Like, how to love, what to do, how to initiate love, how to get girls, and all of these angles. These things you must be able to do yourself, so that's why I usually like to watch the love stories.[12]

This young man's remarks seem to capture much of the ambiguity, tenuousness, and anxiety that many middle-class youth feel in negotiating new identities. His comments about what it means to be "teenage" seemed to be as much a series of questions as confident assertions. While his tastes in film and his interest in "doing love" were extremely common among middle-class young people in Kathmandu, few so explicitly identified mass media as a source of tutorial guidance in the theory and practice of teenness. In describing himself as a "teen" this young man invoked the commercial logic of the cinema, which, not unlike the logic of *Teens* magazine, conflates "teen" identity with consumption: I am a teenager; *therefore* I like to watch films.

Young people were not the only ones to point out a relationship between the concept of "teenager" and particular media. Many adults too made the association. This came through with exceptional clarity in a series of interviews I conducted with retail merchants who specialized in the sale of audiocassette tapes. With surprising consistency the middle-aged proprietors of these cassette shops associated "teenagers" with tastes in imported, Western, "English" music. Typical were the comments of one merchant, whose shop was located on a back street near the Chetrapati section of Kathmandu. Here the proprietor, a local man in his late thirties, explained to me why Hindi cassettes were his biggest sellers:

---

[12] It is fascinating to compare this Nepali young person's comments on the pedagogic role of Indian romance films for youth who need to learn "how to love" with the almost identical language of young people in Sierra Leone (Richards 1996:110) and Kenya (Fuglesang 1994:177). These African young people look to the same Hindi melodramas for answers to the same "how to" questions, as they also work to imagine themselves into a new "modern" (mediated and commercialized) world of "youth and love."

Here Hindi films have had a really big impact. In the cinemas, from the videos, a really big influence. Therefore, those films that are showing in the theaters, or on video, people come here immediately to buy the music cassettes.

He explained that most of his customers were high school students or recent graduates (mostly, but not exclusively, male) from a range of caste, ethnic, and class backgrounds. Given these demographics, I was surprised at his answer when I asked who bought the Western pop music cassettes that accounted for perhaps a third of his stock:

It's the teenagers. They go for the rock, heavy metal, and now rap music is picking up in popularity. We have some of that here too. I mean some of them also like the modern Nepali songs, but these modern teenagers have been mostly influenced by Western music, and they don't go for the [Nepali] folk songs. Here the teenagers only really go for the latest songs. Those songs are really for the teenagers.

Although almost all of his customers were roughly the same age, this cassette dealer used the word "teenager" to distinguish one consumer group from another. For him "teenagers" were those who bought not just "Western" music but the "latest" imported pop songs. They were the ones who were always asking for what was new.

In contrast to the positive connotations that *Teens* magazine and many other business interests associated with the words, for most other adults (as well as many of the school-aged girls we interviewed) the words "teen" and "teenager" almost always described young, unmarried males who were considered unruly or delinquent. For example, after describing how young people these days are often intractable, one young woman pointed particularly to the "teenagers":

Usually I've found that kids [keṭākeṭīharu] are good, but some people have very bad behavior, like when they become teenagers. These days in Nepal, people are using a lot of smack.[13] They don't listen to their parents. All they do is hang out with friends, and if they don't get what they want, they just argue. Mostly it's the boys who do this.

For this young woman, most kids are good, but some, unfortunately, become "teenagers." For her "teenagers" are disobedient, likely to take drugs, and usually male.

Even more than drugs, the subject that most often elicited use of the English word "teenager," as opposed to assorted Nepali words for youth,

---

[13] "Smack" is a slang term for brown heroin in Kathmandu.

was that of "blue" (pornographic) film viewing. One typical set of comments came from a thirty-five-year-old woman, born in India of Nepali parents and now the owner of her own small business in Kathmandu:

Have you ever seen a blue film?

No, [my husband and I] never watched that kind of film. I guess our thought on that matter is like the old people's thought. We don't like it. I think those that do a lot of sex, those who want a lot of entertainment [*manoranjan*], those who want a free life, they watch this kind of film. Like the young, unmarried boys—they watch.

Why do people want to watch this?

It's especially the teenagers who watch these. Because they haven't gotten any experience with this, so they want to know what it is like! Then, if they watch once, they want to watch again, and again. I mean the boys [*keṭāharu*] who haven't watched aren't so interested [in sex] as those who have watched. It's the teenagers who like it.

Aside from expressing her moral indignation, in her last two sentences this woman makes the important distinction between "boys," who do not watch pornographic films, and "teenagers," who do.

Finally, another revealing usage of "teenager" came in the course of a conversation with an upper-caste woman in her forties, the mother of a seventeen-year-old son.

There are so many drug-addicted people who have spoiled everything, even their whole families. The parents are just crying. Oh, how sad this is! I think it's the teenagers usually who use [drugs]. This is the age [*umer*] for spoiling one's life. It is the unmarried ones who take drugs.

Later, when the subject had shifted to films, and finally to "blue" films, she again took up the theme of "teenagers":

Well, it is said that people watch these films, but I feel disgusted just from hearing about them. I don't know who it is that watches these. Maybe some married people, . . . [*pause*], but mostly teenagers. Yes, I think it is the teenagers who don't have any common sense [*buddhi*]. Like my son, he doesn't watch that stuff. He watches only *Sunday Pop* in which there are only English songs [pop music videos].

As in the other examples above, it was telling that this woman could speak of drug-taking, pornography-watching "teenagers," and then contrast these undesirable young males with her own seventeen-year-old son. This comment, and others like it, led me again to the conclusion that the term "teenage" in colloquial Nepali usage was often less a designation of age than an indicator of a certain social type. For these men and women (including many teenage women), "teenager" meant an antisocial, vulgar, and potentially violent young male.

Conclusion

From all of these voices—the publishers of *Teens* magazine, parents, shop-keepers, young people themselves—it is clear that the meaning and nature of modern youth are topics of active debate in Kathmandu. While some promote a "teen" identity, others see it in a negative or ambivalent light, while for still others it is simply a new consumer category. For all of these speakers, the category of youth as a modern consumer has taken root in the form of the "teen," though the way people use the term indicates that they are far from consensus on its meaning.

In the debate over teenness we see the forces of consumer modernity at work in the newly opened "in-between" spaces being pioneered by middle-class youth in Kathmandu; forces which seek to define modernity in material terms and construct identities around commodities. Yet while commercial interests populate this new landscape with beatific images of leisure, pleasure, progress, glamour, and beauty, another perspective in the debate counters with the image of the "teen" as a drug or pornography addict. This critical take links commercialization with the seduction and corruption of youth, *not* some longed-for "teen" epiphany. In the counter-representation of the "teen" as consumer-addict lies an indictment of a commercially sponsored material reductionism that encourages persons to imagine themselves as objects and then set out on a never-ending, ad-dictive quest to find identity in consumption, to purchase reality and meaning, again and again. The battle for the territory of "modern youth" underlines the importance of young people in the future of Kathmandu's middle-class culture. But the conflicting forces that rage across this "in-between" space, and the sharply contrasting images of youth that they offer, leave young people with the challenge of reconciling their own mod-ern identities. As the next chapter's stories of middle-class teenage trauma illustrate, for young people in Nepal the "in-between" space of youth threatens to become a "self"-enveloping gulf, as competing visions of the future clash with the realities of the present.

9

MODERNITY, TIME, AND PLACE: YOUTH CULTURE IN KATHMANDU

> Every earlier present had the tendency to do away with the past and to
> put limits on the future. In our day, for the first time, the forces of the
> present have the objective power to close the horizons of the future ir-
> revocably and to cut off the past. . . . The present could not effect its
> seizure of power over other times if it were not for something in
> human beings in complicity with it. . . . Something remains suspended
> between past and future—and we call this the present. It is something
> different from waiting and something other than life: a new way for
> fate to strike. . . . Something emerges that is neither dream nor reality.
>
> —ALEXANDER KLUGE, *The Assault of the Present on the*
>   *Rest of Time*

This chapter consists of the stories of two young men. Their stories are
like those of thousands of other young people in the city, yet these two
represent the logical extremes—the ultimate consequences—of forces and
trends that most other youths experience only in part, or in diluted form.
These stories exemplify some of the anxieties and aspirations, perspectives and values, opportunities and impediments that constitute the experience of modernity for young people in Kathmandu.

In many ways these are stories about stories: they are stories of how
young people work to reconcile a barrage of conflicting accounts of what
was, should be, can be, and is. Each of these two young men describe
their encounters with the narrative forces of modernity, narratives with
profound implications for how individuals interpret past, present, and
future. In young people's lives, state-promoted narratives of material
progress, development, and achievement fuse with commercially driven
narratives of consumer desire and fulfillment (like those discussed in the
previous chapter) to create powerfully compelling stories of value. By creating new standards with which to gage progress—standards that are

both explicitly material and comparative (with "the West," or "the industrialized world")—these stories quite literally retell the Nepali past and present (as backward and deficient) even while they claim the future (by defining the deferred goals of "development"). At the same time, these stories of material progress and desire implicitly undermine local narratives of value and meaning kept in cultural circulation by members of earlier generations, rendering them less and less likely to maintain the narrative momentum needed to carry these Nepali cultural practices from the past into the everyday lives of young people in the present, let alone into their imaginings of the future.

The two stories in this chapter offer glimpses into the worlds of imagination that young Nepalis construct in order to make sense of their lives in the present and future. It is within these imaginary worlds that state and consumer programs of modernity meld with the particularities of local culture and individual life histories. As both stories illustrate, though these worlds of imagination are cluttered with mediated images and meanings, it is never to the exclusion of a critical awareness that grows from lives lived in contradiction.

THE GENDER OF "YOUTH"

Why are these stories of "youth culture" both about young *men*? Why do women here, and in the previous chapter, begin to slip out of the picture? In chapter 8, "teenagers" were almost by definition male. In chapter 7, out of the thousands of applications to a local film-acting school, none were from women. Chapter 6 discussed how young men act as "gatekeepers" or censors, determining what kinds of films women in their families can see. This chapter, too, will focus on the experiences of males, and for the same reason. In short, one of the things this book suggests is that in Kathmandu young men are more likely to be implicated in the cultural construction of "youth" than are women. What emerges in Kathmandu as an *age-specific* "youth culture" is not only *class-specific* but also largely *gender-specific*. If, as I suggested in the previous chapter, "youth" is a category of middle-class privilege (for example, the privilege of "delaying manhood" through education), it should not be surprising that "youth" may also be a category of gender privilege. Historically youth cultures have almost always started as male cultures.[1] Ironically—just as the pub-

---

[1] For example, Philippe Aries makes the startling point that, in European history, "boys were the first specialized children," because they were selected for education and marked off through the adoption of age-specific dress (Aries 1962:58, cf. Elias 1978 [1935]). Similarly, patterns of military (Loriga 1997) and labor recruitment (Perrot 1997) also isolated male

lishers of *Teens* magazine insisted—"youth culture" may have relatively little to do with age per se, but a great deal to do with creating distinction and naturalizing privilege, in terms of class, but also of gender. To say that "youth culture" in Kathmandu is largely a male experience is to underline again the fact that "youth" is a culturally constructed category: "youth" is a specific cultural construction not only of age but also of class and gender.

This is, obviously, not to say that young women in Kathmandu have been bypassed by processes of cultural transformation; the earlier chapters of this book have made it abundantly clear that young women actively participate in the cultural processes of middle-class modernity (though these cultural experiences are less often marked off by age). Nor is it to say that young women have no "youth culture." But young women, even in the middle class, still have relatively limited access to public space (where a woman's honor [ijjat] is always at risk) and are still likely to have fewer opportunities (and lower expectations) for education, professional employment, and positions of public responsibility. Hence, "youth culture" is still largely (though not exclusively or eternally) male and middle-class.[2]

"OUT HERE IN KATHMANDU": ANXIETY AND PERIPHERAL CONSCIOUSNESS

I had not seen Ramesh for over a year when I glimpsed him out of the corner of my eye while riding my bike down a crowded, narrow Kathmandu street one chilly spring morning in 1991. Ramesh looked considerably more gaunt and tired than I remembered him from our earlier acquaintance, when he was a regular at a drug-free youth center set up for recovering addicts. I had heard from others that Ramesh had relapsed into his heroin habit, and the jittery but probing look in his eyes when I hailed him made me think twice about the wisdom of reestablishing this relationship.

"youth" as a social category long before comparable processes for young women came into place (see, e.g., Peiss 1986).

[2] Although compared to male "youth culture" it is a much less marked or targeted phenomenon—whether in commercial discourse or in public debate—I suspect that female "youth culture" (that is, an age-specific experience of middle-class modernity for young women) exists in Kathmandu, though in more private, domestic settings, relationships, and practices. The fact that these experiences are not represented in this ethnography reflects not only the limitations of the ethnographer (as a male) but also the fact that the middle-class cultural project of "youth" formation has focused primarily on males. For an ethnography of modern, non-Western, middle-class, female youth culture, see Fuglesang 1994.

When we met later that day in the garden of a Thamel restaurant,[3] Ramesh gave me one of what turned out to be many lessons in the nature of street life in Kathmandu. Through his narration the people and places of Kathmandu, and especially the liminal zone of the Thamel tourist district, took on entirely new meanings. In the next hour and a half, in a restaurant I had visited regularly during my stays in Nepal over the previous five years, Ramesh threw light on a different (previously hidden) dimension of reality, one of drug transactions, police surveillance, schoolboys drinking codeine-laced cough syrup, and a junkie tottering out of the bathroom, his face flushed from retching, unable to keep down any food. In Ramesh's company, places I had imagined and inhabited for years would suddenly evaporate, as glimpses of other (and others') places came briefly into view.

At twenty-one Ramesh was living life close to the edge, though seven or eight years earlier no one would have predicted the rough times that lay ahead. Ramesh's parents had moved to Kathmandu from an eastern hill district when he was in his early teens. He had attended a respected English-medium high school in the valley and learned to speak competent, colloquial English. He had first tried heroin as a high school student, and over the course of several years, during which his mother died and his father married a woman with several sons, Ramesh developed a habit that grew out of control. Through a combination of mistrust between him and his family members, a slow-burning resentment over his father's remarriage, and an increasingly disruptive heroin addiction, Ramesh began to spend more and more time living with friends and, eventually, on the streets. The previous year, having gone through a detox program, his good English had landed him a coveted (though typically low-paying) sales job in a retail shop catering to tourists. He swore to me that he had stayed clean and would still be working had not someone told the manager that he was a former junkie. (Others claimed that he had been caught trying to sell drugs to tourists.) By the time I met him, in 1991, he had been in and out of drug rehabilitation seven times and owned little more than the clothes on his back and the few rupees in his pocket. He lived by his wits day to day, hustling tourists, taking profits on petty commodity transactions, and running a variety of scams, such as sewing foreign labels into locally produced garments.

Sitting in the restaurant that afternoon, over tea and Danish pastries, Ramesh meandered through stories from his past, sometimes with fists clenched in anger, sometimes close to tears. Ramesh was the *one-in-ten*,

[3] Thamel is the popular "budget-class" tourist area of Kathmandu, known for its hotels, restaurants, bars, and souvenir shops. For more on interactions between Nepali youth and foreign tourists, see Liechty 1996a.

a living example of what could go wrong, a reference point that both peers and parents looked to in horror. I found that Ramesh's attitudes and opinions rarely differed in *content* from those of his middle-class peers, only in *intensity*. A member of a middle-class family, the product of an English-medium school, a heavy consumer of Hindi and English mass media (from videos to detective novels), Ramesh had much more in common with his peers than many were willing to acknowledge.

Like many others, Ramesh was acutely—sometimes painfully—aware of his life as a Nepali, a life that he repeatedly compared to lives lived in distant power centers. Ramesh constantly evaluated his Nepaliness through his awareness of life in the West and Far East, even though he himself had never traveled farther than North India. Perhaps because of me, he often invoked images of life in America compared to which he found his own life one of extreme deprivation.

Out here young people like me, we want a *fast* life, not this slow life.

What do you mean, a "fast" life?

I mean like in the States, where you can stay out all night until you drop. Here, there's nothing, no [late-night] bars, and we can't even go anywhere to play video games.

When I asked how he knew about bars and video games, he explained that he had learned all about these things from movies and novels.

Indeed, Ramesh was a special connoisseur of films, books, magazine articles—anything he could find—having to do with America, and particularly New York City. He knew all the city's boroughs and landmarks, but he was especially intrigued by "the Bronx," a place he brought up again and again in our conversations. From dozens of tough-guy movies, gangster or mafia novels, and African-American "ghetto" films, Ramesh had constructed a detailed image of a New York street culture full of drugs, thugs, and gangs. He frequently compared Kathmandu's street life with that of New York, as when he explained how Kathmandu "gangs" take "tabs" (certain prescription-drug tablets) before going to a fight, "just like in the Bronx." Ramesh could quote lines from mafioso novels, and he frequently spoke of how one's face should never show feeling, a lesson he learned from *The Godfather*. Ramesh's ultimate goal was to move to "the States" and live in New York City. He often spoke in vague terms of a cousin living in Seattle who might help him get there.

Ironically, sometimes it seemed as though Ramesh already lived in New York. "The Bronx," in particular, seemed like a kind of shadow universe where his mind roamed while his body navigated the streets of Kathmandu. "The Bronx," with its street smarts and antiheroic codes of valor, was often the standard of reality against which he measured his own existence. At times it seemed that Ramesh was only imagining his life in Kathmandu while "the Bronx" was his reality, rather than vice versa. For Ramesh "the Bronx" seemed to offer a way of understanding his own life, a life that he hated, yet which he could link with a way of existence at the modern metropole. Ramesh's vision of "the Bronx" allowed him to identify his own existence as at least some version of "modernity," even if it lacked the all-night bars, the video games, and a host of other modern accoutrements that he had never seen in more than two dimensions.

The mediated images in Ramesh's imagination also had important implications for his perceptions of place. Like many other young adults I met in Kathmandu, when speaking in English Ramesh constantly referred to the place he had spent most of his life as "out here." "Out here in Kathmandu" prefaced so many of his comments that in the course of time the words barely registered in my mind. This persistent self-peripheralization is almost unimaginable outside the context of global media and a host of other marginalizing transnational cultural forces, including tourism and commodity imports. Mass media (as well as tourists and foreign goods) act like a lens that situates the local in an implicitly devalued and diminished "out here" place, while at the same time seeming to provide a window onto modern places that are distant in both time and space. But if the video screen is like a window, it is one with bars that keep viewers like Ramesh outside, "out here" looking in.

But media and tourism only work in conjunction with the Nepali state and its ideology of progress (bikās) and modernization. By assuming the role of recipient and dependent in the global development aid economy, the Nepali state also languishes in this "out here," self-peripheralizing mentality in which modernity is essentially a foreign commodity. Hence, in schools and in the government-run media, young people are frequently reminded of Nepal's status as a "least developed country." Poverty and backwardness are among the primary components of a Nepali identity, or a sense of Nepaliness, for young people in Kathmandu. By almost all the criteria that their education—whether formal or through consumption of commercial mass media—teaches them to value, Nepali conditions are deemed inferior in an evolutionary sense. The rhetoric of backwardness, development, foreign aid, and education collapses time and space such that Nepali youth learn to situate themselves on the margins of a meaningful universe as consumers of an externally generated material modernity (cf. Fabian 1983).

This sensibility came through powerfully in one of Ramesh's comments. Having described his education, problems, and knowledge of life abroad (via foreign media), Ramesh slouched in his chair, looked skyward and sighed:

> You know, now I know so-o-o much. [*Pause*] Being a frog in a pond isn't a bad life, but being a frog in an ocean is like hell. Look at this. Out here in Kathmandu, there is nothing. We have nothing. We even have to stand in line for kerosine.

Turning in disgust to politics, and the recently revived multiparty political scene, Ramesh went on to blame the country's condition, and his own, on the government.

> Why should Nepali people work hard? There's no hope. Nothing will ever change. If I had a gun, I'd go and shoot them, the whole fucking lot of them. At least then someone would notice and something might change.

Ramesh's perspective is only the logical extreme of a vision shared by thousands of other middle-class Nepali young people. A combination of personal misfortune and susceptibility to substance addiction led Ramesh to an uncommon level of despair and marginalization, but many others were also caught in this wasteland between two worlds: the lived experience of "out here" and the dream of modernity. As summed up by a Nepali psychologist who had spent years working with young people in Kathmandu, the biggest contradiction that young people face is "the incongruence between their expectations and their real life."

As I have suggested above, this is a systemic incongruence born of modernism and dependence as a state rhetoric; of education, commercial interests, global mass media, and tourism; and of the fantastic interconnections of all of these. These interests and processes converge to provide an "education" for young people that is "alienating" to the extent that it instills a self-peripheralizing consciousness. Yet Ramesh's "ocean" of alienation is not simply an enormous mass of knowledge. It is a particular *kind* of knowledge, one that vastly expands his frames of reference and successfully pushes his own lived experience to the margins of an ever expanding world of modernization and desire. Much of this knowledge/education comes from interactions with mass media. Like Ramesh, many youth use media to make sense of their own lives and to imagine what Arjun Appadurai calls other "possible lives." Appadurai emphasizes how mass media and other transnational cultural processes "deterritorialize" local experience by multiplying the "imaginative resources" that people use to make sense of their lives (1991:196). Yet I would add that while forces such as mass media now guarantee that local experience almost anywhere on the globe will be thoroughly permeated by transnational cultural processes, this same cultural "deterritorialization" has a very real "territorializing" effect on the minds of people like Ramesh. The entire discourse of modernization, progress, and development fuse with the image worlds of media to give people like Ramesh an acute sense of marginality.

"This Nowhere Place": Life in the Consumer Present

As consumers of modernity, always scanning the mediated horizons awaiting its arrival, middle-class youth live in a constantly dissolving and reconfiguring sequence of "modern" presents that wash over the valley in successive waves (cf. Jameson 1983). As Alexander Kluge suggests in this chapter's epigraph, the commercial and mass-mediated narrative forces of late-capitalist modernity may now have the objective power to swamp our personal experiences of both past and future—to overpower both historical consciousness of other possible conditions and dreams of fundamental structural change—with a relentlessly reified (and mechanically reproduced) present; a present that hovers somewhere between "waiting" and "life," between "dream" and "reality," a present that is itself "a new way for fate to strike." Middle-class youth in Kathmandu often inhabit a commercially mediated "nowhere place," a present that seems to resolve the contradictions between a devalued local past and an unreachable foreign future.

I first met Suman one late-summer evening in 1991 in a Thamel bar where I had gone to meet a European friend. It was only after my friend left, as I sat writing out some ideas in a notebook, that the young Nepali man sitting next to me for the past hour introduced himself. Suman was twenty-two years old and had lived in the city since boyhood, after his father had moved from central Nepal to Kathmandu to set up a business with a group of relatives. When his father took a second wife, Suman and his mother established a separate residence. Here they led a precarious middle-class existence, combining income from his father's business, his mother's low-paying office job, and, after Suman finished high school, his own low-paying job at a relative's travel agency.

Suman was one of the few young people I met for whom experiences of misfortune and anxiety had led to introspection and a growing sense of critical self-awareness. More than anything else, Suman helped me gain some understanding of what the past, present, and future meant for middle-class youth like himself. Suman expressed an extreme version of sentiments that I often heard when young people spoke about the future. Especially for those "first-generation modern" youth—those who were the first in their extended families to have grown up in a cosmopolitan setting, with sustained formal education and a variety of other powerful extrafamilial socializing influences—the future was often an uncharted void. In school and at home young people learn that they are responsible for their own modern future. Yet for most youth, not only are there extremely few "modern" role models, the "successful" adults around them often set repugnant examples, as they did for Suman.

Suman found himself in a position where the past (as embodied in his father, his relatives, and their village background), if not actively devalued in the state rhetoric of progress, was simply irrelevant to his efforts to imagine and implement his own future. Without a valued past and carrying a concept of the future as something, like modernity, that arrives preassembled from foreign places, Suman was left in an extremely nebulous and vulnerable position. On several occasions he told me, "I don't have any place to stand. I don't know where I stand. I'm in this nowhere place." What he lacked was a sense of continuity, a sense of "place" in a meaningful sequence from past to future.

Suman had spent his early childhood in a hill village, his teen years in a Kathmandu English-language boarding school, and the last five years in almost daily contact with foreigners. Once, he had actually accompanied foreign tourists to his natal village, a visit that triggered some painful soul-searching. Suman had been unprepared for the experience of viewing his "past"—embodied in relatives who could just as easily have been himself—through the eyes of foreign tourists. The same state-disseminated discourse that leads people across rural Nepal to locate "progress" (bikās) in urban centers leads urban Nepalis to view "the village" as the land of ultimate undevelopment (Pigg 1992). For Suman, like many thousands of other residents of Kathmandu who grew up on the "village-side," one's natal village and rustic cousins are unsettling reminders of a personal past that the state devalues, modernity negates, and foreign tourists consume as an exotic commodity. Wedged in this in-between space—between the future as distant foreign commodity, and the past as commodity for distant foreigners—it is not surprising that young urban Nepalis have trouble identifying a place for identity or, in Suman's words, a "place to stand." One evening Suman told me:

> When I look at you, I can see a person clearly. I can look at your behavior, what you say, and the little things you do, and I see who you are. But when I try to look at myself, I don't see anything. I mean, what I see is only unclear, it's so unclear. There's nothing really there, just bits and pieces, floating.

Suman, like many others, can find no firm ground on which to unite a range of often stunningly contradictory identities into a viable, coherent sense of self. The past is devalued, yet a "modern" future is out of their grasp, seemingly defined by the standards of "development" as something that is not Nepali.

For many middle-class young people, the only place left to stand is with class peers, on the shifting grounds of day-to-day existence, the "nowhere place" of the present. Youth are terrified at the prospect of being left behind in the poverty and backwardness of the past, but terrified too by the seeming impossibility of the modern future that society expects them to construct. It is for these people that peer groups become extraordinarily important. Young men especially turn to these groups, with sometimes almost desperate attachment. Yet more often than not these groups permit members to evade their individual futures by focusing their attentions, as a group, on the present. Peer groups allow young people to abandon themselves in the utter banality of a day-to-day material existence, consciously avoiding the future by living for each other in the present.[4]

Suman was one of the few young people I met who had reflected on the experience of peer dependence. He described how, over the course of his high school years, he had become extraordinarily dependent on a circle of friends, which continued to hold together after graduation. Only recently had Suman realized that for years he had lived in terror of losing these affiliations. Self and group had become so intermeshed that even the thought of jeopardizing these relationships had been tantamount to threatening the only valued sense of social identity that he had. He told of how he had once been willing to do almost anything to please his friends and avoid their disapproval; often he had conformed to their wishes even when they went against his own sense of propriety. For Suman and others, group identity revolved mostly around conformity to group-dictated standards of taste in dress and other consumer goods from food and music, to drugs—including, in his case, one nearly disastrous brush with heroin addiction. Yet the price of falling away is being left behind, Suman explained, which makes people cling even tighter to their peer circles.

Living in the present, with often extremely insecure senses of identity based on peer affiliation, young people are often susceptible to commercial interests clambering to provide youth with commoditized means of imagining themselves as members of groups. Like *Teens* magazine and its host of commercial backers, various businesses are only too eager to fill the space of the present with the trappings of an imagined future. Often desperate to claim modern identities, middle-class youth themselves appropriate these commercial offerings: with "fashions," haircuts, fitness programs, and modern foods, young people can become modern by purchasing their own modern bodies. (Or, in the words of one young man, "Actually now, in a way, fashion has become a part of our bodies.") But

[4] For more on everyday "boredom" and the experience of youth in Kathmandu, see Liechty 1996a.

like the ice cream advertised in magazines and sold on Kathmandu street corners, the apparently solid commodities soon melt away in the anxious heat of the present, leaving young people again to confront their own futures. Life in the consumer present is like an addiction: as Suman found in trying to break away from his peer dependence, an identity built on consumer fashion goods is one that needs to be purchased again and again. Yet this is the price middle-class youth pay to distance themselves from the past and forestall a future that seems to preclude them.

For many young people in Kathmandu, this life in the present is the experience of modernity. It is a life of ambiguity in an "in-between" space: between desire and reality; between past and future; between the village and an external, modern metropole; between childhood and adulthood; between high and low class; between education and meaningful employment. The experiences of youth like Ramesh and Suman are strongly inflected by the marginalizing and mediated forces of modernity, though their lives are far from the sublime images of youth offered in the pages of *Teens*. Media and education stake claims in their imaginations, though the possible futures they offer rarely seem to fit the realities of Nepal. Kathmandu's high school and college campuses produce graduates far in excess of the service and business sector's ability to provide meaningful employment. Even if a young person is employed, wages barely pay for minimal necessities, much less the consumer lifestyles the graduates covet. While the children of the elite typically expect *their* modern futures to be in *foreign places*, middle-class youth are left to reconcile the foreign images of a modern future with the realities of present-day Nepal.

What then *is* "youth culture" in a place like Kathmandu—where, to a considerable extent, "youth" as a distinctive phase between child- and adulthood did not really exist in most social sectors a generation or two ago? Is all youth activity now de facto "youth culture," or are some aspects of young people's lives dictated by cultural traditions in which the young are expected to assume adult roles? Without suggesting that young people (or anyone else) move between autonomous spheres of existence— that the values and rationales from one set of experiences do not spill over into, inform, or frame other experiences—I would contend that the cultural spaces encountered by young people in Kathmandu are not homologous. From home to temple to campus to movie theater to marketplace, young people move between cultural spaces sometimes lacking clear boundaries,[5] yet nevertheless enclosing certain expectations, certain valued ways of being, certain "epistemological styles" (Appadurai

---

[5] For example, the religious themes common in South Asian popular film (Mishra 1985) blur the boundaries between cinema and temple, and television's place in domestic space blurs the boundary between shopping arcade and home.

1990b:207) that are sometimes conflicting and contradictory. What might be most meaningfully called "youth culture" in Kathmandu is the public cultural practice that emerges from this modern mode of being.

To the extent that young people in Kathmandu find themselves in a new "in-between" domain of "youth" that opens up at the intersection of new patterns of education, labor, consumption, and class formation, it is clear that these "youth" are themselves actively engaged in constructing the new cultural space, marking it off as their own, and imagining themselves as its inhabitants. From the young men who appropriate certain items of "ethnic Nepali" clothing (produced for the tourist trade) as parts of their own uniforms as modern youth (Hepburn 1993) to the local rock band whose members recorded an all-original, Nepali-language album in the style of the Beatles, examples abound of new forms of youth expression that are clearly local, "youthful," and modern. So also is the lifestyle of young, middle-class men hanging out on street corners or in tea shops, exchanging gossip and small talk, slinging jibes at girls passing by.[6] These young men often congregate into peer groups, whose interactions with other such groups occasionally erupt in "gang fights," where local "heroes" try out their martial-arts skills, or even weapons. It is in these groups that local youth fashions are negotiated, whether in clothing, music, hairstyles, videos, or slang. Within and between these peer groups, styles and behaviors take on meanings that are locally determined, even if they are often deployed in commercially mediated images, ideas, practices, and other consumer goods. Young people as groups of peers assemble the components of a youth identity with which they seek to mark off the new cultural space in which modernity has deposited them.

Thus, "youth culture" in Kathmandu is that distinctive public practice through which young people mobilize resources that give shape to the space of "youth" that they are forced to pioneer. Because this new cultural space has few roles (aside from "student") to anchor it into social practice, it tends to be a highly expressive culture, one in which distinction is unusually dependent on images and image-bearing goods, and their attendant cultural practices. As I have shown in this chapter and the last, "youth culture" is a contested space: a variety of forces—the state (through education), commercial interests like *Teens* and its "member establishments," and society at large (where critical voices emerge)—compete to "assist" young people in their project of imagining themselves as "modern youth."

The agency of young people in constructing "youth culture" has to be seen in light of these competing images of "youth." Young people have choices, but they are not unlimited. To return to a spatial metaphor, if

---

[6] See Liechty 1996b for women's perspectives on harassment and male aggression.

"youth" is a newly opened space, there are many interests with vast resources scrambling to develop that space. Commercial and state "developers" invest heavily in lavish new structures of imagination for "youth," offering up sparkling mansions for the mind but demanding a price for the "furnishings" or goods needed to inhabit and enjoy these spaces. Many middle-class young people must make their choices within these "prefab" imaginative structures, for few have the resources, confidence, and cultural authority to construct their own alternative, nonmediated visions of valued, modern, and Nepali selves. In the rush to claim the newly opened space of "youth culture," young people are key actors, but their agency can never be unraveled from the actions of other interests also seeking to colonize the space of "modern youth."

CONCLUSION: SUMAN'S DREAM

One of the most powerful memories I have of Suman concerns the story he told me of his feelings upon watching the American film *One Flew over the Cuckoo's Nest*. Suman's reactions to this film, and especially the dream story that his mind created to retell the film's message in Nepali terms, are powerful indicators of the narrative and ideological forces at work in the lives and imaginations of Nepali young people.

Suman regularly went to friends' homes to watch Hindi video films but also made a point of seeing Western films, both for entertainment and to improve his English. Yet, according to Suman, no film had ever affected him as did *Cuckoo's Nest*, which he had seen several nights earlier: "After seeing it at my friend's house, I just wanted to go out and scream. I wanted to start hitting someone. It was all I could do to keep from hitting my friend." Trying to imagine why he would have reacted this way, I asked if he meant that he empathized with the main character, if perhaps he felt like a sane person surrounded by lunatics. At this he gave me a puzzled look and replied that this was not really what he meant. He seemed to have trouble articulating his feelings about the film but said that mainly he had been shocked, even terrified, to think that something like this could happen in "America."

While trying to explain his feelings and reactions, Suman brought up the dream he had had the night after watching *Cuckoo's Nest*:

> In the dream I was a street vendor, sitting by the side of the road, selling some small things, when a big three-wheeler[7] completely full

[7] "Three-wheelers" are boxy, open-air commuter vehicles, noisy and fume-ridden, that ply the roads in the Kathmandu valley, transporting mostly middle-class workers and students from their homes in the suburbs to the offices and campuses of the city.

with people came by and covered me with dirty water from a big puddle by the road.

The next thing I remember was seeing someone—he was a friend of mine—riding on a bicycle, peddling as fast as he could, trying to go away from something. Then the three-wheeler that was already full went after him and with a big mechanical arm grabbed him by the head and pulled him inside.

Although I do not hold that dreams have intrinsic meaning, I believe that dreamers can assign them meaning. That Suman remembered this dream, and that he consciously associated it with the film, gives it a special significance.

Youth in Kathmandu often view Western films as stories of modernity—a modernity that is virtually always constructed as an *object* of desire. What was so shocking to Suman about *Cuckoo's Nest* was that it depicted modernity's dark side, something he had perhaps never before seen in a Western film. But what made *Cuckoo's Nest* doubly terrifying was that its horrifying vision of modernity matched something he had already intuited from his experience as a Nepali youth. The powerlessness of the mental-patient "hero" in *Cuckoo's Nest* and his ultimate domestication and total subjugation to the irresistible will of the "modern" institution seemed to resonate powerfully with a dark premonition that Suman harbored of his own Nepali future. The vivid images of his dream speak to this connection: the three-wheeler hurtling like a juggernaut, drenching in filth a petty street merchant crouched by the roadside selling trinkets, and finally pursuing a young man on a bicycle, only to grab him by the head and stuff him into its maw—this is an authentically Nepali scenario that Suman self-consciously linked with the film.

Suman seemed to equate the three-wheeler of his dream with the mental hospital of the film. Both were images of modernity gone wrong, technologies that turned on their makers. Perhaps not insignificantly, Suman's three-wheeler seemed to distinguish, or even produce, two kinds of people: the petty vendor of baubles, left behind, defiled and sputtering in its toxic wake; and the young man, fleeing but eventually forcefully incorporated (coopted) into its course. In a sense, these two fates are the "options" that stories of "modernization" or "development" seem to offer the new Nepali middle class: either to be forever left behind, wallowing in the noxious effluent of "progress," or to be appropriated by some dehumanizing, mechanistic modernity. Suman's dream story twists the "official" narratives of *bikās* and consumerism into a nightmare vision of modernity, a modernity whose narratives construct futures of either abandonment or cooption.

Narratives of development and consumer fulfillment are stories that tell the future (a deferred, essentially foreign, "modernity") in ways that sever the future's ties with the Nepali past, leaving middle-class young people to experience the present, in Kluge's terms, as "something different from waiting and something other than life . . . neither dream nor reality" (1990:20). Thus, the experience of Kathmandu as a "nowhere place," and the nervous boredom of everyday life spent with peers, must be seen as much more than merely the self-pitying whining of middle-class youth. As I have shown in this chapter, to be young and middle-class in Kathmandu is to be on the front lines—the vanguard—of the cultural project whereby an emerging middle class attempts to selectively weld a local past to a global future. Yet because the narratives of progress and consumer value that the middle class uses to construct its own cultural life tend to locate modernity in distant times (the future) and spaces (the "developed world"), middle-class youth are left to bear the full brunt of the spatial and temporal contradictions of "Third World" modernity. The stories of Ramesh and Suman demonstrate that the contradictions of modernity do not go unnoticed, but are instead viscerally felt.

Suman's dream vision encapsulates both the gut-wrenching anxieties that lie at the heart of the experience of modernity for young people and a powerful critique of consumer capitalism as it exists on the "Third World" periphery. As a *story*, Suman's dream can be read as a critical *alter-narrative* (if not *alternative*) to the dominant narratives of progress and development that his story mimics and critiques. The challenge for people like Suman is to envision alternative modernities, to claim narratives of value and fulfillment that are not tied to the commodity form, to construct (and enact) futures that are not already appropriated by the state or the forces of consumer modernity. They must acquire the "imaginative resources" to erect alternative modernities that transcend, or diverge from, the unilinear narrative of "modernization" *projected* onto the future by global structures of transnational state modernism/dependence and commodity markets. I stress the verb *project* to emphasize the fact that narratives, as stories of and for life, are "real" only to the extent that they can successfully compel. In these chapters I have explored some of the factors in the lives of young people that make these narratives of modernity compelling, but I have also suggested that their influence is never total.

PART V

CONCLUSION

10

THE SPACE OF CLASS: TOWARD AN ANTHROPOLOGY OF MIDDLE-CLASS CULTURAL PRACTICE

This book includes lengthy ethnographic accounts of consumer culture, mass media, and youth culture in Kathmandu; yet, paradoxically, it is not "about" any of these topics. Instead, I have argued that all of these—consumption, media, and youth—are constitutive elements of a larger process of cultural formation that is underway in the lives and practices of middle-class people in Kathmandu. It is impossible to make sense of the class-cultural politics of consumption and the moral narratives that circulate through it, the worlds of imagination and desire opened up by the windows of mass media, or the contested terrain of the modern "teen" consumer without each of these cultural dynamics making reference to the others. They are, in effect, "joint productions." But even more importantly, it is impossible to make sense of these interdigitating cultural processes outside of the context of Kathmandu's emerging middle class. The middle class carves out and populates these domains in its larger task of pioneering a space of cultural middleness between its local and global class others, both above and below.

Instead of systematically reviewing the contents of the book, this final chapter considers some of its implications for understandings of culture, process, and class. After brief considerations of global/local cultural dynamics and the cultural politics of class practice, the chapter concludes with a discussion of class and space. I argue that the spatial dynamics of class practice help us understand *what class is*, but much more importantly, *what class does*. It is through the endlessly repeated and reenacted spatial claims of class practice that class becomes a reality—a "social fact."

GLOBAL PROCESS, LOCAL PRACTICE

Although consumerism and its interrelated processes of mass mediation and youth culture are surely global cultural processes at work in shaping middle-class cultures worldwide, this book has made it clear that shared global cultural processes do not lead to shared cultural lives. Even while vastly expanding consumer markets continue to draw Kathmandu's middle class further and further into the webs of transnational consumer capitalism, local consumer lifestyles should not be read simply as so many instances of the global market triumphant. When we see how middle-class householders describe the irresistible terror of new consumer demands, how local television administrators lament their loss of control to foreign media products, how people in Kathmandu critique the commercial construction of the new "teen" identity, or how urban youth experience the alienation of a "modernity" that condemns them to lives in a futureless present, we begin to sense the profound feelings of resistance, compromise, and even violation that accompany the middle class's embrace of consumer lifestyles. The "new consumerism" described in this book represents not brainwashing but the converging imperatives of market forces and social pressures. To the extent that they become part of the local social currency, consumer goods and media images become necessary components in projects of class formation. In spite of the ambivalence, moral hesitation, and even anger that many people express toward the unstable and constantly expanding realm of goods and images, few in Kathmandu's middle class can afford *not* to participate in the new consumer economy.

"Cultural homogenization," "Americanization," "westernization," the "global village," even "modernity" itself, are all variants of a myth— a cultural narrative, to use the terms of this study—whereby the West imagines its own being and becoming, and that of the rest of the world. This study challenges the myth of global homogenization in a number of ways. It shows that Nepal, although peripheral to the global economy, relates not to one cultural and economic center but to a range of centers. East and Southeast Asia, South Asia, Europe and America, and increasingly, the Gulf states all converge upon the lives and imaginations of middle-class people in Kathmandu in complex ways. But much more importantly, this study shows that global cultural processes alone cannot account for, or determine, local cultural lives. An array of local cultural narratives—stories of honor, value, prestige, and piety—flow in and around global narratives of "progress," modernity, and consumer fulfillment, simultaneously adopting and critiquing these stories, braiding and mixing their narrative strands into a local middle-class cultural life that is as unpredictable as it is unique.

Those who would stake a claim in this middle-class project must daily navigate the compelling inertia of diverse cultural currents—the pull of powerful forces both local and global—that converge in the "middle ground" of middle-class life. To the extent that these currents are often contradictory (as in the conflict between "old" and "new" ideas of consumer value described in chapter 4) or shifting (as in local fashion practices), the challenge is to ride them into a future shared with one's class peers without being overwhelmed and swept away in modernity's wake. In their daily performances of middle-classness, actors must make sometimes agonizing decisions about which stories (progress, piety, fashion, education, ijjat) they will use to *tell themselves*.

The ways that people manage these narratives of modernity—stories of being and becoming modern that people tell, and that tell people— underline the fact that the global must be seen in the context of the local. This study has documented a range of potent "global forces" in the lives of people in Kathmandu, from mass media and fashion to "development" and "youth." But these "foreign influences" are not so much instances of cultural domination or imposed meaning than models for cultural practice, ways of doing that can be harnessed (along with other practical logics) to the imperatives of local cultural projects. In particular, this study shows how elements of a now global consumer-cultural logic are appropriated by people seeking to carve out a class-cultural space and constitute themselves in class-cultural practice.

Like everything else on the global cultural market, these models of cultural practice, and the stories of reality, value, and meaning that they tell, do not come without cost. These new cultural narratives and their attendant logics and implications offer useful leverage to those seeking to pry open a middle-class cultural niche, but they also threaten to leave their mark on the people who use them. In other words, the people that these modern narratives "tell" are not always the people that those telling the stories wish to be. The "fashion prostitute," the family driven to sell gold in order to buy a television, the corrupt government worker who takes bribes in order to improve his family's "standard of living," the elderly parent disrespected because he has no money, the drug- and pornography-addicted "modern youth": these are only a few examples of the undesired people that are "told by" the forces of modern consumerism. These ill-omened figures reside in Kathmandu's middle class somewhere between fact and fantasy; they are as important for their symbolic roles in the moral economy as for their flesh-and-blood existence. Indeed, as we have seen, a fundamental part of the middle-class cultural project is precisely to *circulate* these tales of modern propriety and impropriety. The person who tells them maintains his or her place in the ongoing moral/ cultural dialogue/practice that is class. This moral economy is the place where the middle class attempts to manage the narratives of modernity, appropriating its promises while excluding its evil emanations. These discontents of modernity—the repellent beings (and ways of being) that its narratives tell—must be perpetually deflected onto one's class others, above and below (chapters 3 to 5). It is in that collective, selective critique of modernity that the middle class constantly marks its external boundaries and reaffirms its internal solidarity.

These processes of narrative management, whereby the middle class hopes to claim the blessings of modernity while rejecting its curses, are an important collective (and class-constitutive) project, even if ultimately it fails to effectively exclude the "evils" of consumer modernity. By trying to divert them onto other classes, Kathmandu's middle-class moral economy may succeed in *symbolically* identifying, containing, and expelling the evils of modernity, but in the end these evils take root within the space of the middle class itself. The endlessly retold stories of sons/daughters/fathers/brothers/neighbors/friends gone bad ultimately stand as testimony to the moral compromises the middle class itself has made in exchange for the class-constructing power of modern consumer society. The "evil spirits" of modernity take up residence in the new middle class even as they are symbolically exorcised in its endlessly circulating moral economy.

It is this cultural compromise—the inextricable simultaneity of using and being used, telling and being told, narrative and narrativity—that perhaps best characterizes the relationship between the local and the global in middle-class cultural process. Middle-class cultural practice is the "middle ground" in which both the local and the global are mediated, melded, and braided into cultural forms and patterns that are "neither here nor there."[1] This study has documented the middle class's profound sense of betweenness, of "hanging between high and low," of anxious unresolvedness and irresolution. Middle-class cultural practice is fundamentally, inescapably, about the tension of perpetually negotiating betweenness. To the extent that words like "local" and "global" are able to convey the spatial origins of cultural forms in the contemporary world, the emerging middle classes on the "global periphery," in Kathmandu and countless other locations, are key sites for the cultural mediations of an ever more potent transnational modernity.

The challenge for anthropology is to clearly distinguish (ethnographically and theoretically) the now-global cultural processes of middle-class emergence from the assumptions of worldwide cultural homogenization that have often accompanied understandings of "globalization." The transformative work of cultural compromise that takes place as part of

[1] It was only after this manuscript was completed that I read Richard White's masterful study (1991) of the cultural "middle ground" constructed between Europeans and Native Americans in the Great Lakes region during the seventeenth and eighteenth centuries. Although the two books are vastly different in both their descriptive and theoretical intent, the basic premise—that cultural contact is often not a matter of "domination" and "resistance" but of transformative compromise on both sides of the equation—is similar.

these global middle-class projects is less about "westernization" than about the making of local class culture. Middle-class cultural practices link Kathmandu to the modern world not through some inherently insidious system of transferred meanings but through a growing network of shared processes that link class-based projects of cultural production around the world. Global cultural processes are always localized in cultural practice, even if that new cultural practice exists "somewhere in the middle," manifesting itself in forms that are neither local (in the sense of "traditional") nor global (in the sense of "foreign").

THE CULTURAL POLITICS OF CLASS

This book has built its portrayal of middle-class cultural practice in Kathmandu on the basic foundation of Marxian and Weberian theories of class. As I argued in chapter 1, an anthropology of middle-class cultural practice must combine a Weberian concern for the role of culture in social life (lifestyle, education, status goods, etc.) with a Marxian insistence that cultural practice be located in the context of the unequal distribution of power and resources between classes. Although this book has not focused directly on interclass relations (that is, relations *between* class groups), it has shown how middle-class economic authority is culturally mediated. For example, I have shown how the middle-class "social currency" of consumer goods and images serves to deflect attention away from an even more basic form of currency—cash—without which participation in a commercialized prestige economy is impossible. Indeed, much of middle-class practice is about the *transformation* of cash into social currency, the *translation* of market privilege into cultural privilege, and the *deployment* of a limited resource to create a limiting form of cultural life. Middle-class privilege is always depoliticized, its economic advantage "naturalized," behind cultural screens of status, lifestyle, honor, education, achievement, and so on. This is not to say that middle-class culture is in any way simply the product of economic determinations. Instead, it illustrates the profound role that cultures of privilege play in producing and reproducing hierarchies of economic privilege. Culture and economics are mutually constitutive, neither reducible to the other.

Because Weber was among the first, and still most important, theorists of middle-class culture, this study draws on several of his original insights into middle-class cultural dynamics, and, as for Weber, consumption emerges here as a defining characteristic of middle-class cultural life. Neither "mere" laborers nor owners of industrial or finance capital, earning neither "wages" nor "dividends," middle classes are situated in the productive process not as producers but as consumers. Consumption is the cultural labor of the middle class: its forms of practice, its stories of morality and value, its competing modes of "cultural capital" and rival lifestyles are all conveyed in and through goods and consumer practices.

These very patterns of status emulation and competition constitute a second Weberian theme that pervades this study. Throughout I have emphasized the precariousness of middle-class claims to status in the always contested middle-class economy of prestige. Ironically, even while shared experiences as owners of individual "capital" assets—whether material (consumer goods, homes, small businesses, etc.) or cultural (education, social connections, training, etc.)—helps *unite* the middle class in a common socioeconomic position, it is precisely the *diversity* (and often nonconvertibility) of these forms of capital that promotes competition between rival forms of prestige. Kathmandu's middle-class ijjat, or prestige, economy is the distinctly Nepali expression of the profoundly status-oriented and status-conscious cultural dynamic within middle-class societies that Weber reported a century ago. What Weber describes as the struggle within middle-class groups to "usurp 'status' honor" (1946:188) takes shape in Kathmandu as an anxious middle-class dance of emulation and competition in registers of prestige from the material to the moral.

Looking beyond the Weberian concern for *intra*class cultural dynamics, this study has shown how middle-class cultural practice also has important implications for Marxian perspectives on *inter*class relations. The language and practice of "middleness" explicitly locates the middle class within the local terrain of interclass associations and antagonisms (a point I will return to shortly). The constant efforts to displace immorality onto those "above" and "below" the middle class, the endlessly debated standards of middle-class suitability, acceptability, and propriety "between high and low," the local cultural contests over who "counts" and who doesn't—all of these overtly positional cultural confrontations show how middle-class practice is as much about exclusion as it is about inclusion. The cultural politics of "middleness" is simultaneously a Weberian domain of status emulation and competition and a Marxian domain in which the middle class naturalizes its economic and political privileges vis-à-vis its class "others" in noneconomic, nonpolitical narratives of morality, respectability, achievement, and progress. This study has shown how an *intraclass* debate over standards of class inclusion and an *interclass* program of class exclusion are inextricably bound together in the cultural politics of middleness. That many in the "industrialized world" have lost sight of this dual project of middle-class life stands as testimony to the success of the middle-class endeavor to de-politicize the cultural politics of class.

THE CULTURAL SPACE OF CLASS: MAKING SPACE,
TAKING PLACE

Throughout this book I have used phrases such as "cultural project," "cultural performance," and "cultural practice" as ways of conceptualizing how members of Kathmandu's middle class jointly and individually construct class-cultural lives. Thinking of class in terms of "project," "performance," and "practice" highlights the fact that class is a cultural process—active, fluid, contested, in-the-making—not a timeless, objectlike, social category. It is through a wide range of shared cultural processes (even if some of them are processes of intraclass competition) that the people described in this study carve out a new cultural domain, what I have called a new middle-class "cultural space."

In this final section, I argue that the idea of "cultural space" is crucial to an understanding of class as cultural practice: the production of class-cultural space is the fundamental outcome of class-cultural practice. But what are the spatial dynamics of class practice, and what implications do these have for a processual theory of middle-class culture? How does "practice"/"process" produce "space"? It is in fact through the "performance" of middle-class life that the middle class makes and claims space.

If the experience of class is bound up in ways of doing and being, practice and performance, then the outcome of that doing and being—the product of class-cultural practice—is cultural space. Class is an inescapably locational idea: it necessarily implies a geography in which difference (however imagined and/or enforced) is mapped onto social space. Class as cultural practice and performance is about locating one's self and one's class "others" in social space. But these very cultural practices of locating in turn produce cultural locations, cultural spaces that are both conceptual and physical. By linking class with space we run the risk of again immobilizing class in the material, static, objective realm of things. Yet if we can begin to see how space is itself culturally constructed—filled with cultural meaning and substance through cultural practice—we can begin to appreciate the profoundly important role that class-cultural practice plays in the cultural production of space, especially in modern, urban settings. It is the endlessly enacted spatial declarations of class practice—the construction and locating of class difference, the mapping of social space, the annexation of physical spaces as class domains—that make class a "fact." Class is real, but its reality is something that never exists outside of its continuous production and reproduction in cultural practice.

This study has ethnographically documented middle-class culture in Kathmandu. It has shown how the middle class locates itself and its class others in a wide range of spatial registers (from the moral to the material) and in so doing produces its own cultural life and lays claim to its own class domain. The production of class-cultural space is accomplished through two conceptually distinct forms of cultural practice: discursive, narrative, or linguistic practice on the one hand and embodied, physical, or material practice (including the use of goods) on the other.

Discursive and narrative constructions of class cultural space are the most obvious. Chapters 3 and 4 offered detailed insights into the language of middle-class life. This is a language fixated on ideas of "middleness" and "betweenness," a language that explicitly constructs a moral space between social others, "high" and "low," between transnational discourses of tradition and modernity, and between local understandings of old and new. Middle-class discourse works incessantly to position itself in a sociomoral universe that is both local and global, with local elites associated with the immorality of global modernity and local poor with the immorality of tradition. Elaborate stories of honesty, propriety, suitability, and acceptability are the cultural narratives that, in their telling and retelling, locate the space of middle-class life between the poles of upper- and lower-class deficiencies. The delicate balance between not-too-much and not-too-little, between the vulgarity of the poor and the vulgarity of the rich, is endlessly negotiated in middle-class discourses of "suitability." It is through these subtle stories of betweenness that the middle class attempts to displace the contradictions of modern consumerism—a practice that promises status but at the cost of moral dereliction—by recognizing, yet distancing itself from, the dangers that they pose.

More than simply locating (excluding) the middle class's "others," these same narrative practices are also central to the project of creating an inclusive, collective space for the middle-class social self. Here the *language of consumption*—how people *talk about* middle-class consumer goods and consumer desire—is especially important. As I discussed in chapters 3 and 4, the everyday linguistic constructions that link the Nepali verb for "to do" (*garnu*) with English words like "fashion" or "makeup" (e.g., "doing fashion") point to the importance of consumer *practice* in the collective *performance* of middle-class culture. Similarly, the stories of personal anguish and moral compromise that emerge from people's experiences in Kathmandu's new consumer economy (chapter 4) underline the fact that the (sometimes fatal) attraction of consumerism is much less about the *goods themselves* than about the *social imperatives to consume*. The often-repeated colloquial Nepali phrase "to do fashion" (*fashion garnu*)—so integral to the local discourse of class—neatly captures the sense of how members of the middle class constitute consumption less as a domain of goods, objects, or passive possession than as an active communicative sphere. In a local middle-class world in which "everything has become fashion," it is the *doing* of fashion (and all of the commoditized dimensions of life that "fashion" encompasses) as much or more than its *having* that underlines the importance of consumer *practice* in the ongoing construction of middle-class culture.

When we understand consumer behaviors to be more about participation than possession, we can begin to see how local patterns of consumerism are less about the desire for things than about the desire for sociality. (It is telling that within the middle-class consumer economy, ijjat (prestige, honor, respectability)—as something that can be gained or lost, preserved or expended—often seems to be the most *thinglike* object of desire.) In this light, "doing fashion" becomes an important act in the performance of class. The word "fashion" designates those goods and images with currency in the local middle-class cultural economy, but as fashions change, maintaining one's *place* in that system of exchange becomes the real object of consumer desire.

If the narrative and linguistic strategies that middle-class people use to locate themselves and others are about the discursive production of cultural space, it is equally important to see how a range of material practices, embodied cultural behaviors, and actual objects contribute to the middle-class project of constructing and claiming physical space. The notion that class-cultural practice "takes place" is more remarkable than might appear at first glance. From one perspective, "taking place" reminds us that cultural practice *actually occurs*: it *happens* in real time and space; it is *done*, and in the doing it *does something*. From another perspective, it is crucial to see how one of the things that cultural practice can do is actually *take place*. That is, because it is performed by people in actual localities at specific times, class-cultural practice can claim space by filling it with bodies, images, goods, and logics that render that space meaningful. Class cultural practice "takes place" by transforming specific spaces into arenas, or stages, for the performance of its own class logics and narratives. To the extent that any physical space comes to be dominated by the cultural values, goods, and bodies of a particular class collectivity, that space becomes the "natural" space of that class culture and, even more importantly, the space in which that class culture is "naturalized."

Chapters 4 and 5 described a variety of ways in which the middle class maps its own cultural logic onto urban space, reconstituting public space as middle-class space. Here we return to another fundamental implication of the middle-class practice of "doing fashion." Fashion as consumer practice "takes place" in the city. At the most abstract level, middle-class consumer logic colonizes the imaginations of urban young people, implanting visions of "commodity futures"—narratives of consumer desire that are literally unimaginable to their rural, lower-class peers (chapter 4). But middle-class consumer practice also turns "real" space into commodity zones. Middle-class people spoke repeatedly of the new demands of the new public spaces. City streets and shopping districts, college campuses and offices, cinemas and restaurants—all have been transformed into middle-class cultural spaces where "doing fashion" is not an option but a necessity. These new public spaces are consumer spaces: spaces of, for, and by consumption; public to the extent that all are "free" to participate in the class-cultural rituals of consumer practice. As I discussed in chapter 5, reconstituting the public as a consumer domain (a democracy of goods) allows the middle class to naturalize, and even embody, its class privilege, even while it claims public space as its own "natural" class territory. Public spaces that manifest different, older forms of cultural/ritual logic (spaces of communal production and caste-based community rituals) still exist in the city (chapter 5), but their abilities to "take place"—to encompass city spaces within their governing narratives of meaning and value—are rapidly eroding.

Because this large-scale colonizing of urban public space by a new middle-class consumer logic is something that has occurred only in the last few decades, many people—not least those seeking to claim and maintain a position within the space of the middle class—are distinctly aware of the new demands of public practice. People constantly spoke of the growing tyranny of fashion and the inescapable demands placed on individuals when they venture outside the house (*ghar bāhira*). The unfashioned body enters the new public space at the risk of being included among those who "don't count," those who make no claims to middle-class respectability. In effect, the new public spaces render the unfashioned body socially invisible, a fate few people in Kathmandu are willing to contemplate, at least as long as they are able to stake any claims in the cultural space of the middle class. Transforming public space into consumer space serves to exclude those who cannot participate in its consumer "freedoms," even while setting the inescapable standards by which people make "visible" their aspirations to middle-class standing. It is precisely the physicality of consumer goods that allows middle-class cultural logics to claim public space by defining reality as a material condition. In this way middle-class culture becomes "nature," its class-cultural practices naturalized by its appropriation of public space.

Thus far my discussion of the cultural space of class has been mainly limited to a review of the spatial implications of the ethnographic material presented in part 2 of this book (chapters 3 to 5, which sketch the basic ethnographic elements that contribute to an understanding of class as cultural practice). But just as parts 3 and 4 (on media consumption and youth, respectively) provided additional layers of detail to the image of class culture in Kathmandu, they also offer further insights into the construction of class-cultural space.

Patterns of media consumption exhibit some of the most graphic examples of the mapping of class onto space. Chapter 6 described how Kathmandu cinema halls in the 1960s and 1970s were vivid microcosms of the city's social universe, with different class groups arrayed (literally) from low to high along the ticket gradient that separated the cheap seats down front to the pricey ones in the balcony. Cinemagoers described how the distribution from low to high also charted out a cultural gradient of affect, with the more refined and sedate patrons above looking down distastefully upon the restless, indecorous riffraff below. The arrival of VCR technology in the early 1980s gradually put an end to this cross-class consumer experience of the cinema hall and re-mapped the patterns of class and media consumption. With VCR ownership becoming more and more essential to claims to middle-class status, the cinema halls were increasingly left to the lower classes as the middle class retreated to the comforts and privacy of their homes. Once again patterns of media consumption helped produce and naturalize class distinctions by confining different class practices within different spaces.

Equally important in the middle-class move from "hall to home" is the shift in this key domain of consumer practice from public to private. Media consumption went from being a public performance of class (in the cinemas) to being a central feature of the daily production of middle-class domestic life. Chapters 6 and 7 discussed the dominant role that acts of media consumption (video, television, magazines, radio, music, etc.) have come to play in defining middle-classness. Just as other middle-class consumer practices have constituted and commandeered new forms of public space in the city, new patterns of media consumption have reconstituted the private spaces of middle-class life, transforming them into new arenas for the display of middle-class privilege and the collective production of middle-class culture. The circulation and joint consumption of media products between and within middle-class homes becomes a principal form of exchange in the middle-class cultural economy.

But the mediation of middle-class cultural life is about more than just setting up exclusive (excluding) patterns of exchange: it also has more subtle implications for the spatialization of class. Massive middle-class investments in media (in terms of both money and time) are also investments in a new, class-privileging form of reality. Chapter 6 described the middle-class discourse of "film realism." Even if different age and gender categories within the middle class disagreed on what films were "realistic" (a matter that I will not revisit here), all of them shared a fixation on realism as the defining attribute of "good" media products. Good films are "just like life"; they thus offer lessons that willl prove useful for the future. In chapter 6 I argued that this middle-class identification of lived reality with media reality is an instance of the "cultivation effect," the phenomenon whereby heavy consumers of media are more likely to "perceive the real world in ways that reflect the most common and recurrent messages" in the medium they consume (Shanahan and Morgan 1999:4).

I also suggested that media cultivation has implications for the construction of class culture. When middle-class viewers identify *certain* media products as "real"—while labeling other products phony, cheap, uncouth, and fit only for the lower classes who favor them—they are also identifying *certain* "realist" cultural logics. I argued that the middle-class privileging as "real" of certain narrative constructions of causality (centered on individual achievement and personal responsibility) and of certain visual/material systems of value is part of the larger cultural project whereby the middle class attempts to "realize" its own highly consumer-oriented cultural values. The middle-class discourse of media realism is about naturalizing the cultural values and practices of the middle class.

There are several important spatial implications of this process of middle-class media "realization." First, the privileging of a middle-class consumer realism through a discourse of media realism helps account for the profound role of media consumption in influencing patterns of middle-class consumer practice more broadly. The seamstress who (in chapter 5) marvelled at how film fashions now instantly shape fashion demands in the city (and keep her well employed) is only one of countless examples throughout this study of how media representations become models for middle-class reality. If, as I have argued above, fashion practice is a key element in the middle-class project of making space, media consumption (and the narrative and material models of reality that it provides) helps to naturalize the cultural logics that the middle class uses to "take place." The privileging of media reality helps make middle-class cultural values appear to be inherent and spontaneous attributes of the new public space, characterized by its hyperconsumer aura of commodity promotion and display. The increasingly seamless transition between media realism and lived reality helps disguise the artifice by which middle-class systems of cultural value are transposed onto public space.

Mass media play another important role in the construction of middle-class cultural space. Here I return to the theme of the "media assemblage" (discussed in chapters 7 and 8), a concept that stresses the extraordinarily complex ways in which different mass media play off of (and mutually promote) one another, as well as a host of other allied commodities. Even in an apparently "out-of-the-way" place like Kathmandu, a range of commercial media (local, regional, and global) constantly play off of and refer to each other, forming an intricate web of linkages that promote and channel consumer desires in never-ending circuits from one product to the next. As I argued in my discussion of *Teens* magazine in chapter 8, individual media products link with other media products (videos, music, TV shows, etc.) and with consumer goods (from the magazine's dozens of "member establishments") in self-substantiating, "inter-effective" (Grossberg 1988:34) systems of value.[2] From the image worlds of local youth magazines (where media and other business interests coalesce to create and service a middle-class youth consumer market) to interactive radio programs to media-driven fashion regimes, the notion of the media assemblage points to how, rather than functioning as isolated meaning systems, a vast range of mass media, as well as other commodities, mix together and resonate with each other in a sphere of mutually referencing, mutually reinforcing ideas and images.

The concept of the media assemblage reminds us that media products *are* consumer goods: the consumption of media cannot be separated from the consumption of other commodities, either in theory or in practice. While euphemistically known as "communications industries," capitalist media enterprises might be better understood as distribution systems for commercial products.[3] Because media products are commodities, they are natural allies for the promotion of other consumer goods.[4] As commodities, media products share with other goods a common interest in a kind of "consumer ethic," or "consumer logic," that attempts to blur the boundary between self and commodity (like the *Teens* articles that equate being with consuming). The heart of the commercial project is not to produce a "satisfying object" but to produce the "needing subject" (Haug 1987:122). This is the project that producers of media share with other

---

[2] Many other commentators have also pointed to the saturation of daily life with continuous and overlapping media inputs (e.g., Bausinger 1984), or what Sklair has called "the systematic blurring of the lines between information, entertainment, and promotion of products" in contemporary capitalism (1995:87).

[3] According to Raymond Williams, "We fail to realize . . . that much of what we call communication is, necessarily, no more in itself than transmission: that is to say, a one-way sending. Reception and response, which complete communication, depend on other factors" (1958:302).

[4] There are now many studies from a variety of disciplines that explicitly link media products with the promotion of consumerism. Eckert describes the "almost incestuous hegemony that characterized Hollywood's relations with vast reaches of the American economy by the mid-1930s," such that films had "the effect of a direct sales agency" for a huge number of American corporations working hand-in-glove with film studios (1978:4–5). Hidden but carefully planned corporate advertising *within* commercial films and television programs continues unabated today (Wells 1995). Friedman (1985) reports similar patterns of commercialization in popular print "entertainment" media. Perhaps the ultimate example of the "public promotion" of private capitalist interests is the U.S. government's "Market Promotion Program," which in the early 1990s was handing out 200 million dollars per year to corporations like McDonald's, Campbell Soup, and Seagram & Sons for overseas advertising (Rauch 1992).

commodity producers and which unites all commodity promotion in a common enterprise.

Significantly, this assemblage of media forces helps to produce the auras of meaning that encompass consumer goods, rendering them desirable through their association with other objects of seemingly intrinsic value (from film stars to fitness clubs). The intereffective powers of media promotion work to conjure up and privilege worlds of visuality, surfaces, and display in which commodities and public consumer settings (restaurants, shops, cinemas, hotels, "attractions") are marked as objects of desire, means of distinction, or signifiers of value. As exemplified in the relationship between media and fashion consciousness in Kathmandu, electronic and print media play a crucial role in creating the imaginary spaces of meaning that surround contemporary commodities like penumbrae of signification. From the clothing fashions, beauty parlors, and fast-food joints in *Teens* magazine to the stereo systems, birthday parties, and private villas in Nepali films, media assemblages surround commodities (either literally or through association) not only with a whole host of complementary commodities[5] but with intangible meanings in the realms of style, modernity, newness, eroticism, "hepness" and so on.[6] Like the films and music that appear in magazines, and the magazines and music that appear in films, before long these penumbrae of signification overlap in a conglomeration of mutual referencing to form a continuous, eventually enormous, transnational sphere of imagination. This sphere invites people to live their lives around its structures of imagination and to experience their own reality through a world of signification built up around commodities.[7]

---

[5] For other perspectives on the idea of "complementary commodities," see Baudrillard on commercially generated "object paths" and "networks of objects" (1988:31), and Negt and Kluge's remarks on the role of commercial media in promoting commodified "cycles of fulfillment which embody the basic conditions of life" (quoted in Knödler-Bunte 1975:73).

[6] In his study of direct advertisement in American commercial films, Eckert describes how cinema fetishizes filmed objects and how desire is created and displaced onto consumer goods that have been made "libidinous, haunted" through filmic associations (1978:11).

[7] Haug argues that, due to their commercial aestheticization,

> commodities are surrounded by imaginary spaces which individuals are supposed to enter and to fill in with certain acts. If an individual acts within them, these spaces organize his/her way of experiencing these acts and personal identity. These spaces organize the imaginations of those who enter them. The use of these imaginations is the social identity of the individuals. . . . The commodities function now as real imaginations; the mythical supersigns built up around them present images of realized identity with the promise that the buyers become their representations. They present an imaginary identity; the purchase enables one to have an imaginary representation of one's identity. (1987:123)

These auras of meaning play a crucial role in middle-class public practice, surrounding consumer goods as they circulate from locally-con-
sumed (and often locally produced) films and magazines to the streets and
other public spaces of Kathmandu. As I described in chapter 5, Western
clothing styles began to "take off" in Kathmandu not with the arrival of
foreign tourists in the 1960s but only with the arrival of VCRs in the late
1970s. In short order disco films constructed a sphere of signification
around certain consumer goods that a decade of Western visitors had not.
Once animated by commercial media, goods begin to "speak for themselves," touting their own value and promising the fulfillment of identification. It is a very direct line that links the images on the cinema screen
to the images in the film magazine sitting in the tailor's shop, and these
to the shop displays and "fashions" on middle-class bodies on the streets
and campuses. Mass media help not only to make consumer goods omni-
present and constantly visible in the public realm but also to provide these
objects with auras of meaning, value, and desirability.

Whether they appear on middle-class bodies or in the shop windows
of the new commercial districts, these auras assist in the middle-class's
project of "taking place," of making space meaningful in the terms of its
own class values. Media's powerful signifying and validating effect on
consumer goods may be, ultimately, among the main reasons why the
middle class invests so heavily in media and its constructions of reality.
Middle-class culture has in common with commercial mass media a new
kind of "common sense," a consumer sensibility that comes through
clearly in the articles in *Teens* magazine that insistently and incessantly
equated reality with materiality and encouraged readers to find identity
in consumption. It is this common sense—one that naturalizes and privileges forms of consumer subjectivity—that is common to both media
promotion and middle-class cultural practice. To the extent that middle-
class cultural practice hinges on the promises (and pitfalls) of modern
capitalist consumerism (as I and others since Weber have argued), processes of commercial media promotion act as "natural" allies in the middle-class project of making space and taking place. The assembled pro-
motional powers of commercial mass media in effect affirm, validate,
and verify ("make true") the very strategies of cultural distinction that
the middle class uses to naturalize its own class privilege and carve out
a space for its own class culture.

Finally, what do youth and youth culture (part 4) have to do with the
production of middle-class cultural space in Kathmandu? If, as I have
argued, the production of "youth" (as a distinct sociocultural category
between childhood and adulthood) is an integral part of the larger project
of constructing a middle class, not only is modern "youth culture" almost
by definition middle-class but middle-class space is often highly youth-

oriented. Most obvious are the proliferating educational institutions designed to isolate, contain, and produce youth (chapter 8). Middle-class education has a range of spatial implications. First, Kathmandu's thousands of schools and campuses are physical spaces largely of, by, and for the middle class.[8] Second, as a consumable product, education both marks off a conceptual space of middle-class privilege ("achievement") and constitutes a key element of middle-class cultural practice. To invest in education is to stake a claim in the cultural space of the middle class. And third, over time education marks off the temporal "space" of youth. Unlike class (and race, ethnicity, and gender), youth is a temporary condition, its temporal existence largely framed within the space of education.[9] In effect youth help to construct the middle-class cultural space within which they are defined and confined.

The experience of youth in Kathmandu takes place within this confining and defining middle-class cultural space. Because youth is, like the middle class itself, a new "in-between" space, middle-class young people are doubly implicated in the ambiguities, tensions, and contradictions of "pioneering the middle." A major theme of the ethnographic material in chapters 8 and 9 was the competing forces at work in the new space of youth, each hoping to "tell" the "modern youth" within its own narrative of being and becoming. These forces ranged from the powerful consumerist narrative of *Teens* magazine (which offered a new "silent language" to interpellate its readers into its systems of meaning and value) and state-promoted narratives of progress and development to biting local critiques of modern youth as good-for-nothing "teens" and foreign media products that (in conjunction with the Nepali state's "development aid" industry) locate modernity beyond the boundaries of Nepal. Adults too must confront the competing and contradictory narratives of middle-class modernity, but youth carry an added burden: they must not only create a coherent present but imagine a coherent future. Caught somewhere between local, "traditional" narratives of value struggling to retain their "telling" power and carry their cultural meanings into the present, not to mention the future, and commercial images of foreign modernities that seem to locate the future in distant places, youth are left, in the words of one of the young men described in chapter 9, in the "nowhere place" of the present. If middle-class practice in Kathmandu produces a local cultural

---

[8] Elites send their children abroad or to a handful of very expensive local schools. Lower-class children, if their parents can afford any education for them at all, are segregated in low-quality public schools.

[9] Employment, marriage, or the establishment of a career, also serve to frame the condition of youth, but, as discussed in chapter 8, when young people confront a glutted middle-class labor market that forces them to postpone marriage, education continues to define the experience of youth, as adulthood is delayed further and further.

space, youth—the people who experience perhaps the greatest discontinuity between what they can imagine and what they can expect[10]—often experience that space as a prison located on the periphery ("out here") of an imagined world.

Conclusion

This final chapter has not been a summary in any formal sense, even though it has brought together many of the book's more significant arguments and insights. More than summarize, this chapter has sought to take the study's ethnographic perspectives on class culture and use them to reexamine the problems of what class is and does. If, as I have argued, class is not a "thing" but rather a practice or project, then we need to move beyond the passive, objectifying, immobilizing question "What *is* class?" to the active, processual question "What does class as cultural practice *do*?" By focusing on the spatial dynamics of class practice in Kathmandu, I have argued that what class *does* is make space and take place. Through a complex set of cultural processes—from the most conceptual to the most physical and material—middle-class practice is about carving out a cultural space in which people can speak and act themselves into cultural existence. Whether through language techniques, stories of morality and value, negotiations of status and honor, consumer practices and the deployment of consumer goods, media consumption, the creation of new sociocultural categories such as the "modern youth," or other methods, class practice *locates people* (either inside or outside the collectivity) and *creates locations*, conceptual and material spaces of, for, and by class. It is through everyday practice–in the deployment of language, goods, ideas, values, and embodied culture—that people produce the cultural space of class.

Asking "What is class?" freezes the concept within ahistorical, universalizing, and ultimately heuristic terms. Asking what class *does* allows us to understand it in its full historical, cultural, and cross-cultural complexity. I have argued that while processes of class formation are increasingly global, the reality of class is always produced in local cultural practice. In this study, class emerges not as a theoretical tautology imposed on the data but as a vivid ethnographic fact, perpetually produced and reproduced in cultural practice.

[10] This is what Appadurai identifies as "the ironic compromise between what [people can] imagine and what social life will permit" (1991:198).

BIBLIOGRAPHY

Abercrombie, Nicholas, Scott Lash, and Brian Longhurst.
    1992. Popular Representation: Recasting Realism. In *Modernity and Identity*. Scott Lash and Jonathan Friedman, eds. Pp. 115–40. Oxford and Cambridge, MA: Blackwell.
Adams, Vincanne.
    1996. *Tigers of the Snow and Other Virtual Sherpas: An Ethnography of Himalayan Encounters*. Princeton: Princeton University Press.
Adorno, Theodor W., and Max Horkheimer.
    1979 [1944]. *Dialectic of Enlightenment*. London: New Left Books.
Aglietta, Michel.
    1987. *A Theory of Capitalist Regulation*. London: Verso.
Ahearn, Laura. 2001. *Invitations to Love: Literacy, Love Letters, and Social Change in Nepal*. Ann Arbor: University of Michigan Press.
Akela, Vijay.
    1991. Big Is Back. *Filmfare* (Bombay) 40(9)(September):22.
Allen, Michael.
    1993. Hierarchy and Complementarity in Newar Eating Arrangements. In *Anthropology of Tibet and the Himalaya*. Charles Ramble and Martin Brauen, eds. Pp. 11–18. Zurich: Ethnological Museum of the University of Zurich.
Allison, Anne.
    2000. *Permitted and Prohibited Desires: Mothers, Comics, and Censorship in Japan*. Berkeley: University of California Press.
Alter, Joseph.
    1992. The *Sanyasi* and the Indian Wrestler: The Anatomy of a Relationship. *American Ethnologist* 19(2):317–36.
Anderson, Robert T., and Edna M. Mitchell.
    1978. The Politics of Music in Nepal. *Anthropological Quarterly* 51:247–59.
Ankerson, Robert W.
    1992. Nepal Is Not a Part of China. *The Independent* (Kathmandu), 26 August, p. 11.
Appadurai, Arjun.
    1986. Introduction: Commodities and the Politics of Value. In *The Social Life of Things: Commodities in Cultural Perspective*. A. Appadurai, ed. Pp. 3–63. Cambridge: Cambridge University Press.
    1988. Putting Hierarchy in Its Place. *Cultural Anthropology* 3(1):36–49.
    1990a. Disjuncture and Difference in the Global Cultural Economy. *Public Culture* 2(2):1–24.
    1990b. Technology and the Reproduction of Values in Rural Western India. In *Dominating Knowledge: Development, Culture, and Resistance*. F. Marglin and S. Marglin, eds. Pp. 185–216. Oxford: Clarendon Press.
    1991. Global Ethnoscapes: Notes and Queries for a Transnational Anthropology. In *Recapturing Anthropology: Working in the Present*. Richard G.

Appadurai, Arjun.
    Fox, ed. Pp. 191–210. Santa Fe, NM: School of American Research Press.
    1996. *Modernity at Large: Cultural Dimensions of Globalization.* Minneap-
    olis: University of Minnesota Press.
Appadurai, Arjun, ed.
    1986. *The Social Life of Things: Commodities in Cultural Perspective.* Cam-
    bridge: Cambridge University Press.
Appadurai, Arjun, and Carol Breckenridge.
    1991. Marriage, Migration and Money: Mira Nair's Cinema of Displace-
    ment. *Visual Anthropology* 4(1):95–102.
Appiah, Kwame Anthony.
    1991. Is the Post- in Postmodernism the Post- in Postcolonial? *Critical In-
    quiry* 17(2):336–57.
Aries, Philippe.
    1962. *Centuries of Childhood: A Social History of Family Life.* New York:
    Knopf.
Armbrust, Walter.
    1996. *Mass Culture and Modernism in Egypt.* Cambridge: Cambridge Uni-
    versity Press.
Aryal, Manisha.
    1992. Women in Development: What's in It for Me? *Himal* 5(2):24–25.
Audience Research.
    1989. *Television India (April, 89).* New Delhi: Directorate General Doordar-
    shan.
Babb, Lawrence A., and Susan S. Wadley, eds.
    1995. *Media and the Transformation of Religion in South Asia.* Philadelphia:
    University of Pennsylvania Press.
Baniya, Prem.
    2045 v.s. Chalchitrako Bikas: Kehi Charcha. In *Nepal Chalchitra Sang Rajat
    Jayanti: Smarika 2045.* Pp. 49–55. Kathmandu: Nepal Chalchitra Sang.
Baral, Dyuti.
    1990. Television and Children in Nepal: An Assessment of Viewing Patterns.
    In *Occasional Papers in Sociology and Anthropology.* S. Mikesell, ed. Pp.
    67–76. Kathmandu: Tribhuvan University.
Barry, Jonathan, and Christopher W. Brooks.
    1994. *The Middling Sort of People: Culture, Society and Politics in England,
    1550–1800.* New York: St. Martin's Press.
Barthes, Roland.
    1983. *The Fashion System.* New York: Hill and Wang.
Baudrillard, Jean.
    1988. Consumer Culture. In *Jean Baudrillard: Selected Writings.* Mark
    Poster, ed. Pp. 29–56. Stanford: Stanford University Press.
Bausinger, Herman.
    1984. Media Technology and Everyday Life. *Media, Culture and Society*
    6(4):343–51.

Bennett, Lynn.
    1983. *Dangerous Wives and Sacred Sisters: Social and Symbolic Roles of High-Caste Women in Nepal.* New York: Columbia University Press.
Bhattarai, Binod.
    1992. Watch Out: Is Nepal Television CNN, BBC, or Doordarshan? *The Rising Nepal,* 3 January, p. 5.
Bishop, R.N.W.
    1952. *Unknown Nepal.* London: Luzac and Co.
Bista, Dor Bahadur.
    1991. *Fatalism and Development: Nepal's Struggle for Modernization.* Calcutta: Orient Longman.
Bista, Sichendra.
    1993. It's a Gas. *The Independent* (Kathmandu), 15 September, p. 6.
Bjonness, Hans C.
    1990. Urban Eco-Development: Some Perspectives-Examples from Nepal and the Nordic Countries. Paper presented at the Fourth Asian Congress of Architects, New Delhi, 27–29 September.
Blaikie, Piers, John Cameron, and David Seddon.
    1980. *Nepal in Crisis: Growth and Stagnation at the Periphery.* Delhi: Oxford University Press.
Blanc, Cristina Szanton.
    1997. The Thoroughly Modern "Asian": Capital, Culture, and Nation in Thailand and the Philippines. In *Ungrounded Empires: The Cultural Politics of Modern Chinese Transnationalism.* Aihwa Ong and Donald M. Nonini, eds. Pp. 261–86. New York and London: Routledge.
Bledsoe, Bronwen.
    1984. Jewelry and Personal Adornment among the Newars. Unpublished paper prepared for the College Year in Nepal Program (University of Wisconsin, Madison), Kathmandu.
Bottomore, Tom.
    1966. *Classes in Modern Society.* New York: Vintage.
Bottomore, Tom, ed.
    1983. *A Dictionary of Marxist Thought.* Oxford: Basil Blackwell.
Bourdieu, Pierre.
    1977. *Outline of a Theory of Practice.* Cambridge: Cambridge University Press. 1980. *The Logic of Practice.* Stanford: Stanford University Press. 1984 [1979]. *Distinction.* Cambridge: Harvard University Press.
    1985. The Forms of Capital. In *Handbook of Theory and Research for the Sociology of Education.* John G. Richardson, ed. Pp. 241–58. New York: Greenwood Press.
Bourdieu, Pierre, and Jean-Claude Passeron.
    1990 [1970]. *Reproduction in Education, Society and Culture.* Second edition. London: Sage.
Breckenridge, Carol, ed.
    1995. *Consuming Modernity: Public Culture in a South Asian World.* Minneapolis: University of Minnesota Press.

Brosius, Christiane, and Melissa Butcher.
    1999. *Image Journeys: Audio-Visual Media and Cultural Change in India.*
    New Delhi: Sage.
Buck-Morss, Susan.
    1991. *The Dialectics of Seeing: Walter Benjamin and the Arcades Project.*
    Cambridge: MIT Press.
Burghart, Richard.
    1984. The Formation of the Concept of Nation-State in Nepal. *Journal of
    Asian Studies* 44:101–25.
Burke, Timothy.
    1996. *Lifeboy Men, Lux Women: Commodification, Consumption, and Clean-
    liness in Modern Zimbabwe.* Durham and London: Duke University Press.
Burris, Val.
    1987. The Neo-Marxist Synthesis of Marx and Weber on Class. In *The Marx-
    Weber Debate.* Norbert Wiley, ed. Pp. 67–90. Newbury Park, CA: Sage.
Butler, Judith.
    1990. *Gender Trouble: Feminism and the Subversion of Identity.* New York
    and London: Routledge.
Caplan, Lionel.
    1970. *Land and Social Change in East Nepal.* Berkeley: University of Califor-
    nia Press.
Caughey, John L.
    1984. *Imaginary Social Worlds.* Lincoln: University of Nebraska Press.
Cavarero, Adriana.
    2000. *Relating Narratives: Storytelling and Selfhood.* London and New
    York: Routledge.
Central Bureau of Statistics (CBS).
    1991. *Statistical Year Book of Nepal.* Kathmandu: CBS.
    1995. *Statistical Year Book of Nepal.* Kathmandu: CBS.
    1996. *Statistical Pocket Book.* Kathmandu: CBS.
Chakravarty, Sumita S.
    1993. *National Identity in Indian Popular Cinema, 1947–1987.* Austin: Uni-
    versity of Texas Press.
Chaudhuri, K. C.
    1960. *Anglo-Nepalese Relations from the Earliest Times of British Rule in
    India till the Gurkha War.* Calcutta: Modern Book Agency.
Chetwode, Penelope.
    1935. Nepal: The Sequestered Kingdom. *National Geographic* 120:319–52.
Chhetri, Subarna.
    1994. Those Magnificent Products in Their Flying Machines. *The Indepen-
    dent* (Kathmandu), 9 March, p. 8.
Cohen, Colleen B., Richard Wilk, and Beverley J. Stoeltje, eds.
    1995. *Beauty Queens on the Global Stage: Gender, Contest, and Power.* Lon-
    don and New York: Routledge.
Cohn, Bernard S.
    1968. Notes on the History of the Study of Indian Society and Culture. In

Structure and Change in Indian Society. M. Singer and B. Cohn, eds. Pp 3–28. Chicago: Aldine.

1984. The Census, Social Structure and Objectification in South Asia. *Folk* 29:25–51.

Csordas, Thomas.
1990. Embodiment as a Paradigm for Anthropology. *Ethos* 18(1):5–47.

Custen, George.
1987. Fiction as Truth: Viewer Use of Fictive Films as Data about the "Real" World. In *Visual Explorations of the World.* Martin Taureg and Jay Ruby, eds. Pp. 29–46. Aachen: Edition Herodot.

Dahal, Rajendra.
2000. Nepal's Remittance Bonanza. *Samachar Bichar* (Boston) 16 (summer): 7–8, 19.

Darian-Smith, Eve.
1999. *Bridging Divides: The Channel Tunnel and English Legal Identity in the New Europe.* Berkeley: University of California Press.

de Certeau, Michel.
1984. *The Practice of Everyday Life.* Steven Rendall, trans. Berkeley: University of California Press.

Derne, Steve.
1995. *Culture in Action: Family Life, Emotion, and Male Dominance in Banaras, India.* Albany: SUNY Press.

Des Chene, Mary.
1991. Relics of Empire: A Cultural History of the Gurkhas, 1815–1987. Ph.D. dissertation, Stanford University.

Dickey, Sara.
1993. *Cinema and the Urban Poor in South India.* Cambridge and New York: Cambridge University Press.

Dixit, Ajaya.
1992a. Little Water, Dirty Water. *Himal* 5(1):8–9.
1992b. The Bagmati Scorned. *Himal* 5(1):25–6.

Dixit, Kanak Mani.
1992. Compact Development: Kathmandu Tried It First. *Himal* 5(1):39.

Douglas, Mary, and Baron Isherwood.
1979. *The World of Goods.* New York: Basic Books.

Dumont, Louis.
1970. *Homo Hierarchicus.* Chicago: University of Chicago Press.

Dwyer, Rachel.
2000. *All You Want Is Money, All You Need Is Love: Sex and Romance in Modern India.* London and New York: Cassell.

Earle, Peter.
1989. *The Making of the English Middle Class.* Berkeley: University of California Press.

Eckert, Charles.
1978. The Carole Lombard in Macy's Window. *Quarterly Review of Film Studies* (winter):1–21.

Eckert, Penelope.
    1989. *Jocks and Burnouts: Social Categories and Identity in the High School.*
    New York: Teachers' College Press.
Egerton, Francis. 1852. *Journal of Winter Tours in India with a Visit to the Court
    of Nepal.* Two vols. London: John Murray.
Ehrenreich, Barbara.
    1989. *Fear of Falling: The Inner Life of the Middle Class.* New York:
    Pantheon.
Eickelman, Dale F., and Jon W. Anderson.
    1999. *New Media in the Muslim World: The Emerging Public Sphere.*
    Bloomington: Indiana University Press.
Elias, Norbert.
    1978 [1935]. *The History of Manners. The Civilizing Process,* vol. 1. New
    York: Pantheon.
    1978 [1968]. Introduction to the 1968 Edition. In *The History of Manners.
    The Civilizing Process,* vol. 1. Pp. 219–63. New York: Pantheon.
Eley, Geoff.
    1994. Nations, Publics, and Political Cultures: Placing Habermas in the Nine-
    teenth Century. In *Culture/Power/History: A Reader in Contemporary Social
    Theory.* Nicholas Dirks, Geoff Eley, and Sherry Ortner, eds. Pp. 297–335.
    Princeton: Princeton University Press.
Escobar, Arturo.
    1995. *Encountering Development: The Making and Unmaking of the Third
    World.* Princeton: Princeton University Press.
Ewen, Stuart, and Elizabeth Ewen.
    1982. *Channels of Desire: Mass Images and the Shaping of American Con-
    sciousness.* New York: McGraw-Hill.
Fabian, Johannes.
    1983. *Time and the Other.* New York: Columbia University Press.
Farmer, Victoria.
    1994. Politics and Airwaves: The Evolution of Television in India. Paper pre-
    sented at the Annual Meeting of the Association for Asian Studies, Boston,
    23–27 March.
Ferguson, James.
    1994 [1990]. *The Anti-Politics Machine: "Development," Depoliticization,
    and Bureaucratic Power in Lesotho.* Minneapolis: University of Minnesota
    Press.
Fisher, James.
    1990. *Sherpas: Reflections on Change in Himalayan Nepal.* Berkeley: Univer-
    sity of California Press.
Fiske, John.
    1989a. *Reading the Popular.* Boston: Unwin Hyman.
    1989b. *Understanding Popular Culture.* Boston: Unwin Hyman.
Foley, Douglas E.
    1990. *Learning Capitalist Culture: Deep in the Heart of Tejas.* Philadelphia:
    University of Pennsylvania Press.

Forbes, Ann A.
    1989. *Settlements of Hope: An Account of Tibetan Refugees in Nepal*. Boston: Cultural Survival.
Foucault, Michel.
    1979. *Discipline and Punish: The Birth of the Prison*. New York: Vintage.
    1980. *The History of Sexuality*. Vol. 1. New York: Vintage.
Fox, Richard G.
    1985. *Lions of the Punjab: Culture in the Making*. Berkeley: University of California Press.
    1989. *Gandhian Utopia: Experiments with Culture*. Boston: Beacon Press.
    1991. For a Nearly New Culture History. In *Recapturing Anthropology: Working in the Present*. Richard G. Fox, ed. Pp. 93–113. Santa Fe, NM: School of American Research Press.
Frank, Thomas.
    1997. *The Conquest of Cool: Business Culture, Counterculture, and the Rise of Hip Consumerism*. Chicago: University of Chicago Press.
Freire, Paulo.
    1970. *Pedagogy of the Oppressed*. New York: Seabury Press.
Friedman, Monroe.
    1985. The Changing Language of Consumer Society: Brand Name Usage in Popular American Novels in the Postwar Era. *Journal of Consumer Research* 11:927–38.
Frykman, Jonas, and Orvar Lofgren.
    1987 [1979]. *Culture Builders: A Historical Anthropology of Middle-Class Life*. New Brunswick and London: Rutgers University Press.
Fuglesang, Minou.
    1994. *Veils and Videos: Female Youth Culture on the Kenyan Coast*. Stockholm: Department of Social Anthropology, Stockholm University.
Fujikura, Tatsuro.
    1996. Technologies of Improvement, Locations of Culture: American Discourses of Democracy and "Community Development" in Nepal. *Studies in Nepali History and Society* 1(2):271–311.
Gaines, Donna.
    1990. *Teenage Wasteland: Suburbia's Dead End Kids*. Chicago: University of Chicago Press.
Galbraith, John Kenneth.
    1969. *The Affluent Society*. Second edition, revised. Boston: Houghton Mifflin.
Gallagher, Kathleen M.
    1991. An Exploration into the Causes of Squatting in the Kathmandu Valley. Master's thesis, Tribhuvan University, Kathmandu.
Gellner, David, and Declan Quigley, eds.
    1999. *Contested Hierarchies: A Collaborative Ethnography of Caste Among the Newars of the Kathmandu Valley, Nepal*. Oxford: Oxford University Press.
Gerbner, George, and Larry Gross.
    1976. Living with Television: The Violence Profile. *Journal of Communication* 26(2):173–99.

Gerbner, George, Larry Gross, Michael Morgan, and Nancy Signorielli.
    1994. Growing Up with Television: The Cultivation Perspective. In *Media Effects: Advances in Theory and Research*. Jennings Bryant and Dolf Zillman, eds. Pp. 17–41. Hillsdale, NJ: Lawrence Erlbaum.
Gerth, H. H., and C. Wright Mills.
    1946. Introduction. In *From Max Weber: Essays in Sociology*. H. H. Gerth and C. Wright Mills, eds. Pp. 1–74. New York: Oxford University Press.
Gewertz, Deborah, and Frederick Errington.
    1999. *Emerging Class in Papua New Guinea: The Telling of Difference*. Cambridge: Cambridge University Press.
Giddens, Anthony.
    1971. *Capitalism and Modern Social Theory*. Cambridge: Cambridge University Press.
Gillespie, Marie.
    1989. Technology and Tradition: Audio-Visual Culture among Asian Families in West London. *Cultural Studies* 3(2):226–39.
    1995. *Television, Ethnicity, and Cultural Change*. New York: Routledge.
Ginsburg, Faye, Lila Abu-Lughod, and Brian Larkin, eds.
    (forthcoming) *The Social Practice of Media*. Berkeley: University of California Press.
Giuseppe [da Rovato], Father.
    1790. An Account of the Kingdom of Nepal. *Asiaticke Researches* 2:307–22.
Goldschmidt, Walter.
    1950. Social Class in America: A Critical Review. *American Anthropologist* 52:483–98.
    1955. Social Class and the Dynamics of Status in America. *American Anthropologist* 57:1209–17.
Gombo, Ugen.
    1985. Tibetan Refugees in the Kathmandu Valley: A Study in Sociocultural Change and Continuity, and the Adaptation of a Population in Exile. Ph.D. dissertation, SUNY, Stony Brook.
Gramsci, Antonio.
    1971. *Selections from the Prison Notebooks*. Quentin Hoare and Geoffrey N. Smith, eds. New York: International Publishers.
Griffin, Christine.
    1993. *Representations of Youth: The Study of Youth and Adolescence in Britain and America*. Cambridge: Polity Press.
Grossberg, Lawrence.
    1988. The In-difference of Television. *Screen* 28(2):28–45.
Gumperz, John.
    1982. *Discourse Strategies*. Cambridge: Cambridge University Press.
Habermas, Jurgen.
    1989 [1962]. *The Structural Transformation of the Public Sphere*. Cambridge: MIT Press.
Hall, John, R.
    1997. The Reworking of Class Analysis. In *Reworking Class*. John R. Hall, ed. Pp. 1–37. Ithaca and London: Cornell University Press.

Hall, Stuart.
    1986. Gramsci's Relevance for the Study of Race and Ethnicity. *Journal of Communication Inquiry* 10(2):5–27.
Hall, Stuart, Bob Lumley, and Gregor McLennan.
    1977. Politics and Ideology: Gramsci. In *On Ideology*. Centre for Contemporary Cultural Studies, ed. Pp. 45–76. London: Hutchinson.
Halle, David.
    1984. *America's Working Man: Work, Home and Politics among Blue-Collar Property Owners*. Chicago: University of Chicago Press.
Haque, Anisul.
    1992. Bollywood and Indian Society. *Deep Focus* 4(1):59–63.
Harvey, David.
    1996. *Justice, Nature and the Geography of Difference*. Oxford: Blackwell.
Harvey, Neil.
    1998. *The Chiapas Rebellion: The Struggle for Land and Democracy*. Durham: Duke University Press.
Haug, Wolfgang Fritz.
    1987. *Commodity Aesthetics, Ideology and Culture*. New York: International General.
Hedrick, Basil C., and Anne K. Hedrick.
    1972. *Historical and Cultural Dictionary of Nepal*. Metuchen, NJ: Scarecrow Press.
Hepburn, Sharon.
    1993. Fashion and Ethnic Tourists in Nepal: Whose Authenticity Is This? Paper presented at the Twenty-second Conference on South Asia, Madison, Wisconsin, November.
Hinchman, Lewis P., and Sandra K. Hinchman.
    1997a.
    Memory, Identity, Community: The Idea of Narrative in the Human Sciences. Albany: SUNY Press.
    1997b. Introduction. In *Memory, Identity, Community: The Idea of Narrative in the Human Sciences*. Lewis P. Hinchman and Sandra K. Hinchman, eds. Pp. xiii–xxxii. Albany: SUNY Press.
Hodgson, Brian H.
    1834. On the Law and Legal Practice of Nepal, as Regards Familiar Intercourse between Hindu and Outcaste. *Journal of the Royal Asiatic Society of Great Britain and Ireland* 1:45–56.
    1847. Production and Consumption of a Newar Peasant of the Valley of Nepal; Cultivating with the Spade Seven Standard Ropini of Nepal. In *On the Aborigines of India*. Pp. 195–200. Calcutta: Baptist Mission Press.
    1972 [1874]. *Essays on the Languages, Literature, and Religion of Nepal and Tibet, Together with Further Papers on the Geography, Ethnography, and Commerce of Those Countries*. Reprinted as vol. 7, series 2, *Bibliotecha Himalayica*. New Delhi: Manjusri Publishing House.
Höfer, Andras.
    1979. *The Caste Hierarchy and the State in Nepal: A Study of the Muluki Ain of 1854*. Innsbruck: Universitätsverlag Wagner.

276

BIBLIOGRAPHY

Holland, Dorothy C., and Margaret A. Eisenhart.
1990. *Educated in Romance: Women, Achievement, and College Culture.* Chicago: University of Chicago Press.

Howes, David, ed.
1996. *Cross-Cultural Consumption: Global Markets, Local Realities.* London and New York: Routledge.

Hunt, Margaret.
1996. *The Middling Sort: Commerce, Gender and the Family in England, 1680–1780.* Berkeley: University of California Press.

Hurlock, Elizabeth.
1929. *The Psychology of Dress: An Analysis of Fashion and Its Motive.* New York: Ronald Press.

Isaacson, Joel M.
1990. A Structured Examination of Some Links between Political, Economic, and Social Change, and Architecture in Nepal. Master's thesis, Antioch University.

Jameson, Fredric.
1983. Postmodernism and Consumer Society. In *The Anti-Aesthetic: Essays on Postmodern Culture.* Hal Foster, ed. Pp. 111–25. Port Townsend, WA: Bay Press.
1989. Nostalgia for the Present. *South Atlantic Quarterly* 88(2):517–37.

Joshi, Bikas.
1997. Foreign Aid in Nepal: What Do the Data Show? *Himal South Asia* 10(2):70–71.

Joshi, Prayag Raj.
2045 v.s. Nepalma Chalchitra Nirmani Evan Pradarshan. In *Nepal Chalchitra Sang Rajat Jayanti: Smarika 2045.* Pp. 35–39. Kathmandu: Nepal Chalchitra Sang.

Joyce, Patrick.
1997. Forward. In *Reworking Class.* John R. Hall, ed. Pp. xi–xiii. Ithaca and London: Cornell University Press.

Justice, Judith.
1986. *Policies, Plans, and People: Foreign Aid and Health Development.* Berkeley: University of California Press.

Kakar, Sudhir.
1989. *Intimate Relations: Exploring Indian Sexuality.* New Delhi: Viking.

Kellner, Douglas.
1990. *Television and the Crisis of Democracy.* Boulder: Westview.

Kett, Joseph.
1977. *Rites of Passage: Adolescence in America, 1790 to the Present.* New York: Basic Books.

Khatri, Kem B.
1983. *Nepal's Mass Media.* Kathmandu: HMG. Ministry of Communication.

Kirkpatrick, William.
1969 [1811]. *An Account of the Kingdom of Nepaul.* Reprinted as vol. 3, series 1, Bibliotecha Himalayica. New Delhi: Manjusri Publishing House.

Kleinman, Arthur.
   1988. *The Illness Narratives: Suffering, Healing, and the Human Condition.*
   New York: Basic Books.
Kluge, Alexander.
   1990. The Assault of the Present on the Rest of Time. *New German Critique*
   49:11–22.
Knödler-Bunte, Eberhard.
   1975. The Proletarian Public Sphere and Political Organization: An Analysis
   of Oskar Negt and Alexander Kluge's *The Public Sphere and Experience.*
   New German Critique 4:51–75.
Kottak, Conrad Philip.
   1990. *Prime-Time Society: An Anthropological Analysis of Television and
   Culture.* Belmont, CA: Wadsworth Publishing.
Kumar, Nita.
   1988. *The Artisans of Banaras: Popular Culture and Identity, 1880–1986.*
   Princeton: Princeton University Press.
Landon, Percival.
   1928. *Nepal.* Two vols. London: Constable.
Lears, T. J. Jackson.
   1983. From Salvation to Self-Realization: Advertising and the Therapeutic
   Roots of the Consumer Culture, 1880–1930. In *The Culture of Con-
   sumption.* Richard Fox and T. J. Jackson Lears, eds. Pp. 3–38. New York:
   Pantheon.
Leuchtag, Erica.
   1958. *With a King in the Clouds.* London: Hutchinson.
Levy, Robert I., and Kedar Rajopadhyaya.
   1991. *Mesocosm: Hinduism and the Organization of a Traditional Newar
   City in Nepal.* Berkeley: University of California Press.
Lewis, Todd T.
   1984. The Tuladhars of Kathmandu: A Study of Buddhist Tradition in a
   Newar Merchant Community. Ph.D. dissertation, Columbia University.
   1993. Himalayan Frontier Trade: Newar Diaspora Merchants and Bud-
   dhism. In *The Anthropology of Tibet and the Himalaya.* Charles Ramble
   and Martin Brauen, eds. Pp. 165–78. Zurich: Ethnological Museum of the
   University of Zurich.
Liebes, Tamar, and Elahu Katz.
   1990. *The Export of Meaning: Cross-Cultural Readings of Dallas.* New
   York: Oxford University Press.
Liechty, Mark.
   1994. Fashioning Modernity in Kathmandu: Mass Media, Consumer Culture, and the Middle Class in Nepal. Ph.D. dissertation, University of Pennsylvania.
   1995. Modernization, Media and Markets: Youth Identities and the Experience of Modernity in Kathmandu, Nepal. In *Youth Cultures: A Cross-Cultural Perspective.* Vered Amit-Talai and Helena Wulff, eds. Pp. 166–201.
   London: Routledge.

Liechty, Mark.
    1996a. Kathmandu as Translocality: Multiple Places in a Nepali Space. *Geography of Identity*. Patricia Yaeger, ed. Pp. 98–130. Ann Arbor: University of Michigan Press.
    1996b. Paying for Modernity: Women and the Discourse of Freedom in Kathmandu. *Studies in Nepali History and Society* 1(1):201–30.
    1997. Selective Exclusion: Foreigners, Foreign Goods, and Foreignness in Modern Nepali History. *Studies in Nepali History and Society* 2(1):5–68.
    2001. Women and Pornography in Kathmandu: Negotiating the "Modern Woman" in a New Consumer Society. In *Images of the "Modern Woman" in Asia: Global Media/Local Meanings*. Shoma Munshi, ed. Pp. 34–54. London: Curzon Press.
Lipsitz, George.
    1990. *Time Passages: Collective Memory and American Popular Culture*. Minneapolis: University of Minnesota Press.
Loriga, Sabina.
    1997. The Military Experience. In *A History of Young People in the West*, vol. 2. Giovanni Levi and Jean-Claude Schmitt, eds. Pp. 11–36. Cambridge and London: Harvard University Press.
Luger, Kurt.
    2000. *Kids of Khumbu: Sherpa Youth on the Modernity Trail*. Kathmandu: Eco-Himal/Mandala Book Point.
Lutgendorf, Philip.
    1990. Ramayan: The Video. *Drama Review* 34(2):127–76.
Lyons, Harriet D.
    1990. Television in Contemporary Urban Life: Benin City, Nigeria. *Visual Anthropology* 3:411–28.
Lyotard, Jean-François.
    1984 [1979]. *The Postmodern Condition: A Report on Knowledge*. Minneapolis: University of Minnesota Press.
Macfarlane, Alan.
    1994. Fatalism and Development in Nepal. In *Nepal in the Nineties*. Michael Hutt, ed. Pp. 106–27. Delhi: Oxford University Press.
Mankekar, Purnima.
    1999. *Screening Culture, Viewing Politics: An Ethnography of Television, Womanhood, and Nation in Postcolonial India*. Durham and London: Duke University Press.
Manuel, Peter.
    1993. *Cassette Culture: Popular Music and Technology in North India*. Chicago: University of Chicago Press.
Marcus, George.
    1990. The Modernist Sensibility in Recent Ethnographic Writing and the Cinematic Metaphor of Montage. *Visual Anthropology Review* 6(1):2–12, 21, 44.
Marcus, George, ed.
    1983. *Elites*. Albuquerque: University of New Mexico Press.

Marcus, George, and Michael M. J. Fischer.
    1986. *Anthropology as Cultural Critique: An Experimental Moment in the Human Sciences*. Chicago: University of Chicago Press.
Marx, Karl.
    1973 [1857–58]. The General Relation of Production to Distribution, Exchange, Consumption. In *Grundrisse: Foundations of the Critique of Political Economy*. Pp. 88–100. New York: Vintage.
Mathema, Pushkar.
    2047 v.s. 2047 Salbhitra: Nepali Telichalchitra. *Gorkhapatra*, 30 Chaitra (13 April 1991), p. gh.
Mattingly, Cheryl, and Linda C. Garro.
    2000. *Narrative and the Cultural Construction of Illness and Healing*. Berkeley: University of California Press.
McCracken, Grant.
    1988. *Culture and Consumption*. Bloomington: Indiana University Press.
Melkote, Srinivas R., Peter Shields, and Binod C. Agrawal, eds.
    1998. *International Satellite Broadcasting in South Asia: Political, Economic and Cultural Implications*. Lanham, MD: University Press of America.
Meyrowitz, Joshua.
    1985. *No Sense of Place: The Impact of Electronic Media on Social Behavior*. New York and Oxford: Oxford University Press.
Michaels, Eric.
    1993. *Bad Aboriginal Art: Tradition, Media, and Technological Horizons*. Minneapolis: University of Minnesota Press.
Michaud, Eric.
    1997. Soldiers of an Idea: Young People under the Third Reich. In *A History of Young People in the West*, vol 2. Giovanni Levi and Jean-Claude Schmitt, eds. Pp. 257–80. Cambridge and London: Harvard University Press.
Miller, Daniel.
    1987. *Material Culture and Mass Consumption*. Oxford and New York: Basil Blackwell.
    1994. *Modernity: An Ethnographic Approach: Dualism and Mass Consumption in Trinidad*. Oxford: Berg.
    1995a. Consumption Studies as the Tranformation of Anthropology. In *Acknowledging Consumption*. Daniel Miller, ed. Pp. 264–95. London and New York: Routledge.
    1995b. Consumption and Commodities. *Annual Reviews of Anthropology* 24:141–61.
    1995c. Consumption as the Vanguard of History. In *Acknowledging Consumption*. Daniel Miller, ed. Pp. 1–57. London and New York: Routledge.
Miller, Daniel, ed.
    1995. *Worlds Apart: Modernity through the Prism of the Local*. London and New York: Routledge.
    1998. *Material Cultures: Why Some Things Matter*. Chicago: University of Chicago Press.

Miller, Sarah.
    1992. Twice-Born Tales from Kathmandu: Stories That Tell People. Ph.D.
    dissertation, Cornell University.
Mishra, Vijay.
    1985. Toward a Theoretical Critique of Bombay Cinema. *Screen* 26(3–
    4):133–46.
Mitsui, Toru, and Shuhei Hosokawa, eds.
    1998. *Karaoke around the World: Global Technology, Local Singing.* Lon-
    don and New York: Routledge.
Moreiras, Alberto.
    1998. Global Fragments: A Second Latinamericanism. In *The Cultures of
    Globalization.* Fredric Jameson and Masao Miyoshi, eds. Pp. 81–102. Dur-
    ham: Duke University Press.
Morris, John.
    1963. *A Winter in Nepal.* London: Rupert Hart-Davis.
Mosse, George.
    1985. *Nationalism and Sexuality: Middle-Class Morality and Sexual Norms
    in Modern Europe.* Madison: University of Wisconsin Press.
Nacify, Hamid.
    1989. Autobiography, Film Spectatorship, and Cultural Negotiation. *Emer-
    gences* 1:29–54.
Nag, Dulali.
    1991. Fashion, Gender and the Bengali Middle Class. *Public Culture*
    3(2):93–112.
Nandy, Ashis.
    1998. Introduction: Indian Popular Cinema as a Slum's Eye View of Politics.
    In *The Secret Politics of Our Desires: Innocence, Culpability and Indian Pop-
    ular Cinema.* Ashis Nandy, ed. Pp. 1–18. London: Zed.
Nash, June, and Maria Patricia Fernandez-Kelly, eds.
    1983. *Women, Men and the International Division of Labor.* Albany: SUNY
    Press.
Nava, Mica.
    1992. *Changing Cultures: Feminism, Youth and Consumerism.* London: Sage.
Nepal Administrative Staff College
    2048 v.s. *Solid Waste Management at Thamel, Kathmandu and Its Impact
    (A Sectoral Analysis).* Jawalakhel, Lalitpur: NASC.
Nepali, Gopal Singh.
    1965. *The Newars: An Ethno-Sociological Study of a Himalayan Commu-
    nity.* Bombay: United Asia Publications.
Newman, Katherine S.
    1988. *Falling from Grace: Downward Mobility in the Age of Affluence.*
    Berkeley: University of California Press.
    1993. *Declining Fortunes: The Withering of the American Dream.* New
    York: Basic Books.
Ong, Aihwa.
    1987. *Spirits of Resistance and Capitalist Discipline: Factory Women in Ma-
    laysia.* Albany: SUNY Press.

Ong, Aihwa, and Donald M. Nonini, eds.

1997. *Ungrounded Empires: The Cultural Politics of Modern Chinese Trans-nationalism.* New York and London: Routledge.

Onta, Pratyoush.

1994. History of Photography in Nepal. *The Sunday Post* (Kathmandu), 28 August, 4 September, 11 September, 18 September, 25 September, 2 October.

1996. Creating a Brave Nation in British India: The Rhetoric of *Jati* Improvement, Rediscovery of Bhanubhakta, and the Writing of *Bir* History. *Studies in Nepali History and Society* 1(1):37–76.

Orlove, Benjamin.

1997. *The Allure of the Foreign: Imported Goods in Postcolonial Latin America.* Ann Arbor: University of Michigan Press.

Ortner, Sherry B.

1984. Theory in Anthropology since the Sixties. *Comparative Studies in Society and History* 26:126–66.

1991. Reading America: Preliminary Notes on Class and Culture. In *Recapturing Anthropology: Working in the Present.* Richard G. Fox, ed. Pp. 163–89. Santa Fe, NM: School of American Research Press.

1994. Ethnography among the Newark: The Class of '58 of Weequahic High School. *Michigan Quarterly Review,* summer, 410–29.

1997. Fieldwork in the Post-Community. *Anthropology and Humanism Quarterly* 22:61–80.

1998. Identities: The Hidden Life of Class. *Journal of Anthropological Research* 54(1):1–17.

1999a. Generation X: Anthropology in a Media-Saturated World. In *Critical Anthropology Now.* George Marcus, ed. 55–87. Santa Fe, NM: School of American Research Press.

1999b. *Life and Death on Mt. Everest: Sherpas and Himalayan Mountaineering.* Princeton: Princeton University Press.

Owens, Bruce McCoy.

1989. The Politics of Divinity in the Kathmandu Valley: The Festival of Bungadya/Rato Matsyendranath. Ph.D. dissertation, Columbia University.

Pahari, Anup.

1992. Fatal Myth: A Critique of *Fatalism and Development.* Himal 5(1):52–54.

Palladino, Grace.

1996. *Teenagers: An American History.* New York: Basic Books.

Parkin, Frank.

1979. *Marxism and Class Theory: A Bourgeois Critique.* New York: Columbia University Press.

Passerini, Luisa.

1997. Youth as a Metaphor for Social Change: Fascist Italy and America in the 1950s. In *A History of Young People in the West,* vol 2. Giovanni Levi and Jean-Claude Schmitt, eds. Pp. 281–341. Cambridge and London: Harvard University Press.

Paudel, Phanindreshwar.

1990. Employment, Working Conditions and Mode of Living: The Case of

Paudel, Phanindreshwar.
    Nepali Watchmen in Bombay. In *Occasional Papers in Sociology and Anthropology*. S. Mikesell, ed. Pp. 59–66. Kathmandu: Tribhuvan University.
Peiss, Kathy.
    1986. *Cheap Amusements: Working Women and Leisure in Turn-of-the-Century New York*. Philadelphia: Temple University Press.
Peissel, Michel.
    1966. *Tiger for Breakfast: The Story of Boris of Kathmandu: Adventurer, Big Game Hunter, and Host of Nepal's Famous Royal Hotel*. Bombay: Allied Publishers.
Pendakur, Manjunath.
    1990. India. In *The Asian Film Industry*. John Lent, ed. Pp. 229–52. Austin: University of Texas Press.
Perrot, Michelle.
    1997. Worker Youth: From the Workshop to the Factory. In *A History of Young People in the West*, vol. 2. Giovanni Levi and Jean-Claude Schmitt, eds. Pp. 66–116. Cambridge and London: Harvard University Press.
Pieper, Jan.
    1975. Three Cities of Nepal. In *Shelter, Sign and Symbol*. Paul Oliver, ed. Pp. 52–69. London: Barrie and Jenkins.
Pigg, Stacy.
    1992. Inventing Social Categories through Place: Social Representations and Development in Nepal. *Comparative Studies in Society and History* 34(3):491–513.
    1996. The Credible and the Credulous: The Question of "Villagers' Beliefs" in Nepal. *Cultural Anthropology* 11(2):160–201.
Pinney, Christopher.
    1998. *Camera Indica: The Social Life of Indian Photographs*. Chicago: University of Chicago Press.
Pokhryal, Yadunath.
    1966. Stuti Padhya 1. In *Purano Kavi ra Kavita*. Baburam Acharya. ed. Pp. 81–91. Kathmandu: Sajha Prakashan.
Proksch, Andreas, ed.
    1995. *Images of a Century: The Changing Townscapes of the Kathmandu Valley*. Kathmandu: GTZ.
Proweller, Amira.
    1998. *Constructing Female Identities: Meaning Making in an Upper Middle Class Youth Culture*. Albany: SUNY Press.
PuruShotam, Nirmala.
    1998. Between Compliance and Resistance: Women and the Middle-Class Way of Life in Singapore. In *Gender and Power in Affluent Asia*. Krishna Sen and Maila Stivens, eds. Pp. 127–66. London and New York: Routledge.
Quigley, Declan.
    1993. *The Interpretation of Caste*. Oxford: Clarendon Press.
Radway, Janice.
    1984. *Reading the Romance: Women, Patriarchy and Popular Literature*. Chapel Hill: University of North Carolina Press.

1991. Interpretive Communities and Variable Literacies: The Functions of Romance Reading. In *Rethinking Popular Culture*. Chandra Mukerji and Michael Schudson, eds. Pp. 465–86. Berkeley: University of California Press.

Rajagopal, Arvind.
2001. *Politics after Television: Religious Nationalism and the Retailing of "Hinduness."* Cambridge: Cambridge University Press.

Rajadhyaksha, Ashish, and Paul Willemen.
1999. *Encyclopedia of Indian Cinema*. New Revised Edition. Delhi: British Film Institute and Oxford University Press.

Rana, Brahmesvar Jangabahadur.
1935. *Nepalko Mahabhukampa*. Kathmandu: n.p.

Rana, Pramod Shamshere.
1978. *Rana Nepal: An Insider's View*. Kathmandu: Mrs. R. Rana.
1995. *Rana Intrigues*. Kathmandu: Mrs. R. Rana.

Rankin, Katharine N., and Madan Gopal Shrestha.
1995. The Implications of Local Credit Markets for Financial Policy. *ECO-News* (Kathmandu) 6(2) (May).

Rauch, Jonathan.
1992. Subsidized Ads. *National Journal*, 27 June pp. 1509–12.

Regmi, Mahesh Chandra.
1978. *Thatched Huts and Stucco Palaces: Peasants and Landlords in Nineteenth-Century Nepal*. New Delhi: Vikas.
1988. *An Economic History of Nepal, 1846–1901*. Varanasi: Nath Publishing House.

Richards, Paul.
1996. *Fighting for the Rain Forest: War, Youth and Resources in Sierra Leone*. Portsmouth, NH: Heinemann.

Roberts, Sam.
1997. Another Kind of Middle-Class Squeeze. *Los Angeles Times*, 18 May, section 4, pp. 1, 6.

Robison, Richard, and David S. G. Goodman.
1996. The New Rich in Asia: Economic Development, Social Status and Political Consciousness. In *The New Rich in Asia*. Richard Robison and David S. G. Goodman, eds. Pp. 1–16. London and New York: Routledge.

Robison, Richard, and David S. G. Goodman, eds.
1996. *The New Rich in Asia: Mobile Phones, McDonalds and Middle-Class Revolution*. London and New York: Routledge.

Rodowick, David.
1988. *The Crisis of Political Modernity: Criticism and Ideology in Contemporary Film Theory*. Urbana: University of Illinois Press.

Rosser, Colin.
1966. Mobility in the Newar Caste System. In *Caste and Kin in Nepal, India and Ceylon*. C. von Furer-Haimendorf, ed. Pp. 68–139. London: Asia Publishing House.

Rudolph, Lloyd I., and Susanne Hoeber Rudolph.
1967. *The Modernity of Tradition: Political Development in India*. Chicago: University of Chicago Press.

Rutz, H. J., and Benjamin Orlove, eds.
    1989. *The Social Economy of Consumption*. Lanham, MD: University Press of America.
Sacks, Karen Brodkin.
    1989. Toward a Unified Theory of Class, Race, and Gender. *American Ethnologist* 16(3):534–50.
Sato, Ikuya.
    1991. *Kamikaze Biker: Parody and Anomy in Affluent Japan*. Chicago: University of Chicago Press.
Schein, Louisa.
    1999. Performing Modernity. *Cultural Anthropology* 14(3):361–95.
    2000. *Minority Rules: The Mioa and the Feminine in China's Cultural Politics*. Durham: Duke University Press.
Schlegel, Alice, and Herbert Barry.
    1991. *Adolescence: An Anthropological Inquiry*. New York: Free Press.
Seidman, Steven.
    1994. *Contested Knowledge: Social Theory in the Postmodern Era*. Oxford: Blackwell.
Sen, Krishna, and Maila Stivens, eds.
    1998. *Gender and Power in Affluent Asia*. London and New York: Routledge.
Sever, Adrian.
    1993. *Nepal under the Ranas*. New Delhi: Oxford and IBH Publishing Co.
Shanahan, James, and Michael Morgan.
    1999. *Television and Its Viewers: Cultivation Theory and Research*. Cambridge: Cambridge University Press.
Sharma, Pitamber.
    1989. *Urbanization in Nepal*. Papers of the East-West Population Institute, no. 110 (May 1988). Honolulu: East-West Center.
Sharma, Prayag Raj.
    1975. Inventory of Individual Monuments and Monument Sites in Kathmandu. In *Kathmandu Valley: The Preservation of Physical Environment and Cultural Heritage, A Protective Inventory*, vol. 2. Pp. 6–125. HMG Department of Housing, Building and Physical Planning, in collaboration with the United Nations and UNESCO; coordination and production, Carl Pruscho. Vienna: Anton Schroll and Co.
Sharma, Sudhindra.
    2001. *Procuring Water: Foreign Aid and Rural Water Supply in Nepal*. Kathmandu: Nepal Water Conservation Foundation.
Shiva, Vandana.
    2000. *Stolen Harvest: The Hijacking of the Global Food Supply*. Cambridge, MA: South End Press.
Shrestha, Bijaya Lal.
    1992. Valley Tourism: The Shine Is Off. *Himal* 5(1):19–20.
Shrestha, Chandra B., Prem K. Kharty, Bharat Sharma, and Hamid Ansuri.
    1986. *The Historic Cities of Asia: Kathmandu*. Kathmandu: CNAS.

Shrestha, Nanda R.
1990. *Landlessness and Migration in Nepal*. Boulder: Westview.
Shrestha, Padma Prakash.
1986. *Nepal Rediscovered: The Rana Court 1846–1951, Photographs from the Archives of the Nepal Kingdom Foundation*. New Delhi: Time Books International.
Shrestha, Pushkar Lal.
2047 v.s. Kamanale Malai Dhani Banaeko Cha. *Kamana* 50:137–39.
Shrestha, Uma.
1990. Social Networks and Code-Switching in the Newar Community of Kathmandu City. Ph.D. dissertation, Ball State University.
Siegel, James T.
1986. *Solo in the New Order: Language and Hierarchy in an Indonesian City*. Princeton: Princeton University Press.
Simmel, Georg.
1950. *The Sociology of Georg Simmel*. K. H. Wolff, ed. New York: Free Press.
Singh, Najar Man.
1990. *Nepal in Transition*. Kathmandu: the author.
Sitton, John F.
1996. *Recent Marxian Theory: Class Formation and Social Conflict in Contemporary Capitalism*. Albany: SUNY Press.
Sklair, Leslie.
1995. *Sociology of the Global System*. Second edition. Baltimore: Johns Hopkins University Press.
Slater, Don.
1997. *Consumer Culture and Modernity*. Cambridge: Polity Press.
Sloane, Patricia.
1999. *Islam, Modernity and Entrepreneurship among the Malays*. New York: St. Martin's Press.
Slusser, Mary Shepherd.
1982. *Nepal Mandala: A Cultural Study of the Kathmandu Valley*. Princeton: Princeton University Press.
Smith, Raymond.
1984. Anthropology and the Concept of Social Class. *Annual Reviews of Anthropology* 13:467–94.
Somers, Margaret R.
1994a. The Narrative Constitution of Identity: A Relational and Network Approach. *Theory and Society* 23:605–49.
1994b. Reclaiming the Epistemological "Other": Narrative and the Social Constitution of Identity. In *Social Theory and the Politics of Identity*. Craig Calhoun, ed. Pp. 37–99. Oxford: Blackwell.
1997. Deconstructing and Reconstructing Class Formation Theory: Narrativity, Relational Analysis, and Social Theory. In *Reworking Class*. John R. Hall, ed. Pp. 73–105. Ithaca and London: Cornell University Press.
Spiegler, Marc.
1996. Marketing Street Culture: Bringing Hip-Hop Style to the Mainstream. *American Demographics* 18(11):28–35.

Spitulnik, Debra.
    1993. Anthropology and Mass Media. *Annual Review of Anthropology*
    22:293–315.
Springhall, John.
    1986. *Coming of Age: Adolescence in Britain, 1860–1960*. Dublin: Gill and
    Macmillan.
Stiller, Ludwig F., S.J.
    1968. *Prithvi Narayan Shah in the Light of the Dibya Upadesh*. Kathmandu:
    Himalaya Book Centre.
    1973. *The Rise of the House of Gorkha: A Study in the Unification of Nepal,*
    1768–1816. Ranchi: Catholic Press.
    1976. *The Silent Cry: The People of Nepal, 1816–1839*. Kathmandu: Sahay-
    ogi Prakashan.
    1981. *Letters from Kathmandu: The Kot Massacre*. Kirtipur: Tribhuvan Uni-
    versity Press. 1993. *Nepal: Growth of a Nation*. Kathmandu: Human Re-
    sources Development Research Center.
Stivens, Maila.
    1998a. Theorising Gender, Power and Modernity in Affluent Asia. In *Gender*
    and Power in Affluent Asia. Krishna Sen and Maila Stivens, eds. Pp. 1–34.
    London and New York: Routledge.
    1998b. Sex, Gender and the Making of the New Malay Middle Classes. In
    Gender and Power in Affluent Asia. Krishna Sen and Maila Stivens, eds. Pp.
    87–126. London and New York: Routledge.
Subrahmanyam, Sanjay.
    1997. Connected Histories: Notes towards a Reconfiguration of Early Mod-
    ern Eurasia. *Modern Asian Studies* 31(3):735–62.
Susman, Warren.
    1984. *Culture as History: The Transformation of American Society in the*
    Twentieth Century. New York: Pantheon.
Tagg, John.
    1988. *The Burden of Representation: Essays on Photographies and Histories*.
    London: Macmillan.
Tarlo, Emma.
    1996. *Clothing Matters: Dress and Identity in India*. Chicago: University of
    Chicago Press.
Task Force on Migration.
    1999. *Internal and International Migration in Nepal: Summary and Recom-*
    mendations. Kathmandu: Tanka Prasad Acharya Memorial Foundation.
Taynbee, Polly.
    1996. The Sinister Sound of Democracy. *The Independent* (Kathmandu), 4
    December, p. 4.
Thomas, Rosie.
    1985. Indian Cinema: Pleasures and Popularity. *Screen* 26(3–4):116–31.
Thompson, Edward P.
    1966 [1963]. *The Making of the English Working Class*. New York: Vintage.
    1978. Eighteenth-Century English Society: Class Struggle without Class? *So-*
    cial History 3(2):133–65.

Thompson, F.M.L.
    1988. *The Rise of Respectable Society: A Social History of Victorian Britain, 1830–1900.* Cambridge: Harvard University Press.
Tiwari, Ashutosh.
    1992. Planning: Never without Aid. *Himal* 5(2):8–10.
Tomlinson, John.
    1991. *Cultural Imperialism.* Baltimore: Johns Hopkins University Press.
Tomory, David.
    1996. *A Season in Heaven: True Tales from the Road to Kathmandu.* London: Thorsons.
Tufte, Thomas.
    2000. *Living with the Rubbish Queen: Telenovelas, Culture and Modernity in Brazil.* Luton, Bedfordshire, U.K.: University of Luton Press.
Turow, Joseph.
    1997. *Breaking Up America: Advertisers and the New Media World.* Chicago: University of Chicago Press.
Tyler, Stephen A.
    1984. The Vision Quest in the West, or What the Mind's Eye Sees. *Journal of Anthropological Research* 40(1):23–39.
Upadhyaya, Shreeram Prasad.
    1992. *Indo-Nepal Trade Relations: A Historical Analysis of Nepal's Trade with the British India.* Jaipur and New Delhi: Nirala Publications.
Upadyaya, Laxman.
    1991. Nepalma Bigyapan Byabasaya: Sabchchhan-data ra Niyaman. *Gorkhapatra*, 15 November, p. 4.
Uprety, Hari.
    1991. Banking Reform: Dhukutis Are Doing It. *The Rising Nepal*, 14 November, p. 4.
van der Veer, Peter.
    1994. *Religious Nationalism: Hindus and Muslims in India.* Berkeley: University of California Press.
van Spengen, Wim.
    1987. The Nyishangba of Manang: Geographical Perspectives on the Rise of a Nepalese Trading Community. *Kailash* 13(3–4):131–277.
    2000. *Tibetan Border Worlds.* London: Kegan Paul International.
Vasudevan, Ravi.
    1989. The Melodramatic Mode and the Commercial Hindi Cinema: Notes on Film History, Narrative, and Performance in the 1950s. *Screen* 30:29–50.
Veblen, Thorstein.
    1953 [1899]. *The Theory of the Leisure Class.* New York: Mentor.
Vergati, Anne.
    1995. *Gods, Men and Territory: Society and Culture in the Kathmandu Valley.* Delhi: Manohar.
von der Heide, Susanne.
    1997. *Changing Faces of Nepal: The Glory of Asia's Past.* Kathmandu: UNESCO/HimalAsia.

Wallerstein, Immanuel.
    1974. Dependence in an Interdependent World: The Limited Possibilities of Transformation within the Capitalist World Economy. *African Studies Review* 17:1–26.
Walvin, James.
    1982. *A Child's World: A Social History of English Childhood, 1800–1914.* Harmondsworth, U.K.: Penguin.
Watkins, Joanne C.
    1996. *Spirited Women: Gender, Religion, and Cultural Identity in the Nepal Himalaya.* New York: Columbia University Press.
Watson, James, ed.
    1997. *Golden Arches East: McDonalds in East Asia.* Stanford: Stanford University Press.
Weber, Max.
    1946. *From Max Weber: Essays in Sociology.* H. H. Gerth and C. Wright Mills, eds. New York: Oxford University Press.
    1947. *The Theory of Social and Economic Organization.* Talcott Parsons, ed. New York: Free Press.
    1958 [1904–5]. *The Protestant Ethic and the Spirit of Capitalism.* New York: Charles Scribner's Sons.
Weiss, Brad.
    1996. *The Making and Unmaking of the Haya Lived World: Consumption, Commodification, and Everyday Practice.* Durham and London: Duke University Press.
Wells, Alan, and Lee Chun Wah.
    1995. Music Culture in Singapore: Record Companies, Retailers, and Performers. In *Asian Popular Culture.* John A. Lent, ed. Pp. 29–41. Boulder: Westview.
Wells, Melanie.
    1995. Nation's Top Advertisers Plan Big Screen Blitz. *USA Today,* 29 November, B-1.
Weyland, Petra.
    1993. *Inside the Third World Village.* London and New York: Routledge.
Whelpton, John.
    1983. *Jang Bahadur in Europe: The First Nepalese Mission to the West.* Kathmandu: Sahayogi Press.
White, John Claude.
    1920. Nepal: A Little Known Kingdom. *National Geographic* 105:245–83.
White, Richard.
    1991. *The Middle Ground: Indians, Empires, and Republics in the Great Lakes Region, 1650–1815.* Cambridge: Cambridge University Press.
Wilk, Richard.
    1992. Consumer Goods as Dialogue about Development. *Culture and History* 7:79–100.
    1995. Learning to Be Local in Belize: Global Systems of Common Difference. In *Worlds Apart.* Daniel Miller, ed. Pp. 110–33. London and New York: Routledge.

Williams, Linda.
    1989. *Hard Core: Power, Pleasure, and the "Frenzy of the Visible."* Berkeley:
    University of California Press.
Williams, Raymond.
    1958. *Culture and Society, 1780–1950.* New York: Harper and Row.
    1974. *Television: Technology and Cultural Form.* New York: Schocken.
    1977. *Marxism and Literature.* Oxford: Oxford University Press. 1985. *Keywords.* Revised edition. Oxford: Oxford University Press.
Willis, Paul.
    1977. *Learning to Labor: How Working Class Kids Get Working Class Jobs.*
    New York: Columbia University Press.
    1990. *Common Culture: Symbolic Work at Play in the Everyday Cultures of
    the Young.* London: Open University Press.
Wilson, Elizabeth.
    1985. *Adorned in Dreams: Fashion and Modernity.* London: Virago.
Wong, Deborah.
    1995. Thai Cassettes and Their Covers: Two Case Histories. In *Asian Popular
    Culture.* John A. Lent, ed. Pp. 43–59. Boulder: Westview.
Wright, Daniel, ed.
    1972 [1877]. *History of Nepal, Translated from the Parbatiya.* Second edition. Kathmandu: Nepal Antiquated Book Publishers.
Wright, Eric Olin.
    1985. *Classes.* London: Verso.
    1997. *Class Counts: Comparative Studies in Class Analysis.* Cambridge:
    Cambridge University Press.
Yang, Mayfair Mei-hui.
    1994. *Gifts, Favors and Banquets: The Art of Social Relationships in China.*
    Ithaca and London: Cornell University Press.
    1997. Mass Media and Transnational Subjectivity in Shanghai: Notes on
    (Re)Cosmopolitanism in a Chinese Metropolis. In *Ungrounded Empires: The
    Cultural Politics of Modern Chinese Transnationalism.* Aihwa Ong and Donald M. Nonini, eds. Pp. 287–319. New York and London: Routledge.
Yami, Hisila, and Stephen Mikesell, eds.
    1990. *The Issues of Squatter Settlements in Nepal.* Proceedings of a national
    seminar, 2–4 February. Kathmandu: Concerned Citizen Group of Nepal.
Zivetz, Laurie.
    1992. *Private Enterprise and the State in Modern Nepal.* Madras: Oxford
    University Press.

INDEX